Perestroika and the Party

Perestroika and the Party

*National and Transnational Perspectives
on European Communist Parties in the
Era of Soviet Reform*

Edited by
Francesco Di Palma

NEW YORK · OXFORD
www.berghahnbooks.com

First published in 2019 by
Berghahn Books
www.berghahnbooks.com

© 2019, 2024 Francesco Di Palma
First paperback edition published in 2024

All rights reserved. Except for the quotation of short passages
for the purposes of criticism and review, no part of this book
may be reproduced in any form or by any means, electronic or
mechanical, including photocopying, recording, or any information
storage and retrieval system now known or to be invented,
without written permission of the publisher.

Library of Congress Cataloging-in-Publication Data
Names: Di Palma, Francesco, editor.
Title: Perestroika and the Party : national and transnational perspectives on
  European communist parties in the era of Soviet reform / edited by
  Francesco Di Palma.
Description: New York : Berghahn Books, 2019.
  Identifiers: LCCN 2019017272 (print) | LCCN 2019013866 (ebook) | ISBN
  9781789200201 (hardback : alk. paper) | ISBN 9781789200218 (ebook)
Subjects: LCSH: Communism--Europe--History--20th century. | Communist
  parties--Europe--History--20th century. | Perestroĭka--History. |
  Glasnost--History. | Soviet Union--Politics and government--1985-1991. |
  Communist countries--Politics and government. | Europe, Western--Politics
  and government--20th century.
Classification: LCC HX238.5 .P467 2019 (ebook) | LCC HX238.5 (print) | DDC
  324.2/17509409048--dc23
LC record available at https://lccn.loc.gov/2019017272

British Library Cataloguing in Publication Data
A catalogue record for this book is available from the British Library

ISBN 978-1-78920-020-1 hardback
ISBN 978-1-80539-132-6 paperback
ISBN 978-1-80539-390-0 epub
ISBN 978-1-78920-021-8 web pdf

https://doi.org/10.3167/9781789200201

Contents

Introduction. Perestroika: The Demise of the Communist World?   1
Francesco Di Palma

Part I. Eastern Europe

Chapter 1. The Impact of Perestroika and Glasnost on the CPSU's
Stance toward the "Fraternal Parties" in the Eastern Bloc   27
Peter Ruggenthaler

Chapter 2. Soviet Society, Perestroika, and the End of the USSR   55
Mark Kramer

Chapter 3. Perestroika Made in Hungary? The HSWP's Approach
to the Soviet Reform of the Late 1980s   88
Tamás Péter Baranyi

Chapter 4. Yugoslavia and Perestroika, 1985–1991: Between Hope
and Disappointment   105
Petar Dragišić

Chapter 5. The Polish United Workers' Party and Perestroika   118
Wanda Jarząbek

Chapter 6. SED and Perestroika: Perceptions and Reactions   132
Hermann Wentker

Chapter 7. Between External Constraint and Internal Crackdown:
Romania's Non-reaction to Soviet Perestroika   153
Stefano Bottoni

Part II. Western Europe

Chapter 8. Parallel Destinies: The Italian Communist Party and
Perestroika   179
Aldo Agosti

Chapter 9. "I Felt as If I Were Faced with a French Honecker": The
French Communist Party Confronted with a World Falling Apart
(1985–1991)   202
Dominique Andolfatto

Chapter 10. A Dialogue of the Deaf: The CPGB and the SED
during the Gorbachev Era (1985–1990)   216
Stefan Berger and Norman LaPorte

Chapter 11. Premature Perestroika: The Dutch Communist Party
and Gorbachev   236
Gerrit Voerman

Chapter 12. Perestroika and the Greek Left   256
Andreas Stergiou

Chapter 13. The Austrian Communists and Perestroika   278
Maximilian Graf

Chapter 14. The Spanish Communist Party and Perestroika   298
Walther L. Bernecker

Afterword. Gorbachev and the End of International Communism   323
Silvio Pons

Index   331

Introduction

Perestroika
The Demise of the Communist World?

Francesco Di Palma

With the rise to power of Mikhail Gorbachev as general secretary of the Communist Party of the Soviet Union in March 1985, a range of extensive reforms were initiated under the headings of *glasnost* (openness) and *perestroika* (restructuring). Among other objectives, they sought to make the regime less bureaucratic, to tackle increasing financial woes and to reduce foreign trade imbalances. Given the leading role that Soviet Russia played in bi- and multilateral relations between communist parties on both sides of the Iron Curtain, however, these reforms had important effects not only in the USSR. This book examines both the encounter with Gorbachev's policies by select European communist parties and the historical actors who helped to guide those policies' reception and implementation—topics that the historical literature has hitherto failed to analyze systematically.[1] It is concerned with the parties' responses in two respects: firstly, with regard to their mutual political, cultural, and not least financial connections; and secondly, within the context of their bilateral relationships to the hegemonic CPSU.

While the "export"[2] of Perestroika has been widely acknowledged and extensively described, historians have rarely broached the topic of the independent reformist policies among communist parties that emerged in the 1970s, nor whether and to what extent Gorbachev and his aides may have drawn upon already existing doctrines to buttress their restructuring.[3] Moving beyond the impact of Perestroika on the Soviet Union and its foreign policy (e.g., the abandonment of the Brezhnev Doctrine),

Notes for this chapter begin on page 17.

the following chapters investigate ideological discussions and more concrete political decisions within and between other communist parties.

As all the chapters in this volume show, party communism had not vanished by the beginning of 1990s—but Soviet-ruled world communism had. The title of this Introduction refers directly to the supposed destiny of party communism following the fall of the Berlin Wall and the disintegration of the Soviet Empire. Yet it might be helpful to reflect on the term "demise." It is obvious indeed that Perestroika and Glasnost triggered or perhaps accelerated a vast array of mechanisms that led to the end of a certain form of communism. But was communism, as such, erased and overcome? Would it be more accurate to look at this breakthrough as a major transformation? Or had communism as a cohesive phenomenon already been long dead—possibly since 1968?

Communist ideas would continue to inform and inspire politicians, opinion leaders, intellectuals, students and workers for years to come, both in Eastern and Western Europe. Yet we cannot ignore the fact that the collapse of the Soviet Empire was nothing less than the most disastrous event in communism's relatively young history. Similarly, it would be absurd to believe that single individuals, as influential and charismatic as they might be, can almost single-handedly end a long-standing, internationally organized power network with deep cultural roots. And yet history definitively proves that they can significantly contribute to the conclusion of an already ongoing process of change. So where does Gorbachev rank as the "terminator" of Soviet communism? As Juliane Fürst, Silvio Pons and Mark Selden put it: "[T]he peaceful demise of communist regimes throughout Eastern Europe and the Soviet Union should not be seen as inevitable. It involved complex interactions between long-term processes and contingency, resulting in a decline in legitimacy and self-confidence."[4]

As the historical record shows, Gorbachev and his entourage failed to fully grasp the close connection between market liberalization and the implementation of democratic values and political mechanisms. The consequences of that failure would be manifold and highly unpredictable. It is therefore useful for our work to keep in mind the importance of agency and the impact that personalities can exert on ideas and institutions.[5] With hindsight we can assume that probably nobody could have imagined back in 1985—as Gorbachev was appointed general secretary of the most powerful communist party of the world—that that same party and the nation it had ruled since 1917 would disappear within about six years. However, during the 1980s quite a few people knew and understood that Soviet rule was becoming considerably more volatile, and that any change in political strategy and rhetoric could prove disastrous for the

Soviet federation and all of its satellites. All those involved in communist rule were well aware of the major transformations that all societies were going through during the Cold War. Each and every of them—along with the parties they controlled, belonged to, or solely supported, as well as all communist governments—came up with specific, nationally tailored measures to spot and tackle problems in the future. Some of them cautiously opened up to capitalism, like Hungary and Romania.[6] Others, like the GDR and the French Communist Party,[7] respectively stepped up repression and control to prevent turmoil and politically "deviant" behavior.

Perestroika as "Revolution"?

With the "August coup" of 1991, the most important communist party in the world formally ceased to exist. This of course had immediate consequences. The two biggest West European communist parties, the French PCF and Italian PCI, were shattered by the dissolution of the CPSU. The PCI, the most influential communist organization west of the Iron Curtain, broke apart and was absorbed by other parties, jettisoning its symbols and its long-serving leaders. The PCF, which had been free-falling since at least the mid-1980s, was able to keep its name and organizational structure, yet it very soon faded into political oblivion.

In fact, the end of Soviet rule had repercussions on the political agenda of all communist parties, even those who were rhetorically distant from the "real socialist" ones. After Khrushchev's endorsement of the so-called "peaceful road to power," West European communists responded by adapting their policies to parliamentary strategies. Ultimately, this meant meeting the demands of their conservative followers while pursuing dialogue with the established social democratic parties that had been skeptical of communism and socialism since the end of World War II. This dialogue had begun to develop at a relatively early stage—the PCI, for instance, had been seeking it ever since the late 1960s, serving as an intermediary between the West German SPD and the East German SED. Yet this strategy gave rise to a dilemma: how to find a way to stay loyal to Moscow while potentially collaborating with conservative and/or social democratic forces? Not only was Moscow wary of other parties attempting to reach out to "bourgeois" leaders, but the latter were very often inclined to view the former as potential double agents in the service of the Kremlin. It was this dilemma from which Eurocommunism could eventually originate. Yet, as this book will demonstrate, West European CPs (except for some smaller parties like those of Finland, Sweden, Portugal and Cyprus)[8] were not able to influence, let alone control, national policy making. By the mid-1980s, West European communist parties were on average marginal political forces with only limited impact; the PCI, PCF and PCE constituted the notable exceptions.

Keeping in mind how quickly real communist regimes declined in the second half of the 1980s, and how slowly West European communist parties responded to the need for modernization and reform, we can raise the question of whether Perestroika was the final nail in the coffin for communism, and if so, why. Gorbachev characterized Perestroika as both a reformist and a revolutionary attempt to renew and refurbish — a "revolution" that should be carried out by evolutionary means. Meanwhile, his detractors called it a "counterrevolution" poised to nullify the central tenets of Leninism and Stalinism. So, was Gorbachev able to push through this revolution? It has been argued that he was so wary of the potential turmoil his reforms could have caused that he found himself stuck between the poles of Marxism–Leninism and revisionism à la Eduard Bernstein.[9] Was it his indecisiveness that led to a collapse, rather than to a rebirth? Did he fall prey, like several other West European communist leaders, to the temptation of a third way that not even Enrico Berlinguer or the PCF's Jean Kanapa had been able to convincingly draw up and implement?

If we take an overall look at how socialist and communist parties responded to Gorbachev's Perestroika, one thing stands out: while he embodied for many the hope for a better, more democratic, more prosperous future, for others he was a secessionist rebel attempting to sell the Eastern Bloc to the highest bidder. Gorbachev turned out to be a strongly polarizing figure, in that he reinforced and amplified the inherent contrast between specific national contexts and traditional proletarian internationalism. British communists remained loyal to the CPSU and advocated for his reforms while remaining allies of the SED, while the Austrian KPÖ almost uncritically patterned its policy after the East German model. Despite the supremacy of the USSR and its predominant role in both West European communism and the real socialist "family," nearly every communist party reacted autonomously to the reform impulses from Moscow. It seems reasonable to believe therefore, especially at the international and transnational level, that, borrowing from a book title by Alexander Wendt, "anarchy is what states make of it."[10]

This holds true especially within the context of the waning Cold War; whereas it is widely agreed that Gorbachev's reformist zeal was instrumental in the weak economic condition of the USSR, it is important to recall that his foreign policy convictions and objectives were not conceived of as defensive but rather "transformative" measures.[11] Both material and ideological concerns came equally to bear as the Soviet leader opened up to the West and began advocating universal human rights and disarmament. And yet no other real socialist head of state went as far as to displace class struggle as the sole justification and driving force of politics, nor to promote democracy and international security, even against internal opposition.[12] This would eventually open a Pandora's box, whereby the promotion of self-determination emboldened regime critics and independence seekers, culminating in the fall of the Berlin Wall and the collapse of the entire real socialist system. As Robert S. Snyder rightly put it: "Gorbachev's counterrevolutionary effort to transform international politics into a new peaceful world in order to remake the USSR unwittingly set in motion the forces that pulled the Soviet Union apart."[13]

Actors, Ideas, and Transnationalism

In its analysis of the transnational influence of Gorbachev's reforms in both Western and Eastern Europe, this book focuses on three main areas: *historical actors*, and their individual impact on political, cultural, and social developments; *ideas*, in the sense of a shift or abrupt change within the ideological structure of communism; and *transnational activity*, encompassing both material and intellectual transfer and exchange.

To begin with: *Actors*. To understand this aspect, it is first most useful to put the notions of Perestroika and Glasnost into a broader framework, taking into account what they actually meant both in Eastern and Western Europe. There has been over the last twenty-five years an oversimplification of what Perestroika, with all its prospects for change and long-term modernization, signified. Archie Brown, among others, draws our attention to a few fallacies: that Soviet Russia was already near to collapse as Gorbachev took the reins; that the Soviet Empire, and thus the Cold War, was ended by Ronald Reagan and his administration; and that the dismantling of communism in Russia was mainly caused by Boris Yeltsin and his supposed continuation of Perestroika.[14]

The impact Gorbachev exerted as general secretary intensified the differences between supporters and opponents of general reform. In this respect, it must be recognized that the opponents—driven by legitimate concerns about potential destabilization of power and rule in the communist world—by far outnumbered the supporters. As Silvio Pons and Michele Di Donato succinctly put it: "Although Gorbachev's plans went far beyond the failed pattern of 1965, at the same time they were hardly realistic—and unsuitable for facing the mounting crisis—given that direction and enforcement still relied on centralized institutions. The Soviet reformers were isolated."[15] In such an account, Gorbachev seems to be the "ultimate culprit."

True or false, one important theme comes immediately to the fore: the inclination to identify and attribute the responsibility for major political and cultural upheavals to single individuals or a rather small group of actors. Yet political systems, as is known from historical and empirical experience, take quite a long time to disappear. Were seven years and a small group of men enough to end all of that? And how was it even possible in a country like Soviet Russia, which in the 1980s—as historians such as Matthew Wyman and Stephen Kotkin have pointed out[16]—in fact displayed economic and political stability?

Even the manner in which Gorbachev took power in 1985 has left room for speculation as to what extent the inner leadership of the Soviet Communist Party was looking for substantial reform or not—and if they were, whether it was really Perestroika they were looking for. The CPSU included a broad range of very different elites: reformist elements, orthodox communists, and not least military figures who opposed any kind of liberal overhaul until the very end.[17] So again, how did Gorbachev manage to push his reforms through the party's Central Committee and the Politburo? To start with, he looked to reform the very structure of the party, vocally criticizing it and its approach to policy making. (It was the sort of critique that he extended just as well to the powerful KGB, whose leaders on many occasions openly denounced his visions of a more transparent, more democratic communism.) This was a strategy with transnational implications—due to the multilayered cross-border entanglements the Soviet Union held as a major world power—and yet, at the same time, one dictated by specific Soviet domestic needs.[18] As Alexei Yurchak among others points out,[19] although the attempts to reform communism from within had a long history, their pragmatic implementation had nevertheless repeatedly failed to take place. As Gorbachev pushed reform, the very opposite result ensued: the rapid undermining of equilibrium among the forces that kept Soviet Russia politically stable.

Against this backdrop, much research is still needed to thoroughly assess the individual impact of the Soviet general secretary abroad, and specifically on other communist leaders. If it is true that Perestroika was to a certain extent exported to East European countries—where, in general, communist parties also controlled ministerial functions—how, for instance, was it received in West European, parliamentary democracies? This brings us to our second keyword of *ideas*, along with the institutions in which they were embedded. "Realist" scholars have, since the late 1960s, theorized that the starting point for any political idea, especially in conservative or totalitarian regimes, is power and national interest. Then, in the early 1980s, neoliberal views emerged that attached great importance to international institutions as an additional element to be taken into account. Yet neither approach ultimately did much to supersede materialist, narrowly causal perceptions of policymaking. Today—and indeed over the last twenty years—there has been a wide consensus over a "new constructivist" approach to ideas: in order to break with the traditional materialism–idealism dichotomy, scholars emphasize that ideas and cultural phenomena can be, and in fact happen to be, just as "real" a political and historical phenomenon as power.[20] Neither realist nor liberal approaches can be completely discounted, but it is advisable to analyze ideology in terms of the actual human beings involved and the contexts of meaning they construct around them.

The guiding idea of the present volume is that Communism, as a heterogeneous complex of ideas, manifestly failed to be successfully transmitted and safeguarded by its highest-ranking representative, the Soviet Union. In other words, State Socialism (at least in Europe) was indeed in large part dominated by Moscow—yet the respective rulers and their fellow politicians differed greatly from each other, both in their cultural-political traditions and their specific objectives.

What Gorbachev had in mind demanded a great deal of psychological adjustment in society, within the party, and across the whole Soviet system through its ramifications both in the Eastern Bloc and beyond the Iron Curtain. The task ahead was monumental, and faced resistance from within the CPSU and, in several cases, from abroad. The French Communist Party, for instance, and the Unified Socialist Party in the GDR, vehemently opposed the winds of reform blowing from Moscow. But what was Perestroika all about, in terms of ideological and pragmatic innovation?

It has been argued that Gorbachev's own evolution was in the direction of social democracy. This implied, inter alia, the opening of domestic finance to a broader market economy. Yet, probably the most significant idea the new rulers in Moscow were seeking to realize was to turn away from the long-standing, entrenched top-down hierarchical organization of the communist party as well as of Russian society—which would, in fact, eventually spark and speed up the process of national emancipation in many member states of the former soviet federation.[21]

With this in mind, was Perestroika therefore a complete failure? It could not prevent the domestic economy from eventually going bankrupt; it was not able to reform and restructure the system it operated in, without ultimately laying the groundwork for its disintegration; and it could not reconcile the many diverging interest groups within the highest echelons of power, nor inspire the public in general, with the exception of the rather sparse social and cultural movements that drew directly upon it. It remained—as many critics have pointed out—a top-down imposition. Nonetheless it succeeded in fostering and promoting a "New Thinking," and arguably even brought Soviet Russia closer to the rest of the Western world.

As mentioned above, different analysts theorized that Gorbachev would pattern Perestroika after Western Europe's social democracies. But what model exactly did they have in mind? Gorbachev very frequently cited Lenin and referred to Marxism–Leninism as an important font of inspiration for his own work and as a basic blueprint for understanding the world. His adherence to Leninism is indeed at odds with any kind of parliamentary framework, and in 1990 the Russian leader made the point in an unpublished book that a one-party system would better serve the objective of buttressing democracy and pluralism.[22] So, how do these positions fit with the social democratic body of thought? Was Gorbachev under the theoretical influence of foreign social democrats? Did transnational entanglements and personal affiliations play a role in molding the new trend toward reform?

This brings me to the third and last aspect: *transnational influences and entanglements*. Even the most conservative socialist countries were not immune to influence from abroad, be it in the fields of economics, agriculture or communist theory. It is true that, apart from a very few exceptions in the Eastern Bloc—Yugoslavia comes immediately in mind; Poland of the 1980s is a much more debatable case[23]—no communist state leaders ever abandoned the tenets of Marxism–Leninism, a political orientation that was in fact controlled and supervised from Moscow. Nonetheless, Hungary and Yugoslavia, for instance, had started to open up their markets at the beginning of the 1980s. This obviously generated new relationships and helped to reshape mutual perceptions; it possibly set the frame for debate over theory and ideology with differently minded partners. So what impact, if any, did West European varieties of communism and social democracy have on Eastern Europe, the Soviet Union, and most notably on Gorbachev and his "New Thinking"?

The so-called "third wave" of democratization in Europe, which began around the mid-1970s with the end of fascist rule on the Iberian Peninsula and the ratification of the Helsinki Final Act in 1975, facilitated contact and exchange across the Iron Curtain, notwithstanding the rather defiant attitude of the Brezhnev leadership. That decade also witnessed the emergence of a communist "third way" doctrine, commonly referred to as "Eurocommunism," that was strongly endorsed and promoted by the Italian communist leader Enrico Berlinguer and his party, PCI.[24] Even though Perestroika and Eurocommunism share some similarities, there has been little research on the topic, although several scholars have hinted at the peculiar bond between Gorbachev and Italy. It is known, for instance, that his first visit to Western Europe, in 1971, was to Italy, and that he led the Soviet delegation to Berlinguer's state funeral in June 1984—only a few months before the notorious stopover in Britain where he met Prime Minister Margaret Thatcher.[25] The last general secretary of the PCI, Achille Occhetto, acknowledged in an interview for the Italian Newspaper *Il Messaggero* that "Gorbachev had rediscovered Berlinguer," and added: "Only four men have been able to understand Europe with particular lucidity: Willy Brandt, Olof Palme, Enrico Berlinguer and now Gorbachev."[26] Even Erich Honecker—the "poster boy" of real socialism who had, since the 1970s, criticized the PCI's policies as being a bad precedent for communist parties—in 1987 told Alessandro Natta, Berlinguer's successor as general secretary of the PCI, that apparently "Eurocommunism had not been in vain."[27]

Yet we must again be wary of oversimplification. Obviously West European social democracy and Eurocommunism originated from different cultural contexts and entailed different goals than Perestroika. Despite their common features, it was hard for Gorbachev to set up a direct dialogue with the leadership of the PCI, which even in the late 1980s was still refusing to organize international meetings with the CPSU because of the response to the 1968 Prague Spring. At the same time there is no denying that toward the very end of the Gorbachev era, Perestroika looked very much like the platform of the Social Democratic Party of Germany, with support for universal values and human rights. Alexander Yakovlev, the chief theoretician of the CPSU in that period, recollected in a 1988 interview that "[i]f we had spoken then [back in 1985] as we have spoken today, we would have been considered dissidents."[28]

Understanding Perestroika's influence abroad—how it was developed and implemented, and how it was perceived both by contemporaries and from the perspective of today—also poses problems and raises significant questions. Perestroika undeniably had a major impact on the European communist parties, yet the specifics and the degree of influence varied greatly and without respect to a given party's alignment with West or East. For example, Italy's PCI suddenly fell into a political crisis in June 1984, following the sudden death of Enrico Berlinguer. The crisis resulted from the ideological vacuum that had been growing since the early 1980s and had accompanied the gradual decline of Eurocommunism. Notwithstanding their individual characteristics, the communist parties of France, Britain, Spain, Greece, and other nations had, since around the end of the 1970s but more intensively in the 1980s, developed a more "flexible" communism.[29] The gradual withdrawal of these parties from the influence of Moscow was at that time linked to the project of a transnational, pan-European peace movement that emerged in opposition to the policies of the two superpowers, especially the 1979 NATO Double-Track decision. And while many West and South European communists showed relative open-mindedness towards Gorbachev, the East German SED leadership categorically rejected his reform efforts.

Perestroika must also be understood in the context of another explicitly transnational phenomenon: the decades-long efforts to achieve European unification. For much of the postwar period, the CPSU's politically propagandistic fight against unification was motivated not only by ideology but also by power politics. The idea of unification not only helped to shape bilateral and multilateral relations among communist parties, but it was also for a long time interpreted as a front against communism.[30] Instead of West European postwar hopes for a federated Europe, the top Soviet communists would have preferred fragmented nation-states, allowing the USSR to assume an undisputed hegemonic position after the withdrawal of the Americans.[31] This view did not change fundamentally until the intensifying crisis of state communism at the end of the 1970s.

From the very beginning, the CPSU was distrustful of and hostile to European unification. It interpreted the integration of Western Europe ideologically, seeing it as a defensive strategy of "state monopolistic and imperialist capitalism" against expanding communism. At the same time, the CPSU disapproved of the consolidation of the "Western Bloc" for pragmatic reasons: the successful emergence and expansion of a system aimed at unifying Europe was seen as a direct threat to the unity of the communist community and thus to Soviet supremacy. On the one hand, the party promoted a variety of integrationism with the aim of forming and expanding a counterforce to the European Communities (EC) in its own sphere of power. On the other hand, it fervently sought to make cooperation with West European states less attractive, often through its "brother parties," by deliberately and propagandistically assailing the "Europe of monopolies" by issuing warnings to and exerting direct influence upon the actors involved.

For the CPSU, however, the conflict with the European Economic Community (EEC) specifically, and the EC as a whole, was never its primary focus. Its perspective was largely determined by the broader context of the Cold War. From this point of view, the EC was allegedly an instrument for NATO or American "imperialism." When Moscow reached out to Brussels during the détente period, it was with the aim of positioning itself as a new protective power. However, given the poor prospects for success, the Soviet Union was never able to commit seriously to this strategy.[32]

The "New Thinking" introduced by Gorbachev, which did not oppose the West unconditionally but perceived it as an enemy par excellence and was oriented towards rapprochement, also put the unification agenda in a completely different light. Although the phrase "Common European Home" was originally formulated as an anti-European slogan, Gorbachev took it up during his visit to London in December 1984 without further elaboration.[33] On 30 May 1985, Gorbachev announced to the Italian prime minister, Bettino Craxi, that he would in the future seek a common language with the EC countries "as a political unit" in order to bring about a "radical change" in European policy.[34] A breakthrough was indeed not long in coming,[35] as a bilateral trade agreement was ratified in December 1989.

The overall process of transformation initiated by Gorbachev's rise to power also had a direct impact on the implementation of the Helsinki Final Act. Only a few months after the CSCE follow-up meeting in Vienna in 1989 and the signing of the "Charter of Paris for a New Europe" in 1990, both domestic and foreign "orthodox" communists harshly criticized Gorbachev and his policies. He was accused not only of having arranged the "sellout" of Marxism–Leninism and its distinctive socialist values, but also of potentially depriving the Soviet Union of its ideological and political monopoly within the community of socialist states, and left it to the advances of the West. Only a few months later, in 1991, the USSR collapsed.

Methodology

The chapters in this book draw on the sort of historical-comparative research that has been the subject of intensive methodological and theoretical discussion in recent years. Each contribution deals with relationships, transfers, and interdependencies that took place outside of the primary East–West confrontation that defined the Cold War.[36] They reconstruct and analyze the complex mediation and feedback processes between state and non-state actors with regard to the specific constellations of political parties in European countries. Through empirical evaluation, contributors examine whether and to what extent the cross-border relations between communist parties involved significant transfers or learning processes. To this end, the methods of "entangled" history are combined with traditional comparative methods.[37] In order to avoid the danger of a monocausal interpretation of Perestroika as the "gravedigger" of Socialism and Marxist–Leninism, their effects are explained transnationally. The consequences of Perestroika are examined in terms of not only politics and economics, but also sociocultural processes.

A combination of theoretical approaches from politics, history, social science, and other disciplines is needed to achieve this. In particular, scholarship on the conceptual development of political history has shown since the 1990s that political action—including decision making—is consistently and comprehensively grounded in culture. Contributors thus emphasize processes of definition, communication, and interaction along with perception, representation, and symbolic staging. In this framing, politics are constituted by the social practices and cultural conceptions of specific actors. Rather than assuming a largely autonomous sphere of politics in which influential politicians and their diplomatic relations take center stage, political action is here conceived as the result of social interactions. According to this approach, specific actors can be seen limiting, communicating, and representing policies. They initiate or impede processes of politicization. The boundary between the "political" and the "non-political" is thus a contingent one. At the same time, one can no longer write social or cultural history to the exclusion of politics, and the studies collected here integrate the subjective dimension of the social and political world as well as processes of communication, representation, and symbolic interaction.

The contributions in this book are thus, on the one hand, committed to empirical research, and on the other hand to constructivist historiography, which postulates that human activity, including in the realm of the political, is shaped not only by power and interests, but also by social or normative factors. According to the constructivist model, a "social actor" operates within a network of intersubjective meanings in which he makes "norm- and rule-guided decisions on the grounds of subjective factors, historical-cultural experiences and institutional integration."[38] The social actors, in this volume, are communist politicians and the people with whom they interacted in specific contexts and constellations. These include representatives of other parties, the media, and public life generally.

The Chapters of the Volume

Part I of the book is dedicated to Soviet Russia and the Eastern Bloc. Peter Ruggenthaler introduces this topic by providing an overall picture of developments within the European "real socialist" community. Gorbachev's Perestroika, he argues, meant one thing in particular: that the hitherto valid and regularly reasserted notion of unity of world Communism was no more. It was the historical merit of the Moscow rulers to divine to a certain extent that communist rule was soon bound to fall and to ensure that the process of disintegration would proceed violence-free. Yet, all circulating hopes that Socialism would rise out of the ashes even stronger were shattered, as is now generally known by later events.

Mark Kramer explores the social context, both in Russia and in the Soviet society outside, in which the political revolution set off by Gorbachev unfolded. He makes the case for an "ethnic" explanation for the unraveling of the Soviet Union, pointing out that its cohesion was not so much endangered by the rise of nationalistic discontent at the periphery of the federation, but rather by the size, cultural and political preponderance of Russia. It was Ukraine though, and its demand for independence after the failed coup in August 1991, that proved to be fatal for the existence of the union.

Tamás Péter Baranyi tackles the popular belief according to which Hungarian reforms constituted in their nature an offspring of the Soviet ones from the second half of the 1980s. As he explains, the latter ones gained momentum over the years and were eminently political in scope, whereas the Hungarian ones pivoted on economic benefit. Nonetheless party leaders like János Kádár and, later, Károly Grósz still publicly championed Perestroika and committed to a further upgrade of Comecon (grósznoszty). Yet, the thus triggered reforms, designed to save State Communism, eventually served as fuel for the opposition to call for even more extensive democratization. The author ultimately identifies specific gaps in the research, such as the underexposed role played by the unraveling Comecon in the last years of "really existing socialism" or the interrelationship between major ideological frames like Eurocommunism and Perestroika.

Petar Dragišić reconstructs and explains the main reasons why the political agony of the Soviet Union so strongly affected the Socialist Federal Republic of Yugoslavia and its Communist Party (League of Communists of Yugoslavia—LCY), eventually causing there the same destiny, even though the latter had officially withdrawn from the Eastern Bloc back in 1948. Likewise, he elaborates on how the dismantling of State Socialism proved to serve as a catalyst for the re-emergence of aggressive nationalism in the Yugoslav federal units.

Wanda Jarząbek takes on the reactions of the Polish United Workers' Party (PUWP) to Perestroika, and makes the case for a pragmatic interpretation. She correspondingly emphasizes how Polish interests in Soviet reforms were mainly intended to boost the domestic economy. Vice versa, they were not a major factor in triggering Polish-made political or ideological amendments. Nevertheless, they still had a remarkable impact on the pace of transformation and/or disruption of communist rule.

Hermann Wentker examines the rapid evolution in the understanding of Perestroika by the Socialist Unity Party of Germany (SED), from general approval in 1985 to skepticism and ultimately firm rebuttal starting from 1987. Whereas the State Party rejected any import of reforms, the SED rank and file increasingly looked at Gorbachev as the model to follow, thus contributing to the undermining of the communist regime.

Stefano Bottoni explores Nicolae Ceaușescu's determined refusal to adhere to Perestroika. He argues that this was mainly due to a misinterpretation of the West's readiness to keep helping stabilize the stagnating Romanian economy. The Romanian Communist Party (PCR) soon had to discover that its own special status as a mediator between the West and the Eastern Bloc was irremediably on the wane, which eventually set the scene for its end and Ceaușescu's execution.

Part II of the book examines West European communist parties. Aldo Agosti elaborates on the impact of Perestroika and Glasnost on the Italian Communist Party, PCI. He points out that the great hopes the Italian communists had put in Gorbachev and his reforms in the second half of the 1980s were offset and ultimately leveled by political doubts. After the fall of the Berlin Wall, the PCI focused entirely on the internal debate leading up to the Party Congress set for February 1991, which laid the ground for the relinquishment of the communist tradition. He thus proposes the thesis that both the "refoundation" efforts by the Italian party executive and the demand for a renewal of World Communism from Moscow were parallel paths to demise.

Dominique Andolfatto addresses what impact Perestroika had on the French PCF. He describes the impotence of the party leaders to critically recognize and understand the high topicality of the events that had caused the fall of the Iron Curtain in 1989 as well as the disintegration of the USSR in 1991. The same blindness was accountable for the gradual estrangement between the party and French society, which had been unfolding since the 1970s. Because of ideological commitments—the PCF remaining staunchly orthodox—it recanted Gorbachev's policies, a decision which did not stop its own downfall.

Stefan Berger and Norman LaPorte develop some of the issues posited in this Introduction by looking at how contrasting ideas—such as orthodox Marxist–Leninist and Gramscian—and their social carriers held sway in the Communist Party of Great Britain (CPGB) before Gorbachev came to power in the Soviet Union, and how this influenced its reception of Perestroika itself afterwards. They come to the conclusion—by dint of a fruitful comparison with the Socialist Unity Party of Germany (SED)— that, despite all sympathy for reformist communism, British reform-oriented communists never abandoned "really existing socialism." This happened out of loyalty to an array of theoretical tenets that had their roots in the realm of Socialist Internationalism. Because of this strong interdependence with the soviet "Big Brother," the CPGB eventually collapsed, just like the CPSU after 1989—a prey of its own ideas.

Gerrit Voerman explores the history of the relations of the Communist Party of the Netherlands (CPN) with the Soviet Union, and defines them as "paradoxical." After basically sharing no contacts until the 1980s, the ties between both sides grew tighter because of Gorbachev's reforms. Yet, the downfall of East European socialism was not the main reason for the dissolution of the CPN after 1989, although it surely accelerated it. On the contrary, the end of Dutch Communism has to be traced back to its "autonomous" endorsement of a whole array of reforms, a "premature Perestroika," whose side effects it eventually could not cope with.

Andreas Stergiou examines the long agony of Greek Communism during the 1980s, and identifies Gorbachev's liberalization programs as having had a disruptive influence on it. Confronted with this menacing development, the fragmented Greek left parties engaged in a merger operation, leading up to an electoral alliance and even involvement in a government with right-wing forces. Yet, the end of State Socialism in Europe soon encroached on the unionist experiment and revived orthodox resurgences, like that by the KKE (Communist Party of Greece), which in retrospect firmly rebutted Perestroika.

Maximilian Graf assesses the impact that Gorbachev's call for restructuring had on the Stalinist-oriented Communist Party of Austria (KPÖ) by implying that Austrian communists' fate was closely connected to the demise of the Soviet Union. After a short reformist period, he argues, the electorally insignificant party became one of the closest allies of the SED, and often served as an intermediary between East and West.

Walther Bernecker closes this section of studies and the anthology by describing the role played by Perestroika for the Communist Party of Spain (PCE). Strained by an ideological and political crisis, from 1982 the PCE embraced a "policy of convergence" that paved the way for the creation of the left-wing coalition "Izquierda Unida." The author comes to the conclusion that the rapid evolutions in the Soviet Union in the second half of the 1980s did have visible repercussions on the PCE, albeit that Perestroika's impact on it was rather limited.

Of course, the chapters collected here cannot fully encompass the complexity of Perestroika as a cultural and political-ideological turning point in the history of European Communism, and we can be certain that Gorbachev's controversial policies will remain an object of historiographical inquiry and debate.

"International Communism," conceived as a monolithic and homogenous historical phenomenon, was always an illusion—a fact that Perestroika made especially evident. Regardless of the degree of loyalty that communist regimes and parties displayed, or of the extent of the interdependence between them and Moscow on different relevant (particularly economic) issues, individual parties were unavoidably affected by national specificities. Notwithstanding cross-border exchange and adherence to international communist principles—ideals that were genuinely valued in the nations under investigation here, both before and after the fall of the Berlin Wall—the decisive failure of the Soviet-ruled Communist Bloc was that it was never able to develop a truly functional and supranational body of governance. As political crisis and financial turmoil struck in 1990 and 1991, "parochial" thinking and separatist movements triumphed over transnational solidarity. This is the leitmotif of all the chapters in the present volume.

Gorbachev paradoxically embodied this dilemma: "International Communism" had held together only under conditions of unchallenged Soviet domination—in other words, the imposition of one nation's will. With the advent of Perestroika and Glasnost, this equilibrium was destabilized in favor of a diversity of transnational entanglements and power relations. The reaction to this was astounding. Communist rulers in Eastern and Western Europe (with the sole moderate exception of the PCI) opposed almost unequivocally the unleashing of such reforms. This harsh rejection was simultaneously an "ultranational" and transnational development. It is in this way that the various reactions to Perestroika and Glasnost explored here need to be understood: as national phenomena that can nevertheless be studied as an integrated whole. Whether this "whole" is best understood as the demise of Communism remains a question for further investigation. This book represents a step in that direction, and is a collective argument for a transnational, actor-oriented approach.

Francesco Di Palma is a historian, postdoctoral research fellow and lecturer at the Institute of History and Cultural Studies, Freie Universität Berlin. His main areas of investigation are Communism/Socialism and Fascism/Antifascism, as well as Jewish History in nineteenth- and twentieth-century Europe. His works include, among others: Monographs: *Liberaler Sozialismus in Deutschland und in Italien im Vergleich: Das Beispiel Sopade und Giustizia & Libertà* (Metropol Verlag, 2010); *Die SED, die kommunistische Partei Frankreichs (PCF) und die kommunistische Partei Italiens (PCI) von 1968 bis 1989/90: Beziehungen, Verflechtungen,*

Policy-Making (forthcoming, 2020). Edited books: *Bruderparteien jenseits des Eisernen Vorhangs: Die Beziehungen der SED zu den kommunistischen Parteien West- und Südeuropas (1968 bis 1989)* (Ch. Links Verlag, 2011, with Arnd Bauerkämper); *Kommunismus und Europa: Europapolitik und -vorstellungen europäischer kommunistischer Parteien im Kalten Krieg* (Schöningh Verlag, 2016, with Wolfgang Mueller); *Jewish Minorities between Nationalism and Emigration in Central and Eastern Europe, 1866–1918* (forthcoming, 2020, with Grzegorz Rossoliński-Liebe).

Notes

Special thanks go to Arnd Bauerkämper, who helped organize an early meeting at which this project began to take place. That gathering arose from my own research into three European communist parties, the Partito Comunista Italiano (PCI), the Parti Communiste Français (PCF), and the Socialist Unity Party of Germany (SED), specifically on how they organized and carried out their own trilateral relations from the late 1960s until the disintegration of "really existing socialism" against the background of—or rather despite—the overpowering "Mother Party," the CPSU. See, among other works: *Kommunismus und Europa: Europapolitik und -vorstellungen europäischer kommunistischer Parteien im Kalten Krieg*, ed. Francesco Di Palma and Wolfgang Mueller, Paderborn, 2016; Francesco Di Palma, "Europa als transnationales 'Konstrukt'? Europapolitik und Europavorstellungen bei dem PCI und der SED," in *Kommunismus und Europa*, ed. Di Palma and Mueller, 52–70; *Bruderparteien jenseits des Eisernen Vorhangs: Die Beziehungen der SED zu den kommunistischen Parteien West- und Südeuropas (1968 bis 1989)*, ed. Arnd Bauerkämper and Francesco Di Palma, Berlin, 2011; Francesco Di Palma, "Eurocommunism and the SED: A Contradictory Relationship," in *Journal of European Integration History* 20(2), 2014, 219–31; Francesco Di Palma, "Der Eurokommunismus und seine Rezeption durch die SED (1968–1976): Einige theoretische Bemerkungen," in *Jahrbuch für Kommunismusforschung 2012*, Berlin, 2012, 233–48; Francesco Di Palma, "PCF und SED im späten Kalten Krieg: ein translokales Beziehungsgeflecht?," in *Die DDR in den deutsch-französischen Beziehungen*, ed. Anne Kwaschik and Ulrich Pfeil, Brussels, 2013, 275–88.

1. Among the many works on Perestroika and Glasnost are: Karner, *Der Kreml und die Wende*; Von Saal, *KSZE-Prozess*; Comte, *La perestroïka de Gorbatchev*; Bozo, *Europe and the End of the Cold War*; Savranskaya, Blanton and Zubok, *Masterpieces of History*; Kramer and Smetana, *Imposing, Maintaining, and Tearing Open the Iron Curtain*; Pons, *The Global Revolution*; Pons and Romero, *Reinterpreting the End of the Cold War*; Dallin, "Causes of the Collapse of the USSR"; Malia, *The Soviet Tragedy*; Kotkin, *Armageddon Averted*; Kramer, "Collapse of East European Communism"; Beissinger, *Nationalist Mobilization*; Aron, "The 'Mystery' of the Soviet Collapse"; Gill, *Collapse of a Single-Party System*; Hahn, *1985–2000. Russia's Revolution from Above*.
2. Hardman, *Gorbachev's Export of Perestroika*.
3. Initial, fragmentary approaches to this issue can be found in, among others: Brown, *Seven Years that Changed the World*, esp. 229–33; Hough, "Gorbachev's Endgame."
4. Fürst, Pons and Selden, *The Cambridge History of Communism*, "Introduction to Volume III," 12–13.
5. On the concepts of "agency" and "performance," see among others: Wulf, Göhlich and Zirfas, "Sprache, Macht und Handeln," 9–24, esp. 12.; on the "social construction of politics," see Wendt, *Social Theory of International Politics*; Wendt, Albert and Cederman,

New Systems Theories; Risse-Kappen, "Introduction," in *Bringing Transnational Actors Back In*, esp. 3–33.
6. See the chapters in this volume by Tamás Baranyi and Stefano Bottoni.
7. See the chapters in this volume by Hermann Wentker and Dominique Andolfatto.
8. Dörr, "Die Beziehungen zwischen der SED und den kommunistischen Parteien."
9. See Brumberg, "Moscow: The Struggle for Reform."
10. Wendt, "Anarchy Is What States Make of It."
11. Snyder, "Bridging the Realist/Constructivist Divide," 56.
12. English, *Russia and the Idea of the West*; English, "Power, Ideas, and New Evidence."
13. Snyder, "Bridging the Realist/Constructivist Divide," 67.
14. Brown, *Seven Years that Changed the World*, 4–11. See also Dalos, *Gorbatschow*.
15. Pons and Di Donato, "Reform Communism," 198–99.
16. Wyman, *Public Opinion*; Kotkin, *Armageddon Averted*.
17. See among others: Grachev, Blengino and Stievano, *1985–2005: Twenty Years that Changed the World*, 50–59.
18. See the chapter in this volume by Mark Kramer.
19. Yurchak, *Everything Was Forever*.
20. Realism, the leading paradigm in international relations theory, has over the last twenty years been the object of criticism on the part of constructivist scholars. The seminal work by one of the "founding fathers" of realist–structuralist approaches, Kenneth Waltz's *Theory of International Politics* (1979), has been especially scrutinized from every conceivable angle. The difference between the two schools of thought is clear-cut. Realists assume that the distribution of power and power itself is the main force behind world politics. Constructivists instead specify that structural realism misses one determinant factor: the intersubjectively (or social) shared core of ideas that leads to a certain behavior and indeed constitutes identities and interests of any involved actors. On this debate, see among others: Hasenclever, Mayer and Rittberger, *Theories of International Regimes*, esp. 158–67; Hopf, "The Promise of Constructivism," 172–73; Wendt, "The Agent-Structure Problem"; Wendt, "Anarchy Is What States Make of It."
21. See, among others: Suny, *The Revenge of the Past*; Brunce, *Subversive Institutions*; Brubaker, *Nationalism Reframed*.
22. See Brown, *Seven Years*, 139–42; Brown, *The Demise of Marxism–Leninism in Russia*, 70–100.
23. See the chapter in this volume by Wanda Jarząbek.
24. On "Eurocommunism," see among others: Weinberg, *The Transformation of Italian Communism*; Priester, *Hat der Eurokommunismus eine Zukunft?*
25. See Brown, *Seven Years*, 229–33.
26. Il PCI e il vento di Mosca. Occhetto: "Gorbaciov ha riscoperto Berlinguer," in *Il Messaggero*, 7 November 1987.
27. Archivio del Partito Comunista Italiano (APCI), Fondo Natta, Fasc. 45, *Incontro Honecker-Natta a Berlino*, 12 February 1987.
28. Yakovlev, *A Century of Violence in Soviet Russia*, 79.
29. On the British Communist Party (CPGB), see Andrews, *Endgames and New Times*; on the Greek Communist Party (KKE), see Stergiou, *Im Spagat zwischen Solidarität und Realpolitik*; ibid., "Die Europapolitik der kommunistischen Parteien Griechenlands und Zyperns"; on the Spanish PCE, see Baumer, *Kommunismus in Spanien*; on the French PCF, see Andolfatto, *PCF: de la mutation à la liquidation*.
30. Zubok, "The Soviet Union and European Integration"; Narinski, "La construction européenne"; Rey, "Le retour à l'Europe?"; Mueller, "Die UdSSR und die europäische Integration"; Kansikas, "Room to Manoeuvre?"
31. Pechatnov, "The Big Three after World War II," 7–8.

32. See the "Einleitung" (Introduction) to Di Palma and Mueller, *Kommunismus und Europa*, 13–26.
33. Brezhnev had coined it in 1981 to exert pressure on the United States. On this, see Rey, "Europe is our Common Home."
34. See Mueller, "Die KPdSU und Europa," 48.
35. Official negotiations began in September 1986, which, despite striking differences over the inclusion of West Berlin, eventually led to a joint declaration and bilateral and multilateral agreements between the EC and the individual CMEA states. Regular contacts between the West European institution and the CMEA were established on 25 June 1988; and diplomatic relations between the EC and the USSR were established in November. See Stent, *Russia and Germany Reborn*, 67.
36. Johnston, "Revisiting the Cultural Cold War," 295.
37. Pernau, *Transnationale Geschichte*; Bauerkämper, "Wege zur europäischen Geschichte"; Kocka, "Comparison and Beyond"; Haupt, "Comparative History."
38. Schaber and Ulbert, "Reflexivität in den Internationalen Beziehungen," 143; Zubok, "The Collapse of the Soviet Union," 272–73.

Bibliography

Andolfatto, Dominique. *PCF: de la mutation à la liquidation*, Monaco, 2005.

Andrews, Geoff. *Endgames and New Times: The Final Years of British Communism 1964–1991*, London, 2004.

Aron, Leon. "The 'Mystery' of the Soviet Collapse," *Journal of Democracy*, Vol. 17, No. 2 (April 2006), 21–35.

Bauerkämper, Arnd, and Francesco Di Palma (eds). *Bruderparteien jenseits des Eisernen Vorhangs: Die Beziehungen der SED zu den kommunistischen Parteien West- und Südeuropas (1968 bis 1989)*, Berlin, 2011.

_____. "Wege zur europäischen Geschichte: Erträge und Perspektiven der vergleichs- und transfergeschichtlichen Forschung," in *Vergleichen, verflechten, verwirren? Europäische Geschichtsschreibung zwischen Theorie und Praxis*, ed. Agnes Arndt, Joachim C. Häberlen and Christiane Reinecke, Göttingen, 2011, 33–60.

Baumer, Andreas. *Kommunismus in Spanien: Die Partido Comunista de España — Widerstand, Krise und Anpassung (1970–2006)*, Baden-Baden, 2008.

Beissinger, R. Mark. *Nationalist Mobilization and the Collapse of the Soviet State*, New York, 2002.

Bozo, Frédéric (ed.). *Europe and the End of the Cold War: A Reappraisal*, London, 2008.

Brown, Archie (ed.). *The Demise of Marxism–Leninism in Russia*, London, 2004.

_____. *Seven Years that Changed the World: Perestroika in Perspective*, Oxford, 2007.

Brubaker, Rogers. *Nationalism Reframed: Nationhood and the National Question in the New Europe*, Cambridge, 1996.

Brumberg, Abraham. "Moscow: The Struggle for Reform," *New York Review of Books*, 30 March 1989, 37–42.

Brunce, Valerie. *Subversive Institutions: The Design and the Destruction of Socialism and the State*, Cambridge, 1999.

Comte, Philippe (ed.). *La perestroïka de Gorbatchev: piteuse déconfiture ou réussite historique*, Paris, 2012.
Dallin, Alexander, "Causes of the Collapse of the USSR," *Post-Soviet Affairs*, Vol. 8, No. 4 (October–December 1992), 279–302.
Dalos, György. *Gorbatschow: Mensch und Macht. Eine Biographie*, Munich, 2011.
Di Palma, Francesco. "Der Eurokommunismus und seine Rezeption durch die SED (1968–1976): Einige theoretische Bemerkungen," in *Jahrbuch für Kommunismusforschung 2012*, Berlin, 2012, 233–48.
———. "Eurocommunism and the SED: A Contradictory Relationship," *Journal of European Integration History*, Vol. 20, No. 2 (2014), 219–31.
———. "Europa als transnationales 'Konstrukt'? Europapolitik und Europavorstellungen bei dem PCI und der SED," in *Kommunismus und Europa*, ed. Di Palma and Mueller, Paderborn, 2016, 52–70.
———. "PCF und SED im späten Kalten Krieg: ein translokales Beziehungsgeflecht?," in *Die DDR in den deutsch-französischen Beziehungen*, ed. Anne Kwaschik and Ulrich Pfeil, Brussels, 2013, 275–88.
Di Palma, Francesco, and Wolfgang Mueller (eds). *Kommunismus und Europa: Europapolitik und -vorstellungen europäischer kommunistischer Parteien im Kalten Krieg*, Paderborn, 2016.
Dörr, R. Nikolas. "Die Beziehungen zwischen der SED und den kommunistischen Parteien West- und Südeuropas," in *Bruderparteien jenseits des Eisernen Vorhangs: Die Beziehungen der SED zu den kommunistischen Parteien West- und Südeuropas (1968 bis 1989)*, ed. Bauerkämper and Di Palma, Berlin, 2011, 48–65.
English, Robert D. "Power, Ideas, and New Evidence on the Cold's War End: A Reply to Brooks and Wohlforth," *International Security* Vol. 26 (2002), 70–92.
———. *Russia and the Idea of the West*, New York, 2000.
Fürst, Juliane, Silvio Pons and Mark Selden (eds). *The Cambridge History of Communism*, Volume III, *Endgames? Late Communism in Global Perspective, 1968 to the Present*, Cambridge, 2017.
Gill, Graeme. *The Collapse of a Single-Party System: The Disintegration of the Communist Party of the Soviet Union*, Cambridge, 1994.
Grachev, Andrei, Chiara Blengino and Rossella Stievano (eds). *1985–2005: Twenty Years that Changed the World*, Rome, 2005.
Hahn, Gordon M. *Russia's Revolution from Above, 1985–2000: Reform, Transition and Revolution in the Fall of the Soviet Communist Regime*, New Brunswick, NJ, 2002.
Hardman, Helen. *Gorbachev's Export of Perestroika to Eastern Europe: Democratisation Reconsidered*, Manchester, 2012.
Hasenclever, Andreas, Peter Mayer and Volker Rittberger. *Theories of International Regimes*, Cambridge, 1997.
Haupt, Heinz-Gerhard. "Comparative History," in *International Encyclopedia of the Social and Behavioral Sciences*, Vol. 4, ed. Neil J. Smelser and Paul B. Baltes, Amsterdam, 2001, 2397–403.
Hopf, Ted. "The Promise of Constructivism in International Relations Theory," *International Security*, Vol. 23, No. 1 (Summer 1998), 172–73.

Hough, Jerry F. "Gorbachev's Endgame," *World Policy Journal*, Vol. 7, No. 4 (Fall 1990), 645–46.
Johnston, Gordon. "Revisiting the Cultural Cold War," *Social History*, Vol. 35 (2010), 290–307.
Kansikas, Suvi. "Room to Manoeuvre? National Interests and Coalition-Building in the CMEA 1969–74," in *Reassessing Cold War Europe*, ed. Sari Autio-Sarasmo and Katalin Miklossy, London, 2011, 193–209.
Karner, Stefan (ed.). *Der Kreml und die Wende 1989: interne Analysen der sowjetischen Führung zum Fall der kommunistischen Regime*, Innsbruck, 2014.
Kocka, Jürgen. "Comparison and Beyond," *History and Theory* Vol. 42 (2003), 39–44.
Kotkin, Stephen. *Armageddon Averted: The Soviet Collapse, 1970–2000*, New York, 2001.
Kramer, Mark. "The Collapse of East European Communism and the Repercussions within the Soviet Union," *Journal of Cold War Studies*, Vol. 5, No. 4 (Fall 2003), 178–256.
Kramer, Mark, and Vit Smetana (eds). *Imposing, Maintaining, and Tearing Open the Iron Curtain: The Cold War and East-Central Europe 1945–1989*, Cambridge, MA, 2014.
Malia, Martina, *The Soviet Tragedy: A History of Socialism in Russia, 1917–1991*, New York, 1994.
Mueller, Wolfgang. "Die KPdSU und Europa im Kalten Krieg: Blockpolitik im Osten, Antiblockpolitik im Westen," in *Kommunismus und Europa*, ed. Di Palma and Mueller, Paderborn, 2016, 29–51.
———. "Die UdSSR und die europäische Integration," in *Vom gemeinsamen Markt zur europäischen Unionsbildung*, ed. Michael Gehler, Vienna, 2009, 617–62.
Narinski, Mikhail. "La construction européenne vue par l'URSS de 1948 à 1953," in *L'Europe de l'Est et de l'Ouest dans la Guerre froide 1948–1953*, ed. Saki Dockrill et al., Paris, 2002, 61–72.
Pechatnov, Vladimir O. "The Big Three after World War II: New Documents on Soviet Thinking about Post-War Relations with the United States and Great Britain," Cold War International History Project Working Paper 13, Washington, DC, 1995.
Pernau, Margrit. *Transnationale Geschichte*, Göttingen, 2012.
Pons, Silvio. *The Global Revolution: A History of International Communism 1917–1991*, Oxford and New York, 2014.
Pons, Silvio, and Michele Di Donato, "Reform Communism," in *The Cambridge History of Communism*, Volume III, *Endgames? Late Communism in Global Perspective, 1968 to the Present*, ed. Fürst, Pons and Selden, Cambridge, 2017, 178–202.
Pons, Silvio, and Federico Romero (eds). *Reinterpreting the End of the Cold War: Issues, Interpretations, Periodizations*, London, 2005.
Priester, Karin. *Hat der Eurokommunismus eine Zukunft? Perspektiven und Grenzen des Systemwandels in Westeuropa*, Munich, 1982.
Rey, Marie-Pierre. "'Europe is our Common Home': A Study of Gorbachev's Diplomatic Concept," *Cold War History*, Vol. 4, No. 2 (2004), 33–65.

———. "Le retour à l'Europe? Les décideurs soviétiques face à l'intégration ouest-européenne, 1957–1991," *Journal of European Integration History*, Vol. 11, No. 1 (2005), 7–27.
Risse-Kappen, Thomas. "Introduction," in *Bringing Transnational Actors Back In: Non-state Actors, Domestic Structures and International Institutions*, ed. Risse-Kappen, Cambridge, 1995.
Savranskaya, Svetlana, Thomas Blanton and Vladislav M. Zubok (eds). *Masterpieces of History: The Peaceful End of the Cold War in Europe, 1989*, Budapest, 2010.
Schaber, Thomas, and Cornelia Ulbert. "Reflexivität in den Internationalen Beziehungen: Literaturbericht zum Beitrag kognitiver, reflexiver und interpretativer Ansätze zur dritten Theoriedebatte," *Zeitschrift für Internationale Beziehungen* (ZIB), Vol. 1 (1994), 139–69.
Snyder, Robert S. "Bridging the Realist/Constructivist Divide: The Case of the Counterrevolution in Soviet Foreign Policy at the End of the Cold War," *Foreign Policy Analysis*, Vol. 1, No. 1 (2005), 55–71.
Stent, Angela. *Russia and Germany Reborn*, Princeton, NJ, 1999.
Stergiou, Andreas. "Die Europapolitik der kommunistischen Parteien Griechenlands und Zyperns," in *Kommunismus und Europa*, ed. Di Palma and Müller, Paderborn, 2016, 205–20.
———. *Im Spagat zwischen Solidarität und Realpolitik: die Beziehungen zwischen der DDR und Griechenland und das Verhältnis der SED zur KKE*, Mannheim, 2001.
Suny, Ronald Grigory. *The Revenge of the Past: Nationalism, Revolution and the Collapse of the Soviet Union*, Stanford, CA, 1993.
Von Saal, Yuliya. *KSZE-Prozess und Perestroika in der Sowjetunion: Demokratisierung, Werteumbruch und Auflösung 1985–1991*, Munich, 2014.
Waltz, Kenneth. *Theory of International Politics*, New York, 1979.
Weinberg, Leonard. *The Transformation of Italian Communism*, New Brunswick, NJ, 1995.
Wendt, Alexander. "The Agent-Structure Problem in International Relations Theory," *International Organization*, Vol. 41, No. 3 (Summer 1987), 335–70.
———. "Anarchy Is What States Make of It: The Social Construction of Power Politics," *International Organization*, Vol. 46, No. 2 (Spring 1992), 391–92.
———. *Social Theory of International Politics*, Cambridge, 1999.
Wendt, Alexander, Mathias Albert and Lars-Erik Cederman (eds). *New Systems Theories of World Politics*, Basingstoke, 2010.
Wulf, Christoph, Michael Göhlich and Jörg Zirfas. "Sprache, Macht und Handeln—Aspekte des Performativen," in *Grundlagen des Performativen: eine Einführung in die Zusammenhänge von Sprache, Macht und Handeln*, ed. Wulf, Göhlich and Zirfas, Weinheim, 2001.
Wyman, Matthew. *Public Opinion in Postcommunist Russia*, London, 1997.
Yakovlev, Alexander N. *A Century of Violence in Soviet Russia*, New Haven, CT, 2002.
Yurchak, Alexei. *Everything Was Forever, Until It Was No More: The Last Soviet Generation*, Princeton, NJ, 2006.

Zubok, M. Vladislav. "The Collapse of the Soviet Union," in *The Cambridge History of Communism*, Volume III, ed. Fürst, Pons and Selden, Cambridge, 2017, 250–77.
_____. "The Soviet Union and European Integration from Stalin to Gorbachev," *Journal of European Integration History*, Vol. 2, No. 1 (1996), 85–98.

Part I

Eastern Europe

Chapter 1

The Impact of Perestroika and Glasnost on the CPSU's Stance toward the "Fraternal Parties" in the Eastern Bloc

Peter Ruggenthaler

The ruling communist parties in the Eastern Bloc reacted to the advent of Mikhail S. Gorbachev's perestroika by splitting into different camps,[1] a process encouraged by the Kremlin's insight—along the lines of the "New Thinking"—that the unity of the global communist movement had long ceased to have any basis in actual fact. One of the consequences of this development was the need for a continuous reshaping of relations between the "fraternal countries." The reason for this, rather than being framed as a question of reform or revolution formulated in the terms of Marxist–Leninist ideology, was the hard and bitter fact that the Socialist countries' productivity and technological development were lagging behind the West by roughly twenty years.[2]

The Stalinist-planned economy had unwittingly smothered productive forces, as a comparison with the Western market economies made only too painfully obvious. Gorbachev made the fate of the Soviet-style Socialist social order dependent on this insight, telling the "fraternal parties" that the Soviet Party would refrain in future from practicing the traditional centralism that had been the order of the day since the times of the Communist International (Comintern), and from continuing to interfere in the internal affairs of the Socialist countries.[3]

Gorbachev had put the legitimization of the Communist parties' power on a new basis. Rather than primarily relying on the self-pleasing monopoly of Marxism–Leninism on historical truth, the parties were to justify their existence by serving the interests and needs of their people.

Notes for this chapter begin on page 47.

This was the precondition in Gorbachev's eyes for the establishment of a socialist democracy, an idea he consistently upheld in his struggle to dismantle the USSR's entrenched Stalinist structures. His reformist zeal now met with opposition from newly formed camps to which the ruling "fraternal parties" withdrew. From the outset, Gorbachev's most outspoken opponents were the Romanian dictator, Nicolae Ceaușescu, and the leader of the SED, Erich Honecker. To quell demands for reform straightaway, both claimed that perestroika was only a new name for a policy that was already being implemented in their respective countries, and had been ongoing for a long time.[4]

The countries crucial for the reform process, which had to a certain extent spearheaded in their different ways the development now proclaimed by Moscow, were Hungary and Poland. Janos Kádár, who had been installed in Budapest by the Soviet Union after the suppression of the Hungarian Uprising in 1956, had already experimented with economic reform in the 1960s, notably in agriculture, with a view to improving the standard of living in Hungary. His goal was the stabilization of the country in terms of domestic policy. Kádár was an internationalist in the Soviet sense of the word, and loyal to Lenin's and Stalin's country, but at the same time his party needed national legitimization in Hungary to consolidate its rule. Both the ruler in the Kremlin and the Hungarian leadership knew that the top priority for communist policy in Hungary had to be the prevention of a replay of 1956.[5]

This chapter is based on archival materials of the Russian State Archives on Contemporary History (RGANI), which were analyzed for the first time, especially those of the International Department of the Central Committee of the Communist Party of the Soviet Union. It discusses the Soviet estimations of the positions of the communist regimes in the East European satellite states toward Gorbachev's perestroika.

The Reform Policy of the Polish United Workers' Party (PUWP) in the Assessment of the Central Committee in Moscow

The example of Poland is best suited to illustrate how, by the summer of 1989 at the latest, the Soviet Union had accorded higher priority to interstate relations than to relations at the party level. Gorbachev's hand is clearly discernible—despite the persistent denial of his role by the Polish communists—in the process of the "voluntary" resignation of the monopoly on power by the Polish Communist Party.

Along with Hungary, Poland had become one of the pioneers of reform politics in the 1980s. General Wojciech Jaruzelski reinvented himself as one of Gorbachev's closest allies and comrades-in-arms within the Warsaw Pact. Like the initiator of perestroika, he was convinced of the need for far-reaching economic reforms. While Jaruzelski's role is highly controversial to this day, and nowhere more so than in Poland, he was valued by Gorbachev as an "ally and kindred spirit."[6]

On taking office, Jaruzelski managed at first to neutralize the trade union movement Solidarność, but he was later forced to come to terms with it, albeit very much against his will. For a long time, the CP had been strongly opposed to any dialogue with Solidarność.[7] Moscow played the role of patient mediator in this process. In the eyes of the Soviets, involving Solidarność in the political process was the only way to end the proliferation of mass strikes that were crippling the Polish economy.[8] In the next phase, the strategy and tactics of the negotiating partners at the "Round Table" were kept under close scrutiny.[9] While remaining neutral, Moscow continued to bank on dialogue as the only possibility of facing up to reality and of preventing an exacerbation of Poland's social and economic situation.[10] Poland had run out of other options and, according to the Soviet embassy in Warsaw, there was a real risk of further polarization.[11] Moscow was well aware of the desperate state the Polish economy was in, and Western analyses of Poland's economy were studied with great care. Given that these also presented a uniformly bleak picture and that the hope for generous Western economic aid was totally unrealistic, the KGB concluded that there was no danger of the West gaining a foothold in Poland and cementing it with financial and economic assistance.[12]

The Polish communists were looking forward with great self-confidence to the elections that had been agreed on by the Round Table for June 1989. With the benefit of hindsight, the reason for this self-confidence verges on the bizarre: "We simply assumed that we would win. This, after all, had always been the case in the past."[13] The Soviet embassy in Warsaw blamed the first-round defeat of the communists partly on a lack of funds, which put effective canvassing beyond their reach—the opposition's election campaign was bankrolled by sponsors from abroad—but in the embassy's view the general lack of agitation and the complacency the PUWP had displayed had been even more damaging.[14] In his prediction of the election results, the head of the KGB, Vladimir Kryuchkov, was wide of the mark: he had assumed that the elections would pave the way for twin rule by Solidarność and the communists for the next year or two, and that the communists would be assured of a role in governing the country.[15]

The mandate to form a government given to non-communist Tadeusz Mazowiecki in the summer of 1989 marked the start of the democratic transformation process in Poland. The Polish communists, however, did not, to put it mildly, fall over themselves in their efforts to support the first non-communist-led government. They opted for a delaying tactic by haggling over ministries until Jaruzelski, now president of Poland, publicly declared in late July 1989 that "neighboring countries," notably the Soviet Union, were "eyeing" developments in Poland "with concern." It was obvious that he had not yet given up the hope that the Soviet leadership would step in to halt the process that was unfolding.[16] When Gorbachev did step in, he did so on a mandate he had requested from the Politburo to speak to Mieczysław Rakowski on the telephone.[17] In a conversation lasting more than forty minutes, he assured Rakowski of forthcoming Soviet assistance and advised him to "go on the offensive" with regard to the opposition—but what he did above all was to ask him to face up to reality. He told the leader of the Polish CP that he had to embark on a "path of mutual understanding" with the opposition. Gorbachev also shared his view with Rakowski that the PUWP was not going to make it if it continued to rely on the "same old fogeys."[18] By requesting a mandate from the Politburo, Gorbachev had made sure that the entire Soviet leadership was committed to the tenor of his words, which were to prove decisive for the implementation of regime change.

Moscow subsequently supported the forces in Warsaw that were interested in maintaining close Soviet–Polish relations. The question of the social order had become secondary. The USSR had, of course, an ace up its sleeve that it could play at any time: Poland's energy policy was to a large extent dependent on the Soviet Union—and Poland was a member of the Warsaw Pact. Fears that Poland's membership in the pact might be hollowed out until only a facade was left were kept at bay by Moscow for the time being.[19] The Soviet leadership gave top priority to the preservation of Europe's postwar order. At the Warsaw Pact Summit in Warsaw in late October 1989, the members were reminded of the obligations arising from the alliance, and of the need for unity.[20]

In 1989, a certain readiness for fundamental change made itself felt in the leadership of the Polish CP. Whether this readiness could have matured into the eventual power-sharing arrangements and the change of the social system without Moscow's—and above all Gorbachev's—intervention is anybody's guess.

The Hungarian Communists, the "Most Ardent Reformist" in the Eyes of the CPSU, Cut Back Their Own Power Monopoly

Hungary was the first country in the Eastern Bloc to introduce a multiparty system. The implications of the resolution passed in early February

1989 by the Hungarian Socialist Workers' Party (HSWP) were grossly underestimated, not only in Budapest but also in Moscow. While the Hungarian reform communists assumed it would take several years for a multiparty political landscape to develop,[21] Moscow, too, failed to realize that the "socialist principles" of Hungary's people's republic were under imminent threat.[22] When 150,000 Hungarians, paying their last respects to the national martyr of 1956, turned out in mid-June 1989 for Imre Nagy's reburial, the Soviet embassy described the event in rather feeble terms as another "stage on the road to a new model of societal development."[23] It actually recommended seriously considering the viability of introducing the Hungarian concept of a market economy in the USSR.[24] The establishment of the "National Round Table" was seen by the embassy as the "transition to a new model of social development."[25]

Nevertheless, the picture drawn by the Kremlin's Hungary watchers was realistic enough to make the Soviet leadership see what a predicament the HSWP was in. It was obvious that drastic reforms were needed to remedy the country's economic woes, and there was no doubt that the HSWP's maneuvering room was shrinking fast, thus depriving the party of what little capacity it had left of regaining control over the political development of the country.[26]

Moscow paid hardly any attention to the dismantling of the Iron Curtain along Hungary's western border. Having decided to play it safe, the Hungarian reform communists proceeded with extreme caution in this matter, probing as it were the limits of perestroika and glasnost with great care. Moscow did not object to the unrestricted freedom of travel, which had been in place since 1988, as Hungarians almost invariably returned to Hungary after their holidays in the West. Since Khrushchev's days, Hungary had also always set great store by keeping good neighborly relations with their western neighbor, Austria. In 1983, Moscow even sent a guideline to the Soviet Bloc leaders, pointing out how useful it was "to intensify our relations and contacts with the neutral countries of capitalist Europe in every respect and area."[27]

The topic of the dismantling of the Iron Curtain was broached in Moscow for the first time in March 1989. Almost in passing, Miklós Németh mentioned to Gorbachev that "measures had been taken … to remove the electronic and technical barriers altogether at Hungary's western and southern borders." He justified this step quite candidly by saying that the sole purpose the border barriers continued to serve was to stop refugees from Romania and the GDR from leaving the country. Gorbachev confined himself to a brief answer: "We still have a strict border regime in place but we, too, are becoming more open."[28]

However, Moscow's limits of tolerance were not long in reasserting themselves. Calls for neutrality à l'autrichienne or at least à la finlandaise were not acceptable. Gorbachev made this quite clear to the Hungarian secretary general, Károly Grósz, who arrived in Moscow a few days after Németh: "The main objective ought to be the modernization of the Warsaw Pact and not neutrality."[29] The Hungarians took these signals seriously and adopted a pragmatic attitude to the Warsaw Pact, not least on the advice of Western politicians, who were fearful for Gorbachev's standing in the Kremlin.[30] The message to the reform-minded Hungarians could not have been clearer: Yalta and the European postwar order were not to be called into question.

The Hungarian leadership began to dismantle the border fortifications, and the Iron Curtain was discreetly demolished step by step. In reports by the Soviet embassy in Budapest, the onset of the removal was apparently not even mentioned.[31] Austria's foreign minister, Alois Mock, then took the initiative and proposed to his Hungarian colleague, Gyula Horn, to bring the dismantling of the Iron Curtain to the attention of the world.[32] What was at stake was after all not just a media event that was sure to cause a great stir but Hungary's future course predicated on the key question of to what extent Hungary could be—or would be allowed to be—in charge of its own foreign policy. Would the symbolic act of the removal of a border fortification amount, in Moscow's eyes, to a violation of the interests of the Warsaw Pact?

After this initial period of hesitation, the Austrians and the Hungarians launched themselves into the preparation of the symbolic opening of the border. Whether Moscow was consulted at all is as yet impossible to say. Mock was certainly aware of the risks involved. Couching his statements in terms borrowed from Gorbachev's own public utterances—the project was part of the much larger undertaking of building the House of Europe—he tried to provide as much cover for the Hungarians as possible.[33] The production of pictures suggesting that the border was now open amounted to something like "Austria's contribution" to the disintegration of the Eastern Bloc. Their propaganda effect was such that it has been claimed that "the Austro-Hungarian prelude in the summer of 1989" was "crucial for the rapid pace of developments in the fall of 1989 in Germany."[34] The country that was most sensitive to those pictures was the GDR, where the impression was created that "crossing into Austria was a cakewalk."[35] The prospect of an escape route across the green border, even though that route was still heavily guarded, attracted more and more people determined to escape to the West. By mid-July, roughly one hundred East Germans had succeeded in doing so—but many more had been apprehended by the Hungarians, admonished (this was how soft the border regime had become in the meantime) and told to stay away from the border.[36]

The Soviet embassy in Budapest characterized the formal removal of the Iron Curtain by Horn and Mock in terms bordering on the banal as a "bilateral event." As a symbolic expression of an increasingly close relationship, it was of exclusive concern to the two countries immediately involved in it, Hungary and Austria.[37] Not even the "Pan-European Picnic" in August 1989, an initiative by local residents of the regions bordering on the now increasingly defunct Iron Curtain in Austria and Hungary,[38] which provided hundreds of GDR holidaymakers with an opportunity for the largest mass exodus since 1961, set alarm bells ringing in Moscow. Seething with rage, the SED leadership, which had asked Moscow for assistance in its struggle with Hungary over the refugee crisis, was coolly informed by the Soviet foreign minister, Eduard A. Shevardnadze, that this issue was "of no direct relevance to USSR–GDR relations."[39] Only a few days earlier, his Hungarian opposite number, Horn, had told the East German foreign minister, Oskar Fischer, that it was impossible for Hungary "to return to its previous border regime with regard to Austria." Budapest had to be mindful of the "paramount importance of its relationship with Austria."[40]

In line with the drive for the elimination of ideology from Soviet foreign policy and the deliberate abstention from direct intervention in interstate crises, Gorbachev told Chancellor Helmut Kohl when the latter inquired about Hungary that the Hungarians were "good people." Kohl interpreted this as Gorbachev giving him the green light for direct negotiations with Hungary.[41] Budapest had thus crossed the point of no return and was now for the first time pursuing a foreign policy that was independent of Moscow and tailored to its own needs. The problems arising from the onslaught of refugees were, from then on, solved on the basis of humanitarian guidelines and not of Hungary's still existing Alliance commitments within the Warsaw Pact or the obligations arising for Hungary from contractual agreements it had entered into with the GDR. Hungary's politicians took their bearings from the way they had previously dealt with the Ceaușescu regime. The cautiously prepared accession to the Geneva Refugee Convention enabled Budapest to prioritize its international obligations over those arising from within the Warsaw Pact, and to argue convincingly that Hungary was under no obligation to send Romanian refugees back to Bucharest.[42]

While there is no doubt that at this stage a guarantee for multibillion loans by the FRG played a major role in the minds of Hungary's reform communists,[43] emancipation from Moscow and the Warsaw Pact "fraternal states" by concentrating on genuinely Hungarian concerns was even more important. And the Kremlin raised no objections.

Even in late 1989, the Central Committee in Moscow was at pains to give the impression of being completely unperturbed. The possibility that Hungary might completely drift away "to the West" was ruled out, above all on economic considerations.[44] Hungary was going to "remain within our gravitational field also in the long term since there is no other way for the country to safeguard its economic and political interests." In addition to this, the "majority of Hungary's population ... believe in the ideas of Soviet perestroika and in the [Soviet] leaders."[45] Even the KGB confidently asserted in late 1989 that the Hungarian Socialist Party would be able to cope with the new conditions.[46]

Perestroika Put on the Spot: The Czechoslovak Communists, the Legacy of 1968, and Diverging Viewpoints in Moscow

After the suppression of the "Prague Spring," orthodox communists were in power in Prague, to whose lot it fell after 1968 to do Moscow's bidding by purging the party of reformists and driving tens of thousands Czechoslovaks into exile. In December 1987 Gustáv Husák was forced to resign as party leader of the Czechoslovak Communist Party (KSČ). He was succeeded by Miloš Jakeš. Unlike the election of Vasil Bil'ak to the post of party leader, about which no one in Moscow gave a hoot, Jakeš was not an old Stalinist. Passing the baton from Husák to Jakeš meant there would be next to no change in ideology or political alignment, and thus it was considered to be unproblematic by Moscow.[47] Jakeš was Husák's junior by ten years but also complicit in the purges at the time of the consolidation of the rule of the CP, the period of "Normalization" after 1968. Even though he promised to energize the party, he was unlikely to show any zeal for innovation. Nor was there any need for such zeal, at least as far as the economy was concerned. Compared to other East European countries, the Czechoslovak economic situation was enviable. Foreign debt was low, growth rates relatively good, public finances in order, and inflation very low—all this presented a welcome contrast to the increasingly tension-fraught situation in countries like Poland. The KSČ leadership therefore considered itself to be in a position where it could forego significant changes and push reforms to the back burner. By late 1988, however, even the Czechoslovak CP leadership could no longer deny that their country was in the grip of an all-pervasive general crisis; what had (half-heartedly) been attempted by way of economic reforms had ended in failure. V. Bil'ak, in 1968 one of the driving forces behind the violent termination of reform policy,⁴⁸ showed himself concerned in Moscow that the opposition might try to "infest perestroika as parasites." In this way he put his finger on the sore point with regard to understanding why real perestroika was impossible in the ČSSR: it would have endangered the positions held by M. Jakeš and V. Bil'ak. Bil'ak explicitly warned Moscow of the consequences that a reassessment of the 1968 military intervention might have for socialism in Czechoslovakia.

In the elaboration of the "New Thinking," the violent 1968 suppression of Czechoslovak reform policy and of the Prague Spring was an object lesson for Gorbachev in Soviet foreign policy towards the "fraternal states."⁴⁹ He had announced in the Politburo as early as 1986 that military measures against fraternal states, like in Hungary in 1956 and in Czechoslovakia in 1968, must never be repeated—"they are inadmissible."⁵⁰ When Gorbachev visited Czechoslovakia in April 1987, KPČ leader Gustáv Husák asked him to abstain from mentioning the Prague Spring.⁵¹ Yet wherever Gorbachev went in Prague the topic kept cropping up. Back in Moscow he reviewed the highlights of his journey and raised the question in the Politburo: "What is our official line with regard to this event?" One thing he had made entirely clear in Prague was that perestroika was not something Moscow was going to ram down the Czechoslovak CP's throat. This was the guiding principle Gorbachev stood by in the ensuing years when it came to redefining the relationship between the Soviet Union and other socialist countries. The Soviet principle of non-intervention made it imperative for Gorbachev to abstain from criticizing the leadership in Prague. All that was ever mooted in talks behind the scenes was the causes of the present predicament. Jakeš, according to the Soviet embassy, knew he was in a tight spot.⁵²

In March 1989 the Economics Institute of the Academy of Sciences of the USSR, led by Oleg T. Bogomolov, presented their analysis of the situation in Czechoslovakia to one of the members of Gorbachev's inner circle, Aleksandr N. Yakovlev.⁵³ This analysis can also be read as a commentary on the dilemma resulting from the "New Thinking" in Soviet foreign policy, which was predicated on non-intervention. According to the analysts, the consequences of the KPČ leadership's insistence on painting the suppression of the Prague Spring as the salvation of socialism had potentially disastrous consequences. In their view, the USSR could not afford to continue its strict policy of non-intervention because this was interpreted in many quarters as tacit support for the orthodox hardliners in the CP regime. And there was worse to come: the confrontational line taken by the KPČ hardliners was beginning to impinge on perestroika in the Soviet Union itself, in that it could not be ruled out that the confrontation with the opposition in the ČSSR would escalate to a point where the Soviet Union might be forced once more to send in its troops: "This turn of events would suit the interests of the anti-perestroika forces in the Soviet Union. In this scenario, which would be interpreted as a 'success' by those forces, they would be given the chance to call for robust measures under the pretext of 'saving' the Socialist system from final collapse and of 'defending' the military-strategic interests of the USSR."[54] In what effectively amounted to a double-bind, Moscow was no longer able to prevent such a situation from occurring by direct intervention. Demanding a reshuffling of cadres was no longer on the cards. What the analysts held out some hope for was "exerting a certain indirect influence." In their view, the first measure to be taken was exchanging the staff at the Soviet embassy in Prague because the diplomats accredited there dragged their feet over support for perestroika. The Soviet leadership failed to follow up this proposal. Czechoslovakia may thus serve as an example in illustrating the relationship between developments in the Soviet Union and other socialist countries.

In June 1989 the moment of truth had come in Prague regarding the problem of public debt. Even though Czechoslovakia's foreign debts were relatively low, they were nevertheless becoming increasingly irksome. Efforts to cut back on debts in the West failed.[55] Pouring oil onto the fire, the Czechoslovak Academy of Sciences discovered in its mid-1989 opinion polls a significant drop in the authority of the Communist Party as perceived by the populace. In the explanations the Soviet embassy devised for this, it cited the reform processes in Poland and Hungary, and the lack of readiness for reform on the part of the Czechoslovak regime.[56] Notable in its absence was any kind of critical reflection by the leadership on the policies they were pursuing. Like the SED leadership, the KPČ leaders blamed the influence that Western, especially German and Austrian, media were having on the perception of the rapidly emerging crisis.[57] Impervious to what was happening in Poland and Hungary at that time, the core of the Czechoslovak leadership remained hostile to reform.

Far from being willing to enter into a political dialogue with the opposition, they took "measures to neutralize" their opponents in October 1989.[58] Moscow was assured that "the battle against the opposition" was being "fought resolutely, but within the framework of the law".[59] The result was the onset of student protests, which were supported by hundreds of thousands in all parts of Czechoslovakia.[60] The army and the security apparatus were poised for action but the disproportionate force and brutality they showed in the first clashes only made resistance on the part of the population more determined. No shots were fired in Prague and the question remains of why the regime made only half-hearted attempts to stay in power, as they did not unleash the full force of the security apparatus and the army.

A clue is to be found in the speech Prime Minister Ladislav Adamec delivered to the party leadership on 24 November, in which he pleaded against the use of force.[61] The gains would be minimal, he argued, amounting to no more than a brief respite. Gone were the times when, in a situation like this, one could count on assistance from other Socialist countries. It is obvious that the prime minister was referring here above all to the Soviet Union. To make matters worse, he went on that the West would react to a show of force by imposing a political and economic boycott. The upshot of the meeting was that KPČ Secretary General Jakeš handed in his resignation along with the entire presidium, in the hope of paving the way to a dialogue that would end the crisis. This also reflected the shrewd calculation that without a new set of faces it would be impossible to break the deadlock. While all this was undoubtedly true, the switch to dialogue and the pretended personnel changes precipitated the end of the dictatorship.

The Soviet Union was willing to go along with all this as long as the foreign policy dimension remained untouched. Membership of the Warsaw Pact and the European security order were not in any way affected, as the Soviet foreign minister Shevardnadze made abundantly clear when his Czech opposite number, Jiří Dienstbier, came to Moscow for his inaugural visit.[62]

Window Dressing in Sofia: Bulgaria, the Soviet Union's Most Faithful Satellite?

When Gorbachev took office as the secretary general of the CPSU, Todor Zhivkov had been in charge of the Communist Party's fate in Sofia for more than three decades. He was the longest serving CP leader in the Eastern Bloc and had left his mark on three-quarters of the communist era in Bulgaria. After de-Stalinization, Zhivkov had introduced a number of reforms in the Bulgarian CP that increasingly prioritized the interests of the Bulgarian nation over purely Marxist–Leninist ideology. He was committed to overcoming national nihilism, which he tackled by emphasizing Bulgaria's national cultural heritage. This involved Zhivkov's opening the country to the West—at least to a certain extent.[63] He gradually mutated from "proletarian internationalist" to Bulgarian nationalist.[64]

In the arena of Bulgaria's ethnic groups, Zhivkov's increasingly nationalistic course resulted in the Turkish minority being completely deprived of its rights, which led to Bulgaria's international isolation in the 1980s.

Bulgarian Turks were to be assimilated by force. Exploiting the serious illness of Gorbachev's predecessor, Konstantin U. Chernenko, for his purposes, Zhivkov launched the "Process of Rebirth" in 1984. The Turkish minority were forced to change their names from Turkish or Arabic to Bulgarian. This measure was justified with reference to the danger that Bulgaria might otherwise go down the same road as Cyprus.[65]

In the Cold War, Bulgaria had basked in the reputation of being the most faithful satellite of the Soviet Union. This had earned Bulgaria significant financial and economic advantages within the Eastern Bloc, such as generous loans and raw materials, and energy at subsidized rates. In this new phase, the rapprochement with the West in cultural terms went hand in hand with an interest in technological collaboration to bring about a modernization of Bulgaria's industrial sector. It was hoped that a massive injection of Western state-of-the-art technology would make Bulgaria competitive again. This path, however, was largely blocked by CoCom regulations[66] and the Jackson–Vanik Amendment.[67] Bulgaria's foreign debt continued to soar. Selling surplus oil that Bulgaria had received from the Soviet Union was one of the few measures at Bulgaria's disposal to put the budget on a more even keel. After Brezhnev's death, however, the Kremlin decided to discontinue such "gifts." Zhivkov's rigid stance on the question of Bulgaria's Turks finally lost him Moscow's support. It was left to Gorbachev to inform Zhivkov of his fall from grace in October 1985. Meanwhile, Bulgaria's economy continued its downward slide, triggering social unrest.[68]

Zhivkov subsequently proclaimed *preustroistvo* without, however, seriously intending to implement the reform ideas included in this version of "perestroika light." It was merely an exercise in window dressing designed to restore his credibility in Moscow,[69] and it was understood in Moscow in precisely those terms.[70]

In 1987, Zhivkov proposed far-reaching reforms in a package called the "July Concept." Superficially in line with the main trend of all reform proposals since the 1960s, the July Concept advocated market mechanisms and market principles. What Zhivkov was aiming for, however, was not a serious course of reforms but draping his power in pseudo-democratic ornament. On his visit to Moscow in October 1987 he wanted to impress Gorbachev with his readiness to embark on reforms that were so radical they were beyond even Gorbachev's reach, and had to be rejected for precisely this reason. Gorbachev even accused Zhivkov of deliberately delaying reforms and of attempting to undermine the Socialist system. He even alleged that Zhivkov was trying to turn Bulgaria into a miniature version of the FRG or Japan. The only promising way forward, as Gorbachev pointed out to Zhivkov, was socialism and its dynamic development.[71]

It took until January 1989 for economic liberalization to be tackled in earnest.[72] Only now were the necessary foundations laid for the introduction of new business models and of private enterprise. By now, however, it was too late. Running out of time and resources, Zhivkov was forced to admit that "the race against capitalism has been lost."

Repression under the Zhivkov regime was such that for a long time the development of any organized form of opposition seemed to be out of the question; there were hardly any dissidents. The "Process of Rebirth," which was directed primarily against the country's Turkish minority, met with no opposition worth mentioning from within Bulgaria—except of course from the Turks themselves. Opposition groups, which were beginning to put forth tender shoots, such as the "Discussion Club for the Support of Glasnost and Perestroika," had their origin above all in the slowly emerging ecological movement protesting the devastation of the environment by Bulgaria's mining, chemical, and metal processing and metal working industries. Throughout 1989, Bulgaria's Turkish policy remained the dominant topic.[73] The mass exodus of hundreds of thousands of Turks to Turkey further exacerbated the country's economic woes by striking, above all, at Bulgaria's agriculture. These were the preconditions that were to enable the ousting of Zhivkov after almost thirty-five years of dictatorial rule.[74]

On 10 November 1989, one day after the fall of the Berlin Wall but otherwise unconnected to that event, the Zhivkov era ended in Bulgaria. In the official version, the dictator had asked to be allowed to hand in his resignation; in fact, he was ousted by a "palace revolt." This, however, did not yet spell the end of Bulgaria's communist era, as the transformation process took a different course in Bulgaria from other East European countries.[75]

The coup had been prepared long in advance by Andrei Lukanov and Petăr Mladenov. Not much is known so far about this chapter of Bulgarian history. There are extreme discrepancies between how it is remembered and retold by those who were immediately involved in the events. Reliable sources are scarce.[76] What has been established with certainty is that Mladenov tendered his resignation to the Politburo of the BCP in writing on 24 October—ostensibly on the grounds that Zhivkov had decided to use force against eco-Glasnost activists. He forwarded a copy of his letter of resignation to Moscow. By then at the latest the Kremlin must have been aware that Zhivkov no longer enjoyed the full support of his party. On his trip to China, Mladenov stopped off in Moscow twice. On these and other occasions he was encouraged to demand that Zhivkov step down. The most powerful single act of support for Mladenov came on 7 November, when Soviet ambassador Viktor

Sharapov explicitly advised Zhivkov to step down.[77] Even though the significance of "advice" from Moscow had changed drastically under Gorbachev, and there was no longer any need to fear that it was only one step away from the use of force to have it implemented, it may be assumed that this particular piece of advice fell on fertile soil.

As newly installed leader of the Bulgarian CP, Mladenov's top priority was mending fences with Moscow and overcoming the effects of the alienation that Zhivkov's policies had caused. He purged the party leadership and maintained close contact with Moscow.[78] Zhivkov was put on trial; the procedure quickly degenerated into farce.

Giving in to pressure from the street, the new CP leadership finally renounced their monopoly on power. This put them in a league of their own in Eastern Europe, regardless of their reluctance. Earlier than most of their colleagues, they had read the signs of the time and had stepped down. They refrained from creating artificial obstacles and opened up the way to free elections. In what was truly a historic premiere in Eastern Europe, the post-communists, now going under the name of socialists, not only won the elections in the summer of 1990 but won with an absolute majority. They sat out the mass protests that followed the elections. The key question now was the relationship with the MPs of the Turkish party. As a factor that was capable of tilting the balance towards a two-thirds majority (which was lost again in the 1991 elections), the Turkish MPs were in strong demand as partners in parliament. In this way they held an important role in Bulgaria's transformation process. All this was played out against the backdrop of a "centuries-old tradition of interethnic harmony," which set Bulgaria apart from Yugoslavia and constituted at the same time one of the "ironies of history but, for once, not a bitter one."[79]

Entrenched Opponents of Perestroika: Ceauşescu and Honecker

To begin with, Gorbachev repeatedly poked fun to people in his inner circle at the self-styled Romanian Conducător ("Leader") Ceauşescu.[80] Over the years he came to view the Romanian leader as an object of contempt rather than of ridicule. SED leader Erich Honecker moved along a similar trajectory in Gorbachev's judgment.

The rigorous policy of autarky and the repayment of all foreign debts ordered by Ceauşescu turned Romania into Europe's poorhouse in the 1980s.[81] While the GDR offered its citizens a much higher standard of living, it was becoming increasingly clear in light of its debts to the West that it could not go on doing so indefinitely. The SED leadership had become aware of the precarious situation it was in early on, but Honecker preferred to turn a blind eye to it.[82]

In May 1987, Gorbachev went to Bucharest for a three-day visit and discussed Soviet reform policy with Ceaușescu. An inveterate opponent of Gorbachev's perestroika right from the start, the Romanian dictator refused to be impressed. Towards the end of 1987 he told the Party Conference of the Romanian CP that reforms of the kind implemented at that time in the Soviet Union were already "old hat" in Romania.[83] This claim was the ace he used to pull from his sleeve whenever he wished to terminate a discussion on the necessity of switching to a reformist policy in Romania. Honecker tended to take a similar line, which was outwardly perhaps less outspoken and less direct but equally tough in substance. In a conversation with the SED leader at the 11th Party Conference of the SED in April 1986, Gorbachev had not failed to notice that "Honecker had displayed a certain reservation regarding the internal development of the Soviet Union."[84]

Honecker and Ceaușescu became close allies in their struggle against perestroika. Only a few days before Honecker banned the sale of the widely read Soviet magazine *Sputnik* in the GDR in November 1988, he awarded the Karl Marx Order to Ceaușescu. The reason he banned the sale of the magazine was an article critical of Stalin's policy before 1941. Honecker did not, as he told his Romanian guest, believe in "digging up negative facts in history." He was, after all, well aware of the dangers a critical discussion of the past might entail for the standing of the SED and indeed of himself.[85]

Gorbachev nevertheless kept his own counsel in East Berlin. He extended no support to Honecker's opponents lined up in the party, even though he was presumably convinced that the SED would benefit from a change of leadership. Gorbachev, however, again proved to be a man of strong principles, and strictly adhered to the policy of non-intervention.

Ceaușescu had one more trump card left that would ensure a certain amount of maneuvering space for him. As Romania became increasingly isolated on the international stage and found itself bereft of support from the socialist camp, Ceaușescu threatened to subject collaboration within the framework of the Warsaw Pact to a close review. Shevardnadze and Yakovlev therefore recommended "cranking up" political contacts with Romania.[86] Yet another instance of Romania stepping out of line was hardly in the Kremlin's best interest. The stick was no longer an option, there was no doubt about that, but there was still something to be said for the carrot. The Politburo in Moscow therefore passed a resolution in April 1989 containing several measures designed to "crank up" trade relations.[87] Ceaușescu himself did not budge and remained an entrenched critic of reform. At a meeting of the Romanian Defense Council he even gave short shrift to technological innovations in the armaments sector.[88]

On 7 July 1989, Ceaușescu hosted the meeting of the Political Consultative Committee of the Warsaw Pact in Bucharest. In the order of rotation, it was Bucharest's turn to serve as venue and it was in Bucharest, of all places, that the Warsaw Pact passed a resolution emphasizing the paramount importance of the principles of equality and independence of the member states, and the "right of each state to develop its own political course, strategy and tactics without outside interference." This was the death knell for the Brezhnev Doctrine.[89] Ceaușescu deplored the events in Poland, and insisted in such cases on the justification of "assistance" supplied by "fraternal countries." The meeting made the lack of consensus among the member states painfully obvious.[90] Honecker fell ill and had to leave prematurely. As Ceaușescu took leave of him, he said: "Gorbachev wants to build a common European house. Meanwhile the rest of us are set to wreck our own houses." [91]

When the stage was being set in Poland for the formation of the first non-communist-led government in the Eastern Bloc, with Honecker sidelined for health reasons, Ceaușescu saw that socialism in Poland and, by extension, in the entire Warsaw Pact was in danger. Gorbachev, however, refused to discuss Poland with Ceaușescu in person. The Romanian leader had proposed to fly to Moscow, but Gorbachev chose to ignore Ceaușescu's explicit wish. Ceaușescu demanded that measures be taken against the "liquidation of socialism."[92] Deprived of its leadership, his potential ally, the SED, was completely adrift. This did not prevent Ceaușescu from appealing to them, and to Honecker in person, to "express the hope that everything will be done to prevent a course from being continued that will stamp out socialism in Poland." The aggressive determination that Ceaușescu had hoped for from the SED was more than this leaderless party, which had already been overtaken by a fatalistic mood, could muster.[93]

On 21 August 1989—ominously enough the anniversary of the invasion of Czechoslovakia in 1968—the Politburo in Moscow formally rejected Ceaușescu's demands, succinctly citing, in defense of its decision, the fact that the "possibilities for joint measures that do not violate the sovereignty of the People's Republic of Poland ... are extremely limited."[94] The only course of action left to Ceaușescu was to criticize Gorbachev harshly, as he did at the 14th Party Conference of the Romanian Communists in November 1989. He lambasted Gorbachev's reforms once more, comparing them to concessions to the "class enemy" of the order of the 1939 Hitler–Stalin Pact.[95]

At the Warsaw Pact summit in early December 1989, which rose to the task of formulating an apology for the invasion of Czechoslovakia in 1968, Gorbachev gave proof once more of his hallmark irony. He singled out Ceaușescu for praise for his refusal in 1968 to participate in the intervention of the Warsaw Pact troops.[96] By that stage Ceaușescu had lost his last close ally in the Eastern Bloc, Erich Honecker, and found himself completely isolated at the Moscow summit in a sea of new faces.[97] It was to be his last appearance outside Romania. Only a few days later, the Romanian people rose against him in revolt.[98] Moscow supported what appeared to be the will of the people and Ion Iliescu's National Front in the same way it supported the shift of power to Egon Krenz in East Berlin.

Gorbachev deplored Honecker's failure to make "fundamental corrections to his policy" of his own accord. Had he done so, "losses and problems of the kind currently experienced would neither have been necessary nor possible."[99] The GDR was bankrupt, the Berlin Wall had fallen, perestroika had obviously made it to the GDR—at last. But it was too late. Now the question was no longer how best to reform socialism but whether the SED state should continue to exist. For the SED-PDS (Party of Democratic Socialism), the Soviet Union remained the GDR's only sponsor and the only guarantor of its existence. The problem, however, was that the guarantor was now both unable and unwilling to guarantee anything. Gorbachev's line was clear: tottering CP regimes could not count on Soviet tanks to prop them up. After Gregor Gysi had been elected as chairman of the SED-PDS, he asked the deputy leader of the International Department of the CC CPSU, Rafael P. Fedorov, who had come to Berlin for the party conference, the one question that would be decisive for the fate of the GDR: to what extent was the "USSR prepared to assist the GDR in an emergency?" He was told, "the Afghanistan trauma and lessons learnt from 1956 and 1968 were making the matter extremely difficult for the USSR." No one in the CPSU leadership was prepared "to order the use of military force or speak out in favor of it." [100]

This was the result of a long process initiated by Gorbachev. This was what the "New Thinking" was basically all about. It was the core of Gorbachev's foreign policy.

Conclusion

Gorbachev's perestroika and the realization on the part of the Kremlin that the monolithic unity of global communism was no more than wishful thinking led to the formation of camps for the "fraternal parties" of the Soviet Empire to withdraw to. His concept of socialist democracy put the legitimacy of the power of communist parties on an entirely new basis. In this view, the primary purpose of communist parties was to serve the needs of their own populations. The Polish and the Hungarian communist parties were Gorbachev's closest allies in the implementation of the "New Thinking" in the Eastern Bloc.

General Jaruzelski was seen above all as an "ally and a kindred soul" by Gorbachev. This did not deter Moscow from occasionally exerting pressure on Warsaw in order to make the CP leaders see that there was no alternative to engaging Solidarność in a dialogue. This was considered by the CPSU to be an indispensable precondition for breaking the deadlock in Poland. During the crucial "Round Table" negotiations the CPSU observed strict neutrality. After the decisive semi-free elections in the summer of 1989, Gorbachev nudged the Polish communists toward supporting the non-communist prime minister, Tadeusz Mazowiecki. There were manifold reasons for this, the most important being Gorbachev's primary concern in this phase with not losing face or credibility in the eyes of the West. Being seen to pay no heed to the will of the Polish people would have exacted a huge price from the Soviet Union. That the power and authority of the Polish communists were obviously dwindling was not seen in Moscow as a warning that Poland might go off at a tangent and leave the gravitational field of Soviet politics altogether. The Kremlin felt relatively certain that Poland would continue to be dependent on the Soviet Union, notably in its energy policy, that the West would—according to "assurances" George H.W. Bush had given to Gorbachev—not provide assistance to Poland, and that Poland would continue to honor its alliance commitments within the Warsaw Pact. At the top of Moscow's list of priorities—and therefore more important than the PUWP's fate—was the maintenance of good, reliable interstate relations.

The reforms that had long been implemented by Hungary's reform communists met not only with the Kremlin's appreciation but with its active support. The CPSU largely failed to see to what extent Hungary's "socialist principles" would come under pressure from the reform process. The implications of the introduction of a multiparty system were hugely underestimated. Imre Nagy's reburial and the "National Round Table" were merely seen as another "stage on the road to a new model of societal development." The understanding the Kremlin showed for the rapidly dwindling number of options open to the HSWP contrasted starkly with the treatment meted out to Alexander Dubček's KPČ in 1968. Despite the prophesies of doom issuing from East Berlin, the CPSU seemed to pay hardly any attention to the demolition of the Iron Curtain, and even condoned it as a measure whose time had come. The Hungarian government was the first in the Eastern Bloc to strike out in a new direction in its foreign policy, crossing the point of no return in so doing. The Hungarians showed great skill in exploring how far Moscow was prepared to let them go. Calls for neutrality on the model of Austria were countenanced neither in Moscow nor the West. Keeping the Warsaw Pact intact and safeguarding Gorbachev's reform policy were top priorities in Western eyes also. With regard to the opening of borders, the situation was different: in 1988, when Hungarians were permitted to travel to the West, Moscow did not use its veto to block this development. Nor did Gorbachev object to the demolition of the Iron Curtain. The refugee crisis marked the climax of this development and led to a rapprochement between Hungary and the FRG. Again, Gorbachev saw no reason for putting his foot down. That Hungary might drift away to the West completely was, in the eyes of the CC in Moscow, such a distant possibility that it could safely be ruled out. The CC felt quite confident that the HSWP would be capable of remaining in control.

Developments in Czechoslovakia revealed the entire dilemma of Gorbachev's "New Thinking." Given its specific predicament, the KPČ could only pay lip service to perestroika. Any genuine advocacy of reforms would have irreparably damaged the power of the ruling elite, who were heirs to the suppression of the Prague Spring. A potential reassessment of the 1968 intervention would have put the positions of Vasil Bil'ak and Miloš Jakeš in jeopardy. Gorbachev insisted that perestroika must not be implemented at the expense of the KPČ. Throwing contrary advice to the wind, he did so not because he felt especially close to the Czechoslovak comrades, but for political reasons. The victory of the "Velvet Revolution" paved the way to an indictment of the 1968 military intervention in Czechoslovakia.

From the start, Erich Honecker and Nicolae Ceaușescu were the most implacable opponents of perestroika. The contempt Gorbachev felt for these two politicians grew by leaps and bounds. Moscow was in no position to exert significant pressure on Bucharest, and there was little it could do to ease the tense Hungarian–Romanian relations. The Kremlin pinned its hopes on the CSCE process and the obligations that were taking shape in the negotiations in Vienna, which Bucharest would have to abide by whether it wanted to or not. When the Romanian dictator called for an intervention in Poland in order to prop up the communist monopoly on power, Gorbachev ironically reminded him of the wisdom he had shown by not taking part in the 1968 invasion of Czechoslovakia. Even though both Honecker and Ceaușescu lost no opportunity to lambast Gorbachev's perestroika, the secretary general of CPSU steadfastly adhered to his policy of not imposing perestroika on anyone against their will.

Todor Zhivkov, the perennial leader of the Bulgarian CP who ruled his country with an iron fist, was neither an entrenched opponent of perestroika nor its advocate. Having lost Gorbachev's backing owing to his rigorous Turkish policy, the former "most loyal vassal of the Soviet Union" proceeded to de-ideologize his party on his own. "Preustroistvo," allegedly a homemade version of perestroika, was in fact a cheap piece of make-believe rather than a bona fide copy of the Soviet "original." As an exercise in window dressing it was designed to restore his credibility in Moscow and was quickly understood in Moscow to be just that. When Zhivkov tried to impress Gorbachev in 1987 with his allegedly radical economic reforms, the secretary general of CPSU accused him of trying to transform Bulgaria into a capitalist country. Zhivkov had fallen out of favor in Moscow, but the same was not true of the entire party apparatus. The extent to which Moscow may or may not have been complicit in the "palace revolt" in November 1989 is still a moot point. What has been established beyond doubt is that Zhivkov's enforced resignation was welcomed by the CPSU, even if it may not have had a hand in it. Zhivkov's successors lost no time doing a U-turn to mend Bulgaria's fences with Moscow.

While the opinion was widespread in the CC CPSU that the ruling communist parties in Poland and Hungary were in control of their reformist policies and were likely to retain it, and that both countries were highly likely to remain both economically and politically dependent on Moscow, this did not mean there was no such thing as a Plan B. At an early date, Moscow was already eyeing the fall of regimes and the "fraternal parties'" potential loss of power as a distinct possibility, and prepared for it. In such a case the USSR would refrain from military intervention on behalf of the "fraternal parties."[101]

Spirits were relatively high in the CC in Moscow as the revolutionary "annus mirabilis" 1989 drew to a close. There was every reason to hope that, after a temporary eclipse, the Socialist ideology was headed for a comeback in the long term, given that the other parties were equally at a loss when it came to radically reviving economic growth. By the end of 1989 a fundamental readjustment was gaining ground. Moscow's East European allies had to stand on their own legs and rely on their own resources to cope with their problems. Relations with individual countries were put on an entirely new basis: Moscow had made its peace with the fraternal parties' loss of power. It was also decided that contacts between the parties should not become too close anymore: first of all, it was regarded as "unreal to continue the former practice" and summon meetings on economic questions; and secondly, the CC claimed, it would cause suspicions.[102] Much more importantly, the new and future governments in these countries had to abide by the commitments they had entered into within the Warsaw Pact. Maintaining the status quo and safeguarding the continued existence of the traditional blocs, NATO and Warsaw Pact, was not only in Moscow's interest but was seen as an indispensable precondition in Washington and other Western capitals. The demands for a withdrawal of Soviet troops first voiced in Hungary and Czechoslovakia, Moscow's compliance, and the German reunification process starting in 1990, subsequently called the entire Warsaw Pact and, inevitably, the European postwar order into question.[103]

Peter Ruggenthaler is deputy director of the Ludwig Boltzmann Institute for Research on War Consequences, Graz, Austria. Numerous publications, among them the monography *The Concept of Neutrality in Stalin's Foreign Policy, 1945–53* (Harvard Cold War Studies Book Series, 2015); *Soviet Occupation of Romania, Hungary, and Austria 1944/45–1948/49* (Co-editor, 2015); *Warsaw Pact Invasion of Czechoslovakia in 1968* (Harvard Cold War Studies Book Series, co-editor, 2010); *Stalins großer Bluff: Die Geschichte der Stalin-Note in Dokumenten der sowjetischen Führung. Schriftenreihe der Vierteljahrshefte für Zeitgeschichte Bd. 95* (2007).

Notes

Translated from German into English by Otmar Binder, Vienna. Preparatory work for this essay was conducted at the Ludwig Boltzmann Institut für Kriegsfolgenforschung, Graz–Vienna–Raabs in collaboration with Graz University and the City of Graz. It was supported by Austria's Federal Ministry of Science and Research in the context of the research projects "Der Kreml und die Wende 1989" [The Kremlin and the 1989 *Wende*] and "Zerfall der Sowjetunion 1991" ["The Collapse of the Soviet Union"] . See Karner et al., *Der Kreml und die "Wende" 1989*.

1. On M. Gorbachev's awareness of the camp formation, see the minutes of a Politburo session dealing with the Coordinating Committee on Multilateral Export Controls (CoCom) meeting and of a session of the Political Advisory Committee of the Warsaw Pact in Moscow, 13 November 1986, reprinted in Chernyaev, Medvedev and Shakhnazarov, *V Politbyuro TsK KPSS*, 105–12.
2. Cf. for instance his speeches to Eastern Bloc leaders in February and April 1985. Archive of the Gorbachev Foundation (hereafter: AFG), F. 3, Document 4487, M. Gorbachev's speech on behalf of the secretary general of the CPSU, K. Chernenko, delivered to party leaders of the "fraternal states" in Moscow, 18 February 1985; RGANI, F. 10, op. 3, d. 149, ll. 1–14, M. Gorbachev's speech at the summit meeting of the Warsaw Pact states in Warsaw, 26 April 1985.
3. Ibid (both documents). On the consequences of Gorbachev's economic reforms, see Karner, "Von der Stagnation zum Zerfall"; see also Kellerhoff, "Die wahren Ursachen."

4. Chernyaev, *V Politbyuro TsK KPSS*, 105–12; Russian State Archive of Contemporary History (hereafter: RGANI), F. 5, op. 101, d. 954, ll. 119–21, Analysis of the CC CPSU, n.d. [2 August 1988 at the latest]. For the SED's views on perestroika, see most recently Wilke, "The SED and Gorbachev's Reform Policies," and the literature cited there. On Romania, see Deletant, "Romania and the End of Ceaușescu's Rule".
5. See Baráth, "Ungarn und die Sowjetunion."
6. See Gorbachev's memories of Jaruzelski in Gorbatschow, *Erinnerungen*, 863–78.
7. RGANI, F. 5, op. 101, d. 896, ll. 73–78. Report by the CC CPSU Department for Ties with Communist and Workers' Parties of Socialist Countries, 2 September 1988.
8. Kramer, "The Demise of the Soviet Bloc," 1560.
9. RGANI, F. 5, op. 102, d. 762, ll. 39–42. Report by the Soviet embassy in Warsaw, 2 March 1989.
10. RGANI, F.5, op. 102, d. 758, ll. 51–55. Report by the Soviet embassy in Warsaw, 20 April 1989.
11. RGANI, F. 5, op. 102, d. 762, ll. 85–87. Report by the Soviet embassy in Warsaw, 20 April 1989.
12. RGANI, F. 5, op. 102, d. 766, ll. 26–27, KGB to the International Department CC CPSU, 3 March 1989. President George H.W. Bush is said to have addressed this topic in his meetings with the Polish leadership during his visit to Warsaw in July 1989 ("What I don't understand is why the average American or the average Briton should have to aliment the Poles."). See AFG, F. 2, op. 1, Minutes of a meeting between M. Gorbachev and the First Secretary of the CC PUWP, M. Rakowski, 11 October 1989. See also Rakowski, *Es begann in Polen*, 331. For the policy of the United States, see the seminal paper by Bischof, "Running Against a Clock."
13. AFG, F. 2, op. 1, Minutes of a meeting between M. Gorbachev and the First Secretary of the CC PUWP, M. Rakowski, 11 October 1989.
14. RGANI, F. 5, op. 102, d. 763, ll. 45–49. Report by the Soviet embassy in Warsaw, 13 June 1989.
15. RGANI, F. 5, op. 102, d. 763, ll. 70–76. Report by the head of the KGB, V. Kryuchkov, 9 June 1989.
16. Kramer, "The Demise of the Soviet Bloc," 1567.
17. RGANI, F. 3, op. 103, d. 180, l. 63, Politburo resolution "Regarding the appeal for help put forward by Cde. Rakowski," 21 August 1989; from M. Rakowski's political diary, 22 August 1989, reprinted in Rakowski, *Dzienniki Polityczne 1987–1990*, 497–98.
18. Rakowski, *Dzienniki Polityczne 1987–1990*, 497–98. In his memoirs published in German in 1995, Rakowski plays down the significance of what he himself considered to be a routine call by Gorbachev, and only quotes pep talk from it. See Rakowski, *Es begann in Polen*, 337–40.
19. RGANI, F. 3, op. 103, d. 183, S. 21–25, 103–12, Politburo resolution, 28 September 1989.
20. RGANI, F. 3, op. 103, d. 186, ll. 2, 30, 114–17, Politburo resolution, 23 October 1989.
21. Békés and Byrne, *Political Transition in Hungary*; Borhi, *Dealing with Dictators*, 364–433.
22. RGANI, F. 5, op. 102, d. 771, ll. 29–31. Report by the head of the CC CPSU International Department, V. Falin, 16 February 1989. See also RGANI, F. 5, op. 102, d. 774, ll. 94–98. Report on a meeting between A. Dobrynin and the chairman of the Hungarian National Assembly, M. Szűrös, 14 July 1989.
23. RGANI, F. 5, op. 102, d. 772, ll. 101–105. Report by the Soviet embassy in Budapest, 24 August 1989.
24. RGANI, F. 5, op. 102, d. 773, ll. 40–44. Report by the Soviet embassy in Budapest, 9 March 1989.
25. RGANI, F. 5, op. 102, d. 772, ll. 101–105. Report by the Soviet embassy in Budapest, 24 August 1989.

26. GARF, F. 9654, op. 10, d. 264, ll. 144–154. Analysis by the Soviet Foreign Ministry, n.d. [not before May 1989].
27. Quoted in Békés, "Detente and the Soviet Bloc," 170.
28. AFG, F. 1, op. 1. Excerpts from the minutes of a meeting between M. Gorbachev and M. Németh, 3 March 1989.
29. Békés and Kalmár, "Political Transition in Hungary and the End of the Cold War, 1988–1991."
30. Borhi, "Es ist die Pflicht Ungarns."
31. See the great number of reports by the Soviet embassy in Budapest and/or the CC or other agencies to the CC CPSU in seven fascicles comprising between several dozen and several hundred pages in RGANI, F. 5, op. 102, d. 771–77. On the basis of sources notably in the holdings of the Gorbachev Foundation, the same conclusion was reached in Savranskaya, Blanton and Zubok, *Masterpieces of History*, 450.
32. Wohnout, "Vom Durchschneiden des Eisernen Vorhangs," 189.
33. Oplatka, *Der erste Riß in der Mauer*, 108.
34. This is the conclusion Michael Gehler reaches using a wide range of sources. See Gehler, "Bonn–Budapest–Wien," 162.
35. This was the view expressed by the ambassador of the GDR, G. Vehres. Quoted in ibid., 143.
36. Ibid.
37. RGANI, F. 5, op. 102, d. 774, ll. 99–110. Report by the Soviet embassy in Budapest, 27 July 1989.
38. See Karner and Lesiak, *Der erste Stein aus der Berliner Mauer*.
39. SAPMO-BA, SED, ZK, J IV 2/2A/3238. Letter from E. Shevardnadze to O. Fischer, 1 September 1989, reprinted in Stephan, *Vorwärts immer*, 113–14.
40. Quoted in Graf, "Österreich und das Verschwinden der DDR," 232–33.
41. Kohl, *Erinnerungen 1982–1990*, 923.
42. Oplatka, *Der erste Riß in der Mauer*.
43. See Küsters, "Entscheidung für die deutsche Einheit," 42–45.
44. RGANI, F. 5, op. 102, d. 771, ll. 165–70. Report compiled by the International Department CC CPSU, 22 November 1989.
45. Ibid.
46. RGANI, F. 5, op. 102, d. 777, ll. 187–88. Report compiled by the deputy head of the KGB, Colonel General G. Ageev, 5 December 1989.
47. Cf., for instance, Shakhnazarov's memoirs, *Tsena svobody*, 108.
48. Bischof, Karner and Ruggenthaler, *The Prague Spring*, 16, 22.
49. In 1970 the ČSSR was made to sign a treaty of alliance with the Soviet Union, in which the two states committed themselves to protecting "socialist achievements" if these were in danger from an internal "counterrevolution." This retrospective legitimation of the August 1968 invasion of Czechoslovakia gave the Soviet Union's right to intervene a semblance of legality.
50. See Chernyaev, *V Politbyuro TsK KPSS*, 60–61.
51. Ibid., 180–83.
52. RGANI, F. 5, op. 102, d. 782, ll. 66–70. Report by the Soviet embassy in Prague, 7.02.1989.
53. RGANI, F. 5, op. 102, d. 782, ll. 91–98. Report by O.T. Bogomolov to the CC CPSU, 16 March 1989.
54. Ibid.
55. RGANI, F. 5, op. 102, d. 794, ll. 69–75. Report by the Soviet embassy in Prague, 6 June 1989.
56. RGANI, F. 5, op. 102, d. 782, ll. 139–40. Report by the Soviet embassy in Prague, 6 June 1989.

57. This coincides with the view taken by the Soviet embassy in Prague. See RGANI, F. 5, op. 102, d. 783, ll. 87–90. Report by the Soviet embassy in Prague, 18 September 1989.
58. RGANI, F. 5, op. 102, d. 783, ll. 101–103. Report by the Soviet embassy in Prague, 17 October 1989.
59. RGANI, F. 5, op. 103, d. 190, ll. 31–36, here l. 36. Report by N. Slyun'kov to the CC of the CPSU "On the results of the meeting of the CC secretaries from the Comecon brother parties about economic questions," 14 November 1989. The meeting took place 9–10 November in Prague.
60. See Blehova, *Der Fall des Kommunismus*.
61. Savranskaya, Blanton and Zubok, *Masterpieces of History*, 608.
62. See Karner et al., *Der Kreml und die "Wende" 1989*, document 96. Minutes of the meeting between the foreign ministers of the ČSSR and the USSR, J. Dienstbier and E. Shevardnadze, 20 December 1989.
63. A dedicated research institute was founded in Vienna with the remit to present "fundamental theses concerning Bulgarian history and culture." The communist era remained outside consideration. See Bachmaier, "Die Rolle der Kulturpolitik," 251, 257; Kalinova and Baeva, *Bălgarskite prekhodi 1939–2005*, 417.
64. See Baeva, *Todor Zhivkov*, 98–102.
65. Ibid., 104; Baeva and Kalinova, *Bulgarien von Ost nach West*, 65–66.
66. The Coordinating Committee on Multilateral Export Controls (CoCom) was founded in 1949 to put clamps on West–East trade. Its aim was to impose limits on the export of strategically sensitive technology to the USSR and other COMECON countries such as China in order to ensure continued Western technological supremacy. The export of sensitive goods required special permits.
67. The Jackson–Vanik Amendment put restrictions on trade between the United States and the Soviet Union. It was signed into law in 1975 by President Gerald Ford. It still affects US trade relations with those communist or former communist countries that restrict freedom of emigration and other human rights.
68. Baeva, "Bulgaria from the 1980s to 1991."
69. Ibid.
70. RGANI, F. 5, op. 102, d. 743, ll. 108–12. Report by the Soviet embassy in Sofia, 30 June 1989.
71. Baeva, "Bulgaria from the 1980s to 1991."
72. RGANI, F. 5, op. 102, d. 743, ll. 2–6. Report by the head of the KGB, V.A. Kryuchkov, to A. N. Yakovlev on the situation in Bulgaria, 3 January 1989.
73. RGANI, F. 5, op. 102, d. 746, ll. 26–32. Report by the head of the International Department CC CPSU, V. Falin, 31 July 1989.
74. Baeva, "The Year of the Palace Coup."
75. Troebst, "Bulgarien 1989."
76. Dalos, *Der Vorhang geht auf*, 161–65.
77. Baeva, "Bulgaria from the 1980s to 1991."
78. RGANI, F. 5, op. 102, d. 743, ll. 134–38. Minutes of a meeting between Bulgaria's ambassador in the USSR, Georgi Pankov, and staffers of the International Department CC CPSU, 21 November 1989.
79. Troebst, "Bulgarien 1989," 383.
80. See e.g., the minutes of a Politburo meeting dealing with a recent COMECON conference and of a meeting of the Political Advisory Committee of the Warsaw Pact in Moscow, 13 November 1986, reprinted in Chernyaev, *V Politbyuro TsK KPSS*, 105–12.
81. For an overview on Romania, see Deletant, *Romania under Communist Rule*. "Systematization," the destruction and reconstruction of villages, dealt Romanian agriculture another heavy blow. On the one hand, this was a blatant attempt to

forcibly assimilate national minorities, notably the Hungarians of Transylvania, and, on the other, it was supposed to mark the culmination of socialism according to the preconceptions of the dictator. Relations with the "fraternal state" Hungary, which was forced to host an ever-increasing number of refugees from Romania, deteriorated apace.
82. Karner et al., *Der Kreml und die "Wende" 1989*, 37, 42.
83. Deletant, "Romania and the End of Ceaușescu's Rule."
84. Quoted in Wilke, "The SED and Gorbachev's Reform Policies."
85. Ibid.
86. RGANI, F. 3, op. 103, d. 169, S. 111–12. E. Shevardnadze and A. Yakovlev to the CC CPSU, 24 March 1989.
87. RGANI, F. 3, op. 103, d. 169, S. 22. Politburo resolution of the CC CPSU, 12 April 1989.
88. Deletant, "Romania and the End of Ceaușescu's Rule."
89. Altrichter, *Russland 1989*, 333.
90. Ibid., 308.
91. Quoted in Krenz, *Herbst 89*, 28.
92. RGANI, F. 5, op. 102, d. 780, ll. 107–10. Entry by the Soviet ambassador in Romania, E. Tyazhel'nikov, in his official diary, 21 August 1989; RGANI, F. 3, op. 103, d. 180, ll. 2, 7, 76; ibid., d. 181, ll. 140–41, Politburo resolution of the CC CPSU, 21 August 1989.
93. Wilke, "The SED and Gorbachev's Reform Policies."
94. RGANI, F. 3, op. 103, d. 180, ll. 2, 7, 76; ibid., d. 181, ll. 140–41. Politburo resolution of the CC CPSU, 21 August 1989.
95. Deletant, "Romania and the End of Ceaușescu's Rule."
96. See RGANI, F. 10, op. 3, d. 164, ll. 48–70. M. Gorbachev's speech delivered to the Warsaw Pact Summit in Moscow, 4 December 1989.
97. Hoover Institution, Stepanov–Mamaladze Papers, Diary Nr. 10, entry, 4 December 1989, reprinted in Karner et al., *Der Kreml und die "Wende" 1989*, document 90/2.
98. For the revolution in Romania in 1989, see the seminal work by Siani-Davis, *The Romanian Revolution of December 1989*; and Weiss, "Traumatische Befreiung," 323.
99. Quoted in Wilke, "The SED and Gorbachev's Reform Policies."
100. See "Note on a meeting between G. Gysi and R. Fedorov on 10 December 1989 in Berlin," reprinted in Nakath, Neugebauer and Stephan, *"Im Kreml brennt noch Licht"*, 83–84.
101. For details, see Kramer, "The Demise of the Soviet Bloc," 1555–59; AFG, F. 3, Document 7179, Vadim V. Zagladin's analysis of Soviet military assistance commitments, 24 January 1989.
102. RGANI, F. 5, op. 103, d. 654, ll. 1–8, here l. 4. Report by the CC CPSU International Department, n.d. [1990].
103. For details, see the seminal paper by Mark Kramer, "The Warsaw Pact Alliance."

Bibliography

Altrichter, Helmut. *Russland 1989: Der Untergang des sowjetischen Imperiums*, Munich, 2009.

Bachmaier, Peter. "Die Rolle der Kulturpolitik in den Beziehungen zwischen Österreich und Bulgarien 1962–2008," in *Österreich und Bulgarien 1878–2008: Geschichte und Gegenwart*, ed. Peter Bachmaier, Andreas Schwarcz and Antoaneta Tcholakova, Vienna, 2008, 251–70.

Baeva, Iskra. "Bulgaria from the 1980s to 1991: The Price of Being the Most Faithful Satellite of the Soviet Union," in *The Fate of Communist Regimes, 1989–1991* (3 vols), ed. Mark Kramer et al., Harvard, forthcoming.

———. *Todor Zhivkov*, Sofia, 2006.

———. "The Year of the 'Palace Coup' or a New Start in Bulgarian History," in *Der Transformationsprozess in Bulgarien und der Weg in die EU*, ed. Peter Bachmaier, Vienna, 2006.

Baeva, Iskra, and Evgenia Kalinova. *Bulgarien von Ost nach West*, Vienna, 2009.

Baráth, Magdolna. "Ungarn und die Sowjetunion," in *Die 'Sechziger Jahre' in Ungarn*, ed. János M. Rainer, Bochum, 2009, 39–78.

Békés, Csaba. "Detente and the Soviet Bloc: From Promoter to Victim, 1975–91," in *The "Long 1970s": Human Rights, East–West Detente, and Transnational Relations*, ed. Poul Villaume, Rasmus Mariager and Helle Porsdam, New York, 2016, 165–83.

Békés, Csaba, and Malcolm Byrne (eds). *Political Transition in Hungary 1989–1990: A Compendium of Declassified Documents and Chronology of Events*, Budapest, 1999.

Békés, Csaba, and Melinda Kalmár (eds). "Political Transition in Hungary in 1989: Selected Documents," in *Cold War International History Project Bulletin*, Issue 12–13 (Winter 2002), 73–87.

Bischof, Günter. "'Running Against a Clock': The Bush Administration and Its 'Beyond Containment' Policy towards Eastern Europe in 1989," in *The Fate of Communist Regimes, 1989–1991* (3 vols), ed. Mark Kramer et al., Harvard, forthcoming.

Bischof, Günter, Stefan Karner and Peter Ruggenthaler (eds). *The Prague Spring and the Warsaw Pact Invasion of Czechoslovakia in 1968*, Lanham, MD, 2010.

Blehova, Beata. *Der Fall des Kommunismus in der Tschechoslowakei*, Berlin, 2006.

Borhi, László. *Dealing with Dictators, the United States, Hungary and East Central Europe, 1942–1989*, Bloomington, IN, 2016.

———. "'Es ist die Pflicht Ungarns, im Warschauer Pakt zu bleiben': Internationale Zusammenhänge des Systemwechsels von 1989 im Spiegel ungarischer Quellen," in *Das Vorspiel für die Grenzöffnung: Das Paneuropäische Picknick in Sopron am 19. August 1989*, ed. György Gyarmati and Krisztina Slachta, Budapest, 2014, 51–76.

Brait, Andrea, and Michael Gehler (eds). *Grenzöffnung 1989: Innen- und Außenperspektiven und die Folgen für Österreich*, Vienna, 2014, 185–219.

Chernyaev, Anatolii, Vadim Medvedev and Georgy Shakhnazarov. *V Politbyuro TsK KPSS: Po zapisyam Anatoliya Chernyaeva, Vadima Medvedeva, Georgiya Shakhnazarova (1985–1991)*, Moscow, 2006.

Dalos, György. *Der Vorhang geht auf: Das Ende der Diktaturen in Osteuropa*, Munich, 2009.

Deletant, Dennis. "Romania and the End of Ceaușescu's Rule," in *The Fate of Communist Regimes, 1989–1991* (3 vols), ed. Mark Kramer et al., Harvard, forthcoming.

———. *Romania under Communist Rule*, Iași, 1999.

Gehler, Michael. "Bonn–Budapest–Wien: Das deutsch-österreichisch-ungarische Zusammenspiel als Katalysator für die Erosion des SED-Regimes 1989/90," in

Grenzöffnung 1989, ed. Andrea Brait and Michael Gehler. *Grenzöffnung 1989: Innen- und Außenperspektiven und die Folgen für Österreich*, Vienna, 2014 135–62.
Gorbatschow, Michail. *Erinnerungen*, Berlin, 1995.
Graf, Maximilian. "Österreich und das Verschwinden der DDR 1989/90: Ostdeutsche Perspektiven im Kontext der Langzeitentwicklungen," in *Grenzöffnung 1989*, ed. Andrea Brait and Michael Gehler. *Grenzöffnung 1989: Innen- und Außenperspektiven und die Folgen für Österreich*, Vienna, 2014, 221–42.
Gyarmati, György, and Krisztina Slachta (eds). *Das Vorspiel für die Grenzöffnung: Das Paneuropäische Picknick in Sopron am 19. August 1989*, Budapest, 2014.
Kalinova, Evgeniya, and Iskra Baeva. *Bălgarskite prekhodi 1939–2005*, Sofia, 2006.
Karner, Stefan. "Von der Stagnation zum Zerfall: Kennzeichen der sowjetischen Wirtschaft der 1980er Jahre," in *Der Zerfall des Sowjetimperiums und Deutschlands Wiedervereinigung* [The Collapse of the Soviet Empire and Germany's Reunification], ed. Hanns Jürgen Küsters, Cologne, 2016, 15–45.
Karner, Stefan, and Philipp Lesiak (eds). *Der erste Stein aus der Berliner Mauer: Das paneuropäische Picknick 1989*, forthcoming.
Karner, Stefan, et al. (eds). *Der Kreml und die "Wende" 1989: Interne Analysen der sowjetischen Führung zum Fall der kommunistischen Regime. Dokumente*, Innsbruck, 2014.
Kellerhoff, Sven Felix. "Die wahren Ursachen für den Untergang der Sowjetunion," in *Die Welt*, 16 May 2016.
Kohl, Helmut. *Erinnerungen 1982–1990*, Munich, 2005.
Kramer, Mark. "The Demise of the Soviet Bloc," *Europe–Asia Studies* Vol. 63, No. 9 (2011), 1535–90.
———. "The Warsaw Pact Alliance, 1985–1991: Reform, Adaption, and Collapse," in *Der Zerfall des Sowjetimperiums und Deutschlands Wiedervereinigung* [The Collapse of the Soviet Empire and Germany's Reunification], ed. Hanns Jürgen Küsters, Cologne, 2006, 69–103.
Krenz, Egon. *Herbst 89*, Berlin, 1999.
Küsters, Hanns Jürgen. "Entscheidung für die deutsche Einheit," in *Dokumente zur Deutschlandpolitik. Deutsche Einheit*, ed. H.J. Küsters and Daniel Hofmann, Sonderedition aus den Akten des Bundeskanzleramtes 1989/90, Munich, 1998.
Nakath, Detlef, Gero Neugebauer and Gerd-Rüdiger Stephan (eds). *"Im Kreml brennt noch Licht": Spitzenkontakte zwischen SED/PDS und CPSU 1989–1991*, Berlin, 1998.
Oplatka, Andreas. *Der erste Riß in der Mauer: September 1989—Ungarn öffnet die Grenze*, Vienna, 2009.
Rakowski, Mieczysław. *Dzienniki Polityczne 1987–1990*, Warsaw, 2005.
———. *Es begann in Polen: Der Anfang vom Ende des Ostblocks*, Hamburg, 1995.
Sabrow, Martin (ed.). *1989 und die Rolle der Gewalt*, Göttingen, 2012.
Savranskaya, Svetlana, Thomas Blanton and Vladislav Zubok (eds). *Masterpieces of History: The Peaceful End of the Cold War in Europe, 1989*, Budapest, 2010.
Shakhnazarov, Georgii Kh. *Tsena svobody: Reformatsiya Gorbacheva glazami ego pomoshchnika*, Moscow, 1993.
Siani-Davis, Peter. *The Romanian Revolution of December 1989*, Ithaca, NY, 2005.
Stephan, Gerd-Rüdiger (ed.). *"Vorwärts immer, rückwärts nimmer!"* Berlin, 1994.

Troebst, Stefan. "Bulgarien 1989: Gewaltsamer Regimewandel in gewaltträchtigem Umfeld," in *1989 und die Rolle der Gewalt*, ed. Martin Sabrow, Göttingen, 2012, 357–83.

Weiss, Peter Ulrich. "Traumatische Befreiung: Die rumänische Revolution von 1989/90 als unbewältigte Gewalterfahrung," in *1989 und die Rolle der Gewalt*, ed. Martin Sabrow, 304–36.

Wilke, Manfred. "The SED and Gorbachev's Reform Policies: A 'Brotherhood' Shatters," in *The Fate of Communist Regimes, 1989–1991* (3 vols), ed. Mark Kramer et al., Harvard, forthcoming.

Wohnout, Helmut. "Vom Durchschneiden des Eisernen Vorhangs bis zur Anerkennung Sloweniens und Kroatiens: Österreichs Außenminister Alois Mock und die politischen Umbrüche 1989–1992," in *Grenzöffnung 1989: Innen- und Außenperspektiven und die Folgen für Österreich*, ed. Andrea Brait and Michael Gehler, Vienna, 2014, 185–219.

Chapter 2

Soviet Society, Perestroika, and the End of the USSR

Mark Kramer

Soviet Russian Society

In the 1960s, numerous Western scholars, influenced by the burgeoning literature on "modernization," argued that long-term changes in Soviet society—increased literacy and education levels, industrialization, increased urbanization, greater occupational differentiation, generational change, the advent of modern communications, and other such trends—were mitigating the Soviet regime's ability to exercise tight political and economic control.[1] Although none of these analysts believed that the Soviet Union would cease to be a communist state, many assumed that the USSR would gradually "converge" with Western societies. This school of thought was challenged by other scholars, notably Kenneth Jowitt, who asserted that the leaders of the Soviet Communist Party (CPSU) would be able to preserve Leninist rule by co-opting or integrating new social groups into the system.[2] These contending views of how the Soviet regime would cope with long-term social change were never fully reconciled, but the topic was revived in the mid- to late 1980s by Jerry Hough, who averred that changes associated with modernization and economic development in the Soviet Union had generated strong pressures "from below" for democratization, pressures that Mikhail Gorbachev was seeking to use to his advantage:

Notes for this chapter begin on page 74.

> During Gorbachev's lifetime, the Soviet people became vastly more sophisticated, urban, and educated ... Even before becoming general secretary, Gorbachev apparently understood the implications of these enormous demographic changes ... Gorbachev had good reason to believe that the Soviet Union was ripe for dramatic political change. Historically, when a country achieves a high level of urbanization and education, the democratic pressure against dictatorship becomes irresistible ... Gorbachev understood that the transformation of Soviet society [in the decades after World War II] had increased the risk of radical popular rebellion ... As a country urbanizes and education becomes more widespread, the threat of popular revolt becomes greater.[3]

Hough's analysis was grounded in the traditional themes of the modernization school, but it also tallied well with contemporaneous Western literature that highlighted the role of key social groups (especially the middle class and new professionals) in pushing for democratization in southern Europe, Latin America, and East Asia.[4]

Although Hough emphasized "the Russian people's receptivity to radical reform," he believed there were limits on how far the Russian public would actually go.[5] Most Russians, he argued in late 1989, were "shocked by the strength of the national feeling" in the non-Russian republics, and were more concerned about the cohesiveness of the Soviet Union than about the prospects for further reform:

> The vast majority of Russians—even highly educated Russians, including the intelligentsia—are very leery of the possibility that a multiparty democracy would lead to the establishment of separatist parties in union and autonomous republics that would gain majority support. ... [Russians] fear that democracy for themselves would mean the breakup of the union. A Boris Yeltsin who is forced to concede that his program means the possibility of independence for the Baltic republics faces a virtually impossible task in winning the populist mandate [in Russia].[6]

Hough claimed that the adverse "effect of the multinational character of the Soviet Union on the Russian attitude toward full democracy" was what had given rise to "the longstanding perception among the Soviet intelligentsia that the Russian people are basically conservative."[7] In Hough's view, Gorbachev did not share the intelligentsia's "mistaken perception," but he did sense that many Russians were worried about the impact of democratization on the survival of the state. Hough maintained that the Soviet leader was seeking to exploit the Russian public's fears by orchestrating "conditions of controlled chaos" that would enable him "to maintain his control" while implementing drastic changes.[8] "Gorbachev's basic decision," Hough wrote, "was to let unrest in the republics—especially the smaller ones—go to an extreme."⁹ Far from viewing the ethnic ferment as undesirable, Gorbachev actually welcomed it and "deliberately [sought] to create an exaggerated sense of crisis" that would heighten "the subjective feeling among Moscow intellectuals that the nationality problem [was] dangerous."¹⁰ This strategy, according to Hough, reflected Gorbachev's "very sound" understanding of the conflicting impulses within Russian society: On the one hand, most Russians were eager for "more freedom and greater integration into the West"; on the other hand, they were, in Hough's assessment, "still several decades away from accepting the breakup of the country."¹¹

The evidence that has emerged over the past thirty years indicates that social trends in the USSR—especially in the Russian Soviet Federated Socialist Republic (RSFSR), the largest and most important of the fifteen Soviet republics—were more complicated than Hough implied. Although Hough was right in predicting that some important social groups in the RSFSR (and in other republics) would be strongly supportive of political and economic liberalization, he was wrong in arguing that the Russian public had a fundamental commitment to the preservation of the Soviet Union in its post-1945 borders. When Soviet troops cracked down in Lithuania and Latvia in January 1991, large crowds of Russians voiced their opposition and signed petitions of solidarity with the Baltic nations at the unofficial Lithuanian and Latvian "embassies" in Moscow.¹² More than 150,000 Russians took part in a protest demonstration in Moscow on 20 January 1991 to denounce the violent clampdown in the Baltics, a turnout that dismayed Soviet leaders.¹³ A few weeks later, some 250,000–300,000 protesters took part in a boisterous demonstration in downtown Moscow, voicing anger not only about the crackdown in the Baltic republics but also more generally. In June 1991, Russians voted decisively for Boris Yeltsin in the Russian presidential election, even though he had spoken strongly in favor of independence for the Baltic republics. When the Baltic states, Moldova, and Georgia gained independence shortly after the rebuff of the August 1991 coup in Moscow, the Russian public barely seemed to notice. Nor were there any mass protests in Russia in December 1991 when Yeltsin joined with his Ukrainian and Belarusian counterparts in signing the Belovezhskaya Pushcha agreements that brought a formal end to the Soviet Union.

Hough had claimed in late 1989 that "the absence of significant demonstrations by the students in Moscow and Leningrad"—at a time of growing unrest in many of the non-Russian republics—was attributable to Russians' "fear of a breakup of the union." A much more plausible explanation for the lack of student protests in Moscow is that a "civil society" had not yet taken root in Russia. Soviet society had gradually taken on a new complexion after the death of Josif Stalin in 1953, and it is clear that many Russians by the 1980s did want greater freedom and contact with the West. Nonetheless, the demographic changes that occurred from the mid-1950s through the mid-1980s did not produce a genuine civil society, either in Russia or in most of the other republics. The barriers to collective action in Russia thus remained formidable.

Although some Western analysts in the late 1980s argued that a civil society had emerged in the RSFSR, subsequent events did not bear this out.[14] During the early Gorbachev years, environmental concerns were the only notable catalyst of social mobilization in Russia and most other republics.[15] The fact that environmental issues played this role is not at all surprising. In the pre-Gorbachev era, the only "unofficial" movement that was tolerated in Soviet Russia was a diffuse coalition led by conservationists, scientists, writers, and other intellectuals who sought to prevent further environmental damage, especially the ongoing pollution of Lake Baikal.[16] From the regime's standpoint, the prominent role of this ad hoc environmental movement in the "save Baikal" campaign in the 1960s and 1970s was relatively innocuous, but the precedent it set was important in a country that had been subjected to environmental depredation throughout the Soviet era. The perceived "safety" of at least some environmental issues as a topic of public debate ensured that long-standing concerns about the effects of pollution and radioactive contamination, voiced by Russian nationalists in the RSFSR as well as by "popular fronts" (newly formed nationalist groups) in many of the non-Russian republics, would become a rallying point during the initial phase of perestroika.

Aside from that one factor, however, there was surprisingly little impetus for social mobilization in Russia (or in most of the other republics) during the early period under Gorbachev. Russians wanted greater freedom and integration with the West, but they were not inclined to organize in support of their demands. Although independent associations had begun to emerge in Russia by 1988, these were not tantamount to sustained grassroots mobilization. Even after Gorbachev introduced a far more radical agenda of liberalization and democratization in July 1988 and permitted much freer discussion of Soviet history and of long-standing social problems in the Soviet Union, these measures did not initially give rise to any broad social movement in Russia. Not until 1989—with the elections in March for the USSR Congress of People's Deputies (resulting in a grassroots victory for Boris Yeltsin, who had been ousted in October 1987 and had to overcome the Soviet regime's efforts to thwart his election to the Congress), the subsequent formation of the Moscow Union of Voters, and the eruption of large-scale coal miners' strikes in July in the Kuznetskii Basin (Kuzbass) and other regions—was there any appreciable manifestation of organized popular ferment in the RSFSR.[17] Even then, the signals "from below" in Russia were hardly overwhelming.

Although organized opposition to the regime increased in 1990 and early 1991—reaching levels unseen in Russia since March 1917—the number of active participants still represented only a small percentage of the total populace. Moreover, even if the rate of participation had been higher, the bitter fragmentation among the various groups would have prevented the emergence of anything like the mass *Solidarność* movement that arose in Poland in 1980. The opposition in Russia was so riven by internal discord that participation began dropping off significantly in the spring and summer of 1991 after it had reached its peak in early 1991. The relative lack of social mobilization in Russia was evident in August 1991 when hardline officials and military commanders launched a coup d'état in Moscow. The vast majority of Russians stayed on the sidelines, waiting to see how events would turn out. Contrary to the popular myth that vast throngs of Russians triumphed over the coup plotters, no more than sixty thousand demonstrators gathered in the capital to oppose the coup—a paltry turnout in a city of more than ten million. (By contrast, in Prague, a city of only about 1.2 million, more than a million demonstrators took to the streets in November 1989 to face down the communist regime during the "Velvet Revolution."[18]) Steven Fish, in a study of grassroots movements in Russia in 1985–1991, attaches considerable weight to the "motley conglomeration of autonomous societal organizations [that] spearhead[ed] a popular movement for democracy," but even Fish concedes that the deep rifts within this "movement" (to the extent it existed as a unified entity) severely attenuated its effectiveness.[19] In a retrospective analysis of the Gorbachev era published in 1997, Hough is largely justified in arguing that "seldom has there been a revolution or process of democratization accompanied by so little direct pressure from society."[20]

Soviet society played a role during the Gorbachev era that entailed strong support for democratization, on the one hand, but a low degree of mobilization, on the other. The increasing complexity of Soviet society in the wake of Stalin's death had led, by the 1970s, to a gulf between the expectations of well-educated young people and the opportunities available to them. This problem was compounded in the late 1970s by the slowdown of Soviet economic growth and the embarrassing spectacle of an increasingly ill and infirm leader, Leonid Brezhnev, who presided over the CPSU. The confluence of these circumstances engendered cynicism and detracted from social morale, especially among those under thirty. Cynicism and declining morale were not tantamount to social revolt, but they did erode the public's willingness to "accept" the Soviet order. Soviet society remained generally stable in spite of these problems, but here I would emphasize two factors: the use or threat of repression, and the modest but steady improvements in living standards after Stalin's death. Both of these elements were severely disrupted by Gorbachev's policies, which brought a fundamental easing of repression and a sharp deterioration of economic performance from mid-1990 on.

The discontent that ensued did not necessarily mean that events would spin out of control, but it did create a more volatile situation than had existed earlier. The potential for instability was augmented by two other hallmarks of the Gorbachev era: the growing salience of information technology, and the much greater exposure of Soviet society to the West. Advances in technology—radio, television, telephones, computers, and so forth—affected Soviet society from the time of Nikita Khrushchev in the 1950s through the advent of Gorbachev in the mid-1980s. Technology can be an instrument of social control (as in George Orwell's *1984*) as well as a means of social diffusion. During the Brezhnev era, a coterie of leading scientists in the Soviet Union (the latter-day Taylorists) advocated mass computerization precisely because they believed it would be an effective means of top-down control and would facilitate "rational" economic planning.[21] For various reasons, however, computerization did not make much headway in the Soviet Union and was concentrated disproportionately in the military sector.

The impact on Soviet society of other technological developments, including shortwave radios and international phone service, was much greater, but still limited. For the most part, Soviet leaders were able to contain the social and political effects of technological advance, even though in some cases they found that a modicum of control had to be sacrificed. Had it not been for the broad political liberalization that Gorbachev introduced, the decrement of control would have been of minor significance and would not have posed any risk for the Soviet regime.[22] But with the inception of far-reaching political reforms, Soviet citizens could make much greater use of technology to operate outside state control and to circumvent the official media.[23]

Information technology also facilitated the enormous growth of contacts with the outside world in the late 1980s and early 1990s. During the Stalin era, Soviet society had been almost completely isolated from the West (aside from the unavoidable contacts that occurred during World War II). Exposure to the West increased somewhat under Khrushchev and expanded still further during the Brezhnev era, with at least a small impact on the regime's efforts to maintain tight control. Although East–West cultural, scientific, and educational exchanges affected only a relatively narrow band of the Soviet population, the exchanges gradually "softened" communist rule—if only minutely—by exposing up-and-coming Soviet elites to the outside world.[24] The Soviet media routinely glossed over the wealth and freedoms of the West, but these traits were hard to miss for Soviet citizens who witnessed them firsthand. Exposure to the outside world waned during the surge of US–Soviet tensions in the early 1980s, but when Gorbachev came to power he was determined to end Soviet isolation. From 1985 on, East–West contacts increased exponentially. More important than the official exchanges and high-level visits were the unprecedented opportunities for ordinary Soviet citizens to travel to the West. In a society that had until recently been kept apart from capitalist countries, the huge proliferation of links with the outside world came as a jolt to many people, who suddenly realized that everything they had been told about their own living conditions compared to those in the West was false.

The illusions that had long prevailed within Soviet society were shattered not only by the surge of contacts with Western countries but also by the electrifying impact of glasnost in the Soviet media. Having been assured for decades that the Soviet Union was the "vanguard of world progress," many Soviet citizens were dismayed to find that their country actually lagged far behind the "civilized" countries. They were also taken aback by the flood of revelations about Soviet history. Although most people had been aware of unsavory events in the Soviet Union's past, they had not fully grasped the dimensions of the Stalinist crimes. Equally unnerving was the sudden outpouring of information about social problems in the Soviet Union—including alcoholism, juvenile delinquency, declining health indices, homelessness, spiritual malaise, crime, poverty, and the disaffection of young people—and about natural disasters and accidents. The stream of disclosures about the Soviet past and about the deficiencies of Soviet society did not spark mass unrest, but it did have the cumulative impact of delegitimizing the Soviet regime in the eyes of many Russians.

This development, combined with the economic hardships that had waxed acute by 1990, mitigated the Russian public's commitment not only to the Soviet regime, but also to the USSR itself. The rebuff of the hardline coup attempt in August 1991 merely accentuated the society's indifference to the survival of the Soviet state. As noted earlier, there were no mass protests—or even minor protests—in Russia when the Baltic states, Moldova, and Georgia gained independence in the immediate aftermath of the failed coup. Nor were there any protests when Russians suddenly learned in December 1991 that the Soviet Union was going to be dissolved at the end of the year. On the contrary, Russian society reacted to the Belovezhskaya Pushcha accords with evident relief. Gorbachev had desperately wanted to preserve the Soviet Union, but his effort to do so was greatly complicated by the public mood in Russia during the final few months of 1991. The dissolution of the Soviet Union had seemed inconceivable before Gorbachev came to power, but one of the consequences of his policies—obviously an unintended consequence—was the growing public perception in Russia that the demise of the Soviet state was inevitable and therefore not worth resisting.[25] Although Russians were not inclined to revolt en masse against Soviet rule, the important thing by the end of 1991 was that all the major social groups in Russia no longer had a stake in the future existence of the USSR.

Soviet Society outside Russia

The muted response of the Russian public to the dissolution of the Soviet Union brings me to the ethnic dimension of the Soviet collapse, a topic that has been discussed and debated at great length by scholars both inside and outside the former USSR.[26] The first thing we need to do is decide whether the Soviet Union should be regarded as an "empire," a term that until the 1980s was rarely applied to the USSR.[27] The reason that very few analysts used the term is not that the Soviet Union bore scant resemblance to large, contiguous empires from the past (the Soviet state did in fact share many of the features of earlier empires), but that the term itself acquired a pejorative sense in the twentieth century, especially after World War II. In the nineteenth century, the great powers in Europe had unabashedly sought colonial empires and adopted imperialist policies, but the connotation of "empire" and "imperialist" changed drastically in the following century, in part because of the rhetorical changes introduced by Vladimir Lenin and other Bolshevik leaders, who claimed to be pursuing an "anti-imperialist" line.[28] The leftward political shift in Europe at the end of World War II led to a further discrediting of the term "empire." By and large, European states no longer wanted to be seen as "imperialist." Although most of them initially were wary of decolonization (and even tried to resist it, as in Indochina and Algeria), they ultimately were willing to grant independence to dozens of former colonies after the war. In the late 1960s and early 1970s, the negative connotation of the term "empire" proved useful to radical left-wing critics of US foreign policy, who denounced the war in Vietnam as an "imperialist" venture and accused the United States of seeking to build a global empire.[29] These accusations ebbed after the US involvement in Vietnam ended, but the stigma associated with the term "empire" persisted.

In the late 1980s, nationalist groups in the non-Russian republics of the USSR increasingly referred to the Soviet Union as an "empire." Their use of an anti-imperialist discourse was intended to legitimize their own claims to independence and to discredit the Soviet state.[30] By the time the Soviet Union ended, the term had also gained favor among Russians, who argued that Russia, too, had been exploited by the communist regime. In the scholarly world as well, characterizations of the Soviet Union as an "empire" suddenly became commonplace. To the extent that "empires in the modern world," as Ian Lustick has pointed out, "are expected to break apart," this new fashion was perfectly understandable.[31] Before December 1991, some scholars had still been leery of describing the Soviet Union as an "empire," lest they imply that the state would definitely unravel, but those concerns became obsolete once the USSR was formally dissolved.[32]

Regardless of whether one finds the term "empire" useful for understanding the Soviet Union, there is no doubt that comparisons with large, contiguous empires from the past can shed useful light on the Soviet case—specifically on the question of whether and how such entities can be held together.[33] The common assumption, as Lustick noted, is that empires always break apart, but the Ottoman, Habsburg, and Tsarist Russian cases suggest that contiguous multiethnic empires can in fact be preserved for a long while. The Ottoman and Habsburg empires held together for centuries, even after they began to grow feeble.[34] Ultimately it took a major war to put an end to them. The Romanov empire likewise remained in place for more than three hundred years—from 1613 to 1917—until the upheavals of World War I led to the overthrow of the Tsar and gave the Bolsheviks an opportunity to seize power. (The new Bolshevik regime temporarily relinquished chunks of territory along the western rim of the former empire, but Stalin eventually regained almost all of it, plus some lands that the Tsars had not occupied.)

These earlier empires were kept together by a number of factors that blended coercion and inducements (in varying proportions over time), but the most crucial factor of all was the demonstrated willingness of the rulers to use force to subdue anyone who would endanger their authority. By the same token, the consolidation of the enlarged Soviet state after World War II was made possible by Stalin's readiness to employ unstinting violence to crush armed separatist movements in the newly acquired regions of western Ukraine, western Belorussia, and the Baltic states.[35] The Soviet government's use of unbridled force against Ukrainian and Baltic insurgents in the 1940s and early 1950s deterred further armed rebellions against Soviet rule. Until the late 1980s, no one in the Soviet Union (or the West) had reason to doubt that the Soviet regime would act as forcefully as necessary to preserve the integrity of the Soviet state.[36] The importance of this perception was underscored—in a different context—by Reinhard Bendix's classic study of monarchical systems in Great Britain, France, Russia, Germany, and Japan. Bendix averred that a monarch's hold on power was ultimately dependent on the widespread belief that "those who rule are able, and will not hesitate, to use force if that is needed to assert their will."[37] Soviet leaders from Stalin through Konstantin Chernenko (Gorbachev's immediate predecessor) amply fulfilled this criterion, but the growing—and well-founded—sense in the late 1980s and early 1990s that Gorbachev would not resort to violence on a consistent basis and in sufficient measure proved to be the undoing of the USSR.[38]

Comparisons with Other Communist Ethnofederal European States

Comparisons are useful not only with earlier empires, but also with two multiethnic European states that no longer exist—Czechoslovakia and Yugoslavia. These two states, like the Soviet Union, were created at the end of World War I and were dissolved in the early 1990s. Both of them were under communist rule for several decades (though the communist regimes there, unlike in the Soviet Union, did not come to power until the 1940s). Most analysts who have sought to ascertain similarities and differences between these cases have emphasized what they see as the inherent fragility of ethnofederalism in communist states.[39] In their view, the ethnic identity of nationalities in the Soviet Union was greatly strengthened over time by the Bolsheviks' decision to set up a federation that was "national in form but socialist in content." According to this argument, the establishment of ethnically based republics, and the inclusion of ethnic background as the "fifth point" in passports (which had to be carried at all times), created an immutable ethnic identity for every citizen, and fostered a sense of national community among the members of the titular ethnic group in each non-Russian republic.[40]

Scholars who attribute the breakup of the Soviet Union to the "subversive" nature of ethnofederal institutions have touched on an important part of the story, but their analyses also have important shortcomings.[41] Their characterizations are too sweeping, and the dynamic they posit for the Soviet Union—whether valid or not—does not seem especially relevant to either Czechoslovakia or Yugoslavia. Czechoslovakia during most of its existence was not a federalized state even in cosmetic terms. Not until late 1968 were federal state institutions set up, and these never acquired any meaningful role during the communist era. Control of most functions remained centralized in Prague, and the proposal advanced by reformers in the Czechoslovak Communist Party (KSČ) during the 1968 Prague Spring to federalize the KSČ was derailed by the Soviet invasion of Czechoslovakia in August 1968.[42] The notion that ethnofederal institutions were instrumental in the formation and strengthening of national identity is clearly inapplicable to Slovak nationalism. Despite the lack of such institutions in pre–World War II Czechoslovakia, Slovak national identity (which had been very weak when Czechoslovakia was formed in 1918) emerged and grew with remarkable celerity in the 1920s and 1930s. Slovak nationalist sentiment was never stronger than during the six years of a nominally independent Slovak state from 1939 to 1945—a period that was remembered with great pride by many Slovaks long after they had been forced back into a unified Czechoslovak state at the end of the war.[43] Slovak nationalism was certainly stronger at that point than it was when the Czechoslovak communist regime collapsed in late 1989. Even though ethnofederal institutions had been nominally in place in Czechoslovakia for two decades by 1989, the Slovaks did not push immediately for an independent state when the opportunity arose after the Velvet Revolution. Instead, they initially sought to work out an accommodation with the Czechs—an accommodation that ultimately proved elusive. Contrary to the "subversive institutions" thesis, the Czechoslovak state did not split apart when it was under, or emerging from, communist rule. The breakup of Czechoslovakia was precipitated by the political maneuvering of democratically elected leaders in Prague and Bratislava in 1990–1992, not by communist-era institutions.[44] The processes of ethnic identity formation and state dissolution in Czechoslovakia were thus fundamentally different from those in the Soviet Union.

In Yugoslavia, too, policies and institutions diverged markedly from the practices in the Soviet Union. Long before ethnofederal institutions and communist rule existed in Yugoslavia, ethnic identities had emerged and intensified, as was demonstrated by the murderous conflicts during World War II. The fervor of national identities actually seemed to diminish, not increase, during much of the communist era.[45] Yugoslav citizens did not have to list their ethnicity on their passports, and when they were given the option of putting "Yugoslav" as their ethnic background on census questionnaires and other official documents, a large (and growing) number chose it. The federal system that Josip Broz Tito established soon after he took power at the end of World War II was heavily centralized for many years (like the Soviet system), but in the 1960s the Yugoslav League of Communists was federalized, and in 1974 Tito consented to a decentralized state structure that gave extensive latitude to the country's six republics and two autonomous republics—far more latitude than the Soviet republics ever enjoyed.[46] In other respects as well, the arrangements that Tito bequeathed to his successors when he died in 1980 were markedly different from the much more centralized system in the Soviet Union.[47] Even if one wants to focus solely on structure at the expense of agency—and to leave out what Daniel Bell once described as "the variabilities of accident, folly, and simple human cantankerousness"[48]—the structural differences among these three cases provide ample grounds for skepticism about the deterministic accounts that have appeared.[49]

Even in the case of the Soviet Union, the notion of "subversive institutions" is facile in its depiction of the rise of ethnic assertiveness. Although the federal structure of the USSR may have institutionalized ethnicity in some regions and thereby reinforced (or even created) ethnic identities among certain segments of the population, this did not automatically lead to separatism when the opportunities for ethnic-related political action suddenly increased in the late 1980s. The federal structure arguably had its greatest impact on ethnic identity formation in Central Asia (where national identities were nonexistent before the Soviet era), but no secessionist movements emerged in the region.[50] On the contrary, sentiment in favor of preserving the Soviet Union was much stronger in Central Asia than anywhere else, including Russia.

In other republics of the USSR, the impact of institutions on ethnicity was at least partly offset by policies adopted in the late 1950s to assimilate ethnic minorities. The assimilationist measures made greater headway than is often realized, even though they were in place for only a short period of time (less than thirty years).[51] The extent of assimilation varied among republics and regions as well as among the minority groups (for example, those who lived outside their titular homelands or lacked a titular homeland were particularly vulnerable to assimilation, as were those who lived in large urban areas), but the results of the 1959, 1979, and 1989 censuses as well as other demographic evidence presented by Barbara Anderson and Brian Silver suggest that assimilation in many areas was indeed occurring.[52] Whether measured by the increasing number of non-Russians who re-identified themselves as "Russian," the expanding number who regarded Russian as their "native language," the declining number who knew their titular language, the growing rate of intermarriage, or some other commonly used indicator, a gradual trend toward assimilation was certainly evident from the late 1950s through the mid-1980s. Indeed, despite the impact of ethnofederal institutions and passport policies, there is abundant evidence that many members of non-Russian ethnic groups belonged to those groups in name only. They did not regard their ethnic identity as important, and shared few if any of the group's cultural and linguistic characteristics. They were also far more likely to marry outside their group.[53] During the Soviet period, the children from mixed marriages overwhelmingly identified themselves as Russian. This two-generation assimilation process was beginning to have a significant demographic impact by the mid-1980s—at the very moment that Gorbachev reversed it. Had the Soviet Union remained under the direction of Brezhnevite leaders, the trend toward assimilation would likely have continued.

Although Soviet policies vis-à-vis nationalities were certainly contradictory—some were conducive to the deepening of ethnic identity, whereas others encouraged assimilation—the overall balance may ultimately have favored assimilation. The notion that Soviet policies and institutions uniformly led to an immense strengthening of ethnic identity in the pre-Gorbachev era, and that this in turn was bound to spawn separatist movements once the "structure of political opportunities" expanded in the late 1980s, is simplistic.[54]

Comparisons with Existing Multiethnic States

In addition to comparing the Soviet Union with empires and states that no longer exist, it is essential to draw comparisons with large, multiethnic countries that are still around. One obvious example is India, a country with a huge, ethnically diverse, and rapidly growing population (projected to be even larger than China's by the year 2024), an ethnofederal political structure, nationalist political parties, egregious disparities of wealth, widespread poverty, long-standing insurgencies (especially in Kashmir and Punjab), periodic instances of extreme ethnic and religious intolerance and violence, and a vast number of languages.[55] Despite all these fissiparous elements, India has remained intact and reasonably democratic since gaining independence in 1947. Even the authoritarian policies introduced by Indira Gandhi in 1975 did not outlast her rule.

Another country that is well worth comparing with the Soviet Union is Indonesia, which became independent in 1949. Indonesia, unlike India, was under authoritarian rule from the late 1950s through the late 1990s (with "Guided Democracy" under Sukarno and the "New Order" under Suharto), and is therefore more directly analogous to the communist system in the Soviet Union. Indonesia shares many of the features that are often cited as having contributed to (or "caused") the breakup of the Soviet Union: a vast population (the world's fourth largest); an immense and sprawling territory consisting of ethnically concentrated regions; a highly centralized government (until 2001, when a policy of decentralization was implemented); a multitude of languages (more than 330); a multitude of distinct ethnic groups with strong ethnic identities; and localized separatist insurgencies. Under international pressure, Indonesia agreed in 1999 to end its occupation of East Timor (a territory it invaded in 1975 and annexed the following year), but that in no way adumbrated the dissolution of Indonesia itself. On the contrary, despite the onerous impact of the Asian financial crisis in the late 1990s and the continued separatist fighting in Aceh and Irian Jaya, Indonesia has remained intact and has moved toward a more democratic system in the wake of Suharto's resignation in 1998.

One other obvious candidate for comparison with the Soviet Union is the post-Soviet Russian Federation. Anyone who wants to understand the disintegration of the Soviet Union has to explain why the collapse did not continue in Russia. Although the percentage of Russians in the Russian Federation is much higher than in the Soviet Union (81 percent versus 52 percent), Russia is an ethnically heterogeneous country with an ethnofederal configuration left over from the communist era. In the immediate aftermath of the Soviet Union's collapse, many Western scholars predicted that Russia, too, was likely to break apart.[56] Those predictions largely disappeared after Yeltsin secured passage of a new constitution in December 1993 and launched a brutal campaign in Chechnya a year later, but it is still interesting to consider why Russia has been able to stay intact in the face of great political and economic upheavals. Many explanations have been offered of this phenomenon, but the factors that seem most important are fivefold: (1) the high percentage of Russians in many of the ethnofederal regions,[57] (2) the historical, geographic, economic, and demographic circumstances that militate against attempts at secession,[58] (3) Yeltsin's success in forging compacts with potentially troublesome regions (all except Chechnya), (4) the Russian government's demonstrated willingness to use force on a massive scale to put down separatist challenges,[59] and (5) the lack of a dominant component in the Russian Federation that could seek to eclipse the central government in the way that Yeltsin gained ascendance over the Soviet regime from his base in Russia in 1991.

It is common nowadays to argue that the collapse of the Soviet Union was inevitable—whether because of a state structure and nationality policies that bred ethnic separatism, the imperial nature of Soviet Communist rule, the puissance of ethnonationalist movements, the inability of Marxist–Leninist regimes to reform themselves, the inherent rigidity of closed one-party systems, or some other factor—but the survival of India, Indonesia, post-Soviet Russia, and numerous other multiethnic states (some democratic, some authoritarian) suggests, all the more, that claims of inevitability are simplistic. Relatively small alterations in circumstances, events, or policy choices in the Soviet Union might have led to a different outcome.

The Leeway for Ethnic Unrest and Defiance

The notion that ethnic pressures were bound to become unmanageable in the Soviet Union is especially problematic in light of new evidence from the former Soviet archives. Although some of the relevant documentation is still inaccessible, a vast amount of evidence indicates that mass ethnic disturbances occurred with surprising frequency throughout the Soviet era.[60] By responding promptly and consistently with resolute force, the authorities were able to suppress these disturbances without any long-term impact on the country's stability. In the absence of Gorbachev's decision to proceed with far-reaching political liberalization, it is inconceivable that fissiparous ethnic tensions would have emerged on the scale they did in the late 1980s and early 1990s. The Soviet Union had coped with mass ethnic violence before, and it could have done so again.[61]

Ethnic unrest during the Gorbachev era could have been quelled at any number of points through the consistent application of force. The first large-scale collective protests after 1985 occurred in Kazakhstan in late 1986, when thousands of Kazakh students and workers staged violent demonstrations condemning Gorbachev's decision to replace the long-time Kazakh Communist Party first secretary, Dinmukhamed Kunaev, with an ethnic Russian, Gennadii Kolbin.[62] Clashes between the demonstrators and security forces resulted in hundreds of injuries and three deaths, and the police arrested more than two thousand people (though the large majority were quickly released) and expelled nearly three hundred students from the university (though most of them were soon permitted to return). But instead of completing a full-scale crackdown and imposing martial law, Gorbachev wavered and indirectly legitimized the protesters' actions by hastily bringing in a native Kazakh to serve alongside Kolbin as the "second secretary." This concession set a precedent that was bound to embolden activists elsewhere who were thinking of challenging the central authorities.

Gorbachev's unwillingness to resort to mass repression became far more evident in July 1987 when a group of 120 Crimean Tatar activists, who had been trying unsuccessfully to meet with the Soviet leader, held an impromptu demonstration in Red Square to demand that Crimean Tatars be allowed to return to their traditional homeland, from which they had been deported en masse by Stalin during World War II.[63] In the past, protests by even a few Crimean Tatars were immediately and harshly broken up, preventing any spread or repetition of the unrest. But Gorbachev, far from ordering the demonstration to be crushed, sent high-level emissaries to negotiate with the activists and set up a Politburo commission to review their demands. After the negotiations dragged on for two weeks without results, hundreds of Crimean Tatars staged another demonstration in Red Square, demanding to see Gorbachev and to be given the right to return to Crimea. When the new protest began on 23 July, the Soviet Politburo met to consider forceful "measures to suppress the Crimean Tatars' demonstration," but Gorbachev decided against a crackdown, hoping that the protests would peter out within a day or two.[64] After a week went by and the Crimean Tatars were still ensconced in Red Square—an unprecedented show of defiance in the heart of Soviet power—the police finally moved in and expelled the demonstrators from Moscow. Even so, many of the activists continued to organize large protests outside the capital to press their demands. Under Brezhnev, the prospect of severe repression against Crimean Tatars had been a formidable deterrent and had essentially eliminated the Tatars' hopes of ever being able to return to Crimea. Gorbachev's reluctance to dislodge the protesters in July 1987, and his offers of major concessions, revived the Crimean Tatar movement and transformed it into a conspicuous example of resistance—an example that other Soviet ethnic groups could seek to emulate.

The growing evidence of Gorbachev's inconsistency in the use of force soon spurred other serious challenges and clashes. In late 1987 and early 1988, activists in Armenia organized a mass petition drive calling for the return of the Nagorno-Karabakh Autonomous Oblast (NKAO), a region within neighboring Azerbaijan populated mainly by ethnic Armenians.[65] The petition, signed by hundreds of thousands of Armenians, was the initial stage of what evolved into a full-scale armed conflict between the Armenian and Azerbaijani Soviet republics. Newly released documents make clear that Gorbachev had no intention of transferring Nagorno-Karabakh to Armenia (such a step, he warned at a Politburo meeting in June 1988, would "provoke genocide"), but he was unwilling to take a decisive stance against the Armenian protesters.[66] The Soviet authorities sent security forces to the region in February 1988 after Azeris in Sumgait (a town near the Azerbaijani capital, Baku) carried out grisly attacks against ethnic Armenians; but the troops were given no clear-cut mission. If Soviet leaders had clamped down harshly on the Armenian activists when the petition drive and demonstrations began, they undoubtedly could have forestalled the subsequent violence. Some members of the Soviet Politburo, notably the head of the state security (KGB) organs,

Viktor Chebrikov, advocated a vigorous crackdown from the very start, but Gorbachev and other officials wanted to rely mainly on "political means" and to eschew the sustained use of force for as long as possible.[67] At a Politburo meeting in early March 1988, Gorbachev acknowledged that "it is impossible to remain indifferent when you see what is going on there [in Sumgait]." He said he could "understand the concerns of Chebrikov and others," but he insisted that the use of large-scale violence would be unacceptable: "Yes, the soldiers we sent to Sumgait were unarmed. But what would we have gained if they had been armed with sub-machine guns? What would have happened then in view of these atrocities?"[68]

At Gorbachev's behest, the CPSU Politburo decided to rely on the Soviet parliament to indicate that Nagorno-Karabakh would have to remain part of Azerbaijan—an action that conveyed no clear message and failed to stem the unrest.

When enmity between the Azeris and Armenians deepened and violence escalated in the summer of 1988, it appeared that Gorbachev would have to take a more forceful stance. Both parties to the dispute expected that an all-out crackdown was imminent, but no such crackdown occurred. As a result, activists in Armenia and Nagorno-Karabakh soon stepped up their efforts to reclaim the NKAO, sparking reprisals by Azeris. Although troops from the Soviet Internal Affairs ministry were again deployed to the region, they were not authorized to clamp down as ruthlessly as was necessary to put an end to the conflict. Despite numerous outbreaks of gruesome interethnic clashes, Gorbachev continued to hesitate, allowing the situation to spin out of control. Order returned for a brief while after an earthquake devastated Armenia in December 1988, giving Gorbachev an opportunity to move against some of the leaders of the Nagorno-Karabakh movement. But in the spring of 1989 he released all of them, and the conflict with Azerbaijan flared up again. By the time Soviet troops were sent to confront Azerbaijani nationalists in January 1990 and Armenian nationalists in the spring of 1991, the situation had deteriorated too far to be defused other than through the use of unrelenting violence—an option that Gorbachev and many of those around him were disinclined to pursue.

In other cases as well—the Baltic states, Moldova, and the Ferghana Valley—Gorbachev was unwilling to use violent repression consistently and on a scale that would have been needed to quell protests and deter further unrest. His reluctance to crack down did not stem from a lack of awareness of the burgeoning instability in the country, but from a conviction that "political solutions" were the only viable way to cope with the situation. At a CPSU Politburo meeting in mid-October 1988, he assured his colleagues that non-violent measures would suffice:

> Looking around the country, we find many problems not only in Armenia and not only in the NKAO. Processes are also under way in the Baltic republics, in Kirgiziya and Kazakhstan, in Moldova and Ukraine. Important questions are arising everywhere. ... But we should not oversimplify this. These processes are natural in conditions of democracy and glasnost. ... I have to say that the information in the Central Committee is one-sided and unconstructive. Often, they simply want to scare us. They think that the Politburo consists of blind fools. Some are already crying "To arms!" And on the basis of disinformation they believe that everything, so to speak, is collapsing. There is no ground for panic or for taking up arms. Such sentiments do not correspond to reality.[69]

Even on the rare occasions when the Soviet regime did use substantial force in response to ethnic challenges, the lack of consistency proved debilitating.[70] After widespread controversy ensued about a deadly crackdown in Georgia in April 1989, Gorbachev disavowed all responsibility for it, and condemned the bloodshed. In the process, he effectively deprived himself of the full latitude he needed to use force in the future, and he antagonized local army commanders, who felt they had been unfairly blamed for an ill-conceived mission. Gorbachev's repudiation of the violence also changed the expectations of potential protesters about the likelihood of encountering repression, giving them greater confidence that defiance would go unpunished. The deterrent effect of the crackdown was thus dissipated. Although Gorbachev ordered a large-scale military intervention in Azerbaijan in January 1990 (and did not subsequently disavow it), he was unwilling after that to use repression consistently enough to hold the country together. A crackdown in the Baltic republics in early 1991 was much more limited and halfhearted than many of his advisers had wanted.

Gorbachev's disinclination to use force with ruthless consistency was a monumental change for a country that had lived under repressive tyranny for seven decades, but it was not necessarily compatible with his desire to preserve the Soviet Union. In *Anatomy of Revolution*, Crane Brinton remarked that when an authoritarian regime began to liberalize and was then faced with a surge of opposition, a diffident response was likely to prove disastrous. According to Brinton, if the authorities were "more than half ashamed to use force, and therefore used it badly, so that on the whole those on whom force was inflicted were stimulated rather than repressed," the whole regime might be destabilized.[71] In numerous Soviet republics, the limited use of force ended up causing a backlash, spurring more people to support and take part in the main nationalist movements. By contrast, in the one case when overwhelming force was used—in Azerbaijan in January 1990—it proved highly effective.

The inconsistency of the use of force elsewhere tended to embolden the opposition and undercut the regime's own "internal consensus" about the prospects for restoring order.[72]

The Challenges from Russia and Ukraine

Gorbachev's unwillingness to rely consistently on violence to keep the Soviet Union from unraveling might not have been a fatal problem if the challenges to central authority had been limited to outlying areas such as the Baltic states, Moldova, and the Caucasus republics. The loss (de facto or otherwise) of those republics would not have been tantamount to the disintegration of the Soviet Union. Far more serious, however, were the challenges posed by Russia and Ukraine. In Russia, Yeltsin exploited the union-republic configuration of the USSR to try to eclipse the Soviet regime and establish Russia as the center of authority. In the context of the far-reaching liberalization introduced by Gorbachev, the federal structure of the Soviet Union proved inimical to the Soviet regime insofar as it enabled the preponderant "ethnic" actor (Russia) to wage a battle against the central government. In the pre-Gorbachev era, no such challenge would have been possible, but in 1990–91 the situation was remarkably fluid, and Russia's bid for ascendance posed a mortal danger to the Soviet regime. The greatly disproportionate size and importance of Russia in the Soviet state prevented Gorbachev from easily fending off this challenge. If the union-republics had been of roughly equal size and strength, Gorbachev might have been able to play them off against one another. But the dominance of Russia in the Soviet federation enabled Yeltsin to confront the Soviet government directly.

The danger that Russia posed, however, was to the Soviet *regime*, not to the Soviet state per se. The ascendance of Russia need not have meant the dissolution of the USSR. Yeltsin was willing to support independence for the Baltic republics and perhaps Georgia and Moldova, but, by all indications, he was hoping to preserve the rest of the union, especially the link with Ukraine and Belarus.[73] In the end, the disintegration of the Soviet Union was driven mainly by Ukraine's bid for independence in the aftermath of the aborted August 1991 coup. Yeltsin did not realize initially how much the coup had changed the prevailing sentiment in Ukraine, and he sought to work out new arrangements for a Slavic union (plus Central Asia). But when a popular referendum in Ukraine on 1 December 1991 resulted in an overwhelming vote for independence, Yeltsin had to change course and abandon further attempts to preserve the union. The result was the Belovezhskaya Pushcha accords.

In that sense, Ukraine was the most important "ethnic" contributor to the breakup of the Soviet Union—an outcome that was tinged with irony. During most of the Gorbachev era, proponents of separatism in Ukraine had made little headway, especially in the central and eastern provinces of the republic. Aside from unrest among coal miners in the Donets'k Basin and Chervonohrad, Ukraine had seemed a veritable island of stability in a sea of turmoil. When the Soviet government held a countrywide referendum in March 1991, nearly three-quarters of voters in Ukraine cast ballots in favor of "preserving the Union of Soviet Socialist Republics as a renewed federation."[74] But in the wake of the failed coup, the "political opportunity structure" in Ukraine expanded so much that the drive for independence became unstoppable. The collapse of central authority after the August 1991 crisis ensured that even a leader who was far more resolute than Gorbachev would not have been able to rely on force to keep Ukraine in the fold.

Mark Kramer is director of Cold War Studies at Harvard University, and a senior fellow of Harvard's Davis Center for Russian and Eurasian Studies. He is also chairman of Harvard's Sakharov Seminars on Human Rights. He is the author of many books and articles on a wide variety of topics, and is the editor of the *Journal of Cold War Studies* and of Harvard's Cold War Studies Book Series.

Notes

1. See, for example, the essays collected in Brzezinski, *Dilemmas of Change*. A related theme is developed by Lowenthal, "Development versus Utopia," which makes a somewhat broader argument about the effect of economic development on the ideological orientation of communist regimes, including Maoist China. See also the essay by Tucker, "The Deradicalization of Marxist Movements."
2. Jowitt, "Inclusion and Mobilization." Jowitt explicitly criticizes Lowenthal and Tucker for "positing a unilinear de-radicalization or de-utopianization of Leninist regimes" (71).
3. Hough, "Gorbachev's Endgame." Hough emphasizes these same basic points in all of his writings in the latter half of the 1980s. See, for example, Hough, *Russia and the West*. In 1997, when Hough published a retrospective analysis of the Soviet collapse, he presented a substantially revised version of this argument, emphasizing the role of a few important social groups (especially bureaucrats and state enterprise managers), but not the society as a whole. See Hough, *Democratization and Revolution*, 31–58.
4. For a cogent overview of the study of democratization as of the early 1980s, see Huntington, "Will More Countries Become Democratic?" Among many subsequent contributions to the democratization literature in the mid- and late 1980s are Pridham, *New Mediterranean Democracies*; O'Donnell, Schmitter and Whitehead, *Transitions from*

Authoritarian Rule; Baloyra, *Comparing New Democracies*. See also Huntington, *The Third Wave*; Di Palma, *To Craft Democracies*; Mainwaring, O'Donnell and Valenzuela, *Issues in Democratic Consolidation*; Yin-wah Chu, "State History"; and Bauzon, *Development and Democratization*.

5. Hough, "Gorbachev's Endgame," 643, 645.
6. Hough, "Gorbachev's Politics."
7. Ibid., 35.
8. Ibid., 38–39.
9. Hough, "Gorbachev's Endgame," 655.
10. Ibid., 662; and Hough, "Gorbachev's Politics," 39.
11. Hough, "Gorbachev's Politics," 39.
12. Simonyan, "Strany Baltii v gody Gorbachevskoi perestroiki."
13. "Zapiska o manifestatsii 20 yanvarya 1991 goda," Memorandum No. 8 (Top Secret) from Yurii Prokof'ev, first secretary of the municipal CPSU committee in Moscow, to the CPSU Politburo and Secretariat, 22 January 1991, in Rossiiskii Gosudarstvennyi Arkhiv Noveishei Istorii (RGANI), Fond (F.) 89, Opis' (Op.) 12, Delo (D.) 31, Listy (Ll.) 1–2.
14. Starr, "Soviet Union: Civil Society"; Ruble, "The Social Dimensions of Perestroika"; Lapidus, "State and Society"; Lewin, *Gorbachev Phenomenon*; Starr, "Voluntary Groups and Initiatives"; Sedaitis and Butterfield, *Perestroika from Below*; Weigle and Butterfield, "Civil Society"; and Hosking, Aves, and Duncan, *The Road to Post-Communism*. For an illuminating overview of the topic and a critique of relevant literature, see Fish, *Democracy from Scratch*.
15. Dawson, *Eco-Nationalism*; Yanitskii, *Ekologicheskoe dvizhenie Rossii*; and Babcock, "Role of Public Interest Groups." In Kazakhstan, the environmental movement during the Gorbachev period was international rather than nationalist in its orientation, but in most of the other republics the orientation of these movements was distinctly nationalist. See Shatz, "Notes on 'the Dog That Didn't Bark'."
16. Weiner, *Little Corner of Freedom*; Kelly, "Environmental Policy-Making," 580–85; Pickvance, *Democracy and Environmental Movements*, 12–14; Mirovitskaya, "The Environmental Movement," 35–38; and Pelloso, *Saving the Blue Heart*. On another issue during the Brezhnev era that was a catalyst of environmental concern and activity—the proposed southward diversion of the Ob River in Siberia—see Darst, "Environmentalism in the USSR"; and Micklin and Bond, "Reflections on Environmentalism."
17. For a large number of sources on the Soviet coal miners' strikes of 1989, see footnote 153 in Kramer, "Collapse of East European Communism." Shortly after the miners' strikes ended, Hough wrote that "very little has happened in the last year that was not the [desired] consequence of [Gorbachev's] conscious policy." Although Hough conceded that "the coal strikes were *probably* unintended," he implied that Gorbachev may even have orchestrated the strikes as part of his long-term "plan." See Hough, "Gorbachev's Politics," 34 (emphasis added).
18. Social mobilization in Czechoslovakia had come to a halt after 1968, but when the "moment of truth" arrived in November 1989 on the heels of momentous changes elsewhere in Eastern Europe, a civil society suddenly coalesced. As the barriers to collective action rapidly faded, the number of participants in the demonstrations rose precipitously, reaching a "tipping point" for the Velvet Revolution.
19. Fish, *Democracy from Scratch*, 51.
20. Hough, *Democratization and Revolution*, 11.
21. The most outspoken proponent of this view was Viktor Glushkov (1923–1982), the well-known mathematician and computer engineer who served for twenty-five years as director of the Institute of Cybernetics of the Ukrainian Academy of Sciences (an

institute that now bears his name). See Mikhailovskii, *Akademik V. Glushkov*; Gerovitch, *From Newspeak to Cyberspeak*, 267–83; and Beissinger, *Scientific Management*. Among the economists advocating this same approach was Stanislav Strumilin; see, for example, Strumilin, *Aktual'nye problemy ekonomicheskoi nauki v trudakh S.G. Strumilina*. On the social implications of computerization in the Soviet Union, see Kanygin, *Informatizatsiya upravleniya*; Judy and Clough, *Implications of the Information Revolution*.

22. On the dilemmas facing earlier Soviet leaders in this regard, see Hoffmann and Laird, *Technocratic Socialism*; and Parrott, *Politics and Technology*.
23. See Starr, "New Communications Technologies"; and Goodman, "Information Technologies."
24. An assessment of East–West cultural exchanges in the pre-Gorbachev era can be found in Richmond, *US–Soviet Cultural Exchanges*, as well as Richmond's subsequent study, *Cultural Exchange and the Cold War*, which also covers the Gorbachev era and provides a net assessment of Cold War-era exchanges. Under Stalin, Soviet society was so tightly controlled and divorced from the West that exchanges had little salutary effect, and were intended almost solely for propaganda purposes. Even then, however, some exchanges did cause at least a modicum of ferment. See Fokin, *Mezhdunarodnyi kul'turnyi obmen i SSSR v 20-30-e gody*.
25. This is not to say that a majority of Russians were actively *hoping* for the demise of the Soviet Union, especially before August 1991. In the March 1991 referendum, Russians voted heavily in favor of preserving the Soviet Union as a "renewed federation of equal sovereign republics." Sentiment in Russia (as everywhere else) changed after the aborted coup in Moscow in August 1991, but the likelihood is that if a referendum had been held shortly after the coup, a majority of Russians would once again have voted in favor of retaining the union minus the Baltic states, Georgia, and Moldova. (Actually, a substantial number of Russians might have been willing to relinquish Central Asia as well, but the Central Asian states themselves were not inclined in that direction.) The point to be emphasized, however, is that support for the union in Russia was mostly passive. Even those Russians who wanted to preserve the USSR were not going to take to the streets or engage in collective protests to demand that the Belovezhskaya Pushcha accords be annulled.
26. For a sophisticated analysis of this issue, see Beissinger, *Nationalist Mobilization*. My own view of the Soviet collapse differs from Beissinger's, but his book is admirably presented and argued, and he rightly emphasizes the importance of contingency, unintended events, and human agency. It is unfortunate, though, that Beissinger failed to draw on the vast store of declassified archival sources now available in the former Soviet Union. Among the many other analyses worth consulting on the role of ethnic and nationalist unrest in the disintegration of the USSR, see Cheshko, *Raspad Sovetskogo Soyuza*; Lapidus, Zaslavsky and Goldman, *From Union to Commonwealth*; Suny, *The Revenge of the Past*; Zaslavsky, "Success and Collapse"; Zaslavsky, "Nationalism and Democratic Transition"; Beissinger, "Demise of an Empire-State"; Roeder, "Soviet Federalism"; Roeder, *Red Sunset*; Fowkes, *Disintegration of the Soviet Union*; Senn, *Gorbachev's Failure in Lithuania*; Krickus, *Showdown*; and Karklins, *Ethnopolitics and Transition*.
27. Among the exceptions were d'Encausse, *L'empire éclaté*; Wolf et al., *The Costs of the Soviet Empire*; Bennigsen and Wimbush, *Muslims of the Soviet Empire*; and Conquest, *The Last Empire*. Wolf and his colleagues distinguish between the "external empire" (Eastern Europe, Cuba, Afghanistan, Vietnam, etc.) and the "internal empire" (the Soviet state itself).
28. Seton-Watson, "Nationalism and Imperialism."
29. See, for example, Kolko, *Roots of American Foreign Policy*; Horowitz, *Empire and Revolution*; Magdoff, *The Age of Imperialism*; Alperovitz, *Cold War Essays*; and Selden, *Remaking Asia*.

30. Beissinger, "Demise of an Empire-State," 93–115.
31. Lustick, *Unsettled States, Disputed Lands*, 22–23.
32. As late as 1991, David Laitin wrote that the term "empire"—which was the title of a book he was reviewing—"obscures far more than it reveals. The problem with calling the Soviet Union an empire today is that by analogy with Austria-Hungary, it allows one to assume its ultimate decomposition. I do not wish to presuppose the collapse of the Soviet Union. I want to analyze those factors that can enhance the integrity of the Union." See Laitin, "Review Article," 140–41.
33. Some valuable comparative work along these lines has appeared—see, for example, Dawisha and Parrott, *The End of Empire?*; Lieven, *Empire: The Russian Empire and Its Rivals*; Barkey and von Hagen, *After Empire*; Demandt, *Das Ende der Weltreiche*; Rudolf and Good, *Nationalism and Empire*; Lieven, *Empire*, 288–339; Lundestad, *The Fall of Great Powers*; Snyder, *Myths of Empire*, esp. 194–244; Motyl, *Imperial Ends*; Strayer, "Decolonization, Democratization, and Communist Reform"; and Wohlforth, "The Russian-Soviet Empire," 175–94; and Jervis, "Variation and Change," 250–66. But much remains to be done.
34. This bears on one of the main points in Kalyvas, "Decay and Breakdown." Kalyvas rightly stresses the importance of distinguishing between the decay and the breakdown of communist systems.
35. Countless declassified materials about the Soviet campaigns against underground nationalist movements in these republics are available in the archives of Estonia, Latvia, Lithuania, and Ukraine (Kyiv and L'viv). In Moscow, the bulk of documents about this topic in the Presidential Archive and the State Archive of the Russian Federation (in Fond R-9478, "Glavnoe upravlenie po bor'be s banditizmom MVD SSSR, 1938–1950 gg.") are still classified, but many important items have been released since 1992. Photocopies of many thousands of pages of relevant documentation are available at the Cold War Studies collections, Harvard University.
36. The likelihood that ethnic groups in the USSR would be deterred from challenging Soviet authority, or would be harshly suppressed if they did challenge it, was stressed in Motyl, *Will the Non-Russians Rebel?*
37. Bendix, *Kings or People*, 27.
38. Mark Beissinger acknowledges, in *Nationalist Mobilization and the Collapse of the Soviet State*, that "the failure of the Soviet regime to defend itself through severe force was partially a matter of Gorbachev's personal commitment to nonviolence" and the way "Gorbachev altered the long-standing regime of repression characteristic of the Brezhnev era" (328). But Beissinger claims that "this lack of commitment to the use of severe violence as a tool for reimposing order" was characteristic of almost all high-level officials in the late 1980s and early 1990s: "It was not only Gorbachev but the vast majority of his conservative critics as well who eschewed a Tiananmen-style crackdown" (328–29). This argument is problematic. It is certainly true that Gorbachev altered the parameters for the use of repression and that this in turn changed the expectations of officials and activists about the prospect of a harsh crackdown. But it is also true that those parameters could have been altered again. No doubt, Abraham Lincoln did not want to use force against the South when he was elected president of the United States in November 1860, but when he was faced with the secession of South Carolina and other Confederate states, he went to war to undo it. If high-level Soviet officials like Valentin Varennikov and Vladimir Kryuchkov had been authorized by Gorbachev to use any means necessary to counter dire threats to the survival of the USSR, they undoubtedly would have been willing to adopt draconian measures— measures that most officials ordinarily would not have countenanced. But unless the top leader, Gorbachev, went along with that option (no matter how grudgingly), the officials around him were unwilling to take responsibility for large-scale bloodshed,

as became evident during the August 1991 coup attempt. The tradition of deference to the CPSU general secretary (and the Soviet president, a post that Gorbachev created for himself in March 1990) was too entrenched for them to undertake severe repression without authorization from the top. Gorbachev's role was crucial. He was the one who altered the "regime of repression" in the first place, and he was the one who would have had to shift it back to the norms of earlier Soviet leaders.

39. Lukic and Lynch, *Europe from the Balkans to the Urals*; Bunce, *Subversive Institutions*; idem, "Peaceful versus Violent State Dismemberment"; idem, "Subversive Institutions"; Leff, "Democratization and Disintegration"; and Vujacvica and Zaslavsky, "Causes of Disintegration." A brief but interesting comparison of the Yugoslav and Czechoslovak cases can be found in Janos, *Czechoslovakia and Yugoslavia*. For a critique of some other works on the breakdown of Soviet-bloc regimes (though not Yugoslavia), see Kalyvas, "Decay and Breakdown."

40. In addition to the sources adduced in the previous footnote, see Roeder, "Soviet Federalism"; Zaslavsky, "Success and Collapse"; Lapidus, Zaslavsky and Goldman, *From Union to Commonwealth*; Suny, *The Revenge of the Past*; Slezkine, "The USSR as a Communal Apartment"; Brubaker, *Nationalism Reframed*; and Cheshko, *Raspad Sovetskogo Soyuza*. An extension of this argument is presented in Walker, *Dissolution*. Walker assumes that, "at the least," the "institutions of Soviet ethno-federalism and nationality policy served as an efficient lubricant of fragmentation" (4), and he therefore believes he does not need to discuss how ethnic identities form or how mobilization occurs. Instead, he focuses on the concept of "sovereignty" to explain why the Soviet Union was divided into the fifteen entities that had been union-republics.

41. My criticisms of analysts who focus on ethnofederal institutions are specifically directed at their depictions of the formation and growth of ethnicity—depictions that are too one-dimensional. I agree with them about the importance of numerous other phenomena they mention, such as the divisions among top elites.

42. Before the August 1968 invasion, the intention had been to set up a separate Czech Communist Party, which would be equal to the Slovak party. Both parties would have existed alongside the central Communist Party of Czechoslovakia (KSČ). After the invasion, Brezhnev pressured KSČ leaders to abandon plans to form a Czech party, apparently because he feared that such a move would weaken the KSČ and set a precedent for the establishment of a Russian party that would detract from the CPSU. During one of the post-invasion negotiations, Brezhnev remarked: "If the Russian Soviet Federated Socialist Republic [in the USSR] has no communist party of its own, why should there be a separate communist party for the Czechs?" At a KSČ Central Committee plenum in November 1968, Czechoslovak leaders succumbed to Moscow's pressure, announcing that plans to establish a Czech party would be postponed indefinitely. A separate communist party of Slovakia continued to exist under the KSČ's auspices, but no separate Czech party was set up. Instead, the November plenum merely created a KSČ "Bureau for the Czech Lands," a modest step that was widely viewed in Slovakia as a disappointing retreat. The failure to establish a separate communist party for the Czech lands implied that the Czechs, represented by the KSČ, were broadly overseeing Slovakia.

43. During the war, Slovak officials tried to ensure that Slovakia would not be reabsorbed into a Czechoslovak state. So desperate were they to avoid having to live under Czech rule again that some even proposed that Slovakia be incorporated into the Soviet Union—a proposal that had first been broached by several leaders of the Slovak Communist Party. Stalin initially displayed interest in the idea, but never followed up on it. See Fierlinger, *Ve službach ČSR*, 326.

44. Innes, *Czechoslovakia: The Short Goodbye*; Musil, *The End of Czechoslovakia*; Pithardt and Spencer, "The Partition of Czechoslovakia"; Stefanovič, *Zrod slovenskej staatnosti*; and Ulč, "Czechoslovakia's Velvet Divorce." For a useful documentary collection covering

this period, see Hlavová and Žatkulík, *Novembrová revolúcia a česko-slovenský rozchod*. See also the detailed chronology compiled by Hovorka, *Kronika dělení: Československo 1990–1992*.
45. Djilas, *The Contested Country*.
46. Ramet, *Nationalism and Federalism*, 214–52.
47. Most proponents of the ethnofederal institutionalist argument are well aware of these differences and have cited the confederal structure in post-1974 Yugoslavia (versus the nominally federal structure in the USSR) to explain why Yugoslavia broke up with far greater violence than the Soviet Union did. But they downplay or fail to mention other implications of these differences that would raise doubts about the ethnofederal institutionalist thesis.
48. Bell, "Ten Theories in Search of Reality."
49. Valerie Bunce acknowledges that she provides a "relatively deterministic framework" in *Subversive Institutions*, but she defends this on the grounds that choices made by elites (and others) were "the product of the very institutional logic of the system itself" (141–42).
50. Roy, *La nouvelle Asie centrale*.
51. Dmitry Gorenburg and I are undertaking an in-depth analysis, based on documentation from the former Soviet archives, of the relative impact of assimilationist policies and ethnofederal institutions and policies. I draw here on some of our preliminary findings.
52. USSR State Committee on Statistics, *Itogi vsesoyuznoi perepisi naseleniya 1989 goda*, 12 vols, Moscow, 1992–1993; Vol. 7 ("Natsional'nyi sostav naseleniya SSSR"); USSR State Committee on Statistics, *Itogi vsesoyuznoi perepisi naseleniya 1979 goda: Statisticheskii sbornik*, Moscow, 1989–1990; USSR State Committee on Statistics, *Itogi vsesoyuznoi perepisi naseleniya 1959 goda*, 16 vols, Moscow, 1962–1968; Anderson and Silver, "Estimating Russification of Ethnic Identity among Non-Russians in the USSR," 461–89; and Anderson and Silver, "Demographic Sources of the Changing Ethnic Composition of the Soviet Union," 612–13.
53. Anderson and Silver, "Estimating Russification," 461–89; and Kenez, *History of the Soviet Union*, 271.
54. The notion of a political opportunity structure, used by Bunce and other proponents of the ethnofederal institutionalist thesis, comes from the sociological and political science literature on protest movements and rebellion. See, for example, Tarrow, "Aiming at a Moving Target." Tarrow writes that "mass outbreaks of collective action are best understood as the collective responses of citizens, groups, and elites to an expanding structure of political opportunities" (13).
55. For comparisons between India and the former Soviet Union, see Narang, *Ethnic Identities*.
56. See, for example, the very gloomy essays in Bloom, *Russia's Future*. For another typical view that Russia would soon collapse, see Stern, "Moscow Meltdown." For a cogent rebuttal to the notion that Russia would disintegrate along ethnofederal lines, see Lukic and Lynch, *Europe from the Balkans to the Urals*, 385–93.
57. Of the eighty-nine entities that make up the Russian Federation, thirty-two are ethnonational territories (twenty-one republics, one autonomous oblast, and ten autonomous regions) and fifty-seven are geographic-administrative units. Only in Chuvashiya, Tuva, and the North Caucasus republics do the titular nationalities constitute a majority. Russians account for a majority of the population in the Buryat, Kareliyan, Komi, Mordovian, Sakha, and Udmurt republics and a plurality in Bashkortostan and Mari El. Large minorities of Russians and Russified Ukrainians live in the Tatar, Kalmyk, and Kabardino-Balkar republics. Overall, Russians account for 42 percent of the population in the ethnonational republics. See Harris, "A Geographic Analysis."

58. Of the eighty-nine entities in Russia, only two (Tatarstan and Tuva) have any history as independent states, and that was in the distant past. Of the approximately 19 percent of Russian Federation citizens who are not ethnic Russians, roughly half live in titular regions well inside the country's boundaries, surrounded by other regions and lacking any access to the sea. Most of the other non-Russians are from diaspora groups, particularly Ukrainians, Volga Germans, Kazakhs, Armenians, and Belarusians, and are scattered across the country. Although a few ethnonational regions (notably Tatarstan and Sakha) have rich deposits of natural resources, most of the regions in Russia still depend heavily on transfers from the central government.

59. Although the Russian army's performance during the first war in Chechnya was decidedly lackluster, the sheer brutality and destructiveness of the campaign served as a lesson to other regional governments and populations of the potential costs of attempts at secession. The army's more impressive showing during the initial phase of the second Chechen war reinforced that lesson, and the protracted stalemate that ensued did nothing to diminish it. No other regional government or regional population would want to end up in the appalling situation that befell Chechnya.

60. The Cold War Studies program of Harvard University has been collecting and cataloguing many thousands of pages of declassified documents on ethnic protests and unrest in the Soviet Union from 1945 to 1991. These materials come not only from the Russian archives but also from repositories in Ukraine, Latvia, Lithuania, Estonia, Moldova, Armenia, and Georgia. Some other important declassified documents have been published in recent years; see, for example, "O massovykh besporyadkakh s 1957 goda," a highly classified memorandum compiled by Soviet KGB chairman, Viktor Chebrikov, at Gorbachev's request in 1987, published in *Istochnik* (Moscow), No. 6 (1995), 146–53. For an interesting monograph covering ethnic as well as other mass disturbances in the years after Stalin's death, see Kozlov, *Massovye besporyadki v SSSR pri Khrushcheve i Brezhneve*. Despite the title of Kozlov's book, it focuses almost exclusively on the Khrushchev era, devoting only one very brief chapter (amounting to less than 2 percent of the total book) to mass unrest during the Brezhnev years.

61. On pp. 54–55 of *Nationalist Mobilization and the Collapse of the Soviet State*, Mark Beissinger implies that ethnic conflicts in the Soviet Union were intensifying in the 1970s and early 1980s compared to previous decades, but elsewhere in the book (e.g., on pp. 71–73) he correctly notes that in fact ethnic conflicts during the Brezhnev era were much less numerous than during the Khrushchev years. Repression, when consistently used, was a powerful means of deterring—or, if necessary, quelling—ethnic unrest.

62. Much about these riots, especially the possibility that the demonstrators were incited by the outgoing leaders, remains murky and speculative. A partial reconstruction of events can be found in Cosman, *Conflict in the Soviet Union*. See also Brown, "Kazakhstan: The Alma-Ata Events." For Kunaev's version of the events, see his two volumes of memoirs: *O moem vremeni: Vospominaniya*, 254–82; and *Ot Stalina do Gorbacheva*, 290–306. For the recollections of Nursultan Nazarbaev, see the interview in Lewandowska, "Między sercem a rozumem," 3. Nazarbaev claims that most of the documentation about these events was destroyed, a claim that does not seem fully plausible.

63. Dzhemilev, *Kratkii analiz*. Further information about the Crimean Tatar movement during the Gorbachev era, along with many valuable documents, can be found in Guboglo and Chervonnaya, *Krymskotatarskoe natsional'noe dvizhenie*, esp. Vol. 1 ("Istoriya, problemy, perspektivy") and Vol. 2 ("Dokumenty, materialy, khronika").

64. "Zasedanie Politbyuro TsK KPSS 23 iyulya 1987 goda: P. 14 Zapiska Otdela TsK KPSS 'O prieme gruppy lits iz chisla krymskikh tatarov' i merakh po nedopushcheniyu ikh demonstratsii," 23 July 1987 (Top Secret), in RGANI, F. 89, Op. 42, D. 17, Ll. 4–5.

65. For background on this dispute, see Melander, "The Nagorno-Karabakh Conflict Revisited."
66. "Rabochaya zapis' zasedaniya Politbyuro TsK KPSS ot 6 iyunya 1988 goda," 6 June 1988 (Top Secret), notes compiled by Anatolii Chernyaev, in Arkhiv Gorbachev-Fonda (AGF), F. 2, Op. 3, D. 7.
67. "Rabochaya zapis' zasedaniya Politbyuro TsK KPSS ot 3 marta 1988 goda," 3 March 1988 (Top Secret), notes compiled by Anatolii Chernyaev, in AGF, F. 2, Op. 3, D. 2. Among other Politburo members supporting this approach were Andrei Gromyko and Egor Ligachev.
68. Ibid.
69. "Rabochaya zapis' zasedaniya Politbyuro TsK KPSS ot 13 oktyabrya 1988 goda," 13 October 1988 (Top Secret), notes compiled by Anatolii Chernyaev, in AGF, F. 2, Op. 3, D. 17.
70. In addition to Tuminez's article, see the articles in the first special issue on "The Collapse of the Soviet Union," *Journal of Cold War Studies*, Vol. 5, No. 1 (Winter 2003).
71. Brinton, *The Anatomy of Revolution*, 57.
72. On the dangers of inconsistency in the use of repression and accommodation, see Lichbach, "Deterrence or Escalation?" as well as the subsequent empirical study by Moore, "Repression and Dissent."
73. See Zlotnik, "Yeltsin and Gorbachev."
74. See the detailed, province-by-province tabulations in *Radyans'ka Ukraina* (Kiev), 23 March 1991, 1.

Bibliography

Alperovitz, Gar (ed.). *Cold War Essays*, Cambridge, MA, 1970.

Anderson, Barbara A., and Brian D. Silver. "Estimating Russification of Ethnic Identity among Non-Russians in the USSR," in *Demography*, Vol. 20, No. 4 (November 1983), 461–89.

_____. "Demographic Sources of the Changing Ethnic Composition of the Soviet Union," in *Population and Development Review*, Vol. 15, No. 4 (December 1989), 612–13.

Babcock, Glenys A. "The Role of Public Interest Groups in Democratization: Soviet Environmental Groups and Energy Policy-Making, 1985–1991," Ph.D dissertation, RAND Graduate School, 1997.

Baloyra, Enrique A. (ed.). *Comparing New Democracies: Transition and Consolidation in Mediterranean Europe and the Southern Cone*, Boulder, CO, 1987.

Barkey, Karen, and Mark von Hagen (eds). *After Empire: Multiethnic Societies and Nation-Building—The Soviet Union and the Russian, Ottoman, and Habsburg Empires*, Boulder, CO, 1997.

Bauzon, Kenneth A. (ed.). *Development and Democratization in the Third World: Myths, Hopes, and Realities*, New York, 1992.

Beissinger, Mark R. "Demise of an Empire-State: Identity, Legitimacy, and the Deconstruction of Soviet Politics," in *The Rising Tide of Cultural Pluralism: The Nation-State at Bay?*, ed. M. Crawford Young, Madison, 1993, 93–115.

_____. *Nationalist Mobilization and the Collapse of the Soviet State*, New York, 2002.

_____. *Scientific Management, Socialist Discipline, and Soviet Power*, Cambridge, MA, 1988.
Bell, Daniel. "Ten Theories in Search of Reality: The Prediction of Soviet Behavior in the Social Sciences," *World Politics*, Vol. 10, No. 2 (April 1958), 358.
Bendix, Reinhard. *Kings or People: Power and the Mandate to Rule*, Berkeley, CA, 1978.
Bennigsen, Alexandre, and S. Enders Wimbush. *Muslims of the Soviet Empire: A Guide*, London, 1985.
Bloom, Douglas W. (ed.). *Russia's Future: Consolidation or Disintegration?*, Boulder, CO, 1994.
Brinton, Crane. *The Anatomy of Revolution*, New York, 1952.
Brown, Bess. "Kazakhstan: The Alma-Ata Events of 1986 Reexamined," *Report on the USSR*, Vol. 2, No. 6 (9 February 1990), 25–27.
Brubaker, Rogers. *Nationalism Reframed: Nationhood and the National Question in the New Europe*, New York, 1996.
Brzezinski, Zbigniew (ed.). *Dilemmas of Change in Soviet Politics*, New York, 1969.
Bunce, Valerie. "Peaceful versus Violent State Dismemberment: A Comparison of the Soviet Union, Yugoslavia, and Czechoslovakia," *Politics & Society*, Vol. 27, No. 2 (June 1999), 217–37.
_____. "Subversive Institutions: The End of the Soviet State in Comparative Perspective," *Post-Soviet Affairs*, Vol. 14, No. 4 (September–December 1998), 323–54.
_____. *Subversive Institutions: The Design and the Destruction of the Socialist State*, New York, 1999.
Cheshko, S.V. *Raspad Sovetskogo Soyuza: Etnopoliticheskii analiz*, Moscow, 1996.
Chu, Yin-wah. "State History, Development Strategies, and the Democratic Movements in South Korea, Taiwan, and Hong Kong," in East Asian Business and Development Working Paper, No. 43, Davis, CA, 1992.
Conquest, Robert (ed.). *The Last Empire: Nationality and the Soviet Future*, Stanford, CA, 1986.
Cosman, Catherine. *Conflict in the Soviet Union: The Untold Story of the Clashes in Kazakhstan*, New York, 1990.
Darst, Robert G. Jr. "Environmentalism in the USSR: The Opposition to the River Diversion Project," *Soviet Economy*, Vol. 4, No. 3 (July–September 1988), 223–52.
Dawisha, Karen, and Bruce Parrott (eds). *The End of Empire? The Transformation of the USSR in Comparative Perspective*, Armonk, NY, 1997.
Dawson, Jane. *Eco-nationalism: Anti-nuclear Activism and National Identity in Russia, Lithuania, and Ukraine*, Durham, NC, 1996.
Demandt, Alexander (ed.). *Das Ende der Weltreiche: vom Persen bis zur Sowjetunion*, Munich, 1997.
d'Encausse, Helene Carrere. *L'empire éclaté: La revolte des nations en URSS*, Paris, 1978.
Di Palma, Giuseppe. *To Craft Democracies: An Essay on Democratic Transitions*, Berkeley, CA, 1990.
Djilas, Aleksa. *The Contested Country: Yugoslav Unity and National Communism, 1919–1953*, Cambridge, MA, 1988.

Dzhemilev, Reshat. *Kratkii analiz sobytii proiskhodyashchikh v Moskve v iyune-iyule 1987 g., svyazannykh s bor'boi krymtsev za vozvrashchenie na rodinu svoikh predkov, v Krym i vosstanovlenie ikh gosudarstvennosti*, Simferopol, 1997.

Fierlinger, Zdeněk. *Ve službach ČSR*, 2 vols, Prague, 1948–1949, Vol. 2.

Fish, Steven M. *Democracy from Scratch: Opposition and Regime in the New Russian Revolution*, Princeton, NJ, 1995.

Fokin, V.I. *Mezhdunarodnyi kul'turnyi obmen i SSSR v 20-30-e gody*, St. Petersburg, 1999.

Fowkes, Ben. *The Disintegration of the Soviet Union: A Study in the Rise and Triumph of Nationalism*, London, 1997.

Gerovitch, Slava. *From Newspeak to Cyberspeak: A History of Soviet Cybernetics*, Cambridge, MA, 2002.

Goodman, Seymour. "Information Technologies and the Citizen: Toward a 'Soviet Style Information Society'?," in *Science and the Soviet Social Order*, ed. Loren R. Graham, Cambridge, MA, 1990, 51–67.

Guboglo, M.I., and S.M. Chervonnaya. *Krymskotatarskoe natsional'noe dvizhenie*, 4 vols, Moscow, 1992–1997.

Harris, Chauncy D. "A Geographic Analysis of Non-Russian Minorities in Russia and Its Ethnic Homelands," *Post-Soviet Geography*, Vol. 34, No. 9 (November 1993), 543–97.

Hlavová, Viera, and Jozef Žatkulík (eds). *Novembrová revoluacia a česko-slovenský rozchod: Od česko-slovenskej federácie k samostatnej demokratickej slovenskej štátností — Vyber dokumentov a prejavov, november 1989–december 1992*, Bratislava, 2000.

Hoffmann, Erik P., and Robbin F. Laird. *Technocratic Socialism: The Soviet Union in the Advanced Industrial Era*, Durham, NC, 1985.

Horowitz, David. *Empire and Revolution: A Radical Interpretation of Contemporary History*, New York, 1969.

Hosking, Geoffrey A., Jonathan Aves and Peter J.S. Duncan, *The Road to Post-Communism: Independent Political Movements in the Soviet Union, 1985–1991*, London, 1992.

Hough, Jerry F. *Democratization and Revolution in the USSR, 1985–1991*, Washington, DC, 1997.

_____. "Gorbachev's Endgame," *World Policy Journal*, Vol. 7, No. 4 (Fall 1990), 645–46.

_____. "Gorbachev's Politics," *Foreign Affairs*, Vol. 68, No. 5 (Winter 1989/90), 35–36.

_____. *Russia and the West: Gorbachev and the Politics of Reform*, New York, 1988.

Hovorka, Rostislav. "Kronika dělení: Československo 1990–1992," *Hodonín: Pedagogické středisko* (June 1995), 31–42.

Huntington, Samuel P. *The Third Wave: Democratization in the Late Twentieth Century*, Norman, OK, 1991.

_____. "Will More Countries Become Democratic?," *Political Science Quarterly*, Vol. 99, No. 2 (Summer 1984), 193–218.

Innes, Abby. *Czechoslovakia: The Short Goodbye*, New Haven, CT, 2001.

Janos, Andrew C. *Czechoslovakia and Yugoslavia: Ethnic Conflict and the Dissolution of Multinational States*, Berkeley, CA, 1997.

Jervis, Robert. "Variation and Change and Transitions in International Politics," in *Empires, Systems, and States: Great Transformations in International Politics*, ed. Michael Cox, Tim Dunne and Ken Booth, New York, 2003, 250–66.

Jowitt, Kenneth. "Inclusion and Mobilization in European Leninist Regimes," *World Politics*, Vol. 28, No. 1 (October 1975), 69–96.

Judy, Richard W., and Virginia L. Clough. *Implications of the Information Revolution for Soviet Society: A Preliminary Inquiry*, Indianapolis, IN, 1989.

Kalyvas, Stathis N. "The Decay and Breakdown of Communist One-Party Systems," *Annual Review of Political Science*, Vol. 2 (1999), 323–43.

Kanygin, Yu. M. *Informatizatsiya upravleniya: Sotsial'nye aspekty*, Kiev, 1991.

Karklins, Rasma. *Ethnopolitics and Transition to Democracy: The Collapse of the USSR and Latvia*, Baltimore, MD, 1994.

Kelly, Donald R. "Environmental Policy-Making in the USSR: The Role of Industrial and Environmental Interest Groups," *Soviet Studies*, Vol. 28, No. 4 (October 1976), 570–89.

Kenez, Peter. *A History of the Soviet Union from the Beginning to the End*, New York, 1999.

Kolko, Gabriel. *The Roots of American Foreign Policy: An Analysis of Power and Purpose*, Boston, MA, 1969.

Kozlov, V. A. *Massovye besporyadki v SSSR pri Khrushcheve i Brezhneve (1953-nachalo 1980-kh gg.)*, Novosibirsk, 1999.

Kramer, Mark. "The Collapse of East European Communism and the Repercussions within the Soviet Union (Part 1)," *Journal of Cold War Studies*, Vol. 5, No. 4 (Fall 2003), 178–256.

Krickus, Richard J. *Showdown: The Lithuanian Rebellion and the Breakup of the Soviet Empire*, Washington, DC, 1997.

Kunaev, Dinmukhamed. *O moem vremeni: Vospominaniya*, Almaty, 1992.

_____. *Ot Stalina do Gorbacheva (V aspekte k istorii Kazakhstana)*, Almaty, 1994.

Laitin, David D. "Review Article: The National Uprisings in the Soviet Union," *World Politics*, Vol. 44, No. 1 (October 1991), 139–77.

Lapidus, Gail. "State and Society: Toward the Emergence of Civil Society in the Soviet Union," in *Politics, Society, and Nationality Inside Gorbachev's Russia*, ed. Seweryn Bialer, Boulder, CO, 1989, 121–47.

Lapidus, Gail, Victor Zaslavsky, and Philip Goldman (eds). *From Union to Commonwealth: Nationalism and Separatism in the Soviet Republics*, New York, 1992.

Leff, Carol Skalnik. "Democratization and Disintegration in Multinational States: The Breakup of the Communist Federations," *World Politics*, Vol. 51, No. 2 (January 1999), 205–35.

Lewandowska, Irena. "Między sercem a rozumem," in *Gazeta wyborcza* (Warsaw), 28–29 September 1996, 3.

Lewin, Moshe. *The Gorbachev Phenomenon*, Berkeley, CA, 1990.

Lichbach, Mark Irving. "Deterrence or Escalation? The Puzzle of Aggregate Studies of Repression and Dissent," *Journal of Conflict Resolution*, Vol. 31, No. 2 (June 1987), 266–97.

Lieven, Dominic. *Empire: The Russian Empire and Its Rivals*, New Haven, CT, 2000.

Lowenthal, Richard. "Development versus Utopia in Communist Policy," in *Change in Communist Systems*, ed. Chalmers Johnson, Stanford, CA, 1970, 33–116.
Lukic, Reneo, and Allen Lynch. *Europe from the Balkans to the Urals: The Disintegration of Yugoslavia and the Soviet Union*, New York, 1996.
Lundestad, Geir (ed.). *The Fall of Great Powers*, Oxford, 1994.
Lustick, Ian S. *Unsettled States, Disputed Lands: Britain and Ireland, France and Algeria, Israel and the West Bank-Gaza*, Ithaca, NY, 1993.
Magdoff, Harry. *The Age of Imperialism: The Economics of US Foreign Policy*, New York, 1969.
Mainwaring, Scott, Guillermo A. O'Donnell and J. Samuel Valenzuela (eds). *Issues in Democratic Consolidation: The New South American Democracies in Comparative Perspective*, South Bend, IN, 1992.
Melander, Erik. "The Nagorno-Karabakh Conflict Revisited: Was the War Inevitable?," *Journal of Cold War Studies*, Vol. 3, No. 2 (Spring 2001), 48–75.
Micklin, Philip P., and Andrew Bond. "Reflections on Environmentalism and the River Diversion Projects," *Soviet Economy*, Vol. 4, No. 3 (July–September 1988), 253–74.
Mikhailovskii, B.N. *Akademik V. Glushkov: Stranitsy zhizni i tvorchestva*, Kiev, 1993.
Mirovitskaya, Natalia. "The Environmental Movement in the Former Soviet Union," in *Environment and Society in Eastern Europe*, ed. Andrew Tickle and Ian Welsh, Harlow, 1998, 30–66.
Moore, Will H. "Repression and Dissent: Substitution, Context, and Timing," *American Journal of Political Science*, Vol. 42, No. 3 (July 1998), 851–73.
Motyl, Alexander J. *Imperial Ends: The Decay, Collapse, and Revival of Empires*, New York, 2001.
_____. *Will the Non-Russians Rebel? State, Ethnicity, and Stability in the USSR*, Ithaca, NY, 1987.
Musil, Jiří (ed.). *The End of Czechoslovakia*, Budapest, 1995.
Narang, Amarjit S. (ed.). *Ethnic Identities and Federalism*, Shimla, 1995.
O'Donnnell, Guillermo, Philippe C. Schmitter and Laurence Whitehead (eds). *Transitions from Authoritarian Rule: Prospects for Democracy*, Baltimore, MD, 1986.
Parrott, Bruce. *Politics and Technology in the Soviet Union*, Cambridge, MA, 1983.
Pelloso, Andrew J. *Saving the Blue Heart of Siberia: The Environmental Movement in Russia and Lake Baikal*, Bloomington, IN, 1993.
Pickvance, Katy. *Democracy and Environmental Movements in Eastern Europe: A Comparative Study of Hungary and Russia*, Boulder, CO, 1998.
Pithardt, Petr, and Metta Spencer. "The Partition of Czechoslovakia," in *Separatism: Democracy and Disintegration*, ed. Metta Spencer, Boulder, CO, 1998, 185–204.
Pridham, Geoffrey (ed.). *The New Mediterranean Democracies: Regime Transition in Spain, Greece, and Portugal*, London, 1984.
Ramet, Sabrina P. *Nationalism and Federalism in Yugoslavia, 1962–1991*, 2nd edn, Bloomington, IN, 1992.
Richmond, Yale. *Cultural Exchange and the Cold War: Raising the Iron Curtain*, University Park, PA, 2003.

_____. *U.S.–Soviet Cultural Exchanges, 1958–1986: Who Wins?*, Boulder, CO, 1987.
Roeder, Philip G. *Red Sunset: The Failure of Soviet Politics*, Princeton, NJ, 1993.
_____. "Soviet Federalism and Ethnic Mobilization," *World Politics*, Vol. 43, No. 1 (January 1991), 196–232.
Roy, Olivier. *La nouvelle Asie centrale ou la fabrication des nations*, Paris, 1997.
Ruble, Blair A. "The Social Dimensions of Perestroika," *Soviet Economy*, Vol. 3, No. 2 (April–June 1987), 171–83.
Rudolph, Richard L., and David F. Good (eds). *Nationalism and Empire: The Habsburg Empire and the Soviet Union*, New York, 1992.
Sedaitis, Judith B., and Jim Butterfield (eds). *Perestroika from Below: Social Movements in the Soviet Union*, Boulder, CO, 1991.
Selden, Mark (ed.). *Remaking Asia: Essays on the American Uses of Power*, New York, 1974.
Senn, Alfred Erich. *Gorbachev's Failure in Lithuania*, New York, 1995.
Seton-Watson, Hugh. "Nationalism and Imperialism," in *The Impact of the Russian Revolution, 1917–1967: The Influence of Bolshevism on the World Outside Russia*, Royal Institute of International Affairs, New York, 1967, 134–205.
Shatz, Edward A.D. "Notes on 'the Dog That Didn't Bark': Eco-Internationalism in Late Soviet Kazakhstan," *Ethnic and Racial Studies*, Vol. 22, No. 1 (January 1999), 136–61.
Simonyan, R. Kh. "Strany Baltii v gody Gorbachevskoi perestroika," *Novaya i noveishaya istoriya* (Moscow), No. 2 (March–April 2003), 65.
Slezkine, Yuri. "The USSR as a Communal Apartment, or How a Socialist State Promoted Ethnic Particularism," *Slavic Review*, Vol. 53, No. 2 (Spring 1994), 414–52.
Snyder, Jack. *Myths of Empire: Domestic Politics and International Ambition*, Ithaca, NY, 1991.
Starr, Frederick S. "New Communications Technologies and Civil Society," in *Science and the Soviet Social Order*, ed. Loren Graham, Cambridge, MA, 1990, 19–50.
_____. "Soviet Union: Civil Society," *Foreign Policy*, No. 70 (Spring 1988), 26–41.
_____. "Voluntary Groups and Initiatives," in *Soviet Update*, ed. Anthony Jones and David E. Powell, Boulder, CO, 1991, 96–116.
Štefanovič, Milan. *Zrod slovenskej štátnosti a zánik česko-slovenskej federácie*, Bratislava, 1999.
Stern, Jessica Eve. "Moscow Meltdown: Can Russia Survive?," *International Security*, Vol. 18, No. 4 (Spring 1994), 40–65.
Strayer, Robert. "Decolonization, Democratization, and Communist Reform: The Soviet Collapse in Comparative Perspective," *Journal of World History*, Vol. 12, No. 2 (Fall 2001), 375–406.
Strumilin, Stanislav. *Aktual'nye problemy ekonomicheskoi nauki v trudakh S. G. Strumilina*, ed. N.P. Fedorenko, Moscow, 1977.
Suny, Ronald Grigor. *The Revenge of the Past: Nationalism, Revolution, and the Collapse of the Soviet Union*, Stanford, CA, 1993.
Tarrow, Sidney. "'Aiming at a Moving Target': Social Science and the Recent Rebellions in Eastern Europe," *PS: Political Science & Politics*, Vol. 24, No. 1 (March 1991), 2–20.

Tucker, Robert C. "The Deradicalization of Marxist Movements," in idem, *The Marxian Revolutionary Idea*, New York, 1970, 172–215.
Tuminez, Astrid S. "Nationalism, Ethnic Pressures, and the Breakup of the USSR," *Journal of Cold War Studies*, Vol. 5, No. 4 (Fall 2003), 81–136.
Ulč, Otto. "Czechoslovakia's Velvet Divorce," *East European Quarterly*, Vol. 30, No. 3 (September 1996), 331–52.
Vujačić, Veljko, and Victor Zaslavsky. "The Causes of Disintegration in the USSR and Yugoslavia," *Telos*, No. 88 (Summer 1991), 120–40.
Walker, Edward W. *Dissolution: Sovereignty and the Breakup of the Soviet Union*, Boulder, CO, 2003.
Weigle, Marcia A., and Jim Butterfield. "Civil Society in Reforming Communist Regimes: The Logic of Emergence," *Comparative Politics*, Vol. 25, No. 1 (January 1992), 1–24.
Weiner, Douglas R. *A Little Corner of Freedom: Russian Nature Protection from Stalin to Gorbachev*, Berkeley, CA, 1999.
Wohlforth, William C. "The Russian-Soviet Empire: A Test of Neorealism," in *Empires, Systems, and States: Great Transformations in International Politics*, ed. Michael Cox, Tim Dunne and Ken Booth, New York, 2003, 175–94.
Wolf, Charles Jr., et al. *The Costs of the Soviet Empire*, Santa Monica, CA, 1984.
Yanitskii, Oleg. *Ekologicheskoe dvizhenie Rossii: Kriticheskii analiz*, Moscow, 1996.
Zaslavsky, Victor. "Nationalism and Democratic Transition in Postcommunist Societies," *Daedalus*, Vol. 121, No. 2 (Spring 1992), 97–121.
_____. "Success and Collapse: Traditional Soviet Nationality Policy," in *Nations and Politics in the Soviet Successor States*, ed. Ian Bremmer and Ray Taras, New York, 1993, 29–42.
Zlotnik, Marc. "Yeltsin and Gorbachev: The Politics of Confrontation," *Journal of Cold War Studies*, Vol. 5, No. 1 (Winter 2003), 128–64.

Chapter 3

Perestroika Made in Hungary?
The HSWP's Approach to the Soviet Reform of the Late 1980s

Tamás Péter Baranyi

A sudden embrace between Hungarian and Soviet reform concepts in the 1980s is a recurring fallacy in some historical assessments. In fact, the two approaches were not really compatible at first, and an alliance of reformist circles was only forged later. This chapter explores the nature and changes of both reform agendas, shedding a fresh light on the very last phase of socialist solidarity. Our starting point is a 1989 assessment by US ambassador to Hungary, Mark Palmer, who observed: "Glasnost and perestroika were in fact invented in Hungary in the 1960s, and I believe Hungary still retains her 20-year advantage."[1] The identification of Hungarian reform and perestroika have since been very common, albeit misleading. This study aims to shed a fresh light on the reception of perestroika by the Hungarian party, with a special emphasis on the fact that perestroika was an evolving notion while HSWP was a party on the verge of tremendous changes.

Perestroika itself was not a unitary concept. Mikhail Gorbachev himself recently told *Rossiyskaya Gazeta*: "Perestroika had various stages. The creators of perestroika were accused of not having a plan, an idea. But there were no ready-made recipes lying around anywhere. The idea of perestroika was created as it developed, as the people were being liberated."[2] That is basically the nature of Gorbachev's reforms—they had been constantly changing and broadening, while certain values remained static.[3] At the very outset, the concept of the Soviet "new thinking" was more like a fresher foreign policy outlook with an ambition to

---

Notes for this chapter begin on page 100.

encapsulate it in something that resembled a new Marxist–Leninist synthesis. Its foreign affairs origins are aptly described by Marie-Pierre Rey, who highlighted that in the early stage, "new thinking" served to decrease the role of ideology in foreign affairs, to shift the emphasis from competition to convergence, and above all, to cut costs in competition and save money for domestic development. Even though there had been earlier attempts and tenets of this kind of policy, it was the new thinking that first made them look coherent and visible.[4] Such a pragmatic, down-to-earth approach had to be sold to the ranks of the apparatus, so it took the form of a new synthesis, developed by Gorbachev and Alexander Yakovlev, chief ideologue at that time. However, it also seems true that at least initially Gorbachev and those around him truly believed they had invented something that could eventually become a general ideology of all humanity—something that would unite East and West.[5]

In other words, new thinking, at least for the beginning, was more like an attitude and an ambition than a policy. This new course, at the very outset, was two-pronged. Gorbachev was convinced that ending the Cold War was a must, and that the Soviet economy needed to gain a new momentum, preferably through integration and decentralization.[6] Notice, when someone talks about Gorbachev's intention to introduce reforms for the sake of maintaining social structures at home and empire abroad, it is not merely a moral judgment. Rather, it emphasizes that the nature of Gorbachev's reforms was not "liberal" in a Western sense of the word: rather, liberal elements were tools, just like the other ones, such as centralization and disarmament.

There is a critical framework that we should apply when analyzing events of the long 1980s from an East European perspective, and that is the conceptual framework of "emancipation." Emancipation is a catchword that can describe the tendency on behalf of the otherwise loyal East European regimes to achieve more elbow room and possible self-sustainability in the face of the Cold War, which was increasingly disregarding the legitimate concerns of the superpowers' allies. This approach has been introduced to historiography by Csaba Békés.[7] If emancipation is taken as a value and a tendency, then the 1980s can be seen as a *dénouement* of this process: emancipation tendencies that may have begun in 1956 had a logical conclusion sometime between 1989 and 1991.[8] Using such a framework of "emancipation" raises the question of whether perestroika or "new thinking" was an element that endorsed or took back the process.

Initial Response to Gorbachev's New Thinking

The relationship between the Soviet new thinking and the East European countries is central to this chapter. However, this relation was not a priority in this first stage of Gorbachev's reform process, or, as Yakovlev put it, during "the silver age of perestroika."[9] Contrary to what Mark Palmer believed, Gorbachev and his circle did not prioritize "the experiences of the East European countries," and believing in the ideological superiority of the Soviet Union, they could not imagine Eastern Europe setting an example for world communism.[10] It is interesting to note that it was not the case with the People's Republic of China, which actively drew on those experiences in its own way to openness and reform.[11]

As for the foreign policy side of Gorbachev's new thinking, the Hungarian party elite could not have agreed more with the Soviets. Moscow's new approach to the global arms race, and its commitment to undo the Second Cold War, was obvious and unanimous.[12] Not so much for the economic revamping of the socialist world system, 1985 was a crucial point in Hungary's history because it turned out that measures taken in the early 1980s were on the verge of exhaustion, and the party elite had just come to the conclusion that further Western integration would be needed to maintain their faltering economy. Under such circumstances, any kind of Soviet advice would have met with three concurring emotions: (1) general suspicion with regard to the nature of centrally sanctioned, top–down reforms; (2) a particular suspicion about the sustainability of reforms in the Soviet Union, and fear of a U-turn; and (3) a general but restrained rejoicing over the "return of vision" to the communist commonwealth.

When introduced, however, unsound reform ideas of the Soviets had different means and ends than those of the Hungarians. While the Soviets wanted to broaden market elements into central planning, they also pursued economic self-reliance within the bloc, and thus longed to ease their dependence on the West. In Hungary, however, market elements had been introduced decades earlier, but their ultimate goal was a more beneficial integration with the West, not a cautious distancing.

On the other hand, Gorbachev emphasized the essentiality of intrabloc integration, while stressing the dangers of Western integration. During the first meeting between Mikhail Gorbachev and HSWP general secretary János Kádár, the former warned: "You depend on us. We depend, in many senses, on everyone. We want this interdependence to become more complete."[13] At this meeting, which took place on 25 September 1985, the Soviet leader repeatedly asked about the Hungarian reform process with a pointedly suspicious overtone. János Kádár defended the Hungarian way in an unusually broad *exposé*. Answering Gorbachev's doubts, Kádár explained that the Hungarian debt spiral had nothing to do with strengthening ties with the West, but instead had some connection with the Soviet refusal of the Hungarian request for a loan in 1974.[14] A month later, at the party leaders' informal meeting after the Sofia summit of the Warsaw Pact, Gorbachev again emphasized the importance of a socialist *phalanx* against the imperialist bloc. He directed a mild attack on Romania and Hungary, stating he did not understand how those two countries had dozens of common enterprises with Western countries but only a few with Comecon countries.[15] He added, however, that it was evidently easier to make a deal with capitalist than communist countries. In his contribution, Kádár answered: "In the past year, Hungary has been praised by the West. However, we never did anything to please imperialism; instead, we acted in the people's interest ... allegedly, capitalist methods are being applied here. But what is being praised so highly by the West today was introduced by Hungary back[16] in the 1950s."[17]

Basic Attitudes to Perestroika

Archival sources from the HSWP reinforces this threefold attitude toward the Soviet reforms. At the Central Committee of the HSWP, the nature of reforms, the fear of a U-turn as well as the general rejoicing can be observed. János Kádár, though praising the overall reform attitude of the Soviet party leader, warned that while, on the one hand, revisionism had indeed penetrated the country, on the other, it has nothing to do with the economy. In his view, some ideological vigilance was needed, as always in times of international turmoil, but Hungary's economic policies were free of harmful influence: "True, correct, and far from being an easy thing, profitable production, especially profitable production for exports, must be given a green light. My deep conviction is that it's not revisionism—this is precisely socialism, and factories should work profitably under socialism as well. This is my conviction, this is not against the system, but for the good of the system."[18] Not only "capitalist elements" were defended against the Soviet new wave, but the overall hurry of reforms was seen as suspicious. Kádár, with a dubious compliment, praised the Soviet sobriety campaign: "There's nothing to smile about it. Comrade Gorbachev ... told me there were twelve thousand fewer accidents on Soviet roads, because there was no driving under influence. I'm not telling you we should launch an ill-conceived anti-alcohol campaign, because what comes out of them is usually something stupid. But we can give it some thought."[19] Perestroika, after all, was a reform initiated from above, a long tradition in Russian politics, and was pressed with some degree of authoritarianism, which was precisely what the HSWP would not like. Generally, in the Eastern bloc, Gorbachev's reforms had the capacity to resemble Russia's historical top–down reform processes, most vividly represented by those of Tsar Peter the Great.[20] Károly Grósz later recounted Kádár's caution against Soviet reforms. Grósz was then first secretary of the Budapest Party Committee and felt that the new Soviet leadership might be more willing to engage in a dialogue, but the leader of the HSWP had another viewpoint: "Kádár didn't realize that circumstances had changed. Moreover, he even cautioned me against everything that could be contentious. *No, no, don't argue with them. It's not worth it.*"[21] Such a perception was still present against the background of the general Soviet attitude that was quite honestly against forcing a reform agenda onto the satellite states, as they were convinced that their ultimate prevailing was an objective historical necessity, and any direct pressure would destabilize the East European countries.[22]

Gorbachev's reforms, though generally considered refreshing and dynamic, gained some popular opposition, as they alienated a wide range of people from diehards through minority leaders to wine-bidders.[23] This was one reason why the HSWP feared a U-turn in reforming the Soviet system. In Budapest, the stop-go nature of socialist reforming was well known from within and without, if one considers Beria, Khrushchev, Dubček or even the faltering of the New Economic Mechanism. Kádár himself asked Gorbachev at their very first meeting whether he had learned from Khrushchev's mistakes.[24] According to Károly Grósz, Kádár saw Gorbachev as a vain and superficial person, though admitted his honesty too. In his view, Gorbachev was interested in quick political success, but the agenda was not thoroughly considered. Political superficiality, vanity, and hasty and immature reforms could lead to "unforeseen consequences."[25]

The next HSWP CC meeting state secretary at the Foreign Ministry, Gyula Horn, commented that the most important words of Gorbachev were "radical reform," adding that there should not even be a backdrop in political liberties: "I think the most important achievements of the past three decades in this country is that one can, in the true meaning of the word, live, think, and express opinion as a man."[26] Rezső Nyers, one time architect of the New Economic Mechanism, and still considered to be of social democratic leaning and dangerous by Kádár, went even further. He expressed his opinion that such reforms are inevitable in the whole socialist world system, though they need to have their own paths from country to country, and adapting Soviet-style new thinking could not mean the undoing of the Hungarian way. As he said: "There is no unitary reform movement or reform model, and there is not even hope for one; country by country, they will be different for a longer historical period. Eventually, however, they would have to converge." Nyers further added that "[n]owadays in the Comecon, the basis of cooperation is commercial; now it's no longer dominated by mutual assistance, which was crucial in the beginning. Now it's on a commercial basis—but on a confusing and contradictory commercial basis. It's pretty strange that, for instance in Hungary, you have to restrict Comecon export to get by somehow, to reach balance."[27]

Another basic attitude was a cautious rejoicing or relief, which is also observable in the very same speech. Nyers expressed his satisfaction at the fact that "panic from reform" has passed from the Soviet dictionary. Another positive tendency, in his view, was that "after ten years, with some minor changes already underway under Andropov, the leadership of our Soviet sister party is now giving up 'scientific' party leadership and statecraft, and sets in motion a 'political' leading, a political activity."[28] Nyers further added that it was a good policy to cling onto the CPSU "party line" instead of particular people. As he put it, "a country cannot follow either Suslov or Kyrilenko, or Rusakov, or Romanov — who was here at our Congress—[29] because *voilà*, they are no longer. And maybe their attitudes aren't, either."[30]

Dead End at the Comecon Allay

A deeper integration of the Comecon had been at the forefront of intrabloc negotiations from the 1960s. Faced with the increasing pace of West European integration, and suffering from their protectionist policies, partly aiming at the breakup of socialist economies, the Eastern bloc was in a constant quest to further integration. Different national concepts emerged, however. The Soviets were lukewarm about it, as their business with the West was predominantly oil and gas, and so it was not affected by the common agricultural policy (CAP) of the European Economic Community (EEC). They were more interested in securing further investments to their own hydrocarbon exploration from the Eastern bloc countries.[31] The East Germans and the Soviets advocated a closed integration process that would not only strengthen ties within the bloc, but would develop a multilateral body that could be easily dominated by the Soviets, while Berlin and Moscow would retain their private channels to Bonn and Paris.[32] The Hungarians, on the other hand, wanted to incorporate elements of their domestic reform agenda into the Comecon integration so as to secure their influence on the whole bloc;[33] meanwhile, Romania opposed all types of integration on the ground that it would necessarily be harmful for their national interests. Gheorghiu-Dej went as far as to say that the socialist program of "nationalization" of the means of production is the opposite of what their "internationalization" would mean in an integrative framework.[34]

The final blueprint of integration eventually became the so-called Complex Programme, which was mostly based on the hard GDR–USSR concept but contained some elements that gave hope to those interested in a process more open to the Western economies.[35] Yet the basic problems—lagging behind in competitiveness, too much import from the West, too much export to the East—did not go away. It was obvious that globalization required the increasing presence of Western technology and capital, but the socialist notion of the two world systems practically impeded the economic changes.[36] The first country whose economic experts and management started a discourse about abandoning the theory of "two systems" was Hungary. In fact, this concept had practically been abandoned in economic circles by the late 1970s. Comecon integration was officially underway, but the countries of the Eastern bloc wanted to strengthen their Western "integration."[37]

The last serious proposal to tighten the cooperation was at the 1984 Comecon meeting. At this session, Soviet party leader Chernenko addressed the representatives and told them that further integration was the only way out of the crisis. He set two targets for the Comecon countries: one was an integrative and intensive economy to develop, and the other was the basis of "class attitude," instead of economic considerations. Obviously, those targets were contradictory.[38] The Soviets, who pressed to tighten cooperation on national and company levels, did not refrain from economic pressure to reach this goal—which was clearly a symptom, rather than a remedy, to the chronic structural disease of socialist economies. The Soviet Union had not, by this time, got enough power to exert appropriate pressure. The West, the capitalist world system, did not let her do so either. Comecon countries, for their part, while conceding the long-term virtues of integration, found it an obstacle to short-term goals. If there had been more time and less pressure, it could have happened—but it did not.

Although the new Soviet approach aimed to further intrabloc integration, one of Gorbachev's measures unintendedly helped disintegrate the Comecon, and in fact, proved to be the coup de grâce for that institution. In mid-1985, the secretary general of the Comecon, Vyacheslav Sychov, sent a letter to the new president of the EC Commission, Jacques Delors, requesting the mutual recognition of the two bodies. It thereby put the

Eastern bloc implicitly into a detrimental position, as the two bodies were not in parity: the EC was supranational with a capacity to negotiate on behalf of its members, whereas the Comecon was a loose organization with only national decision making. The net outcome of the move was that the EC was empowered to negotiate with each separate Comecon state, while the Comecon could only deal with the EC as a whole. This was yet again an instance when Moscow's long-term interests laid elsewhere than those of most satellite countries. While by this time it may have been realized by the Kremlin that such a mutual recognition was detrimental to the Comecon, in Hungary it was praised by the Central Committee as "more lively relations between the integration organizations" that were "now at arm's distance."[39] When the joint declaration of formal recognition was signed in 1988, this made further disintegration within the Eastern bloc not only more likely but inevitable.[40]

Gorbachev, by the end of 1986, had reached the conclusion that short-term Comecon integration may not be in sight. His goal was, until then, threefold: he wanted to reshape the Soviet system, to urge Comecon and overall Eastern bloc integration, and to maintain the Soviet Union's superpower status. By the end of 1986, however, he had figured out that he could only get two out of the three—most likely, he would be able to secure the first (perestroika) and the third (superpower) at the expense of the second (integration). This is precisely the point when the political weight of Eastern Europe rapidly dropped in Moscow, but of course, the region was not at all abandoned.[41] This was precisely the year when Gorbachev, emphatically and with renewed interest, turned to Western Europe.[42]

However, there was another aspect that impeded the sudden identification of Gorbachev's East European perestroika—even for those countries that were considered developed reformers. This was the fact that there was yet another model for reform—the People's Republic of China. Hungary, for its part, wanted to explore possibilities in the relations with China as well, especially given their previous role in inspiring some of the Chinese reforms. János Kádár had already visited Beijing in October 1987,[43] at a time when a Gorbachev visit would not have been possible. This latter only occurred after some amends had been made in the Afghanistan and Cambodia issue in mid-1989. Until then, the USSR's China policy was basically unmoved.[44]

Landslide Changes in Hungary

As Comecon integration proved to be a non-starter and internal trade figures within the Eastern bloc continued to drop steadily throughout the decade,⁴⁵ the perils of Gorbachev's reform ideas ebbed. In 1987, perestroika had still not made it into mainstream Hungarian politics. Moreover, as Gorbachev's reforms did not transcend the scope or depth of the Hungarian reforms, they could have been seen as a backlash to the reform mentality. There are even some who believe that such a perception on the side of Kádár further ossified the system. As the Hungarian reforms went further than the "new ones" of Gorbachev, there was less need to modernize.⁴⁶ One should also add that, by 1988, none of the Gorbachev reforms had achieved much in the field of economy, and there was a general need to further some kind of resuscitation of the economy.⁴⁷

On the other hand, the leadership of the HWSP fully embraced the idea of Soviet reforms from this time on. They started to act as both the "best pupil" and the "master of perestroika," as they started to see it as the late legitimation of their own reform process,⁴⁸ and on many occasions tried to gain advantage of their invented ideological precedence.⁴⁹ It was a radical departure from a time when the party leadership had had to politically "hide" the Hungarian reform, or call it "unfolding" instead of "reform" so as not to provoke Soviet reprisals.⁵⁰ Still, the HSWP often referred to their own sources of economic reforms, most notably the broadening relations with social democrats, mainly West Germans,⁵¹ combined with some Eurocommunist influence.⁵² The real origins of the early Hungarian reforms of the 1960s can, however, be traced back to Evsei Liberman and his 1962 reform proposals, which were short lived in the USSR, but survived in Hungary.⁵³ One should add that the PR identification with Soviet reforms was more a practice of foreign than domestic policy.

If perestroika was used as a foreign policy argument and not introduced early to public speech, glasnost was even less so. In a paper written in July 1986, designed to circulate in the party leadership, it was concluded that the relatively free Hungarian discourse cannot be further relaxed. Furthermore, the Hungarian opposition, they judged, had not become stronger, but had intensified its international support. That is, the Hungarian party had to find a way to silence the opposition without provoking reprisals from Western countries.⁵⁴ But the changes could not be withheld from 1987. This year saw an increased need for radical reform in the economy, but the HSWP still refused pluralization of the political sphere (and it had not yet been endorsed by the Soviet Union, either). That the Soviet brand of reforms was still not unanimous is illustrated by the fact that Kádár traveled to China and had conversations with Deng Xiaoping, who represented a different approach to economic reforms.⁵⁵ A qualitative breakthrough in politics and reform was, however, not that much attached to internal development but to the rapid changes in international politics. This in turn fermented the political change in

Hungary as well. From three distinctive standpoints, the emerging opposition, the Soviet leadership, and Kádár himself all reached the conclusion that Kádár was not up to the challenge to lead the reform. It was the point when economic reforms necessitated a degree of political pluralism where Kádár was by then unable to follow the events: for him, the experience of the revolution of 1956 marked a red line beyond which Hungary could not step, and this was party pluralism. By mid-1988, however, economic and political transformation were no longer extricable.[56]

In May 1988, Kádár and most of his closest co-workers were voted out from the party leadership in a move that was preplanned, but later spiraled out of control. In Rezső Nyers' words, the meeting "turned out to be sovereign in a spontaneous way."[57] It is not necessary here to recall the nature and events of the unraveling of the socialist system in Hungary. Suffice it to say that Károly Grósz, already prime minister from 1987, replaced Kádár as general secretary. Although intended to work with the old guard, he had a whole new set of even more radical reformers while in power. One of them, Rezső Nyers, expressed his views as to the unrealistic nature of any future socialist integration without radical economic and political reforms.[58] Sweeping economic reforms took place in the following months, but they were not based that much on a Soviet blueprint, and rather followed the inner logic of the old Hungarian reforms. This was not often stressed in Hungarian discourse, but it was noticed by contemporary foreign experts.[59]

Károly Grósz's short-lived period was the only one that positively attributed itself domestically with the notion of perestroika and glasnost. The *Frankfurter Allgemeine Zeitung* even coined the term *grósznoszty*, a Hungarian compound of the name Grósz and glasnost. Grósz was of course concerned with the economic situation, but, like the Soviet leader, he considered perestroika to be a tool to preserve the system, not to transform it. As he put it in 1989: "We should not indulge ourselves into illusions; some of our political opponents do not want to fix socialism, but to get rid of it peacefully."[60] Grósz wanted to maximize the PR value of perestroika and glasnost, and garner predominantly foreign respect to gain a firm hold on power. However, with the ascent of younger and more reform-minded people, his attempts ultimately proved to be illusory.[61]

For this period, however, it is even harder to examine the HSWP's attitude towards perestroika, as the party itself was undergoing a period of constant upheaval. It is primarily due to the fact that the opposition, heartened by Gorbachev himself, wanted to go beyond just reforming, while the party membership was confused about the real nature of change. In early 1988, there was an HSWP membership card renewal campaign that resulted in a loss of forty thousand members as well as a long list of grievances against the party.⁶² The normative goal of stabilizing state–party relations did not help, either. Although it was by this time evident that a dualism should be reinstated, it inevitably further deflated the role of the party. As it was said, the "the political structure, and the relationship between the government and the party, should be clarified."⁶³ This had come to a logical conclusion in May 1988 when a resolution decided that the government could overwrite the resolution of the Political Committee. So, while perestroika and glasnost finally became call words for domestic policy even to the Hungarian Socialist Workers' Party, the party itself was on the verge of disintegration. As one leading member of the moderate reformer wing, János Berecz, put it in early 1989, "I think at this moment there is no single ideology that may bog us down in getting through the hardest part of our economic hardships. Nothing should stop us turning around on our constant downward track."⁶⁴

Conclusion

Hungary, often cited as a "best pupil" of Gorbachev's reforms, had in fact a more complicated relationship to them which also evolved with time. Hungarian reforms, originated from the Liberman article of 1962, were mostly about market elements, which were innovative in the 1960s but faltered after the stop–go policy caused by pressures from within and without, following 1972. In the long 1970s, the Hungarian party "learned" to live with their limited reforms, and they wished to avoid a strict Comecon integration that would untie their Western partnerships. Thus, while there was an overall relief that reform was no longer a swearword in Moscow, the party leadership feared the eventual consequences of a Soviet-inspired top–down reform.

This complex made it hard for the HSWP to identify themselves with the perestroika, but for legitimacy and foreign policy reasons they championed it publicly. When the idea of socialist integration proved to be a non-starter, the Soviet reform was embraced and publicly endorsed up to the point when political plurality came to the fore. This was a point that Kádár could not step beyond. His successor, Grósz, tried to implement the maximum number of economic reforms and the minimum number of political ones, thus he became identified with the glasnost brand. This approach did, by then, paradoxically little, as by this time the HSWP had already started to unravel, and the opposition, heartened by the Gorbachev course itself, came up with even more radical political changes. Hungarian reform communism, which had been designed to prolong and fix the system, was thus amended with further reforms that eventually contributed to the admission of the inevitability of a democratic, capitalist transition.

Throughout the whole period, however, there was a certain public acceptance and vindication of perestroika. Indeed, it was deemed opportune to stress Hungary's values and openness vis-à-vis both the West European countries and the East European "allies": it served as an appropriate narrative framing for ever-extending relations with the West, and an adequate contrast to those Eastern bloc countries that had posed the greatest threat to Hungarian national interests—most notably, Romania. The reason why Hungary is often cited as an "eminent in perestroika" may be found in the authenticity and the continuation of this public relations campaign, which has been persistent in the press, both Hungarian and foreign.

Subtopics that may welcome further research in this field are still many. I consider the integration and centrifugal tendencies in the Comecon as one of the most inspiring late Cold War topics. The role of Hungary, undoubtedly the most open and reform-minded country in the bloc, is also worth examining, as its analysis often has elements that are immediately derived from Kádár-era public relations. The precise interrelationships between the currents of Liberman reforms, Eurocommunism, Chinese reforms, social democracy, and perestroika are also worth examining, as the 1980s was characterized by a constant quest to find the great model that could save socialism for the next generations.

Considering the framework of gradual emancipation within the Eastern bloc, it can be concluded that while, from the 1960s on, the Hungarian reform provided ample space in the economic field but no political liberalization, the Soviet "new thinking" ushered in a period when economic interference to ties with the West was perceived as malign, while the political interference to the party's reign was considered dangerous. By the time the Hungarian leaders had changed and the new ones were ready to undertake the reforms, it was no longer enough. While the HSWP's change made it possible to vindicate the values of Gorbachev's reforms, they themselves, coupled with developments in the international field, empowered the country's non-communist opposition. The task for both camps was then to arrange Hungary's transition to democracy.

Tamás Péter Baranyi received his MA degrees in History and American Studies from the ELTE University of Budapest. He started his career as historian at the House of Terror Museum in Budapest in 2010, and in

2012 he became their head of research. In 2015, he joined the Antall József Knowledge Centre, a think tank and research institution, also as head of research. He defended his PhD thesis in 2018 with summa cum laude degree. His main field of study is the international history of the Cold War, Hungarian foreign policy, and transatlantic relations. He has published extensively in both Hungarian and English. Since 2014, he has been teaching at the Modern and Contemporary World History Department of the ELTE University of Budapest. By translating several pieces, he also regularly contributes to bringing international academic literature to Hungary; he is currently working on the Hungarian edition of the memoirs of George F. Kennan.

Notes

1. MNL OL M-KS 288. f. 32./1989/10. ő. e. 151.
2. Mikhail Gorbachev on "Perestroika Today," in *Rossiyskaya Gazeta*. http://in.rbth.com/opinion/2015/03/21/on_perestroika_today_-_mikhail_gorbachev_42123. Last accessed 7 February 2016.
3. The evolving nature of perestroika is a common trait in historiography. Brown succinctly summarizes that Gorbachev's views on the scale of the transformation needed became more radical over time. See Brown, *The Gorbachev Revolution*, 245.
4. Rey, *From Fulton to Malta*, 2–3.
5. Grachev, *Gorbachev's Gamble*, 73–75.
6. Brown, *The Gorbachev Revolution*, 248.
7. Békés, "East Central Europe, 1953–56."
8. Kemp-Welch, "In Search of Sovereignty," 28–42.
9. Grachev, *Gorbachev's Gamble*, 74.
10. Sz. Bíró, "Gorbacsov reformjai és Kelet-Közép-Európa," 16.
11. For the impact economist János Kornai made on the People's Republic of China, see, for example, Farkas, "A kínai kapcsolat," 29–31.
12. Békés, "Why Was There No Second Cold War in Europe?"
13. Földes, *Kádár János*, 457.
14. Földes, *Kádár János*, 455–56.
15. Selvage, "Record of the Meeting," 11–13.
16. This is obviously an overstatement. Elements of the New Economic Mechanism were introduced in the late 1960s. Citing the 1950s instead could have served to further the contrast between the West and Hungary, as in the 1950s, Hungary was a diplomatically isolated country and so could not have received political influences from the West.
17. Selvage, "Record of the Meeting," 31.
18. Kádár János, minutes of the HSWP CC meeting, 4 December 1985. MNL OL MK-S 288. f. 4/215–216 ő. e. 22.
19. Ibid., e. 24.
20. See Wanda Jarząbek's chapter in the present volume.
21. Emphasis in original. Transcript of an interview with Károly Grósz, recorded 24 August 1995. Property of the author, 7.
22. Békés, *Magyarország*, 308–9.

23. Bottoni, *A várva várt Nyugat*, 222.
24. Földes, *Kádár János*, 462.
25. Transcript of an interview with Károly Grósz, recorded 24 August 1995. Property of the author, 7.
26. Gyula Horn, minutes of the HSWP CC meeting, 18 March 1986. MNL OL MK-S 288. f. 4/217–218 ő. e. 25, 28.
27. Rezső Nyers, minutes of the HSWP CC meeting, 18 March 1986. MNL OL MK-S 288. f. 4/217–218 ő. e. 34, 37.
28. Ibid., 33, 35.
29. During the interregnum between Chernenko and Gorbachev, the HSWP held its 13th Party Congress during which Romanov castigated the Hungarians for their extensive Western relations. See Földes, *Kádár János*, 451.
30. Rezső Nyers, minutes of the HSWP CC meeting, 18 March 1986. MNL OL MK-S 288. f. 4/217–218 ő. e. 38.
31. Kansikas, "Calculating the Burden of Empire," 350–51.
32. Kansikas, "Room to Manoeuvre?", 198–200.
33. Földes, *Kádár János*, 112–14.
34. Bottoni, "Unrequited Love," 124–25.
35. Kansikas, "Room to Manoeuvre?", 199.
36. Steiner, "The Globalisation Process," 174–77.
37. Germuska, "Failed Eastern Integration," 276–80.
38. Földes, *Kádár János*, 426.
39. Mátyás Szűrös, minutes of the HSWP CC meeting, 11 November 1987. MNL OL MK-S 288. f. 4/228–229. ő. e. 14.
40. Bideleux and Taylor, *European Integration and Disintegration*, 195–97.
41. Földes, *Kádár János*, 468–69.
42. Chernyaev, *My Six Years with Gorbachev*, 104.
43. 1987 kronológiája. Beszélő, 1999/7–8. http://www.c3.hu/scripta/beszelo/99/0708/15 krono.htm. Last accessed 6 December 2016.
44. Vámos, "Csak kézfogás van, ölelés nincs," 323–24.
45. Bideleux and Taylor, *European Integration and Disintegration*, 198.
46. Kiss, "Politika és percepció," 116.
47. Békés, *Magyarország*, 311.
48. Békés, "Magyar külpolitika," 116.
49. For example, after his trip to China in 1987, Kádár told Gorbachev that Deng Xiaoping believed that the Hungarians "preceded" Moscow in reforms. Gorbachev was unimpressed. See Földes, *Kádár János*, 521.
50. Cf. Békés, *Magyarország*, 156.
51. According to a memoir of Rezső Nyers, the initiator of the New Economic Mechanism. Cf. Nyers, "Visszatekintés az 1988–90-es politikai fordulatra."
52. According to the memoirs of one of the leading members of the Hungarian reform communists, Gyula Horn. Cf. Horn, *Cölöpök*, 37–43.
53. Standeisky, "Újabb történeti irodalom," 18–23.
54. Cynkin, "Glasnost, Perestroika and Eastern Europe", 316.
55. Földes, *Kádár János*, 521.
56. Kalmár, *Történelmi galaxisok vonzásában*, 536–37.
57. Nyers, "Visszatekintés az 1988–90-es politikai fordulatra."
58. Földes, *Kádár János*, 516–17.
59. Cynkin, "Glasnost, Perestroika and Eastern Europe," 317.
60. Károly Grósz, minutes of the HSWP CC meeting, 10–11 February 1989. MNL OL M-KS 288. f. 4/250–252. ő. e. 17.
61. Mink, "Grószsnoszty."

62. For the entire documentation, see Réfi, "Az MSZMP bomlási folyamata."
63. Minutes of the HSWP CC meeting, MNL OL M-KS 288. f. 4/232–235. ő. e. 11.
64. János Berecz, minutes of the HSWP PC meeting, 21 March 1989, MNL OL M-KS 288. f. 5/1058–1059. ő. e. 13.

Bibliography

Archival Sources

Hungarian National Archives (Magyar Nemzeti Levéltár)
MNL OL M-KS 288. f. 32/10. ő. e. 151. (1989)
MNL OL MK-S 288. f. 4/215–216 ő. e. (1985)
MNL OL MK-S 288. f. 4/217–218 ő. e. (1986)
MNL OL MK-S 288. f. 4/228–229. ő. e. 14. (1987)
MNL OL M-KS 288. f. 4/232–235. ő. e. 11. (1988)
MNL OL M-KS 288. f. 5/1058–1059. ő. e. 13. (1989)
MNL OL M-KS 288. f. 4/250–252. ő. e. 17. (1989)

Published Sources

1987 kronológiája, Beszélő, 1999/7–8. http://www.c3.hu/scripta/beszelo/99/0708/15krono.htm. Last accessed 6 December 2016.
Békés, Csaba. "East Central Europe, 1953–56," in *The Cambridge History of the Cold War*, Vol. I: Origins, ed. Melvyn Leffler and Arne Westad, Cambridge, 2010, 334–353.
_____. "Magyar külpolitika a bipoláris világban, 1945–1991," *Külügyi Szemle*, Vol. 4 (2011), 95–127.
_____. "Magyarország, a szovjet blokk és a nemzetközi politika az enyhülés időszakában 1953–1991." Doctoral thesis, Budapest, 2012.
_____. "Why Was There No "Second Cold War" in Europe? Hungary and the East–West Crisis Following the Soviet Invasion of Afghanistan," in *NATO and the Warsaw Pact: Intrabloc Conflicts*, ed. Mary Ann Heiss and S. Victor Papacosma, Kent, OH, 2008, 219–232.
Bideleux, Robert, and, Richard Taylor (eds). *European Integration and Disintegration: East and West*, New York, 1996.
Bottoni, Stefano. *A várva várt Nyugat: Kelet-Európa története 1944-től napjainkig*, Budapest, 2014.
_____. "Unrequited Love?: The Romanian Communist Party and the EEC in the 1960s and 1970s," in *Kommunismus und Europa: Vorstellungen und Politik europäischer kommunistischer Parteien im Kalten Krieg*, ed. Francesco Di Palma and Wolfgang Mueller, Paderborn, 2015, 118–136.
Brown, Archie. "The Gorbachev Revolution and the End of the Cold War," in *The Cambridge History of the Cold War*, Vol. III: Endings, ed. Melvyn Leffler and Arne Westad, Cambridge, 2010, 244–266.
Chernyaev, Anatoly S. *My Six Years with Gorbachev*, University Park, PA, 2000.

Cynkin, Thomas M. "Glasnost, Perestroika and Eastern Europe," *Survival: Global Politics and Strategy*, Vol. 4 (1988), 310–331.
Douglas, Selvage (ed.). "Record of the Meeting of the General Secretaries and First Secretaries of the Central Committees of the Fraternal Parties of the Warsaw Treaty Member States on 23 October 1985 in Sofia. Records of the Political Consultative Committee, 1955–1991," in Parallel History Project on Cooperative Security. Zurich, August 2010.
Farkas, Zoltán. "A kínai kapcsolat," *Mozgó Világ*, Vol. 9 (2010), 29–43.
Földes, György. *Kádár János külpolitikája és nemzetközi tárgyalásai*, Vol. 1, Budapest, 2015.
Germuska, Pál. "Failed Eastern Integration and a Partly Successful Opening up to the West: The Economic Re-orientation of Hungary during the 1970s," *European Review of History: Revue européenne d'histoire*, Vol. 2, 2014, 271–291.
Gorbachev, Mikhail. "On Perestroika Today," *Rossiyskaya Gazeta*, 21 March 2015. http://in.rbth.com/opinion/2015/03/21/on_perestroika_today_-_mikhail_gorbachev_42123. Last accessed 7 February 2016.
Grachev, Andrei. *Gorbachev's Gamble: Soviet Foreign Policy and the End of the Cold War*, Cambridge, 2008.
Grósz, Károly. Transcript of an interview with Károly Grósz, recorded 24 August 1995. Property of the author.
Horn, Gyula. *Cölöpök*, Zenith könyvek, Budapest, 1991.
Kalmár, Melinda. *Történelmi galaxisok vonzásában: Magyarország és a szovjet rendszer, 1945–1990*, Budapest, 2014.
Kansikas, Suvi. "Calculating the Burden of Empire: Soviet Oil, East–West Trade, and the End of the Socialist Bloc," in *Cold War Energy: A Transnational History of Soviet Oil and Gas*, ed. Jeremy Perović, Cham, 2017, 345–369.
_____. "Room to Manoeuvre? National Interests and Coalition-Building in the CMEA, 1969–74," in *Reassessing Cold War Europe*, ed. Sari Autio-Sarasmo and Katalin Miklóssy, London, 2011, 193–209.
Kemp-Welch, Anthony. "In Search of Sovereignty: Central and Eastern Europe, 1956–1989," *Corvinus Journal of International Relations* (COJOURN), Vol. 3 (2016), 28–41.
Kiss, László J. "Politika és percepció: magyar és osztrák (kül)politika az átalakulás éveiben (1988–1991)," *Külügyi Szemle*, Vol. 2 (2013), 102–125.
Mink, Attila. "Grószsnoszty," *Beszélő*, Vol. 9 (1999), 75–79.
Nyers, Rezső. "Visszatekintés az 1988–90-es politikai fordulatra: Magyarország politikai évkönyve. A rendszerváltás, 1988–1998." http://www.politikaievkonyv.hu/online/mp10/2-4-13.html. Last accessed 20 November 2016.
Réfi, Attila. "Az MSZMP bomlási folyamata a párt és tagjai viszonyának tükrében (1985–1989)," *Múltunk*, Vol. 4 (2009), 64–91.
Rey, Marie-Pierre. "From Fulton to Malta: How the Cold War Began and Ended." Lecture held under the same name, organized by the Gorbachev Foundation in 2006. www.gorby.ru/img.php?img=file&art_id=25031. Last accessed 28 January 2016.
Standeisky, Éva. "Újabb történeti irodalom az 1950–1970-es évek Szovjetuniójáról," in *Közelítések a kádárizmushoz*, ed. Pál Germuska, János Rainer and M. János, Budapest, 2008, 11–40.

Steiner, André. "The Globalisation Process and the Eastern Bloc Countries in the 1970s and 1980s," *European Review of History: Revue européenne d'histoire*, Vol. 2 (2014), 165–181.

Sz. Bíró, Zotán. "Gorbacsov reformjai és Kelet-Közép-Európa," *História*, Vol. 12 (2011), 16–20.

Vámos, Péter. "'Csak kézfogás van, ölelés nincs': a kínai–szovjet kapcsolatok normalizálása a nyolcvanas években," *Külügyi Szemle*, Vol. 4 (2007), 312–333.

Chapter 4

Yugoslavia and Perestroika, 1985–1991
Between Hope and Disappointment

Petar Dragišić

From early 1985 to the end of 1991, the Soviet Union underwent an avalanche of changes that radically transformed the Soviet system. Nevertheless, the outcome of the process was fatal, since the "patient" did not survive the treatment. Although Mikhail Sergeyevich Gorbachev and his reform program were met with fierce opposition from the communist elites worldwide,[1] the East European regimes shared the fate of their tutor. Eventually, the belated reforms in the Soviet Union and its communist bloc had profound geopolitical and ideological consequences in Europe—dissolution of the Soviet Union, Czechoslovakia and Yugoslavia, collapse of the socialist systems in Europe, and the expansion of NATO in the former Soviet sphere of influence.

Although Yugoslavia did not belong to the Soviet bloc following the death of Stalin, it cultivated close relations with Moscow, notwithstanding the occasional crisis. Consequently, Yugoslavia was interested in what was happening in Moscow and its client states. Given that Yugoslavs closely monitored the events and processes in the Soviet Union and Eastern Europe, the Yugoslav sources can cast new light on the five years, to paraphrase John Reed, "that shook the world."

Notes for this chapter begin on page 116.

First Impressions

As in March 1985, following the death of Konstantin Chernenko, Mikhail Gorbachev took over the leadership of the Communist Party of the Soviet Union, and the Yugoslav experts in Soviet affairs set to work to profile the new Soviet leader and decipher his first statements. Only a few days after the political earthquake in Moscow, the leading figures of the Yugoslav communist establishment, the president of the State Presidency, Veselin Djuranović, the chairman of the Party Presidium, Ali Šukrija, and the Yugoslav foreign secretary, Raif Dizdarević, attended Chernenko's funeral and got the chance to meet the new Soviet leader. According to Dizdarević's memoirs, the first brief conversation with Gorbachev convinced his Yugoslav interlocutors that they "were dealing with an entirely new political profile on the Soviet political stage … During this brief meeting, Gorbachev was very direct, expressing his interest in developing relations and cooperation between our two countries' leaderships, and in establishing more regular contacts. We were left with the impression that here was an atypical Soviet leader, ready for open dialogue."[2]

The Yugoslavs were anything but surprised by the appointment of Mikhail Gorbachev as a head of the Soviet Communist Party. On 13 March, only a day after Chernenko's death, the correspondent of the Belgrade daily, *Politika*, remarked that Gorbachev's appointment was expected, given that he of all Politburo members was in charge of ideological issues, a function that "traditionally gives the ultimate power."[3] According to Dizdarević, Andropov's intention to appoint Gorbachev as his successor was met with opposition from other Soviet leaders, which subsequently led to the short tenure of Konstantin Chernenko. In his memoirs, the then Yugoslav foreign secretary credited particularly Andrei Gromyko with Gorbachev's appointment as the CPSU general secretary after Chernenko's death in March 1985:

> We had information from the party leadership in Poland that at the end of Brezhnev's rule, in the Soviet Communist Party Politburo those who shared the closest views in their critical and realistic evaluation of the situation and of the need for radical changes in the USSR were Yuri Andropov and Mikhail Gorbachev. We know that Andropov, who was seriously ill, wanted Gorbachev to be appointed in his place as general secretary of the Communist Party of the Soviet Union, and that the line-up among the Soviet leadership was not in favor of his appointment. Chernenko was elected—without doubt the most colorless and least able figure ever to head the USSR in its entire history. He died a year later, and the prevailing view among the leadership was

that someone younger and more dynamic should replace him. The choice fell on Gorbachev, thanks to the particular commitment and influence of Andrei Gromyko in the politburo.[4]

Notwithstanding their sympathy for Gorbachev and his first steps at the head of the Soviet Communist Party, the Yugoslavs did not consider the new Soviet leader a unique phenomenon in the recent history of the Soviet Union. Instead, the comparison with Yuri Andropov was commonplace in the first Yugoslav comments on Gorbachev's appointment. In an internal report of the Yugoslav Institute of International Politics and Economics, produced in October 1985, the connection between the first steps of Mikhail Gorbachev and the reform intentions of his tutor, Yuri Andropov, during Andropov's short tenure, was underlined. According to the authors of this report, Yuri Andropov was well aware of the necessity for profound changes to the Soviet economic system. Besides, the report says, Andropov introduced a new cadre policy by creating a nucleus consisting of young and well-educated leaders. The authors of the Yugoslav report underlined that Andropov's cadre policy had had a substantial impact on the Soviet system, despite the temporary comeback of Brezhnev's followers during Konstantin Chernenko's rule.[5]

Gorbachev's coming to power, his new cadre policy as well as his political orientation were viewed by the authors of the Yugoslav report as a continuation of Andropov's course. They stressed that during the first months of Gorbachev's tenure, new, young and well-educated cadres had taken over the leadership of the party, thus bringing fresh blood into the decrepit Soviet political system.[6]

For Yugoslav observers, the cadre reforms carried out by Gorbachev from 1985 to 1988 were a precondition for a far-reaching transformation of the political and economic system of the Soviet Union. The new generation of Soviet leaders, who had replaced the old-fashioned dogmatists, were seen as staunch supporters of Gorbachev's program in the highest bodies of the Communist Party of the Soviet Union.[7] The Moscow correspondent of the League of Communists of Yugoslavia (LCY) organ *Komunist* described the resignation of Andrei Gromyko and his five coevals (Mikhail Sergeyevich Solomentsev, Vladimir Ivanovich Dolgikh, Pyotr Nilovich Demichev, Ivan Kapitonov and Anatoly Fyodorovich Dobrynin) in autumn 1988 as a successful surgery and a "farewell to the old-fashioned mindset."[8]

The fundamental cadre reform launched by Mikhail Gorbachev gave cause for cautious optimism in Yugoslavia about the outcome of the Soviet perestroika. In 1985 and 1986 the columnists of the *Komunist* predicted that the new political class in Moscow would be able to implement Gorbachev's ambitious project.[9]

The initial stage of perestroika, launched after Gorbachev's appointment as the CPSU general secretary and the April plenum of the Central Committee of the CPSU, was viewed in the report of the Yugoslav Institute of International Politics and Economics as the beginning of a modification to the existing economic and political system in the Soviet Union. Gorbachev's decision to delay the reform until the 27th Party Congress, the Yugoslav report says, was motivated by his intention to meet two preconditions: first, to formulate his reform project; and second, to carry out the cadre reform, given the opposition from the conservatives to perestroika. Although at that point the authors of the Yugoslav report refrained from predicting the outcome of perestroika, they speculated that the delay would increase Gorbachev's chances of success.[10]

Despite the fact that the Yugoslav experts in Soviet affairs did not deny the uniqueness of the Soviet experiment in the 1980s, some of them searched for possible foreign influences on perestroika. In two articles published in 1986 and 1987 in the journal of the League of Communists of Yugoslavia, *Socijalizam*, the authors speculated about the Hungarian impact on the Soviet reform ideas in the early 1980s. Both authors underlined Andropov's diplomatic career in Budapest in the second half of the 1950s, and his knowledge of Hungarian language, which had enabled him to familiarize himself with the "Hungarian experiment."[11] Moreover, the authors of the above-mentioned report of the Institute for International Politics and Economics pointed out that the Soviet reformers had in many respects been inspired by the reforms in Hungary. In addition, the Yugoslav analysts underlined the Soviet interest in monitoring the processes in Bulgaria and the German Democratic Republic, as well as Soviet attempts to use their experiences (East German and Bulgarian) in certain areas (like in the agro-industrial sector).[12]

The Yugoslav observers found no trace of the Yugoslav influence on perestroika, despite the pioneering Yugoslav experiments in the workers' self-management following the Yugoslav–Soviet split in the late 1940s. Although the Yugoslavs were well aware of being carefully monitored by the Soviet reformers, they had no doubt that the mounting crisis in Yugoslavia in the 1980s (high inflation, enormous foreign debt, ethnic tensions) made the Yugoslav model extremely unattractive. In June 1987, at the conference of the Soviet and Yugoslav Marxists in Moscow, the Soviet experts expressed an interest in studying the Yugoslav road to socialism. Nevertheless, given the serious economic troubles in Yugoslavia and the grave crisis in Kosovo in the 1980s, they also expressed doubts about advantages of the Yugoslav experiments.[13]

Similarly, the Yugoslavs closely monitored perestroika and the reform attempts in the socialist bloc in the second half of the 1980s, though without any intention to apply the Soviet innovations. From the very beginning of Gorbachev's ambitious experiment, the Yugoslav press reported on a daily basis on the Soviet perestroika. Numerous comments and reports on the situation in the Soviet Union indicate a positive attitude of the Yugoslav press towards the last Soviet leader and his reform project. Nevertheless, Gorbachev was not portrayed as a revolutionary who questioned the system as a whole, but as one who strove to improve the existing structure.[14]

On Triumphs and Troubles

From 1986 to 1989, the Yugoslav press paid particular attention to the economic consequences of perestroika as well as to the complex process of democratization and liberalization of the Soviet system. The Yugoslav experts in perestroika focused particularly on the Law on State Enterprise, introduced in 1987, which provided Soviet companies with greater autonomy. At the same time, the Yugoslav correspondents from Moscow reported on the disappointing results of the economic reforms, in particular on chronic shortages of consumer goods in the Soviet Union. Nevertheless, the reports on the emerging private sector (particularly in the service industry) updated the Yugoslavs on the beginning of modernization of the Soviet economic system in the early stages of perestroika.[15]

The Yugoslav regime was particularly impressed by results of the democratization of Soviet society in the second half of the 1980s. In 1987, the Croatian political scientist and prominent functionary of the League of Communists of Croatia, Branko Caratan, in his article in the Yugoslav Marxist journal *Socijalizam*, described perestroika as a radical change and revolutionary process, underlining the most impressive aspects of the Soviet liberalization in the Gorbachev era—a new political atmosphere, characterized by the breaking of taboos and the liberalization of intellectual and cultural life.[16]

The Yugoslav press focused particularly on the most eye-catching examples of the democratization and liberalization in the Soviet Union, from open discussions at the conferences of Soviet writers and filmmakers, to the efforts of the Soviet historians to cast new light on the "white spots" of the Stalin era.[17] Besides, in 1987 the vigorous de-Stalinization campaign in the Soviet Union was widely reported in the Yugoslav press. Among other things, the Belgrade daily *Politika* gave considerable publicity to the masterpiece of the Georgian film director Tengis Abuladze—*Repentance*

(Покаяние)—premiered in 1987, in which the author sharply criticized the Stalin era. The *Politika* correspondent was struck by the immense popularity of Abuladze's movie in the Soviet Union, in particular among the young people. Nevertheless, he stressed that *Repentance* had met with a mixed reception, given the reluctance of part of Soviet society to confront the most traumatic episodes in the Soviet past. According to the correspondent of the Belgrade daily, in 1987 it was still possible to see Stalin's pictures in cabs and cabins of trucks, which he ascribed to an inadequate dismantling of Stalin's cult of personality.[18]

Commonplace in the Yugoslav reports and comments on the Soviet perestroika were predictions of the outcome of Gorbachev's reform project, and analysis of major obstacles to perestroika. The Yugoslav observers perceived the huge Soviet bureaucracy as a major threat to Gorbachev and his reform course, stressing that the bureaucracy only verbally supported perestroika, while frantically trying to preserve its privileged status and deliberately obstructing the reforms. From the Yugoslav point of view, it was this opposition that compelled Gorbachev to launch radical political reforms. In this regard, the Yugoslav analysts focused on the first steps towards democratization of the Soviet party and state, taken at the Plenum of the Central Committee of the Communist Party of the Soviet Union in January 1987, which, according to the Yugoslav interpretations, was a major blow to the status of the Soviet bureaucracy.[19] Besides, the Yugoslav observers were full of praise for the elections for the Congress of People's Deputies of the Soviet Union (in spring 1989), which were described in the Yugoslav press as the most democratic elections in the history of the Soviet Union.[20]

In Yugoslavia the bureaucracy was not considered the only obstacle to the progress of perestroika. In 1989 the chronic shortages of consumer goods and the opposition to Gorbachev's course within the leadership of the CPSU (both from conservative and radical circles, led by Yegor Ligachyov and Boris Yeltsin respectively) were perceived by the Yugoslav media as a considerable handicap to Gorbachev's project. In September 1989, the correspondent of the Yugoslav daily *Politika* summarized the mood of pessimism in Yugoslavia about the fate of perestroika in one question: "Can Gorbachev survive?"[21] The party organ *Komunist* described Gorbachev's vulnerable position between those in favor of more rapid reforms and the dogmatists (as well conservatives), by using an illustrative metaphor—"between Scylla and Charybdis."[22] Being confronted with the escalation of ethnic tensions in their own country, the Yugoslavs considered the complex ethnic composition of the Soviet Union to be a potentially serious threat to perestroika and to the future of the Soviet Union. In his paper, published in 1986 in the party journal

Socijalizam, the Croatian political scientist Franjo Butorac underlined the multiethnic character of the Soviet Union, pointing out that the economic decentralization, initiated by perestroika, could lead to requests for political decentralization too.[23] In August 1988, the *Komunist* columnist Branko Stošić underlined the rise of nationalism among Russians, Ukrainians, Belarussians and Baltic regions, which he considered to be a side effect of perestroika.[24] In February 1990, the *Tanjug*[25] correspondent in Moscow ascribed the rebirth of nationalist sentiments in the Soviet Union to the democratization of the Soviet society, which was a result of perestroika.[26]

In his memoirs, Raif Dizdarević recalled that during Gorbachev's visit to Yugoslavia in 1988 he had wondered about Gorbachev's ignoring of the complex ethnic composition of the Soviet Union and its potentially devastating impact:

> In all our previous talks on the changes taking place in the USSR and on perestroika, as well as in these talks with Gorbachev in Yugoslavia, I asked myself two questions: could the Soviet Union successively de-Stalinize itself and instigate the democratic process if these processes were not kept under control, given the vast opposition to them and the explosive national and social charge that had been building up for decades but kept forcibly damped down, as well as all the diversity of unfulfilled national aspirations and regionalism—I had in mind, that is, the danger of spontaneous, stormy and serious resistance and fragmentation. Could these changes proceed safely if everything that had to be abandoned and dismantled was not replaced by the new, specific and achievable—would the line-up in the leadership structure make it possible to draw up a specific programme for change, given that the USSR as a whole, and Russia in particular, could be torn apart by a spontaneous eruption. I have to say that I saw nothing in Gorbachev's speech to suggest that he had considered these dangers.[27]

Although the Yugoslavs closely monitored what was happening in the Soviet Union in the late 1980s, praising the reforms in the Soviet Union as well as in the Soviet client states, perestroika had negligible impact on the political orientation of the Yugoslav communist establishment. In his speech at the 13th Congress of the League of Communists of Yugoslavia, held in June 1986, the member of the presidency of the Central Committee, Vidoje Žarković, commended the determination of the socialist regimes in Eastern Europe to reconsider their strategy.[28] In the following years, a number of high-ranking Yugoslav politicians sympathized with the Soviet experiment, lauding Gorbachev's orientation towards democratization and liberalization, and underlining the importance of perestroika for the socialist and workers' movement.

Despite their overwhelmingly positive attitude towards perestroika, the Yugoslav establishment did not regard it as an inspiration for its own reforms for at least three reasons. First, since 1948 the Yugoslav communists had been firmly convinced of the advantages of their own "road to socialism" and their ability to improve their system on their own. Consequently, they were anything but ready to import and copy foreign models. Thus, with time, Tito's famous motto, born towards the end of the Second World War—"What is others' we do not want, what is ours we shall not give"[29]—received an ideological basis. Besides, given the Yugoslav–Soviet split in 1948, the Yugoslavs had reservations about innovations in the Soviet sphere of influence.

And last but not least, in the late 1980s, the growing ethnic tensions brought Yugoslavia to the brink of a civil war. Consequently, given that the Yugoslav communists gave their ethnic aspirations the highest priority, modernization and reforms vanished from their agenda. At the 14th Party Congress, in January 1990, the League of Communists of Yugoslavia fell apart, which paved the way for the Yugoslav "tragedy."

Death of the Soviet Union—Death of Yugoslavia

The process of disintegration of the multiethnic Yugoslav federation, which accelerated in the late 1980s, precluded any consensus among the Yugoslav leaders about the far-reaching reforms in the Soviet Union and the Soviet East European client states. In other words, the disintegration of Yugoslavia in the early 1990s led to the disintegration of the Yugoslav perceptions of perestroika and its creator, since the political elites of the Yugoslav federal units evaluated differently the reform processes in the Soviet Union and the political role of Mikhail Gorbachev.

The Yugoslav crisis terminated Yugoslavia's traditional (since 1948) balancing between East and West, since the Yugoslav federal units pursued diametrically opposed strategies on the international stage. The western federal units Slovenia and Croatia aspired to decentralization of Yugoslavia, and in 1991 launched a process of separation from Belgrade, seeking the protection of the West—particularly of Germany and the United States. On the other hand, in a bid to prevent the dissolution of Yugoslavia, or rather to strengthen its position on the eve of the Yugoslav wars, Serbia (as well as the leadership of the Yugoslav People's Army) turned to its traditional ally Russia (Soviet Union) for support. The attempts by the Serbian and army leadership to win Soviet support in the final stages of the Yugoslav dissolution culminated in a futile trip by the Yugoslav defense minister, Veljko Kadijević, to Moscow for a conversation with his Soviet counterpart Dmitry Timofeyevich Yazov in March 1991.[30]

The expectation of the Serbian leaders—President Slobodan Milošević and Serbian member of the collective presidency of the Socialist Federal Republic of Yugoslavia, Borisav Jović—that the Soviet Union might support Serbian objectives in the early 1990s profoundly shaped their position on perestroika and its author, Mikhail Gorbachev. The collapse of Soviet Union was a matter of grave concern to the Serbian political class and their allies in the Yugoslav People's Army for two reasons. First, the Serbs were well aware that the breakdown of the Soviet Union, Serbia's only potential ally, would weaken the position of Serbia in the conflict with the western federal units of Yugoslavia. Since perestroika was perceived in Serbia as a catalyst for the Soviet catastrophe in the early 1990s, Mikhail Gorbachev and perestroika both attracted discontent in Serbia. In addition, the rather conservative Serbian communist leadership and the old-fashioned Yugoslav People's Army viewed the liberalization of the Soviet system as a potential threat to the outdated political structure in Serbia and Yugoslavia. Eventually, the sympathies for Gorbachev's experiment in Yugoslavia's largest federal unit, Serbia, degenerated into an aversion, which even today shapes the public attitude in Serbia towards perestroika and its main protagonist—Mikhail Gorbachev.

In his memoirs, General Veljko Kadijević, the Yugoslav defense minister in the final phase of Yugoslav dissolution, strongly condemned Mikhail Gorbachev and his political orientation, which, according to Kadijević had led to collapse of the Soviet Union, consequently upsetting the global balance of power. According to the Yugoslav general, in its ultimate phase perestroika was controlled from abroad. In this regard Kadijević did not attempt to hide his animosity towards two people in Gorbachev's team, whom he labeled as advocates of "pro-American policy and pro-American interests"—Alexander Yakovlev and Eduard Shevardnadze.[31]

In his book, General Kadijević recalls his frequent communication with the Soviet military establishment, underlining its deep dissatisfaction with the final result of the reforms in the Soviet Union. The high-ranking officers of the Soviet army, Kadijević added, had been skeptical about the implementation of perestroika in the Soviet military system. However, Kadijević stressed in his book that in conversations with Marshal Yazov, prior to the attempted coup d'état in August 1991, the Soviet defense minister had never demonstrated disloyalty to Gorbachev.[32]

The collapse of the Soviet Union, Kadijević concluded, had sealed the fate of Yugoslavia, given that Belgrade, after the demise of the Soviet Empire, had become isolated on the international stage, which had consequently dashed any hopes for the survival of Yugoslavia.[33]

The Serbian member of the Yugoslav presidency and the penultimate president of Yugoslavia, Borisav Jović, was also strongly critical of perestroika and of Gorbachev's strategy. In autumn 1989, Jović wrote in his diary ("Poslednji dani SFRJ") about his deep disappointment in the Soviet Union with the results of perestroika. According to Jović, many Soviets perceived perestroika as "deception and treason." Besides, Jović underlined the discontent of the military establishment, the serious shortages of food in the Soviet Union, and the damaged image of Mikhail Gorbachev.[34]

Like Kadijević, Jović saw a causal connection between the demise of the Soviet Union and the breakup of Yugoslavia. In January 1990, Jović lamented the failure of perestroika, the collapse of the Soviet Union and the end of the global balance of power which, the Serbian politician added, had ensured the independence of Yugoslavia.[35] In April 1991, Jović noted in his diary that the situation in the Soviet Union was getting worse, which had consequently weakened the position of Serbia.[36]

In his memoirs, the then Serbian foreign minister, Vladislav Jovanović, compared the Soviet perestroika with "throwing in the towel" in the Cold War competition with the West. With the subsequent collapse of the Soviet Union, Jovanović underlined, Yugoslavia had lost its geopolitical importance, which had eventually encouraged both "domestic and foreign enemies" of Yugoslavia.[37]

The attitude of Croats towards perestroika and its political implications was diametrically opposed to the position of Serbian and army leaders. The memoirs of one of the most prominent Croatian leaders and the last Yugoslav president, Stipe Mesić, reveal that Croatian perceptions of the dramatic changes in the Soviet Union in the early 1990s differed substantially from those of Belgrade. The coup attempt in Moscow, in August 1991, had exposed the lack of consensus among the political elites in Zagreb and Belgrade about Gorbachev and his course. Given that in the process of secession from Yugoslavia, Croatia had counted primarily on Western support, in August 1991 Zagreb favored the pro-Western Gorbachev over his conservative opponents. The passages from Mesić's memoirs on the August putsch in Moscow shed light on the preferences of Belgrade and Zagreb in the Soviet *смутное время* (Time of Troubles):

> In Moscow, on 19 August, the whole world watched while Mikhail Gorbachev was also forced from his office due to violence. The man who started the unstoppable avalanche of anti-socialist dissent through his perestroika had lost omnipotence. His fall had been announced numerous times before, for one reason or another. I know for a fact that in general Yugoslavian circles his departure had been long wished for. ... Prior to flying from Zagreb to Belgrade, I asked the Presidency's deputy general secretary, Ivan Nahtigal,

to call a session that evening, with just one item on the agenda: "Events in the USSR and their influence on the situation in Yugoslavia." The experienced Nahtigal, born in Zagreb, was one of the few high officials I could trust. He took the role of Cassandra when he said: "That could have unfavorable consequences, Mr President, as there are many here who rejoice at the news. My advisor, who had met several of the Army's generals, warned me; they say the smart Russians have cut the spiral of dissipation in the first country of communism, while we here trip over our own feet and watch the crash powerlessly."

In addition to military circles, Milošević's team openly expressed their pleasure over Gorbachev's demise. One of Jović's adjutants in the ruling party, university professor Dušan Marković, publicly supported the coup:

> The journalists, of course, primarily wanted to hear how the Moscow coup may influence the development or halting of activities in Yugoslavia. I had been advised to speak cautiously, but I am not a diplomat of the cloak-and-dagger style, but rather one of those who always publicly states their basic thoughts. It probably has both good and bad sides as far as we are concerned, I said. One of those may have a bad reflection upon us. Conservative forces may adopt the Moscow event, trying to use it as a model for the solution to our problems.[38]

Although Mikhail Gorbachev survived the coup attempt in August 1991, it proved to be his Pyrrhic victory. In December 1991 the Soviet Union dissolved, transforming—following the Belavezha Accords—into the Commonwealth of Independent States. Being de facto deprived of power, Gorbachev had no other choice but to resign as the president of the Soviet Union. The political death of the Soviet Union and its last leader coincided with the death of the Socialist Federal Republic of Yugoslavia, given that, in December 1991, the European Community started a process of international recognition of the Yugoslav secessionist federal units.

The profound impact of perestroika on the fate of Yugoslavia is an incontestable fact. Although at the very beginning of Gorbachev's project, Belgrade observed the reforms in the Soviet Union and the "satellite" countries from a distance, perceiving them as an exclusively Soviet and Eastern Bloc (which Yugoslavia since 1948 did not belong to) phenomenon, perestroika and its ideological and geopolitical consequences strongly influenced the disintegration of Yugoslavia in the early 1990s. The domino effect of the collapse of socialism in the Soviet Union as well as in the other Eastern Bloc countries wiped out the outdated Yugoslav system, thus opening the door to the rise of nationalism in the Yugoslav federal units. Besides, the decline of the Soviet Union upset the balance of power in Europe, eliminating the geopolitical raison d'être of Yugoslavia and thus accelerating its dissolution.

Petar Dragišić (1975) received his PhD in History from the University of Vienna/Institut für Osteuropäische Geschichte. He is a senior research fellow at the Institute for Recent History of Serbia in Belgrade (Institut za noviju istoriju Srbije). In 2013 he was a visiting fellow at the Centre for Southeast European Studies of the University of Graz. His research interests include Yugoslav foreign policy in the Cold War era as well as labor migration from former Yugoslavia. He is author of two books: *Jugoslovensko-bugarski odnosi 1944–1949* (2007), and *Odnosi Jugoslavije i Austrije 1945–1955* (2013).

Notes

1. Pons, *Global Revolution*, 308.
2. Dizdarević, *A First-Hand Report*, 171.
3. *Politika*, 13 March 1985.
4. Dizdarević, *A First-Hand Report*, 171.
5. Arhiv Jugoslavije (AJ), Savez komunista Jugoslavije – Komisija za međunarodne odnose i veze (507), IX, S/a-392, Institut za međunarodnu politiku i privredu – Suština sadašnjih društveno-ekonomskih i političkih kretanja u zemljama Istočne Evrope, oktobar 1985.
6. Ibid.
7. *Komunist*, 17 May 1985; *Komunist*, 7 March 1986.
8. *Komunist*, 7 October 1988.
9. *Komunist*, 17 May 1985; *Komunist*, 7 March 1986.
10. AJ, Savez komunista Jugoslavije – Komisija za međunarodne odnose i veze (507), IX, S/a-392, Institut za međunarodnu politiku i privredu – Suština sadašnjih društveno-ekonomskih i političkih kretanja u zemljama Istočne Evrope, oktobar 1985.
11. Butorac, "Neki aspekti društvenih promjena," 136; Caratan, "Perestrojka u SSSR-u," 129.
12. AJ, Savez komunista Jugoslavije – Komisija za međunarodne odnose i veze (507), IX, S/a-392, Institut za međunarodnu politiku i privredu – Suština sadašnjih društveno-ekonomskih i političkih kretanja u zemljama Istočne Evrope, oktobar 1985.
13. Caratan, "Perestrojka u SSSR-u," 131.
14. *Politika*, 16 June 1985.
15. *Politika*, 7 December 1986; *Politika*, 15 January 1987; *Politika*, 11 April 1988.
16. Caratan, "Perestrojka u SSSR-u," 136–37.
17. *Politika*, 18 May 1986; *Politika*, 21 July 1986.
18. *Politika*, 26 May 1987.
19. *Politika*, 1 February 1987.
20. *Politika*, 26 March 1989.
21. *Politika*, 17 September 1989.
22. *Komunist*, 16 June 1989.
23. Butorac, "Neki aspekti društvenih promjena u socijalističkim zemljama," 138.
24. *Komunist*, 26 August 1988.
25. Tanjug was the Yugoslav press agency (Telegrafska agencija nove Jugoslavije).
26. *Komunist*, 16 February 1990.
27. Dizdarević, *A First-Hand Account*, 180.

28. *Trinaesti kongres Saveza komunista Jugoslavije*, Belgrade, 25–28 June 1986; *Magnetofonske beleške*, Belgrade, 1988, Vol. 1, 64.
29. "Tuđe nećemo—svoje ne damo."
30. Silber and Little, *The Death of Yugoslavia*, 126.
31. Kadijević, *Protiv udar*, 145.
32. Ibid., 29–31.
33. Ibid., 158.
34. Jović, *Poslednji dani SFRJ*, 69.
35. Ibid., 91–92.
36. Ibid., 313.
37. Jovanović, *Rat koji se mogao izbeći*, 10–12.
38. Mesić, *The Demise of Yugoslavia*, 238–41.

Bibliography

Archival Sources

Arhiv Jugoslavije

Published Sources

Butorac, Franjo. "Neki aspekti društvenih promjena u socijalističkim zemljama," *Socijalizam-Časopis Saveza komunista Jugoslavije*, Vol. 12 (1986), 133–40.
Caratan, Branko. "Perestrojka u SSSR-u i mogućnost obnove socijalizma," *Socijalizam-Časopis Saveza komunista Jugoslavije*, Vol. 12 (1987), 129–37.
Dizdarević, Raif. *A First-Hand Report: From the Death of Tito to the Death of Yugoslavia*, Sarajevo and Zagreb, 2009.
Dragišić, Petar. "Članci časopisa Foreign Affairs o jugoslovenskim ratovima 1991–1999," *Istorija 20. veka*, Vol. 1 (2015), 157–71.
_____. "Nemački i austrijski memoari o krizama i ratovima na prostoru bivše Jugoslavije devedesetih godina 20. veka," *Istorija 20. veka*, Vol. 2 (2009), 171–78.
Jovanović, Vladislav. *Rat koji se mogao izbeći: U vrtlogu jugoslovenske krize*, Belgrade, 2008.
Jović, Borisav. *Poslednji dani SFRJ*, Belgrade, 1996.
Kadijević, Veljko. *Protiv udar: Moje viđenje raspada Jugoslavije*, Belgrade, 2010.
Mesić, Stipe. *The Demise of Yugoslavia: A Political Memoir*, Budapest, 2004.
Pons, Silvio. *The Global Revolution: A History of International Communism 1917–1991*, Oxford, 2014.
Silber, Laura, and Allan Little. *The Death of Yugoslavia*, revised edition, London, 1996.
Trinaesti kongres Saveza komunista Jugoslavije, Belgrade, 25–28 June 1986; Magnetofonske beleške, Vol. 1, Belgrade, 1988.

Chapter 5

The Polish United Workers' Party and Perestroika

Wanda Jarząbek

Reform in the Soviet Union at the time of Mikhail Gorbachev attracted much interest, especially when being researched in the context of the ending Cold War. The main purpose of this chapter is to study the nature of the reception of perestroika by the Polish United Workers' Party (Polska Zjednoczona Partia Robotnicza, PZPR). The PUWP was the ruling party in communist Poland, controlling most spheres of life—government, social organizations, media, and publications—so its attitude to glasnost and perestroika can be researched by studying the reactions of former authorities and the picture presented in the press and other media—not just formal bodies of the communist party, such as the Politburo or its departments, and the party's press organs. I will not deal with impressions from the lower level of the party structures, as research on this topic only started recently.

The PUWP and the Internal Situation in Poland after the Imposition of Martial Law, 1981–1983

The ruling Polish United Workers' Party was established in 1948. Strictly speaking, communist Poland had two other parties, but their political influence was very limited prior to 1989. After then, any mid- or high-level careers in the government, the economic sphere, the universities and schools, and in administration were not possible without membership

---

Notes for this chapter begin on page 129.

of the PUWP. It was a mass party—but what should be stressed is that it never gained a vast social support. The system of nomenclature was deeply entrenched in Poland, and this group of beneficiaries of the system became its strong supporters and defenders.[1] In the mid-1980s, as Mikhail Gorbachev became the general secretary of the Soviet Communist Party (CPSU) and started his reforms, the Polish Communist Party was in dire crisis. In 1980, the PUWP counted slightly more than 3 million members and member candidates (out of a Polish population of around 38 million). The first considerable decrease in membership numbers took place in the period after the founding of Solidarność (Solidarity), between fall and winter 1980/81. In June 1981 there were 2.8 million members. After the suspension of martial law this figure dropped to around 2.1 million. What is also interesting is that 52 percent of the party members came from a social group that was referred to during communist rule as the "working intelligentsia"—state functionaries, officials, and administration. The workers constituted about 38 percent of the PUWP's membership, and among them were members of the trade unions, controlled by the authorities.[2] So it was only a "workers' party" in name, as it neither represented workers' interests (this role having been taken over by Solidarność) nor had it been built by the workers. It is worth mentioning that the newly created Solidarność was able to mobilize millions in a relatively short period; until the introduction of martial law on 13 December 1981 there were 10 million of registered members. Among these were also members of the PUWP. The emergence of Solidarność resulted also in attempts to change the role of the communist party. In the PUWP, groupings arose demanding extensive reforms and more transparent contact with the masses, as well as democratization of political and social structures, known as "horizontal structures." In the mid-1980s, the PUWP still constituted the core of the political system. Nevertheless, the center of power shifted to other institutions, such as the army, and a kind of special service controlled by the Ministry of Interior, to which also partly clandestine structures—as the secret police (SB—*Służba Bezpieczeństwa*, Security Service) and the intelligence service—belonged.

The party's first secretary, Wojciech Jaruzelski, was successful in removing his strongest opponents from the political life—among them, the former minister and deputy minister of inner security.[3] The need for rearrangement of the communist system and for economic reforms, undermined by strikes and rejected by the wide majority of society, was a predominant political factor at that time. This is why a restructuring of the communist system started earlier in Poland, mainly due to the domestic situation, and to social and economic demands. It should also be admitted that the nature of the changes in Poland differed from those in the Soviet Union. First of all, the government was aware of the lack of legitimization and was interested in broadening the "social basis" of the authorities. After 1982, many consultative organs to the government and parliament were established—often with the participation of established journalists and professors—such as the Social Economic Council to Parliament (*Rada Społeczno Gospodarcza przy Sejmie*), and the Consultative Economic Council of the Prime Minister (*Konsultacyjna Rada Gospodarcza przy Prezesie Rady Ministrów*). The old National Unity Front (*Front Jedności Narodu*), which had existed since 1957, was replaced in 1985 by the Patriotic Movement of National Revival (*Patriotyczny Ruch Odrodzenia Narodowego*). In December 1985, a Consultative Council to W. Jaruzelski as the head Council of State (*Rada Państwa*, a kind of collective head of state) was created.[4] Several changes were introduced to the Polish constitution, such as establishing the Tribunal of State (which was to become the tribunal for the high-ranking state officials) and the Constitutional Tribunal. These institutions, however, were not really in power: they were meant to show the "democratization" of the communist system, above all to foreign observers.

A turning point in Communist Poland's domestic policy has to be considered the amnesty for political prisoners announced in September 1986. It demonstrated the government's will to start afresh and meet criteria demanded by some Western governments as a prerequisite for bilateral talks. The need to reform the economy, to provide society with everyday products was predominant.[5] The economy was especially important as a means to legitimize the government. Its authority was at a very low level, especially among the younger generations.[6] After the termination of the state of martial law in Poland on 22 July 1983, many attempts were made by the communist party to attract people with non-communist views, among them intellectuals, some of whom were affiliated with the Catholic Church. The party leadership also attempted to broaden its base by attracting young people. The communist youth (and students') organizations lured their members with offers from which many were excluded—for example, almost free-of-charge holidays, and opportunities to earn extra money, to participate in student exchanges with Western countries and to learn languages. Several foundations (e.g., the Friedrich Ebert Foundation) agreed that it would be up to the Polish authorities to choose who should receive a scholarship. The young people who were given good opportunities to kick start their careers in exchange for loyalty to the PUWP were known in Polish society as "Jaruzelski's janissaries." Many of them continued their political careers successfully after 1989 and the transition in Poland. Due to the fact that the process of modifications of the system started shortly after abolishing martial law, there is also a dominant tendency in the Polish historiography to show the events in Poland as having their own genesis.

The PUWP and Changes in the Soviet Union

The Polish diplomatic and party documents only provide readers with scarce direct information on Mikhail Gorbachev and his reforms in the Soviet Union. It seems like the authorities reacted in a way that can be recognized as typical for periods of change of power in the Soviet Union. They restrained from making clear declarations, and adopted a "wait-and-see" approach. They knew that initially Gorbachev's standing within the Soviet apparatus was rather weak.[7] This period of reservation of the PUWP leaders and state authorities lasted more or less up to 1987. When Gorbachev strengthened his position and it became clear that changes in the Soviet Union would continue, his policy of reforms in general gained support as the PUWP tried to adapt to the new situation. The initial reluctance to openly back Gorbachev's plans can also be explained by the fact that he had not made a clear statement about his long-term policy at the beginning, but rather had announced new aspects of it in subsequent speeches. So, as his aims had not been pronounced, they were unknown. In the time under consideration, the 27th Congress of the CPSU (February 1986) was not able to clear the doubts—or at least the documents and the press do not provide us with evidence regarding this. Interestingly, after Gorbachev had gained stronger support at home, the 27th Congress started to be perceived as having been a turning point, paving the way for further reforms. Shortly afterwards, Soviet politicians began speaking more about the democratization of relations between those states belonging to the socialist commonwealth, as Shevardnadze put it in Warsaw during a meeting of the Committee of Foreign Ministers.[8] At the same time, the Soviets attempted to develop inner consultations within the Warsaw Pact structures. Gorbachev's first visit to Poland to the congress of the Polish party in June 1986 was an occasion for closer talks, and it was the first time that General Jaruzelski expressed his backing for Gorbachev's policy in public. The outline of what perestroika should be was given by Gorbachev during the meeting of the Council of Foreign Ministers of the Warsaw Pact in March 1987. He talked extensively about the ideas of "revolutionary changes" in the USSR. According to him, the main principles of perestroika were: acceleration, glasnost, self-criticism and control.[9] He tried to convince the ministers of the other Warsaw Pact countries that in the Soviet Politburo there was a common understanding on this issue, and that insinuations of colliding "fractions" within the

CPSU, which were widespread in the West, were not true. Gorbachev's attempt to convince the other countries of the Eastern Bloc that changes in the Soviet Union were in a sense permanent is valid indirect evidence that the leaders of communist parties treated the changes in Moscow very consciously. Moscow attempted to pour oil on troubled water. As the main opponents to the reforms, Gorbachev singled out "a group of princes, who years before had lost contact with real life and now used to wallow in luxury."[10] He appealed to the "fraternal parties" to keep calm as all Soviet activities were based on "Lenin's teachings." Gorbachev's public announcements enunciating his will to reconstruct relations within the Eastern Bloc were accompanied by a clear hint that Moscow was distancing herself from the economic aid for the bloc countries, which could be understood not only as an indication to conduct internal reforms and rationalize economic policy, but also to try to develop contacts with the non-communist countries in order to gain support from them. At the same time, Moscow suggested a closer economic integration, which was in a sense contradictory to the first declaration.[11] In this situation, leaders of the PUWP tried to define the reasons and goals of the Soviet policy and figure out its impact on Poland. They also attempted to approach the Soviet leaders to learn about the Kremlin's new policy directly from them. They tried to get information about expectations toward the satellite states, and especially Poland. They expected answers to crucial points, such as whether Jaruzelski's group would be supported by Moscow, and what Soviet reforms could eventually mean for the Polish domestic situation, as well as for relations between the party and opposition. As the Soviets spoke about the democratization of relations within the bloc, there arose a very important question: how much room for maneuver would Poland have, both in the domestic dimension and at the international level? And the signals coming from Moscow were not at all univocal.[12] During a talk with the Polish foreign minister, Marian Orzechowski, in February 1988, Gorbachev declared for instance that "in the West many forces were trying to discredit Gorbachev's reforms," and in this context he underlined the "historical role" of Jaruzelski.[13] It might have been understood by the party leadership as an encouragement for the PUWP to engage more closely in domestic changes.[14] The Soviet comments on Jaruzelski could also have been an indication for the Polish comrades that Moscow was interested in keeping him in power as a person who deserved Soviet appreciation for his earlier activities, or because they trusted him and found him useful. And taking into account the authorities' policy in the spring of 1988 — characterized by a hard attitude toward opposition — it is reasonable to assume that, for the communist side, this message from Moscow was not a boost for launching new reforms.

We should also highlight the inconsistency in Soviet declarations. On the one hand, Moscow declared that every country should deal with its economic problems on its own as much as possible and, at that time, it was obvious for everyone that substantial economic assistance was to be obtained only from the West. On the other hand, when such attempts were made by the PUWP, Eduard Shevardnadze suggested that the Polish endeavors to find financial and economic assistance abroad should be consulted within the Warsaw Pact.[15] He also mentioned that the Soviets commended the Polish support for the Soviet conception of perestroika, but according to him it would not be useful for Poland to copy it. We do not know how this remark was perceived by the Polish delegation. They raised doubts though about perestroika and the meaning of Soviet declarations concerning the need to establish more democratic relations between communist countries. Yet, it was not clear what kind of domestic changes would be acceptable for the Kremlin. A tendency to strengthen relations between the Soviets and Poland continued. During the economic talks led by Prime Minister Zbigniew Messner in Moscow in April 1988, CPSU officials spoke much more about a need to give a new impulse to bilateral Polish–Soviet economic contacts, rather than contacts with the West. Gorbachev concentrated on changes in the Soviet Union, and informed the Polish side about the growing support for perestroika in Soviet society.[16] To the Polish delegation it sounded in a sense an encouragement for collaboration with the transforming Soviet Union, which should be recognized because the reforms would make it a more attractive economic partner. The economic relations with the Soviets were to be constructed in a new way, not at the governmental level but led to a greater extent by companies themselves. However, taking into account the technological deficiencies of the Polish economy, the Soviet Union did not constitute the favorite partner, even if the authorities had verbally declared such an interest.

For the Polish side, other aspects of perestroika, like glasnost, were also attention-grabbing. Especially as glasnost was not to be reduced to merely inter-party relations, but also involved the so-called "white stains" in bilateral history and other aspects of bilateral relations. The Polish side attempted to start talks with Moscow on the fate of Poles in the Soviet Union during World War II. Firstly, on 17 September 1939, according to the Hitler–Stalin Pact, the Soviet Union attacked Poland and occupied a significant part of its territory. The Polish inhabitants were suppressed, many were imprisoned or sent to lagers, and others deported to Siberia; and secondly, on the Katyń massacre—a massacre of about 24,000 Polish prisoners of war in 1940, mostly officers of the Polish army who in their civil life had often been intellectuals belonging to the state elite. The Soviets claimed this execution had been organized by the German army in 1941.[17] The Polish authorities expected that it would be possible to find a satisfactory solution for the status of the Polish minority in the Soviet Union, and to receive Soviet permission to open Polish consulates in regions inhabited by Poles, to provide them with broader access to language and culture programs. There were signs of an opening in speaking about the past, such as much more discussion in the press on the history of the communist movement and on prosecution of the members of the Communist Party of Poland (KPP, *Komunistyczna Partia Polski*) in the Soviet Union after 1937. However, for many Poles these topics were of no great interest, and they could not be treated as equivalent to those mentioned above. Finally, the Soviets agreed to build a bilateral commission on historical matters—but its work was sluggish.

The press can also be taken into consideration as a valuable source reflecting the Polish communists' attitude to perestroika. It is easy to notice that there were no domestic reforms implemented in the Soviet Union; but there was a change in Soviet foreign policy, especially on the question of disarmament, and it was this that attracted the most interest initially.[18] Taking into account the top topics in the press, which also reflected inner party debates, it was no coincidence that the Polish communists started to work on a new peace initiative, named after the first secretary, "Jaruzelski's Plan." It was announced on 9 May (in the Communist bloc, the Victory Day) 1987, and after consultations with Moscow it was officially presented during a CSCE follow-up conference in Vienna on 17 July.[19] That same year, the communist press tried to clarify the essence of the changes in the Soviet Union. Much attention was devoted to "acceleration," which was presented as the next stage in building socialism.[20] This way of writing about perestroika corresponded with the Soviet press. An article in Alexandr Yakovlev's "Communist" explaining the objectives of Soviet reforms was reprinted in the main ideological journal of the PUWP, *Nowe Drogi*. One of Gorbachev's closest staff members clarified the essence of perestroika: according to him it was not limited to the economy; "acceleration" should rather be understood as "looking for appropriate ways and means to answer the challenges of domestic and international character."[21] In further articles, Gorbachev's domestic reforms were compared to the NEP (New Economic Policy of Lenin from the 1920s), a policy that was supposed to overcome economic hurdles and allow a deeper inner discussion in the communist party.[22] Perestroika was thus treated as a new stage of building socialism or as a new revolution.[23] Even an overview of Gorbachev's book was published under the title "Why we are talking about a new revolution." Therein it was emphasized that according to Gorbachev the economic and social problems of the Soviet Union were a consequence of slowing the revolution down.²⁴ Starting from the beginning of 1988, more commentaries dealt with the Polish situation against the background of perestroika, in attempt to compare changes in Poland to those in the Soviet Union.²⁵ Due to the heated discussions on relegalization by Solidarność, the question of "pluralism" in political life, as one element of reforms, started to be more frequently discussed.²⁶ Indeed, theoretical assessments of Gorbachev's politics in the Soviet Union occurred predominantly in journals that were addressed to the intelligentsia and not related in a direct way to the party (however, every magazine was under the control of censorship that time), for instance in *Prawo i Życie* (Law and Life).²⁷ Apparently, the most pro-Gorbachev articles were published in 1988 in *Polityka*, a journal considered to be connected to the liberal wing of the communist party.²⁸ A more nuanced analysis could be found in the *émigré* press as well as in underground publications, where critical reports of perestroika also appeared. Gorbachev's book on perestroika and the new thinking from 1986 was published in Poland in 1988, shortly before his visit.²⁹

Gorbachev's Visit to Poland in 1988 and Its Aftermath

In July 1988, Gorbachev and his wife paid a visit to Poland. They travelled around the country and at the end of the stay he took part in a meeting of the Political Consultative Committee, PCC, of the Warsaw Pact. What is striking, and reflected the transformations in Soviet policy, was his willingness to organize gatherings with people other than communist party activists. It was a *signum temporis* and also probably Soviet diplomatic maneuvering. Some prominent Polish individuals refused to meet with Gorbachev, using different excuses, among the most influential being the Primate of Poland, Cardinal Józef Glemp (in the Polish tradition, in the time of foreign rule—and for many people the communist government was an alien rule—a primate served as a kind of inter rex), and the very popular cardinal of Kraków, Józef Macharski. Both were probably aware that it could serve Soviet political aims—as a demonstration of an opening, and it could also be misused as propaganda—the Catholic Church was at that time one of the major opposition powers in Poland, and was treated as a moral authority. The state authorities were nevertheless successful in organizing a meeting with Polish intellectuals, not only those close to the communist party. At a gathering that took place in the Warsaw castle, Professor Michał Krąpiec, Catholic priest and former president of the Catholic University in Lublin, while discussing the topic of sovereignty of states, nations and the problem of human rights, asked about the validity of the Brezhnev doctrine. This same question—if the principles of Brezhnev's doctrine were still valid—was the next one posed by Marcin Król, a person connected with the anti-systemic opposition. Gorbachev refused to answer. This was noticed by many people, as the meeting with intellectuals was transmitted on Polish television. An article reporting on that event was printed the next day in *Trybuna Ludu* (the main party journal). As noted by the author of the press report, there was little time for a convincing explanation, so he had simply commented that "maybe he [Gorbachev] didn't want to discuss this question ad hoc, in a short replica."[30] That was, however, understood by the Poles as a clear answer: the Brezhnev doctrine had not been abolished.

During the meeting of the PCC of the Warsaw Pact, Jaruzelski indicated "perestroika's inspiring role" in the process of renewal in Poland, and mentioned the concurrence of reforms in Poland and the USSR.[31] Jaruzelski supported also the idea of building the Common European House, which according to him was especially important when taking into account the process of European integration, which for him implied cutting out Eastern Europe. However, speaking about the inspiring role of perestroika was not the dominating subject—neither for journalists nor historians. Analyzing the documents from the Politburo and the Ministry of Foreign Affairs, it is evident that the rulers' attitude was much more nuanced. It was indeed usually mentioned that it was the 27th Congress of the CPSU that shaped the general line of changes in the Eastern Bloc, but those amendments differed from state to state and were tailored to the individual needs of each "satellite"—they did not inevitably stem from perestroika. Because of this, any state could consider itself as being "a teacher" to the others—even to the Soviet Union, which, as was apparent, had abandoned this role.[32] The unfolding developments were thus described as both revolutionary and pragmatic. Pragmatism was regarded as the reason why real socialist countries were putting aside some of the "socialist principles." It was a way to withdraw from the centrally planned economy and to introduce elements of market capitalism. These reforms were, however, presented as being convenient for the current stage of communism, and not as tools to do away with Marxist–Leninist tenets, which were limiting the economy. The democratization of political life was seen as arising for similar reasons—namely, the need to meet the demands of the time. Documents show that it first of all meant changes in decision making, and a retreat from the dominant party centralism. Approval for creating new political parties was still not under discussion—although for a large part of the Polish public, it was "the" topic. The end of sanctions against Solidarność became at that time the main postulate for political opposition. The authors of the background report were of the opinion that Gorbachev's policy created more comfortable conditions for "a search for an optimal model of economic and social-political reforms matching the Polish national specificity and for solving occurring problems in a sovereign way."[33] Because of that, it was concluded, the success of perestroika was in Polish interests. However, Polish reforms were not shown as being parallel to the Soviet ones. It was also marked by the wording of official documents, and the press as well used it to describe processes in Poland and the Soviet Union. Changes in Poland were called "socialist renewal" (*socjalistyczna odnowa*), while for those in the Soviet Union the Russian term "perestroika" started to be used more frequently from 1988. Prior to that, Soviet reforms had been called *przebudowa* (reconstruction), which is the Polish translation of perestroika.

The Polish Communist Party, and especially its leaders, have frequently been perceived as having been supporters of Soviet policies, both by eyewitnesses and historians—this seems to hold true, yet according to the accessible primary sources it is not possible to state that there existed a close collaboration as far as reforms are concerned between Warsaw and Moscow. Likewise, it is difficult to provide a clear-cut assessment of the attitude of either the communist leaders or of the party rank and file towards reforms in the Soviet Union. There exist no sociological examinations or memoirs. Research on public opinion was carried out in the 1980s, but no specific inquiry on the communist party occurred. In January 1988, 46.5 percent of respondents answered, for example, that Gorbachev's politics would have positive results. Only 8.2 percent declared to know nothing about that subject.[34] For sure, a certain sympathy for Soviet reforms was also visible in public culture; it was, for instance, a reason for the popularity of Andrzej Rosiewicz's song *Wieje wiosna ze wschodu* (Spring is coming with the wind from the East).[35] Perestroika was perceived by many in Poland as a chance to do better, and some people were even of the opinion that, as far as changes were concerned, the Soviet Union was at that time (1988) way ahead of Poland. What Prime Minister Mieczysław Rakowski declared during his visit to the Soviet Union in October 1988 was therefore presumably true: according to him, Gorbachev's visit to Poland mitigated anti-Soviet feelings in Poland.[36]

Conclusions

It is not easy to describe the PUWP attitude to perestroika, mostly due to the limited number of primary sources that refer to it in a direct way. It is indeed possible to analyze the existing sources to try to learn from the language used in them how the theme covered here was perceived. The term "perestroika" was mostly used in the 1980s to describe changes in the Soviet Union, and generally not applied to Poland. However, after the political transition, it also started to be utilized to define the ongoing reforms in Poland in the late 1980s. Foreign Minister Orzechowski considered Poland to be a "laboratory of perestroika," and some historians wrote about a perestroika "in Polish fashion." Initially, the leaders of the PUWP and the state authorities mostly limited themselves to observing the events in the Soviet Union. Uncertainty predominated, and this probably discouraged them from taking actions. It was on the turn of the year 1987/88 that perestroika began to attract more interest from the center of power (Politburo, government); more attention was also devoted to it by the official media. Apparently, Polish expectations of perestroika concentrated on pragmatic aspects. The government was eager to see how it would impact the country's room for maneuver in the economy, in domestic politics and international activity, as well as whether it would influence the functioning of the communist party and its relations with other countries within the Soviet bloc and with Moscow itself. Less attention was paid to the ideological aspects, albeit that articles about the problems of reforming Marxism–Leninism can be found in the party's ideological publications. It is also not possible to affirm definitely that perestroika and glasnost inspired the PUWP to carry out reforms in Poland. The domestic reforms resulted from the inner needs of the PPR after martial law was suspended, and also from the authorities' perception of Western expectations toward Warsaw. Especially important were those treated by the West as conditions sine qua non to provide Poland with economic aid—among others, the legalization of Solidarność. It is though possible to state that, especially starting from 1988, perestroika impacted the speed of transformations in Poland. Moscow did not obstruct reforms; it did, however, try to keep them under control. In sum, even if glasnost and perestroika cannot be considered to have been decisive for the internal developments in Poland in the second half of the 1980s, they still had a considerable influence on the process of transformation in Poland, and they contributed to the end of the communist system.

Wanda Jarząbek, Dr hab. Professor at the Institute for Political Studies of the Polish Academy of Sciences in Warsaw. She specializes in international relations during the Cold War period, with a special focus on the German question, the CSCE process, and Polish history in the twentieth century.

Notes

1. Dąbek, *PZPR retrospektywny portret własny*; Szumiło, "Elita władzy w Polsce 1944–1989."
2. Leszek Gilejko, "Członkowie PZPR-próba typologii," 134.
3. Paczkowski, "Dowódca czy przywódca?"
4. On this subject, see: Paczkowski, *The Spring Will Be Ours*; on the end of communist rule, see: Dudek, *Reglamentowana rewolucja*.
5. Morawski, "Pełzająca katastrofa," 27–43.
6. Biernacki, "Nie można zdezerterować." See public opinion polls in Badora et al., *Społeczeństwo i władza lat osiemdziesiątych*, 267–68. One should, however, remember that people were often afraid of sharing their true points of view under communist rule.
7. On this, see among others: Brown, *The Gorbachev Factor*; Zubok, *A Failed Empire*.
8. Archiwum Ministerstwa Spraw Zagranicznych (AMSZ, Archive of the Ministry of Foreign Affairs), Departament ds. Stosunków z ZSRR (Department for the Relations with the USSR), z.33/89, w. (volume) 1 (no. pagination), Information note, 23 March 1986.
9. AMSZ, Departament ds. Stosunków z ZSRR, z. 18/91, w. 1, Information note, 30 March 1987.
10. Ibid.
11. AMSZ, Departament ds. Stosunków z ZSRR, z. 18/91, w. 1, Information note, 1 June 1987.
12. Jarząbek, "Na szachownicy wielkich mocarstw," 19.
13. Ibid.
14. AMSZ, Dep. I, z.39/97, w 1. Information note, 21 February 1988.
15. Ibid.
16. "Zapis podstawowych treści rozmowy M. Gorbaczowa ze Z. Messnerem, 6.04.1988", in Dudek, *Zmierzch dyktatury*, 183–89.
17. "Zapis podstawowych treści rozmowy M. Gorbaczowa z W. Jaruzelskim, 14.07.1988," in Dudek, *Zmierzch dyktatury*, 263–68.
18. For example: Wojciech Multan, "Nowe radzieckie inicjatywy rozbrojeniowe," *Nowe Drogi*, no. 1, 452/1987, 10–16. The *Nowe Drogi* (New Ways) journal claimed to be "a theoretical and political organ of the Central Committee of the PUWP."
19. Information note, 23 June 1987, in Jarząbek, *Kłopotliwy*.
20. Ernest Kucza, "Koncepcje i strategie przyspieszenia treścią zjazdów bratnich partii," *Nowe Drogi*, no. 2, 453/1987, 97–107.
21. Aleksander Jakowlew, "Przebudowa a nauki społeczne: O problemach teoretycznych," *Nowe Drogi*, no. 10, 461/1987, 32–38.
22. Mieczysław Krajewski, "Od Lenina do Gorbaczowa," *Nowe Drogi*, no. 11, 1/1987, 75–81.
23. Jerzy Wiatr, "Przebudowa jako rewolucja," *Polityka*, no. 10, 5 March 1988, 6; idem, "Rewolucja wielkich nadziei," *Polityka*, no. 24, 20 August 1988, 1–3.
24. "Gorbachev, Dlaczego mówimy o nowej rewolucji?", *Polityka*, no. 46, 7 November 1987, 12.
25. "Przebudowa i odnowa socjalizmu oraz mechanizm hamowania przemian," *Nowe Drogi*, no. 3, 466/1987.
26. "Pluralizm socjalistyczny: Dyskusja redakcyjna," *Nowe Drogi*, no. 6, 470/1987, 7-14.
27. "Pluralizm rodzi konflikty," *Prawo i Życie*, no. 2, 7 January 1987, 7; Jan Chłopecki, "Polska Przebudowa," *Prawo i Życie*, no. 29, 18 July 1987, 3–4; Roman Kruszewski, "Gorbaczow, trzymaj się!", *Prawo i Życie*, no. 25, 18 June 1988, 12.

28. Jerzy Kleer, "Początek przełomu," *Polityka*, no. 4, 7 March 1987; J. Malczyk, "Jaki jest Gorbaczow," *Polityka*, no. 12, 21 March 1987, 12.
29. Michaił Gorbaczow, *Przebudowa i nowe myślenia dla nas i całego świata.*
30. Janusz Tycner, "Doktryna Breżniewa," *Prawo i Życie*, no. 33, 13 August 1988.
31. AMSZ, Dep. I, z.35/93, w. 3, Information note, 21 July 1988.
32. AMSZ, Dep. I, z.35/93, w. 3, Stosunki między europejskimi państwami socjalistycznymi na tle przebudowy- implikacje dla Polski (Relations with the socialist countries in the context of reconstruction [perestrojka]) , 6 December 1988.
33. Ibid.
34. Badora et al., *Społeczeństwo i władza lat osiemdziesiątych*, 87.
35. This song was presented to Gorbachev and his wife during their trip to Poland in 1988. It had a refrain in Russian addressing Gorbachev directly, with the words: "Mikhail, this is a song for you, a song to give you power for introducing your reforms."
36. "Zapis rozmowy sekretarza generalnego KC KPZR Michaiła Gorbaczowa z premierem Mieczysławem Rakowskim," *Zmierzch dyktatury*, 21 October 1988, 328–43.

Bibliography

Archival Sources

Archives of the Polish Ministry of Foreign Affairs
Archives of the Central Committee of the Polish United Workers' Party in Archives of the Modern Records

Published Documents

Dudek, Antoni (ed.). *Zmierzch dyktatury: Polska lat 1986–1989 w świetle dokumentów*, Vol. 1, Warsaw, 2009.
Jarząbek, Wanda (ed.). *Kłopotliwy sojusznik? PRL w politycznych strukturach Układu Warszawskiego 1980–1991*, Warsaw, forthcoming.

Journals:
Nowe Drogi (New Ways)
Polityka (Policy)
Prawo i Życie (Law and Life)
Trybuna Ludu (Tribune of the People)

Secondary Sources

Badora, Barbara, et al. (eds). *Społeczeństwo i władza lat osiemdziesiątych w badaniach CBOS*, Warsaw, 1994.
Biernacki, Leszek. "'Nie można zdezerterować': młodzieżowy bunt w 1988 roku," in *W przededniu wielkiej zmiany: Polska 1988 roku*, Gdańsk, 2009, 79–97.
Brown, Archie. *The Gorbachev Factor*, Oxford, 1996.
Dąbek, Krzysztof. *PZPR retrospektywny portret własny*, Warsaw, 2006.
Dudek, Antoni. *Reglamentowana rewolucja: Rozkład dyktatury komunistycznej w Polsce 1988–1990*, Cracow, 2004.

Gilejko, Leszek. "Członkowie PZPR-próba typologii," in *PZPR jako machina władzy*, ed. Dariusz Stola and Krzysztof Persak, Warsaw, 2012.
Gorbachev, Mikhail. *Przebudowa i nowe myślenie dla nas i całego świata*, Warsaw, 1988.
Jarząbek, Wanda. "Na szachownicy wielkich mocarstw: Polska w kontekście międzynarodowym roku 1988," in *W przededniu wielkiej zmiany: Polska 1988 roku*, Gdansk, 2009.
Morawski, Wojciech. "Pełzająca katastrofa: Gospodarka polska w latach osiemdziesiątych," in *W przededniu wielkiej zmiany: Polska 1988 roku*, Gdansk, 2009, 27–43.
Paczkowski, Andrzej. "Dowódca czy przywódca? Wojciech Jaruzelski w latach 1981–1989," in *PZPR jako machina władzy*, ed. Dariusz Stola and Krzysztof Persak, Warsaw, 2012, 259–89.
_____. *The Spring Will Be Ours: Poland and the Poles from Occupation to Freedom*, University Park, PA, 2003.
Szumiło, Mirosław. "Elita władzy w Polsce 1944–1989: Studium socjologiczne," in *Władza w PRL. Ludzie i mechanizmy*, ed. Konrad Rokicki and Robert Spałek, Warsaw, 2011, 155–74.
Zubok, Vladislav. *A Failed Empire: The Soviet Union in the Cold War from Stalin to Gorbachev*, Chapel Hill, NC, 2007.

Chapter 6

SED and Perestroika
Perceptions and Reactions

Hermann Wentker

"If we stay behind, life will punish us immediately."[1] With these words Gorbachev tried one last time to persuade the Socialist Unity Party of Germany (SED) Politburo to follow his course of reforming the socialist system. It was 7 October 1989, the fortieth anniversary of the foundation of the GDR. As before, Erich Honecker and the SED leadership opposed all reforms. Although Honecker's successor Egon Krenz tried to convey the impression that he would change course, this was of no avail: the GDR vanished by means of peaceful revolution and Germany's reunification. However, the relationship between Honecker and Gorbachev, and the East German perception of change in the Soviet Union under Gorbachev, had not always been as negative as in 1989. So first it has to be asked where the rupture occurred and why the SED leadership remained so staunchly opposed to any reforms whatsoever. Although Honecker as general secretary was clearly the undisputed leader of the SED, the question will be asked of whether there were any leading members of the party who diverged from his course. The second main concern will be the membership, and special groups within the party and party officials: did they all follow the leadership's course regarding perestroika or did they think and react differently? And how did the party leadership deal with any problems resulting out of these divergences?

Three preliminary remarks are necessary for a better understanding of the SED's perception of Gorbachev and his so-called reform program.

Notes for this chapter begin on page 146.

First, "perestroika" (restructuring) was not a well thought out strategy, which just had to be put into practice. On the contrary, perestroika was more a vague idea and a useful catchword, whose meaning changed immensely in the course of the six years Gorbachev was in power. According to Stephen Hanson, "Gorbachev really did believe what he was saying when he spoke so passionately about the need for a 'radical reform' of Soviet socialism, about perestroika as a 'direct sequel to the great accomplishments started by the Leninist Party in the October days of 1917'. But he had no idea what he was doing."[2] It is no wonder that much of what he said and did was open to interpretation. Second, perestroika could not be separated from its founder. Therefore, the personal relationship between Honecker and Gorbachev mattered just as much as the contrast between East German *Realsozialismus* and Soviet *Reformsozialismus*. However, we have to bear in mind that their scope of action was limited. Gorbachev had neither the power nor the will to enforce reforms in the GDR. The Soviet Union was a world power, but it had suffered from "imperial overstretch" since the beginning of the 1980s, so that Moscow had already secretly buried the Brezhnev doctrine in connection with the Polish crisis of 1980/81.[3] On the other hand, Gorbachev did not want to exert Soviet (military) power to further his aims in the Eastern bloc, but hoped that the other parties would follow the Soviet example out of conviction. Honecker's position was even more difficult: he knew that the GDR was doomed if the Soviet Union withdrew its support—which meant, in the last instance, military intervention—but at the same time he was also convinced that to follow Gorbachev and to introduce serious political reforms would accelerate the downfall of the East German state because it lacked a national identity. This leads us on to the third point, the special geopolitical position of the GDR as part of divided Germany, with the democratic and wealthy Federal Republic on its western border. This implied on the one hand a permanent delegitimization of the GDR and its leading party. On the other hand, the GDR did business with West Germany and was very keen to maintain this profitable relationship. However, since the stationing of Pershing and cruise missiles in 1983, the Soviet Union had perceived Bonn as Washington's minion with whom contacts ought to be reduced. This conflict had a strong negative effect on East German–Soviet relations, and it persisted over the caesura of 1985.[4] So relations between the SED and the CPSU, as the leading parties of their respective states, were encumbered right from the beginning of the Gorbachev era.

As the SED's perceptions and reactions with regard to perestroika, as well as the meaning of perestroika itself, changed over the years that Gorbachev was in power, a chronological structure is necessary. The development of these perceptions and reactions can be divided into the following five distinct phases.

I. The Beginning of the Gorbachev Era (March–January 1986)

Honecker had known Gorbachev since the 1960s.[5] The most memorable incident in their relationship was the meeting of the leaderships of both parties on 17 August 1984 in Moscow. Soviet–East German relations were strained because of two loans to the GDR of 1 billion DM each, arranged by Franz Josef Strauß, with Moscow accusing East Berlin of secret wheeling and dealing with Bonn. On the initiative of Honecker, who wanted to visit Bonn in the same year, the meeting was arranged, in the course of which general secretary Konstantin Chernenko forbade him to meet the West German chancellor, Helmut Kohl. Gorbachev, who had been present at the meeting, had tried to de-escalate, but he had all the same supported his general secretary. In the end Honecker gave in to Soviet pressure, and refrained from his visit.[6]

Although Honecker surely remembered his defeat and did not expect the election of Gorbachev by the CPSU Central Committee, he and the SED leadership welcomed Gorbachev's succession to Chernenko on 11 March 1985. The direction Soviet politics would take was not yet clear. But this uncertainty was overruled by the good news that a relatively young, 54-year-old general secretary was taking over, who had the potential to end the stagnation of the years before.[7] The new Soviet leader seemed intent on reforming the Soviet economy—*uskorenye* (acceleration) was the catchword. This did not imply changes, but just a more efficient way of running the economy. His course was welcomed by leading economy officials in the GDR as well as by the SED leadership. Both saw parallels to the economic course the GDR had been pursuing since the 8th SED Party Congress of 1981.[8] For once, Moscow seemed to be following the GDR. In their meetings in 1985, Honecker reacted positively to Gorbachev's ideas of accelerating socio-economic development in the Soviet Union, and at the same time tried to convince him of the good economic, technological and socio-political performance of the GDR. But Gorbachev did not want to hear anything about the GDR being a model for the other socialist states, and stated clearly: "There is only one model, Marxist–Leninist socialism." Gorbachev laid emphasis on the common basis of the socialist bloc, and Honecker could not but agree with this.[9]

The SED was also in line with Gorbachev's new course in security policy. The party leadership had pursued a peace policy since the end of the 1970s in order to maintain the advantages of détente for the GDR in the inner-German context, and had thereby risked a deterioration of relations with Moscow, who had expected the GDR to follow its line. Since his coming to power, Gorbachev made several spectacular disarmament proposals which culminated in his initiative of 15 January 1986 to abolish nuclear weapons in three phases until the year 2000. Not only Honecker, but also the majority of the East German population welcomed this proposal.[10] Regarding foreign and security policy, the consensus between the SED and the Soviet Union was restored.

II. Beginning Estrangement behind Closed Doors (February–December 1986)

In 1986, not perestroika but the beginning effects of glasnost led to a first estrangement between Honecker and Gorbachev. Although the term *perestroika* had emanated from the 27th CPSU Congress (25 February – 6 March 1986), it did not yet have a great impact. Gorbachev still seemed to concentrate on *uskorenye*.[11] And economically, the SED leaders who were present at the congress felt that they were in the lead and that the CPSU was now following their example. However, Honecker and his entourage found the practice of *glasnost*—openness, transparency—more than irritating. For them, two dimensions of glasnost as practiced at the congress were highly relevant: on the one hand, the criticism of the sloppiness and inefficiency of the Soviet economy in the Breshnev era by Gorbachev and others; and on the other hand, discussions that were much freer than at other party congresses they had experienced so far.[12] Most memorable was Boris Yeltsin's attack on the privileges that party officials enjoyed. In the eyes of the SED leadership this went too far, because they knew that they would be expected to follow Gorbachev's example, which was out of the question.

Gorbachev realized how reserved Honecker was towards Soviet reforms, and he told this to his East German colleague on 20 April 1986, when visiting the 11th Party Congress of the SED (17–21 April). Honecker replied that he had "no reservations against the 27th Party Congress. But there are certain people here [i.e., in the GDR] who have reservations with regard to certain questions."[13] Honecker could only feebly camouflage his misgivings about the course Gorbachev was taking. In his firm opinion, the GDR was following the right course with the SED's socio-political and economic program, so he saw no necessity to copy Gorbachev in his criticism of the existing economic or political conditions, or in his policy of *uskorenye*. But even Gorbachev did not interpret these discords as major differences. In the course of their conversation he said that only the Soviet Union, the GDR, and possibly Czechoslovakia stood "on the firm positions of classic socialism." Honecker consented to this as well as to Gorbachev's statement that there was only one model, the Marxist–Leninist one.[14] Before the background of these reassuring words, Honecker hoped to keep the beginning of the conflict with Gorbachev out of the public eye in order not to damage the picture of a harmonious eastern alliance.

However, his patience came to an end when he spoke to Gorbachev on 3 October 1986. Honecker complained bitterly about Soviet writer Yevgeny Yevtushenko, who had denied the separation of a West and an East German literature and had talked about the necessity of German reunification on West German television. Honecker called these remarks "a provocation"; such conduct was "counterrevolutionary." Gorbachev tried in vain to calm him down. Honecker stuck to his opinion and replied: "For us it is important to fight on one front, and not on two." What he meant was clear: if glasnost in the Soviet Union went too far and endangered Moscow's firm commitment to the status quo in Germany, the GDR could lose the backing it needed from the East in order to sustain the challenge it permanently faced in the West. Although Gorbachev did not share Yevtushenko's openly expressed view, the writers with their opinions about German literature and Germany were in his eyes a minor problem. He felt more critical toward those people "who do not want to change anything, who already have everything they think is worth striving for."[15] Gorbachev was keen on change, and wanted to promote this with glasnost; Honecker saw his policy of preserving the status quo—especially with regard to the German question—endangered by glasnost. These completely divergent attitudes led to the first clash of opinions between the two party leaders.

Honecker was under pressure not only from Gorbachev and the Federal Republic, but also from below. The Stasi reported about the perception of the CPSU congress, especially by party and state officials responsible for the GDR economy. According to the Stasi, these people welcomed Gorbachev's critical words, diagnosed that the same critical points could be found in the GDR economy, and demanded similarly clear and critical comments by the SED leaders at their party congress in April.[16] By transmitting these opinions to the leadership, the Stasi did not want to promote reform of the East German system, but to make its economy more efficient. However, these hopes were dashed by Honecker's speech at the 11th SED Congress, which was full of self-praise and stuck to the success story of *Einheit von Wirtschafts- und Sozialpolitik*.[17] Honecker received less applause than in the past, but after Gorbachev's address, in which the Soviet leader emphasized the self-critical atmosphere of the CPSU congress, the delegates cheered and applauded for minutes.[18] On the one hand, this severely damaged the bright picture of socialism in the GDR that the SED wanted to propagate; on the other hand, the Stasi reports and the applause at the party congress revealed that there was a large amount of discontent with the East German economy, even among the responsible officials. Without the example set by Gorbachev, this discontent would not have been unearthed. Although this did not yet threaten the GDR's stability, the first cracks in the relationship between party leadership and party members became visible.

In spite of their different opinions, Gorbachev never tried to enforce the reforms he deemed necessary in the GDR. At the meeting of party and state leaders of the COMECON on 10–11 November 1986, he made it clear that he wanted to build relations between the socialist states "on the basis of equal rights and of mutual advantage." Preconditions to this were "the independence of each party, its right to decide alone about problems of development in its country, its responsibility to its own people ... No one could claim for himself a special role in the socialist community."[19] So Honecker felt assured that he could deviate from Gorbachev's course without having to fear negative consequences from Moscow.

III. Public Dissent and Dissociation from the Soviet Example (1987)

At the CPSU Central Committee plenum on 27–28 January 1987, Gorbachev went beyond economics. Not only did he criticize the Breshnev era very harshly, but he also propagated real democratization by calling for secret ballots for lower party levels, for the Soviets and for company managements. Although the Central Committee watered down his proposals, he ended the plenum with the words: "We need democracy like air to breathe."[20] For the first time, not only economic but political reforms loomed on the horizon. The SED leadership was horrified. In a paper ordered by Honecker and written by Egon Krenz and the two FDJ officials Hans-Joachim Willerding and Hartmut König, the authors came to the conclusion that the slogan, "To learn from the Soviet Union is to learn how to win," was no longer valid; moreover they emphasized that the GDR was further developed than the Soviet Union.[21] The SED leaders were determined not to take over any of Gorbachev's political reforms. This was not only due to the fact that they were old, inflexible men dedicated to the cause of communism. Crucial was their knowledge that reforms leading to a democratization of the system would in the long run lead to its downfall. The raison d'être of the GDR lay in socialism; a truly democratic East German state had no chance of survival on account of the existence of the Federal Republic just next door.[22]

The SED leadership tried to restrict the effects of Gorbachev's speech in the GDR by having only an abbreviated version printed in *Neues Deutschland*. But this restrictive press policy was not very successful due to the all-German space of communication. On account of reports on West German television and radio, it was illusory to keep the East Germans away from such news from Moscow. Therefore, fourteen days later, the SED-owned Dietz Verlag published a complete version of the proceedings of the CPSU Central Committee meeting, which was soon sold out.[23]

Shortly before this, Honecker decided to change his tactics and to dissociate himself from Gorbachev in public, probably because he knew he could not stop the spread of his ideas into the GDR via West Germany. At a meeting of the SED *Kreissekretäre* (district secretaries) on 6 February 1987, he countered Gorbachev's demand for democratization by speaking of the irreplaceable "socialist democracy in the GDR," without however mentioning Gorbachev by name.[24] This changed when the SED secretary for culture, Kurt Hager, gave an interview with the West German magazine *Stern*. It appeared on 9 April, and was reprinted in *Neues Deutschland* the next day. When asked if the GDR would follow the course of perestroika in the Soviet Union, he answered: "Would you, if your neighbor changes his wallpaper, feel obliged to change your wallpaper, too?"[25] By giving the interview to a West German magazine, the SED leadership had secured itself a maximum media presence. Moreover, besides directly addressing Soviet reform politics, Hager also belittled Gorbachev's efforts, because it had become clear that the CPSU general secretary was not aiming at cosmetic changes but at a fundamental reform of the system.

The reactions of the SED membership are more difficult to make out. Stasi reports suggest that there were two types of reaction. On the one hand, "progressive forces" (i.e., SED members supporting the regime) began to have doubts and worries about the correctness and the future with regard to developments in the Soviet Union. SED officials were unsettled, so they asked for a statement from their leadership—which they got with Honecker's speech of 6 February. From then on, this group took the view that it was impossible to transfer Soviet reforms to the GDR because of the different conditions prevailing in the two countries. On the other side, there were SED members, especially leading state and economic officials, who were more in line with Gorbachev's course and demanded more openness and less whitewashing in order to increase trust in the SED. They demanded that the truth should not be feared, and explicitly rejected the argument that the GDR should restrain itself with regard to reforms because it was located on the dividing line between communism and capitalism. These people also criticized the media policy of the SED, especially the selective reporting that was not telling the whole truth about the Soviet Union.[26]

In one interesting case, we can reconstruct the SED leadership's reaction to the second group. After long internal discussions, the SED group of the state theater in Dresden wrote a letter to Hager on 18 June 1987, protesting about the wording used in his interview. The letter was sent through the official channel, via the first SED district secretary of Dresden, Hans Modrow. The SED group agreed with Gorbachev's interpretation that perestroika was not just a change of decoration but rather "a revolutionary process." And they were of the opinion that a similar process was absolutely necessary for the GDR as well. Modrow did not intervene but passed the letter on to Hager personally. Hager answered the letter on 13 July in a very moderate way, but defended the use of his wallpaper metaphor. Moreover, he passed the correspondence on to Krenz, who was in charge in East Berlin while Honecker was on holiday. Krenz was not prepared to let the matter drop. Instead he interpreted the letter as an attack on the supporting pillars of SED politics. He therefore convened a special session of the SED secretariat in Berlin on 15 July, where not only the letter but also Modrow was harshly criticized for his irresponsibility and his carelessness. Consequently, a commission from the SED secretariat, headed by Krenz, went to Dresden on 17 July to attend a special meeting of the district secretariat under Modrow, who admitted he should not have passed the letter on. At a meeting of the SED group of the state theater on 2 September, Modrow appealed to the conscience of the SED comrades who partly still insisted on inner-party democracy. But in the end the SED group distanced itself from the letter it had written. The aim of the exercise was reached: party discipline was restored and inner-party criticism was silenced—without, however, convincing the local SED members for whom Gorbachev had become the important point of reference.[27] In this process, three points are of relevance to the extent of the opposition to Honecker within the SED leadership and the way in which Honecker and his followers dealt with those who had divergent opinions. First, Modrow was far from being an East German Gorbachev, because he quickly gave in to criticism from the SED leadership. Second, Modrow was forced into self-criticism but was not removed from his position—not because he was well known abroad but because Honecker tried to avoid personnel changes in the higher echelons of the party in order to convey a picture of stability. Third, Honecker and Krenz wanted to make an example of Modrow in order to prevent similar cases from occurring again.

IV. Reinforced Efforts against Perestroika and Censorship of Soviet Media (1987–1988)

In 1988, the SED leadership not only dissociated itself from perestroika but also openly took sides in the conflict in the leadership of the CPSU between the Gorbachev group and his opponents led by Yegor Ligachev. On 13 March 1988, the journal *Sovietskaya Rossiya* published a letter by chemistry lecturer Nina Andreyeva from the Leningrad Technical Institute in which she vehemently criticized perestroika from a neo-Stalinist point of view. The letter, under the title "I cannot forsake my principles," had been revised and completed in the CPSU apparat, with the knowledge and approval of Ligachev. A reply to the letter was not published for three weeks, so that many concluded this was the new party line.[28] The SED leadership, who must have been delighted at this apparent turn of the tide in Moscow, seized the opportunity and had the letter translated and printed in *Neues Deutschland* on 2 April, thus clearly exposing itself as a supporter of Ligachev.[29] It was just too bad that the Gorbachev group retaliated a few days later. Gorbachev reasserted himself after the CPSU Politburo session of 24/25 March, and a counter-article in *Pravda* appeared on 5 April.[30] At first, Honecker declined to publish the article. Only after an intervention by the Soviet ambassador, Vyacheslav Kochemassov, was it reprinted in *Neues Deutschland* on 9 April—without a commentary and together with an anti-reform article directed against the "Prague Spring" from the Czechoslovak paper *Rudé Pravo*.[31]

After this defeat of Gorbachev's opponents within the CPSU Politburo, the general secretary managed to push political reforms in 1988. The most important event in this context was the 19th CPSU conference, which had been publicly prepared since May and which took place from 28 June to 1 July. Two of the main reforms adopted here were the strengthening of the Soviets in comparison with the party, and the introduction of real inner-party elections with more than one candidate.[32] The SED leaders clearly distanced themselves from these plans. In internal papers they declared themselves to be against the reform and restriction of the power of the party, against decentralization, self-administration and the strengthening of the Soviets, and against real elections with several candidates.[33]

According to a Stasi report, party officials and members were again split. On the one hand, there were those for whom the discussions at the CPSU conference went too far, especially with regard to the history of the CPSU, and who were worried about developments in the Soviet Union. Moreover, Gorbachev was, according to this group, exaggerating the criticism of his predecessors, and the extent of the open discussion of mistakes in the Soviet media had been "unjustifiable." Other party members seemed to have welcomed the fact that Gorbachev had limited the time in office for party officials, and to have demanded similar discussions in the GDR.[34] All in all, there seems to have been a lot of enthusiasm for Gorbachev and his reforms at the grass roots of the SED. However, the Stasi report had not touched on the question of inner-party elections with more than one candidate. This theme had evidently been too "hot" for the Stasi writers of the report. The fact that it was discussed widely—not only among the population but also within the party—follows from a letter by an SED member to Modrow, which explicitly took the 19th CPSU conference as a point of departure, and contained exactly this demand. The anonymous writer praised the CPSU for recognizing the wrong development in the past, and for introducing the drastic changes with perestroika and glasnost: "The past congress of this party has shown how the course has to be followed—more democracy leads to more socialism."[35]

However, there were hardly any officials at the top level of the party or state who thought on these lines. One exception was the minister for culture, Hans-Joachim Hoffmann, who according to a former subordinate employee believed "in the possibility of reforming real socialism."[36] In an interview for the West German journal *Theater heute*, he said in June 1988: "There is a 'new thinking' in the Soviet Union, in other socialist countries, in our country. It is not just coming, it is real. What is most certain is that everything is changing [*Das Sicherste ist die Veränderung*]."[37] These words were clearly inspired by glasnost and perestroika. After the interview had been published in September, Hager telephoned Hoffmann and asked him if he had really said those words and if he had consented to them being printed. Hoffmann replied in the affirmative, and Hager ended the conversation with the sentence: "We will have to talk about this." At the beginning of October, the matter was discussed at a meeting of ministers and party officials in the Central Committee, chaired by Hager himself—Hoffmann was absent at a conference in Havana. After his return, Hoffmann had a meeting with Hager in the course of which Hoffmann had a physical breakdown and had to be admitted to hospital. After he had recovered, he was summoned to the meeting of the SED Central Committee on 1–2 December where he was disciplined. Hoffmann apologized, and promised that nothing similar would happen again, so the matter was ended. Hoffmann was left in office, probably because of the expected sensation his removal would have caused at home and abroad, especially among artists.[38]

The other method of dealing with Soviet reforms was to censor potentially dangerous remarks from the Soviet Union. This began with the SED Politburo's decision of 20 October 1987, which said: "Speeches by comrades of the CPSU will in future be published in extracts or summaries."³⁹ This was a feeble attempt by the SED leadership to cut the GDR off from the negative influences of perestroika; on account of the all-German space of communication, this was doomed to fail. In spite of all this the SED leadership had Gorbachev's book "Perestroika" translated and printed. The Politburo was reluctant to take this step but deemed it necessary in order not to affront Moscow. In contrast to the West German translation, which carried the title *Perestroika. Die zweite russische Revolution: Eine neue Politik für Europa und die Welt* [Perestroika. The second Russian revolution: A new policy for Europe and the world], the title of the East German version avoided the term perestroika and was called *Umgestaltung und neues Denken für unser Land und die Welt* [Restructuring and new thinking for our country and the world]. It received four editions of forty thousand copies each, all of which sold out very quickly.⁴⁰

In 1987 and 1988, however, the SED took the first steps in the direction of censoring media emanating from the Soviet Union. Whereas in 1987, the 5th issue and the supplement to the 42nd issue of the Soviet magazine *Neue Zeit* had not been delivered to East German subscribers, the year 1988 started by withholding the first three issues because they contained extracts of the play "Further ... further ... further!" by Mikhail Shatrov, which criticized Stalin. Such a distortion of history was not to be distributed in the GDR. This caused occasional unrest among SED members, and induced individual complaints.⁴¹ However, Honecker overplayed his hand when at his order the Soviet digest *Sputnik* was banned. The 180,000 copies of the October issue were not delivered because they contained articles criticizing Stalin's policy before 1941. On 19/20 November, a short notice was published in *Neues Deutschland* by the press office of the post ministry which informed that *Sputnik* had been withdrawn from the list of post journals because "it was not publishing any contribution serving German–Soviet friendship but only contributions distorting history."⁴² This led to an immense upheaval within the population, and particularly in the party.

Stasi reports for the first time now clearly noted that only a minority of the population called this decision long overdue. They also noted that there were hardly any differences in the opinions and lines of argumentation between party and non-party members. The main argument employed was that with this step the population was declared to be politically immature.⁴³ Moreover, it was deemed an unwise decision because for the first time it brought the GDR leadership into an open confrontation with the politics of the Soviet Union, and because it was counterproductive as the Soviet press and Soviet films were becoming very popular.⁴⁴

With this step, the SED leadership lost much support among its rank and file. This also became clear from the petitions reaching the Central Committee up until the end of 1988: 75 percent out of over 800 petitions had been written by SED members, and 7 percent by party groups.[45] The main point of criticism was that the writers saw themselves deprived of their right to information. But most petitions did not argue from an opinion principally opposed to the regime; they rather argued that the taken step had been imprudent because it showed that the SED was afraid of glasnost, and because it showed weakness and not strength. Therefore, their point of view can be qualified as being inherent in the system ("*systemimmanent*").[46] All in all, the SED leadership lost its grip over a large number of its members. About 11,000 SED members left the party in 1988, and almost 23,000 were expelled—the highest number in the Honecker era.[47] However, their reactions did not challenge the system itself. For the time being, Honecker could continue to feel secure.

The massive outbreaks of discontent did not render the party leadership more receptive towards criticism. Instead it continued with its policy of open confrontation with Moscow. At the meeting of the Central Committee on 1–2 December 1988, Honecker spoke of "the croaking of petit-bourgeois gone wild, who want to rewrite the history of the CPSU and the Soviet Union in a bourgeois sense."[48] SED party members were openly threatened by the district leadership of East Berlin: "Those who want a party of perestroika will be expelled."[49] As the socialism practiced in the Soviet Union was no longer a model, Honecker was only consistent when he proclaimed a "developed socialist society ... in the colors of the GDR" at the commemoration of the 70th anniversary of the KPD on 30 December 1988.[50]

V. Perceptions and Reactions to Democratization and Chaos in the Soviet Union (1989)

In 1989, on the one hand perestroika reached a climax in the Soviet Union with the election of the Congress of People's Deputies in spring and the debates of this semi-democratically elected parliament, which were transmitted on television all over the country. On the other hand, the problems were accumulating: steep economic decline, strikes by millions of miners, and increasingly violent nationality conflicts all threatened the cohesion of the Soviet Union.[51]

Needless to say, the SED leadership remained in stubborn opposition to any political reforms. Already in January 1988 Honecker had said to the Soviet ambassador: "If Gorbachev carries on like this, he will ruin the party and the country within two years."[52] The conflict between him and Gorbachev escalated in 1989 because of the readjustment of Soviet *Deutschlandpolitik* to the Federal Republic. After Kohl's visit to Moscow in October 1988 and Gorbachev's visit to Bonn in June 1989, the leadership in East Berlin was extremely worried that the Soviet Union would reach an agreement with West Germany at the expense of the GDR.[53] Moreover, the East German leadership who had all along supported Gorbachev's security policy became increasingly critical of his course of continuous, unilateral disarmament.[54] In Honecker's view, the problems Gorbachev was facing must have come at the right time. He probably pinned his hopes on the possibility that Gorbachev would be forced to resign and make way for Ligachev and the conservatives in the CPSU leadership. In this context it is remarkable that the latter visited East Berlin from 11 to 13 September 1989, where he was received by the SED secretary for economics, Günter Mittag, as Honecker was ill. On the eve of the peaceful revolution, the anti-reformists from Moscow and East Berlin showed solidarity.[55]

Officials and older members of the SED were unsettled by the social and economic upheaval in the Soviet Union. If the Soviet Union was in this state, what would become of its socialist allies? A mentality of sticking it out spread among these people. Stasi reports about the general development in the Soviet Union suggest that the East German population was turning away from Gorbachev's reform politics. With the spread of knowledge about mass poverty and nationality conflicts in the Soviet Union, admiration for the country was diminishing. The negative sides of glasnost and perestroika became prominent in the Stasi reports. From July on, these suggested that strikes, nationality conflicts, poverty and growing supply problems were increasing doubts about the "Gorbachev-democracy," so that the political and economic stability of the GDR was once more acknowledged. The Stasi seemed to hope that under these conditions GDR citizens would once again rally under the flag of the SED.[56]

The Stasi could not have been more mistaken. In the population and at the grass roots of the SED, Gorbachev and his program remained popular and was seen as an example for the GDR—especially the rejuvenation of the CPSU Central Committee, which was the result of the Central Committee plenum of 25 April 1989.[57] Moreover, in 1988/89 a group of social scientists from Humboldt University were thinking about "modern socialism." The theses they published in 1989 caused unrest in the central party apparatus. Although they adhered to the leading role of the party, to nationally owned property and to a planned economy, they demanded political reforms, especially with regard to electoral law, the legal system, human rights, and regional administrations. A reform of the constitution was planned, especially to achieve the separation of powers.[58] These "reform socialists" were indeed thinking on the lines of Gorbachev's perestroika, but they had come too late for the realization of their plans—they were overtaken by the peaceful revolution in autumn 1989.

The SED leadership went on with its efforts to control and discipline members who did not follow the party line. When the Central Committee announced in December 1988 that the party documents would have to be exchanged in 1989, this was rightly perceived as a method of disciplining party members. However, in the conversations conducted in this context, officials were often confronted by the displeasure of the rank and file of the party. To be expelled from the SED was no longer seen as a threat. On the contrary, the number of resignations from the party increased steadily in the first half of 1989; then from June onwards the numbers almost doubled (1,769 in June to 2,803 in July) and in October more than 10,000 voluntarily left the SED. It is no wonder that the exchange of party documents was stopped in October 1989.[59] Moreover, many of those who remained were no longer willing to follow the party line. When Gorbachev visited the GDR for its fortieth and last anniversary, even the participants of the torchlight procession parading past the official tribune shouted: "Perestroika! Gorbachev! Help us!" Mieczysław Rakowski, first secretary of the PUWP, translated for Gorbachev: "They're demanding: 'Gorbachev, save us once more!' These are party activists! This is the end!"[60]

VI. Conclusion

The SED leadership had welcomed Gorbachev's coming to power in 1985 and had at first supported not only his new foreign policy but also his economic reforms. After 1987, however, it perceived perestroika—which also envisaged political reforms—as a threat to its power and even to the existence of the GDR as a state in its own right. As Honecker and his entourage therefore vehemently opposed any reforms whatsoever in the GDR, they became fierce opponents of Gorbachev's reform policy.

In 1985 the SED rank and file had to a large extent held the same opinion of Gorbachev and his inner politics as the leadership. From 1986 onwards, however, the mass of SED members distanced themselves from their leadership's point of view. For most of them, Gorbachev was a shining example for the GDR, and he thus also contributed to the erosion of the power of the SED. On the other hand, among the SED's upper echelons there was hardly any opposition to Honecker's course. Most of them clung to power just the same as Honecker, and the others were quite easily disciplined. Long-trained party habits could not be shed overnight.

However, although party members could be disciplined, the SED leadership was unable to win them back to its cause. Their disciplining led only to outer adjustment and not to real conviction. In the long run, the party ceased to function in the way it had for the past decades—but in autumn 1989 this was no longer only due to Soviet influence but to a mass exodus from the GDR and peaceful revolution.

Hermann Wentker is head of the Berlin Branch of the Institute for Contemporary History and professor at the University of Potsdam. He has also taught at the universities of Bayreuth and Leipzig. His main interests concern the history of international relations in the nineteenth and twentieth centuries, and the history of the GDR and of divided Germany after 1945. He is author of following monographs: *Zerstörung der Großmacht Rußland? Die britischen Kriegsziele im Krimkrieg*, Göttingen/Zurich, 1993; *Justiz in der SBZ/DDR 1945–1953: Transformation und Rolle ihrer zentralen Institutionen*, Munich, 2001; *Außenpolitik in engen Grenzen: Die DDR im internationalen System 1949–1989*, Munich, 2007. He is co-editor of several other books, which include: *Aufstände im Ostblock: Zur Krisengeschichte des realen Sozialismus*, Berlin, 2004; *Das doppelte Deutschland: 40 Jahre Systemkonkurrenz*, Berlin, 2008; *Zweiter Kalter Krieg und Friedensbewegung: Der NATO-Doppelbeschluss in deutsch-deutscher und internationaler Perspektive*, Munich, 2011; *Die KSZE im Ost-West-Konflikt: Internationale Politik und gesellschaftliche Transformation 1975–1990*, Munich, 2012; *Hauptstadtanspruch und symbolische Politik: Die Bundespräsenz im geteilten Berlin 1949–1990*, Berlin, 2012. He is currently working on a book project about the Germans and Gorbachev. This includes the East and West German perceptions of Gorbachev, as well as the relations between Gorbachev's Soviet Union and the two German states and societies.

Notes

1. "Stenographische Niederschrift des Treffens der Genossen des Politbüros des ZK der SED mit Gorbatschow am 7. Oktober 1989" [Stenographical transcript of the meeting of the comrades of the Politburo of the Central Committee of the SED with Gorbachev on 7 October 1989], in Küchenmeister, *Honecker–Gorbatschow Vieraugengespräche*, 256.
2. Hanson, "Gorbachev," 51.
3. Cf. Adomeit, *Imperial Overstretch*; Ouimet, *Rise and Fall of the Brezhnev Doctrine*.
4. Cf. Wentker, "Zwischen Unterstützung," 137–54.

5. See Honecker's own statement in Andert and Herzberg, *Der Sturz*, 60.
6. Cf. Oldenburg and Stephan, "Honecker kam nicht bis Bonn"; "Niederschrift über das Treffen zwischen Honecker und Tschernenko am 17.8.1984 [Report on the meeting between Honecker and Chernenko on 17 August 1984] (extract)," in Nakath and Stephan, *Die Häber-Protokolle*, 398–422
7. For interviews with former leading SED officials, see Nepit, *SED unter dem Druck*, 63–64.
8. See Gorbachev's speech of 27 November 1985, in Gorbachev, *Ausgewählte Reden und Aufsätze*, Vol. 3, 98–122; "Information über erste Reaktionen von leitenden Wirtschaftsfunktionären auf die Rede Gorbatschows vor dem Obersten Sowjet am 27.11.1985 [Information about first reactions of senior economy officials to Gorbachev's speech to the Supreme Soviet on 27 November 1985]," 29.11.1985, BStU, MfS, HA XVIII, Nr. 18864, fol. 1–6.
9. See especially "Vermerk über ein Gespräch Honeckers mit Gorbatschow am 5.5.1985 [Note on a conversation between Honecker and Gorbachev on 5 May 1985]," in Küchenmeister, *Honecker–Gorbatschow Vieraugengespräche*, 45.
10. See Gorbachev's declaration in Gorbachev, *Ausgewählte Reden und Aufsätze*, vol. 3, 146–59. For Honecker's consent, see "'Miteinander leben, gut miteinander auskommen': Ein Zeit-Gespräch mit Erich Honecker [Living together, getting on well together: A conversation with Erich Honecker]," *Die Zeit*, 31 January 1986. For popular reaction to Gorbachev, see "Reaktionen der Bevölkerung auf die Erklärung Gorbatschows vom 15.1.1986 [Responses of the population to Gorbachev's statement of 15 January 1986]," 22 January 1986, BStU, MfS, ZAIG Nr. 4203, fol. 2–6.
11. Cf. in this context the memoirs of Politburo member Kurt Hager, who wrote that the terms *perestroika* and *glasnost* had been missing in the resolutions of the congress, whereas the term *uskorenye* (acceleration) had been "the central theme of all debates and documents of the party congress": Hager, *Erinnerungen*, 376–77.
12. According to Werner Eberlein, Honecker criticized the "spontaneous" course of the congress and rejected the open and controversial discussions: Eberlein, *Geboren am 9. November*, 448–49.
13. "Information über das Treffen Honeckers mit Gorbatschow am 20.4.1986 in Berlin [Information on Honecker's meeting with Gorbachev on 20 April 1986 in Berlin]," in Küchenmeister, *Honecker–Gorbatschow Vieraugengespräche*, 83–84.
14. Ibid., 93.
15. "Niederschrift über ein Gespräch Honeckers mit Gorbatschow am 3.10.1986 [Transcript of Honecker's conversation with Gorbachev on 3 October 1986]," ibid., quotations on pages 161, 164.
16. "Erste Hinweise über Reaktionen der Bevölkerung der DDR auf den XXVII. Parteitag der KPdSU [First informations about the GDR population's reactions to the 27th CPSU Party Congress]," 3 March 1986, BStU, MfS, ZAIG, Nr. 4205, fol. 2–8; "Hinweise über beachtenswerte Reaktionen der Bevölkerung der DDR in weiterer Auswertung des XXVII. Parteitages der KPdSU und in Vorbereitung auf den XI. Parteitag der SED [Informations about noteworthy reactions of the GDR population in the further evaluation of the 27th CPSU Party Congress for the 11th SED Party Congress]," 21 March 1986, BStU, MfS, ZAIG Nr. 4199, fol. 21–35.
17. Literal translation: "Unity of economic and social policy." This term refers to the concept of consumer socialism being pursued by the SED leadership under Honecker. Thereby economic progress was to be achieved by magnifying the appeal of socialism by giving special consideration to the material needs of the people.
18. See the account of the party official Manfred Uschner: Uschner, *Die zweite Etage*, 127; Dieter Dose and Hans R. Karutz, "Ein Wunschtraum: das ganze Jahr Parteitag," *Die Welt*, 19 April 1986.

19. "Niederschrift über das Treffen der führenden Repräsentanten der Bruderparteien sozialistischer Länder des RGW am 10. und 11.11.1986 in Moskau [Transcript of the meeting of leading representatives of the fraternal parties of the COMECON countries on 10 and 11 November in Moscow]," in Küchenmeister and Stephan, "Gorbatschows Entfernung von der Breshnew-Doktrin," 719–20.
20. See Meissner, *Die Sowjetunion im Umbruch*, 164–69; Schlußwort auf dem Plenum des ZK der KPdSU, 28 January 1987, in Gorbachev, *Ausgewählte Reden und Aufsätze*, vol. 4, 397 (quotation).
21. See Nepit, *SED unter dem Druck*, 152–54; Malycha, *Die SED in der Ära Honecker*, 305–6 (quotation). FDJ stands for Freie Deutsche Jugend, the official youth organization of the GDR.
22. See Wentker, "Die Staatsräson der DDR," 152.
23. See Nepit, *SED unter dem Druck*, 249–50.
24. The speech was printed in *Neues Deutschland* on 7 March 1987, quoted here after the reprint in *Deutschland Archiv* 20 (1987), 442.
25. Quotation after the reprint in *Deutschland Archiv* 20 (1987), 656.
26. ZAIG, "Erste Hinweise über die Reaktion der Bevölkerung auf das Referat Honeckers auf der Beratung des Sekretariats des ZK der SED mit den 1. Sekretären der Kreisleitungen am 6.2.1987 [First informations about the population's reaction to Honecker's lecture at the consultation of the CC of the SED with the 1st District Secretaries on 6 February 1987]," 17 February 1987, BStU, MfS, ZAIG, Nr. 4218, fol. 1–6 (http://www.bstu.bund.de/DE/Wissen/DDRGeschichte/Vorabend-der-Revolution/1987_SED-Perestroika/Dokumente/1987-02-17_Hinweise/_tabelle.html?nn=2635444, 14.7.2016); ZAIG, "Hinweise über die Reaktion der Bevölkerung insbesondere in weiterer Auswertung des Referats von Honecker auf der Beratung des Sekretariats des ZK der SED mit den 1. Sekretären der Kreisleitungen der SED [Informations about the population's reaction in the further evaluation of Honecker's lecture at the consultation of the Secretariat of the CC of the SED with the 1st Secretaries of the SED district leaderships]," 13 April 1987, ibid., fol. 8–11 (http://www.bstu.bund.de/DE/Wissen/DDRGeschichte/Vorabend-der-Revolution/1987_SED-Perestroika/Dokumente/1987-04-13_Hinweise/_tabelle.html?nn=2635444, 14.07.2016).
27. For the most detailed account of this process, see Niemann, *Die Sekretäre*, 304 (quotation); see also Malycha, *SED in der Ära Honecker*, 307–11.
28. See Brown, *Aufstieg und Fall des Kommunismus*, 673–74.
29. "Ich kann meine Prinzipien nicht preisgeben. Brief der Leningrader Dozentin Nina Andrejewa [I cannot forsake my principles. Letter by the Leningrad university lecturer Nina Andreyeva]," in *Neues Deutschland*, 2/3 April 1988. According to a contemporary rumor, the SED leaders had the article printed at a suggestion from Moscow: cf. Süß, "Perestrojka oder Ausreise," 292.
30. See Altrichter, *Russland 1989*, 87–90.
31. "Die Prinzipien der Umgestaltung: Revolutionäres Denken und Handeln [The principles of restructuring revolutionary thinking and acting]," in *Neues Deutschland*, 9/10 April 1988. See Malycha, *SED in der Ära Honecker*, 313; Nepit, *SED unter dem Druck*, 255.
32. See Altrichter, *Russland 1989*, 40–54.
33. See Nepit, *SED unter dem Druck*, 164–69.
34. "Hinweise über beachtenswerte Aspekte aus der Reaktion der Bevölkerung auf die XIX. Unionsparteikonferenz der KPdSU [Informations about noteworthy aspects in the population's reaction to the 19th CPSU Conference]," 11 July 1988, in Joestel, *Die DDR im Blick der Stasi 1988*, 205.
35. "Anonymous letter from Dresden to Modrow," 28 September 1988, in Suckut, *Volkes Stimmen*, 399.

36. Schauer, "Der verdächtige Demokrat," 11.
37. The interview is reprinted ibid., 230–50, quotation 249.
38. Schauer, "Der verdächtige Demokrat," 20; Stephan, "Die letzten Tagungen," 303–4. According to Schauer, Soviet ambassador Kochemassov also advised Honecker not to remove Hoffmann.
39. Quotation in Nakath, *SED und Perestroika*, 17.
40. See Nepit, *SED unter dem Druck*, 251–52; Bortfeld, *Von der SED zur PDS*, 31.
41. See Brie, *Ich tauche nicht*, 44–46.
42. "Information über die Sicherstellung der UdSSR-Zeitschrift *Sputnik* [Information about securing the USSR journal *Sputnik*]," 3 October 1988, BStU, MfS, HA XIX, Nr. 4774, fol. 2 (http://www.bstu.bund.de/DE/Wissen/DDRGeschichte/Vorabend-der-Revolution/1988_Sputnik-Verbot/Dokumente/1988-10-03_information.html?nn=2635460, 12.9.2016); Sabrow, "Die Wiedergeburt des klassischen Skandals," 245–46.
43. Translation of the German phrase: "Damit werde die Bevölkerung der DDR politisch entmündigt."
44. "Hinweise zu einigen bedeutenden Aspekten der Reaktion der Bevölkerung im Zusammenhang mit der Mitteilung über die Streichung der Zeitschrift *Sputnik* von der Postvertriebsliste der DDR [Informations about some important aspects of the population's reaction in the context of the information about the deletion of the journal *Sputnik* from the postal distribution list of the GDR]," 30 November 1988, in Joestel, *DDR im Blick 1988*, 284–88, quotation 285.
45. See Klein, "Reform von oben?", 138.
46. See Werner, "Die 'Sputnik'-Krise in der SED," 135.
47. See Bortfeld, *Von der SED zur PDS*, 38–39.
48. Quotation in Stephan, "Die letzten Tagungen," 304.
49. Quotation in "Ein für allemal," *Der Spiegel*, 28 November 1988.
50. "Was die Gründer vor 70 Jahren begannen, fand seine Krönung im Werden und Wachsen der DDR. Rede Erich Honeckers auf der Festveranstaltung der DDR anläßlich des 70. Jahrestages der Gründung der KPD [What the founders started 70 years ago found its culmination in the development and growth of the GDR]," *Neues Deutschland*, 30 December 1988. Honecker had also used this term at the meeting of the SED Central Committee on 2 December 1988, cf. Süß, *Staatssicherheit am Ende*, 102.
51. See Altrichter, *Russland 1989*, 123–211.
52. Kotschemassow, *Meine letzte Mission*, 73.
53. See Wentker, "Die Deutschen und Gorbatschow," 145–48; idem, "Gorbatschow in Bonn," 277–99.
54. See the conversation between Soviet foreign minister Edward Shevardnadze and his East German colleague Oskar Fischer in June 1989: Kotschemassow, *Meine letzte Mission*, 129.
55. For Ligachev's visit, see Biermann, *Zwischen Kreml und Kanzleramt*, 177–80.
56. ZAIG, "Hinweise über einige beachtenswerte Aspekte der Reaktion der Bevölkerung auf Veröffentlichungen in den Medien der DDR über Entwicklungstendenzen in sozialistischen Staaten [Informations about some noteworthy aspects in the population's reaction to publications in the GDR media about development trends in socialist countries]," 28 February 1989, BStU, MfS, Sek. Neiber 526, fol. 1–7; ZAIG, "Hinweise zur Reaktion der Bevölkerung auf die Informations- und Medienpolitik in der UdSSR und damit im Zusammenhang stehende Probleme [Informations about the population's reaction to the information and media politics in the USSR and connected problems]," 10 May 1989, in Mitter and Wolle, *Ich liebe Euch doch alle!*, 40–41; "Information über Stimmungen und Meinungen von Bürgern der Hauptstadt der DDR [Informations about the sentiments and the opinions of citizens from the captial of the GDR]," Berlin, 29 July 1989, BStU, MfS, BV Bln AKG 4056, fol. 94f.

57. ZAIG, "Hinweise zur Reaktion der Bevölkerung auf das Plenum des ZK der KPdSU am 25. April 1989 [Informations about the population's reaction to the Plenary Session of the CC of the CPSU on 25 April 1989," 5 May 1989, BStU, MfS ZAIG 4250, fol. 2–4; "Information über erste Reaktionen von Bürgern der Hauptstadt der DDR, Berlin, auf die jüngste Tagung des ZK der KPdSU [Information about first reactions of citizens from the capital of the GDR, Berlin, to the recent convention of the CC of the CPSU]," 1 May 1989, BStU, MfS BV Bln AKG 4056, fol. 135–37.
58. For the origins and development of this project, see Segert, *Das 41. Jahr*, 48–74; Malycha, "War die Partei reformfähig?", 157–59.
59. See Malycha, *SED in der Ära Honecker*, 382–83; Mestrup, *Die SED*, 518–23.
60. Gorbachev, *Memoirs*, 524.

Bibliography

Adomeit, Hannes. *Imperial Overstretch: Germany in Soviet Policy from Stalin to Gorbachev: An Analysis Based on New Archival Evidence, Memoirs, and Interviews*, Baden-Baden, 1998.
Altrichter, Helmut. *Russland 1989: Der Untergang des sowjetischen Imperiums*, Munich, 2009.
Andert, Reinhold, and Wolfgang Herzberg. *Der Sturz: Erich Honecker im Kreuzverhör*, Berlin, 1990.
Biermann, Rafael. *Zwischen Kreml und Kanzleramt: Wie Moskau mit der deutschen Einheit rang*, Paderborn, 1997.
Bortfeld, Heinrich. *Von der SED zur PDS: Wandlung zur Demokratie?*, Bonn, 1992.
Brie, André. *Ich tauche nicht ab: Selbstzeugnisse und Reflexionen*, Berlin, 1996.
Brown, Archie. *Aufstieg und Fall des Kommunismus*, Berlin, 2009.
Eberlein, Werner. *Geboren am 9. November: Erinnerungen*, Berlin, 2nd edition, 2009.
Gorbachev, Mikhail. *Ausgewählte Reden und Aufsätze*, vols 3 and 4, Berlin, 1988.
―――. *Memoirs*, London, 1996.
Hager, Kurt. *Erinnerungen*, Leipzig, 1996.
Hanson, Stephen E. "Gorbachev, 'Ideology, and the End of the Cold War,'" in *Der Zerfall des Sowjetimperiums und Deutschlands Wiedervereinigung*, ed. Hanns Jürgen Küsters, Cologne, 2016, 47–67.
Joestel, Frank (ed.). *Die DDR im Blick der Stasi 1988: Die geheimen Berichte an die SED-Führung*, Göttingen, 2010.
Klein, Thomas. "Reform von oben? Opposition in der SED," in *Zwischen Selbstbehauptung und Anpassung: Formen des Widerstandes und der Opposition in der DDR*, ed. Ulrike Poppe, Rainer Eckert and Ilko-Sascha Kowalczuk, Berlin, 1995, 125–41.
Kotschemassow, Wjatscheslaw. *Meine letzte Mission: Fakten, Erinnerungen, Überlegungen*, Berlin, 1994.
Küchenmeister, Daniel (ed.). *Honecker–Gorbatschow Vieraugengespräche*, Berlin, 1993.
Küchenmeister, Daniel, and Gerd-Rüdiger Stephan. "Gorbatschows Entfernung von der Breshnew-Doktrin: Die Moskauer Beratung der Partei- und

Staatschefs des Warschauer Vertrages vom 10./11. November 1986," *Zeitschrift für Geschichtswissenschaft*, Vol. 42 (1994), 713–21.

Malycha, Andreas. *Die SED in der Ära Honecker: Machtstrukturen, Entscheidungsmechanismen und Konfliktfelder in der Staatspartei 1971 bis 1989*, Munich, 2014.

──────. "War die Partei reformfähig? Chancen und Scheitern von Reformansätzen in der Staatspartei," in *Die Geschichte der SED: Eine Bestandsaufnahme*, ed. Jens Gieseke and Hermann Wentker, Berlin, 2011, 136–62.

Meissner, Boris. *Die Sowjetunion im Umbruch: Historische Hintergründe, Ziele und Grenzen der Reformpolitik Gorbatschows*, Stuttgart, 1988.

Mestrup, Heinz. *Die SED: Ideologischer Anspruch, Herrschaftspraxis und Konflikte im Bezirk Erfurt (1971–1989)*, Rudolstadt, 2000.

Mitter, Armin, and Stefan Wolle (eds). *Ich liebe Euch doch alle! Befehle und Lageberichte des MfS Januar–November 1989*, Berlin, 3rd edition, 1990.

Nakath, Detlef, and Gerd-Rüdiger Stephan (eds). *Die Häber-Protokolle: Schlaglichter der SED-Westpolitik*, Berlin, 1999.

Nakath, Monika. *SED und Perestroika: Reflexion osteuropäischer Reformversuche in den 80er Jahren*, Berlin, 1993.

Nepit, Alexandra. *Die SED unter dem Druck der Reformen Gorbatschows: Der Versuch der Parteiführung, das SED-Regime durch konservatives Systemmanagement zu stabilisieren*, Baden-Baden, 2004.

Niemann, Mario. *Die Sekretäre der SED-Bezirksleitungen 1952–1989*, Paderborn, 2007.

Oldenburg, Fred, and Gerd-Rüdiger Stephan. "Honecker kam nicht bis Bonn: Neue Quellen zum Konflikt zwischen Ost-Berlin und Moskau 1984," *Deutschland Archiv*, Vol. 28 (1995), 791–805.

Ouimet, Matthew. *The Rise and Fall of the Brezhnev Doctrine in Soviet Foreign Policy*, Chapel Hill, NC, 2003.

Sabrow, Martin. "Die Wiedergeburt des klassischen Skandals: Öffentliche Empörung in der späten DDR," in *Skandal und Diktatur: Formen öffentlicher Empörung im NS-Staat und in der DDR*, ed. idem, Göttingen, 2004, 231–65.

Schauer, Hermann-Ernst. "Der verdächtige Demokrat," in *"Das Sicherste ist die Veränderung." Hans-Joachim Hoffmann: Kulturminister der DDR und häufig verdächtiger Demokrat*, ed. Gertraude Hoffmann and Klaus Höpcke, Berlin, 2003, 10–24.

Segert, Dieter. *Das 41. Jahr: Eine andere Geschichte der DDR*, Vienna, 2008.

Stephan, Gerd-Rüdiger. "Die letzten Tagungen des Zentralkomitees der SED 1988/89: Abläufe und Hintergründe," *Deutschland Archiv*, Vol. 26 (1993), 296–325.

Suckut, Siegfried (ed.). *Volkes Stimmen. "Ehrlich, aber deutlich": Privatbriefe an die DDR-Regierung*, Munich, 2016.

Süß, Walter. "Perestrojka oder Ausreise: Abwehrpolitik der SED und gesellschaftliche Frustration," *Deutschland Archiv*, Vol. 22 (1989), 286–301.

──────. *Staatssicherheit am Ende: Warum es den Mächtigen nicht gelang, 1989 eine Revolution zu verhindern*, Berlin, 2nd edition, 1999.

Uschner, Manfred. *Die zweite Etage: Funktionsweise eines Machtapparates*, Berlin, 1993.

Wentker, Hermann. "Die Deutschen und Gorbatschow 1987 bis 1989: West- und ostdeutsche Perzeptionen zwischen Kontinuität und Wandel," in *Der Zerfall des Sowjetimperiums und Deutschlands Wiedervereinigung*, ed. Hanns Jürgen Küsters, Cologne, 2016, 119–49.

_____. "Die Staatsräson der DDR," in *Staatsräson in Deutschland*, ed. Günther Heydemann and Eckart Klein, Berlin, 2003, 143–61.

_____. "Gorbatschow in Bonn 1989: Ein historischer Staatsbesuch aus westdeutscher und ostdeutscher Sicht," in *Vergleich als Herausforderung: Festschrift für Günther Heydemann zum 65. Geburtstag*, ed. Andreas Kötzing, Francesca Weil, Mike Schmeitzner and Jan Erik Schulte, Göttingen, 2015, 277–99.

_____. "Zwischen Unterstützung und Ablehnung der sowjetischen Linie: Die DDR, der Doppelbeschluss und die Nachrüstung," in *Zweiter Kalter Krieg und Friedensbewegung: Der NATO-Doppelbeschluss in deutsch-deutscher und internationaler Perspektive*, ed. Philipp Gassert, Tim Geiger and Hermann Wentker, Munich, 2011, 137–54.

Werner, Oliver. "Die 'Sputnik'-Krise in der SED," in *Revolution und Transformation in der DDR 1989/90*, ed. Günther Heydemann, Gunter Mai and Werner Müller, Berlin, 1999, 118–36.

Chapter 7

Between External Constraint and Internal Crackdown
Romania's Non-reaction to Soviet Perestroika

Stefano Bottoni

This chapter analyzes the reaction of Nicolae Ceaușescu's regime to the Soviet quest for an internal reform of the communist system. Was the Romanian choice not to follow Mikhail Gorbachev's advice inevitable? And how was it perceived both at home and abroad in the second half of the 1980s?

Over the last two decades, a large literature has explored the neo-patrimonial turn, the nationalist pervertion, and the repressive practices of the Ceaușescu regime.[1] The few recent archival-based accounts of the Soviet–Romanian relationships offer useful insights into the "inevitable conflict" between the anti-nationalist and supra-national Soviet reform path, and the dogmatic nationalism promoted by Ceaușescu.[2] However, less attention has been paid to the financial and social constraints that late communist Romania had to accept from its Western creditors.[3] On the basis on a wide range of new archival evidence, I argue that it was firstly the debt crisis of the early 1980s that pushed the Romanian communist regime toward self-isolation, after its vaunted independence from Moscow had been jeopardized by the Western-imposed fiscal consolidation. The same international financial institutions (the International Monetary Fund and the World Bank) that Romania had proudly adhered to in 1972 as the first Warsaw Pact country member and had long benefited from before the second oil crisis of 1979–80, suddenly became an instrument of political pressure.[4] Meanwhile, Western countries were beginning to show greater interest in the poor human rights record of the

---

Notes for this chapter begin on page 171.

Ceaușescu regime. This multiple legitimacy crisis helps explain why the Ceaușescu regime reacted negatively after 1985 to the Gorbachev plans to reframe existing socialism. As I will analyze in the second part of the chapter, the Romanian leader looked with suspicion on what he perceived as an entangled (Western *and* Eastern) threat to his rule. It was not an ideological committment, but rather the fear of being overthrown by a Soviet-led conspiracy that made him so vocally unreceptive to perestroika.

The Western Connection: From Mutual Benefit to Imposed Austerity

The first decade of the Ceaușescu regime had been defined by rapid transformations in the socioeconomic structures of the communist state. Corina Marculescu described the first years of the Ceaușescu regime as an important process of learning that won the trust of people and shaped an atmosphere of optimism for the first time after the Second World War.[5] During these "golden years," Ceaușescu displayed—according to Daniel Nelson—a "transient capacity," supported by reforms that identified him as the defender of "the nation" against the implied threats of the USSR, the "regional hegemon."[6] The ostensible alignment with Western attitudes provided Ceaușescu with the opportunity to not only assert Romania's independence from the Soviet Union, but also to empower his economic governance and legitimize his regime in front of the people. In 1975, Romania was granted "Most Favored Nation" (MFN) status by the United States government, and in 1980 the first broad trade agreement between the European Economic Community and a member of the Socialist bloc was signed with Romania, while a joint commission was formed to discuss bilateral issues.

For nearly a decade, the Western financial organizations and private banks provided Romania with easy credit, which the Ceaușescu regime used to finance internal consumption and the industrialization program. Beginning in 1979, and as a result of the second oil shock, the economic situation grew increasingly severe. In 1981 the World Bank approved a three-year loan to Romania; however, it required the country to decrease investment and consumption, to devalue its currency and implement a stability program intended to reform its banking system. It suspended its disbursement after the Ceaușescu regime had refused to implement the stipulated measures, although agreed to release the credit in June 1982 after Romania had agreed to the World Bank's recommended austerity program and to partially acknowledge their true financial situation. The Romanian capitulation stirred concern among the ideologically conservative countries of the Soviet bloc. The East German foreign intelligence (HVA) had been active in Romania for a long period, and made no secret of considering Romania an unreliable ally. In its analytical reports from 1982 to 1983, the HVA argued that the West was still using Romania to weaken the cohesion of the Soviet bloc.[7]

According to Cornel Ban, however, the landing conditions of the early 1980s were very different from the ones during the first oil shock. The energy crisis was sharpened by a "capital crisis," caused by the United States' sudden increase in interest rates.[8] Romania was caught in a vicious circle: it became dependent on foreign loans, and the money was used to back up the national-Stalinist industrialization process, ironically designed to ensure Romania's economic independence. In August 1982, both pillars of Ceaușescu's legitimacy—industrial development and sovereignty—were threatened. The Romanian leader found himself in a vulnerable position without any allies. He was staggered not to receive the preferential treatment he had expected as a reward for the country's earlier opening toward the West. Instead, he watched and worried about the severity of the treatment being applied to Poland, to whom loans were only offered with conditionalities attached. Unlike the Polish leaders, Ceaușescu was not willing to compromise on the developmental agenda. He also took pride in his close relations with the West, but the much-awaited help from the West did not arrive. Romania was essentially cast out from international credit markets. After 1982, the drastic decline in living standards, the introduction of rationing, and the everyday power outages undermined the legitimacy that the Ceaușescu regime had so carefully constructed.

Evidence from the International Monetary Fund Archives in Washington[9] and the internal correspondence between the United Kingdom Treasury, the UK embassy in Bucharest, and the UK Delegation to IMF/IMRD in Washington[10] confirms the notion that the West saw a unique opportunity for evolutive change in the socialist system in the upcoming austerity policies to be implemented in the most indebted East European countries, such as Poland, Hungary, and Romania. As an IMF official stated during the crucial IMF Executive Board meeting of 15 June 1981, at which the Romanian request for a stand-by agreement was discussed and finally approved:

> While the decision to deliberately slow down the growth of the economy was clearly a very difficult one for the Romanian authorities, a change of even more fundamental importance is the acceptance by the authorities of the price and profit mechanism as a guide to the direction of the economy. ... By a process that will start in 1982, retail prices will also be adjusted to reflect costs at a producer level. In conclusion I believe that this program, as contained in the letter

of intent, the performance criteria and the review clauses, give the Fund the assurances it must have, both for the first and for subsequent years, that the very substantial resources it is making available to Romania will be employed to achieve adequate adjustment and to further the purposes of the Fund.[11]

Beyond the soberly worded technocratic approach, one can trace in this statement the driver of the Western attitude to the upcoming economic collapse of the socialist bloc: the very idea that every situation of crisis must be seen as an opportunity to stimulate the internal evolution of these countries, with the cooperation of their ruling elites and—albeit implicitly—regardless of the social costs of austerity. As an IMF official paying a visit to Bucharest in early 1982 put it more bluntly, according to the Foreign Office report: "The first steps toward recovery have been taken. In the short term of course, life will become even harder for the poor Romanian consumer, as imports are cut back and exports increased."[12]

Radio Free Europe (RFE) senior analyst Anneli Ute Gabanyi closely followed the evolution of IMF–Romania talks in that period. On 29 December 1983, quoting confidential IMF sources, she reported that Romania was meeting IMF-imposed economic reform requirements and was expected to receive approval in January of another $400 million credit. Her informants said: "An IMF working group was in Romania two months ago and found that everything seems to be working well under the IMF conditions." The IMF imposed requirements on Romania for reducing hard-currency imports, increasing exports, and instituting wage and price adjustments. The conditions anticipated that to dampen domestic demand and leave more products available for export, the standard of living would have to decline about 10 percent this past year. The sources told Gabanyi that while the figures had not been made public, Romania did meet "the expected 10 percent decline in standard of living, as measured by real income."[13] As the RFE analyst bitterly showed, the sharp cut in purchasing power imposed on the Romanian authorities by the international financial institutions fullfilled their primary expectation of having their money returned but increased the burden of a population already faced with difficulties in producing the most needed foodstuffs. In her global assessment of the Romanian–Western relationships formulated on 31 December 1983, Gabanyi said it was ironic that through the austerity measures imposed on Romania by its Western creditors there has been "growing optimism" in Western banking circles that Romania's tight political system allows it to achieve progress in repaying its debts. She quoted the Country Credit Ratings, according to which "one may not like the system, but it gives the government a free hand in imposing austerity programs."[14]

The analysis of the economic standoff on the eve of the political changes in Moscow is crucial to an understanding of the controversial Romanian rapprochment to the Soviet Union—a desperate step Ceaușescu decided to make in 1984 in an attempt to escape from Western influence. Just after the second wave of "structural reforms" had started, the British ambassador to Bucharest reported that a major factor in Ceaușescu's desire to eliminate Romania's debts quickly, was "a deep dislike of the IMF's interference in Romanian economic policy." Ceaușescu was "probably finding the strings attached to the IMF's stand-by arrangement more restricting than he had imagined," and finding it "hard to tolerate the structural adjustment, which is currently undertaken unwillingly and as slowly as possible by Romania." Then a telling remark followed about the possible "popular discontent" over the worsening supply situation, wage-levels, and social services. According to the report, "many of the ingredients for popular unrest" existed, and "isolated outbursts, protests and strikes" might have occurred. Nevertheless, the regime remained "in firm control" of the "docile" Romanian population, thanks partly to the arbitrary brutal treatment of dissenters by the "all-pervasive secret police." Disturbances were "unlikely to be allowed to reach a level where they would pose any threat to Ceaușescu's position," while Western creditors would be pleased to know that, "for a socialist country," Romania had come "quite a long way down the path of structural adjustment."[15]

The British government had been among those who, since 1981, had been criticizing the "too conciliatory" approach of the IMF to the Romanian debt crisis.[16] Since the primary interest of the Western creditors of Romania was to get the loans they had granted back in due time, they started to voice concern for the internal stability of the country. Public discontent caused by the austerity measures taken by Ceaușescu to comply with the stand-by agreements but never properly explained to the population might have encouraged social turmoil and made the working relations with Bucharest even more conflictual. Thus, keeping Ceaușescu in power despits his poor human rights record has to be regarded as a conscious political move of the Western partners to ensure that Romania would honor its repayments. The comments of the highest British representative in Bucharest were telling of the emergence of a new form of path-dependence in the European (socialist Romania; "embedded neoliberal" Spain of the post-Franco era) and Latin American (Pinochet's Chile; Brazil) semiperipheries: the entanglement of technocratic financial governance and political interests. The British ambassador's remarks also showed the extreme vulnerability of the Ceaușescu regime vis-à-vis the influence of non-political transnational bodies over its own internal affairs.

Around 1984, insiders of Soviet politics, and most probably the Romanian diplomats serving in Moscow too, had already been familiarized with the name of Mikhail Gorbachev, and the Soviet policy making had started to elaborate exit strategies for the empire. Ceaușescu came to the bitter conclusion that the Western "betrayal," and not only the ill-conceived economic policies of his regime, had been responsible for the catastrophic situation of the country. He realized that the West had tactically praised him as long as the hope to open up the Soviet Union with his help could be kept alive. In the oversimplified and outdated global political horizon of Ceaușescu, the West had turned its backs on him because it did not need him anymore. The lack of clemency displayed by the international financial actors led Ceaușescu to a fierce reaction. Repressive population control was tightened within the country, and Romania's financial independence at any costs became a vital interest for the regime. The last IMF office memorandum issued on Romania in November 1989 stated that, after the Romanian government had refused to sign the 1984 standby agreement, Bucharest had broken every working relationship with the Fund and "pursued a policy of repaying all outstanding foreign debt." The Fund acknowledged that the policy was "accelerated in 1988 with early repayments to the IBRD, commercial banks, and the Fund." By March 1989, all foreign debts other than small short-term credits, which at the end of 1985 totalled close to US$7.5 billion, had been fully repaid. According to the IMF, this could only made feasible by a "strong export performance, with goods shifted from the domestic to foreign markets, and severe import compression."[17]

It can be argued that Ceaușescu's Romania fundamentally misinterpreted the nature of the United States' goals in Eastern Europe. According to Anne H. Dannenbaum, the US aimed to enhance East European autonomy from the USSR through the provision of IMF credits, but Washington had no reason to help Romania obtain looser standby conditionality, for such an action would not advance the cause of undermining Soviet influence in Eastern Europe. The American willingness to support Romania within the Fund declined in the 1980s, as Romania's human rights violations became more egregious.[18] The program of cultural liquidation and social disintegration that Ceaușescu had been implementing against the 1.7 million Hungarians living in Transylvania, who constituted almost 8 percent of the population of Romania, increased internal resistance and provoked international protest. In Romania, the Transylvanian question became transformed from a political matter to a cardinal state-security problem, while the issue of Hungarian refugees received the most international publicity.[19] In May 1985, the US ambassador to Romania, David Funderburk, resigned from his post to protest the violation of human rights in the country, as well as his own government's failure to place sufficient pressure on the Ceaușescu regime to improve its human rights record.[20] After the changes had occurred at the Kremlin, the shift of attention from internal stability toward the human rights record in the West and the mobilization of the Hungarian diaspora on the subject of the ethnic Hungarian community in Transílvania undermined Ceaușescu's international credibility. Under growing pressure from advocacy groups like the Hungarian Human Rights Foundation (HHRF), Romania started to be regarded in Washington as a source of embarrassment.[21] The negative consequences of the United States' change of attitude manifested in 1987, when the US Congress passed by a large majority an amendment aimed to suspend the Most Favored Nation status for Romania on the grounds of Ceaușescu's repressive human rights policies, and to provide for a review of it every six months.[22] On the public plan, the greatest blow to Ceaușescu was inflicted by Ion Mihai Pacepa, a former vice-director of the foreign intelligence department and personal advisor to Ceaușescu who defected to the United States in 1978. The changing attitude of US foreign policy toward the Ceaușescu regime emerges from a number of recently declassified US intelligence files, one of which is related to Pacepa.[23] The long silence over the fate of Pacepa was broken in December 1985, when he showed up in a US magazine.[24] The political impact of his revelations about the perverted nature of the Romanian communist system was enormous. Shortly before the article was published, the president of the Jamestown Foundation, William M. Geimer, wrote a short message to the director of the CIA, William J. Casey: "Dear Mr. Casey, I thought you might like to see the gallery of an article by Ion Pacepa which will appear in next month's issue of the *Washingtonian*. I'm convinced that when his manuscript is published it will put an end to Romania's reputation of mister-nice-guy." Casey answered after three weeks: "Thanks for sending me the Pacepa article. I found it very interesting and agree that it will be effective in providing a clearer picture of what is going on in Romania. The President has read it and was impressed."[25] It seems unlikely that Pacepa's 1985 path-breaking piece, or his famous book published two years later, could have been realized without the preliminary knowledge and technical help of the US intelligence agencies. The reactivation of Pacepa following the election of Gorbachev was probably intended in Washington as a sort of "last warning" to Ceaușescu. Moreover, the American warning had been sent on the eve of the last, unsuccessful trip that US secretary of state George Schultz made to Bucharest during his East European tour, on 15 December 1985.[26]

In the meanwhile, the US gathered information on the Soviet maneuvering against the Romanian party leadership. A 1986 memorandum for the director of the CIA contained an intelligence assessment of the speculations arising from several Romanian officials that Mikhail Gorbachev was meddling to influence the Ceaușescu succession. The Soviet leader would have "sought to sponsor officials—like ex-defence minister Olteanu, and Ion Iliescu, a once popular youth leader now in disfavor—who might conceivably become a weak post-Ceaușescu leadership." The US intelligence was undecided about the factors behind the spreading rumors. They might have originated either from Romanian party officials who were beginning to think that Gorbachev might be their only hope in ending Ceaușescu's ever-tightening grip and stopping a dynastic succession by his clan, or from Ceaușescu to "cry wolf" in the hope of Western support for his regime and to discredit his potential challangers. The National Security Agency (NSA) Assistant Officer for Europe seemed to lean toward the latter theory. The CIA knew that Romania was again having "cash flow problems" and was "trying to find a way to wheedle an IMF standby loan by May 1986 without accepting new conditionality." According to the intelligence evaluation, the rumors might have reflected "a serious Kremlin effort to either shape events in Romania or, at minimum, to make a gesture in support of healthy pro-Kremlin forces."[27]

Several months later, in September 1986, the CIA assessed the state of the Romanian regime and the party–society relationship. "Romanian society is deeply divided along ethnic, social, and regional lines, and can fall prey to intense nationalist sentiments. The country's unending economic crisis has added to the strains in this society but a direct challenge to Ceaușescu's rule seems unlikely." The apparent lack of oppositional mobilization was explained by the country's historical experiences and the political culture related to them: "Centuries of cruel and exploitive rule have taught Romanians to survive through simple endurance, suspiciousness of outsiders, and avoidance of direct challenge to authority. In the face of current hardships brought about by exploitive and irrational Stalinist economic policies, the population's typical reaction is to 'hunker down' and look for ways to assure personal and family survival through barter, bribery, personal connections, or exploitation of cracks in the system." According the CIA analysts, in the past, Ceaușescu has been able to deflect discontent through a popular nationalist foreign policy, occasional veiled warnings about an alleged Soviet or Hungarian threat, scapegoating of lesser officials, intimidation by the pervasive security apparatus, and having criticism focus on his powerful but unpopular wife. But this was "no longer working": popular grumbling now focused "on Ceaușescu himself," and wishful thinking led to "widespread rumors on his ill-health." CIA analysts pointed out that "the absence of any national institutions independent of the government and the general climate of stoicism and fatalism" made the concept of nationally organized resistance "alien to most Romanians," but conceded that "an in-house coup, though unlikely, could occur if the situation threatened a nationwide revolt."[28]

Gorbachev, Ceaușescu, and the Hungarian Factor

The spectacular failure of the Western liaison in the mid-1980s provides the framework in which to place the pragmatic Romanian rapprochement with the Soviet Union. According to scholarly common sense, Gorbachev and Ceaușescu never got along well. Ceaușescu was the last East European leader to pay his respects to Gorbachev after his election as general secretary, and Gorbachev returned the slight by visiting Romania only after traveling to all other Warsaw Pact states, in May 1987. Ceaușescu only visited Moscow once more during Gorbachev's rule, and that only for one day (5 October 1988), because of his fear of an assassination attempt in the USSR. According to Soviet diplomats working in Bucharest, despite Ceaușescu's attempt at separating ideological divergences from cooperation in the economic field, this visit deepened the distance between the two leaders, and the Romanian final communiqué even failed to mention Gorbachev's remarks on the necessity to reduce the role of the party in the economy.[29]

However, the Bucharest regime was economically pledged and politically weakened by the effects of the debt rescheduling, and badly needed the Soviet support to survive. The Soviet Union feared that the economic collapse in Romania could bring political turmoil which might spread to Soviet-controlled Moldova. This might explain why it seems very unlikely that Gorbachev and his aides, despite their personal dislike of Ceaușescu, could have promoted or even actively supported an intervention aimed at ousting him from power. Georg Herbstritt extensively quotes a confidential report the CPSU sent in December 1984 to the East German leader Erich Honecker about the talks Soviet leaders had with Emil Bobu, secretary of the Romanian Communist Party for organizational matters and a close surrogate of Ceaușescu. On that occasion the Soviet side openly declared that the Soviet economic aid for Romania would be linked to better political behavior on the Romanian side.[30]

According to RFE analysts, after 1985 the Romanian–Soviet bilateral trade grew by a spectacular 47 percent, compared to the mere 7 percent of the other CMEA countries. In 1986–88, the USSR alone accounted for over one-third of all Romanian trade. Interestingly enough, while the Romanian media kept this evolution under complete silence, the Soviet press gave detailed coverage of cooperation in several fields: steel plants, nuclear energy, oil field equipment, rolling stock, shipbuilding and aircraft production. They were all sensitive and expensive sectors, where highly qualified specialists worked side by side for months. According to Soviet data, several thousand Soviet engineers and workers took part in this second wave of economic cooperation. Soviet exports were mostly in the energy sector, and oil had to be paid for in hard currency.[31]

Anatoly S. Chernayev, a senior analyst at the International Department of the Central Committee of the Communist Party of the Soviet Union and Mikhail Gorbachev's foreign policy advisor, captured in his memories a snapshot of a pragmatic reconciliation that can also be regarded—as Peter Siani-Davies does in his history of the 1989 Romanian revolution—as a sign of mutual dependence.[32] According to Chernayev, the East–West relationship had grown so tense that even most of the allies had distanced themselves from the Kremlin's confrontational line. Gorbachev told him once, jokingly, that "it turns out that Ceaușescu and Kim il Sung are now our best friends, everything with them is just fine and we've forgotten our grievances."[33] After March 1985, the new Soviet leader took a pragmatic stance toward his maverick ally. Gorbachev repeatedly voiced his view that the West was using the Romanian leader as a mere irritant against Moscow, a sort of "Trojan horse" within the socialist camp. According to Cernayev, the CPSU general secretary treated the maneuvers of the "Romanian Führer" (as he sometimes called Ceaușescu) with irony and contempt, and did not consider him a factor in real politics.[34]

An insight on the ambiguous relationship between Gorbachev and Ceaușescu is provided by Yosef Govrin, who served as ambassador of Israel to Romania between 1985 and 1989. According to Govrin, as early as February 1986 the Soviet ambassador in Bucharest had told him that the relations between the two countries were at their lowest point ever. Ceaușescu's cult of personality had a negative impact on the country's leadership, and raised growing concern in Moscow. Moreover, the bad economic situation made Romania a negative example of what a communist country looked like in the 1980s. And finally, the Soviet ambassador mentioned Romania's "impolite" behavior at the 1985 Cultural Forum organized in Budapest by the Commission on Security and Cooperation in Europe. The Romanian delegation caused embarassment and distress among Western delegations in its attempt to prevent any participants from raising the minority issue, claiming that it would be interpreted as an unwelcome interference into Romanian internal affairs.[35]

Bilaterial tension rose in 1987 over the long-awaited visit of Mikhail Gorbachev to Romania. Polish scholar Adam Burakowski maintains that until his trip to Bucharest of 25–27 May 1987, Gorbachev had hoped to turn Ceaușescu toward perestroika. During his stay in the Romanian capital, Gorbachev kept on repeating to all his conversation partners: "You have to do perestroika, this is the most important thing for you to do now; let's do it."[36] However, the Romanian leadership gave much importance to the Gorbachev visit as being a merely diplomatic event, and totally erased its inherent political content from the official news stream. Gorbachev was visibly frustrated by the unusually cold welcome, and when he managed to avoid the security guards, he looked for direct contact with the people gathered, and reproched them ("Why are you silent? Don't tell me please everything is all right in your country, because I'm not going to believe it!"). No one dared yet to enter into dialogue with him.[37] Speaking to RCP officials, Gorbachev offered obliquely worded attacks on Romania's harsh mistreatment of ethnic Hungarians and on Ceaușescu's nepotism. The Romanian party officials present in the convention hall also made known their own displeasure with Gorbachev by interrupting his speech with applause on almost twenty occasions, visibly irritating the Soviet leader.

The issue of the Hungarian minority in Transylvania also contributed to sparking tensions between Moscow and Bucharest during Gorbachev's visit. According to the Hungarian Press of Transylvania (HPT), a source of great value for what concerns the minority policies of the late Ceaușescu regime, the local Soviet embassy managed to arrange a short non-official meeting on 27 May between Gorbachev and Károly Király, a former ethnic Hungarian party official who had become a vocal critic of Ceaușescu's assimilationist policy.[38] Király, who had long been placed under strict police monitoring in his hometown, was taken to Bucharest aiport in a car of the Soviet embassy. Király had spent a long time in the USSR as a student, and so spoke fluent Russian. According to HPT, no direct witnesses or translators attended the 15-minute meeting, but high-ranking Romanian officials with access to the Soviet diplomats later confirmed that Király had described the oppression of the Hungarian minority in Transylvania.[39]

Contemporary analysts and scholars tend to agree that the Soviet delegation left Bucharest in late May 1987 with the clear impression that any change in Romania would be impossible unless Ceaușescu disappeared from political life. The newly released files from the Hungarian counterintelligence unit in charge of Romania help us understand how the Soviet Union (and its closest allies as far as Romania was concerned, Poland and Hungary) came to elaborate and implement the task of strenghtening pro-Soviet and/or reform-oriented party officials, so as to be prepared in case of sudden change. Notwithstanding the persistent lack of relevant Romanian sources on the late 1980s, the Hungarian intelligence leaks on Romania's (un)reception of Soviet perestroika represent a valuable source for analysis. Starting from the late 1970s, intelligence information on Romania was gathered in Hungary, but only in 1983 was a "counterintelligence" (defensive) *residentura* set up in Bucharest to better cover the situation on the ground. It must be pointed out that the freely accessible Hungarian state security archives keep no single record that might corroborate the popular notion in Romania that the Hungarian security services might have helped the USSR plot against Ceaușescu before 1989.[40] From the mid-1980s, the Hungarian intelligence stations in the United States and Western Europe began to collect pieces of information regarding the Romanian internal affairs and the deteriorating situation of the Hungarian minority; but only in June 1989 did an order from the Hungarian minister of interior upgrade the Romanian Securitate to the level of "theatening enemy," due to the massive infiltration of undercover Romanian agents among refugee people.[41] This step made possible the creation of a small "offensive" subunit of the Hungarian civil intelligence in charge of operative work in Romania. In the last months of the Ceaușescu regime, Hungarian undercover officers provided logistic and informational support to the local opposition forces, especially among the ethnic Hungarians in Transylvania.[42]

The first Romanian reaction to the election of Gorbachev was recorded by the Hungarian counterintelligence in April 1985. The "veterans" and the "displaced" close to Moscow—presumably the former chief ideologue and diplomat Silviu Brucan and his associates—were becoming increasingly active following the death of Konstantin Chernenko. However, conditions necessary for a turn in the domestic policy had not in the least been met:

> The group of "otherwise thinkers" have not yet emerged, either on a personal or conceptual level. Those who might constitute its core are the currently "tolerated" politicians in the leadership (such as Ilie Verdet, Paul Nicolescu, Dimitru Popescu, Mihály/Mihai Gere), members of the "displaced intelligentsia" (e.g., Maxim Berghianu, chairman of National Plan Office; and Cornel Burtica and János Fazekas, former deputy prime ministers), still living veteran "greats," and their closest disciples, high-ranking but adulating technocrats and party leaders (ministers, first secretaries of county political committees and their deputies, CEOs of industrial centers and corporations) and "repressed military leaders". On the one hand, they are aware that Romania could overcome the deepening economical and political crisis only with the help of the Soviet Union; on the other hand, they are personally fit to radically review the current political line and draw the necessary consequences. An "explosion" due to the frustration of the masses, "spontaneous actions of the people" are still unlikely to happen. ... A "palace coup" (in which even family members might participate) possibly triggering nationwide changes is likely

to take place only in the event of the emergence of a powerful and relatively unanimous "group of reformers."

According to the Hungarian intelligence, there was a feeling in Bucharest that Ceaușescu's unreliable leadership would "fail to resist this challenge on the long run." A self-modernizing Soviet leadership could choose "to simply ignore the Romanian maverick foreign policy, and come to better terms with the West, with China, and possibly with the Arab world from a superpower standpoint." Thus, the Romanian foreign policy would "likely face a serious downgrading, both in the Warsaw Pact and in the West."[43]

The gradual deepening of the Romanian crisis and the increasingly active role of the Hungarian emigration is well reflected in two reports of May 1985. The first informed of a sudden turn in the Romanian–American relations after the US ambassador in Bucharest resigned in protest when the US Congress extended Romania's MFN status despite objections by human rights organizations. On 20 May, a leading personality of the Hungarian emigration in Spain informed his intelligence contact in Hungary that "the Transylvanian organizations operating in the US consider the resignation of the ambassador as a sign that Reagan's Romanian policy has failed, and believe that the situation is fit for launching a major campaign in defense of minority rights."[44]

By autumn 1985, international pressure on the Romanian government had increased, partly due to the advocacy of the Western Hungarian emigration. The president of the Transylvanian World Federation informed his diplomat contact that the activists of the movement had collected reliable data proving that the Romanian government had provided substantial financial and moral support to the anti-communist Romanian emigration for an anti-Hungarian propaganda in Transylvania. István Zolcsák said that the BBC had also been informed, and the news agency would cooperate in airing confidential information during the Gorbachev–Reagan summit scheduled for November.[45] While it was obvious for experts that the United States was preparing to "let go" of Ceaușescu's hand,[46] the mills of grand politics were grinding slowly. The press campaign was launched during Secretary of State George Schultz's East European tour, which included a visit to Romania. During his stay in Bucharest, the emigrant groups criticizing the Ceaușescu regime enjoyed unprecedented media attention in the United States and Western Europe.[47] A summary report for the Hungarian party leadership claimed that Schultz's Bucharest visit took place in a rather tense atmosphere. When Schultz made an innocuous remark, namely that "Washington applaudes Romania's independent decisions in foreign policy as much as it is intrigued by Hungary's relatively unfettered economic policy," Ceaușescu responded furiously and stated that it had been clear to him that the "current Hungarian leadership" aimed in the long run to revise the borders; that even in their propaganda they followed the line adopted by Horthy's Hungary, and he resented the Soviet Union for "tolerating" it all.[48] Hungarian intelligence had it that Schultz deliberately refused to take a stand in the matter, and only requested the Romanian leaders to grant minority rights and, most of all, the right to emigrate. Contemporary experts accounted for the wariness of the US by emphasizing that the Western powers were concerned that if the Romanian leadership were to lose its "remaining independence" it would forge even closer bonds with Moscow. Bucharest also felt the increasing pressure, and took countermeasures. In the autumn of 1985, prior to Schultz's visit, Viktor Meier, correspondent of the *Frankfurter Allgemeine Zeitung* in Vienna, informed his Hungarian contact—a member of the intelligence network—that the local Romanian embassy had been organizing for the correspondents of Western newspapers an informal discussion on the Transylvanian nationality issue. The embassy also wanted to utilize the occasion for propaganda purposes, and to gather information about Hungary.[49] There are very few intelligence documents from 1986 relating to Romania, and these are of little interest for our research. The reason for the lack of materials is hard to identify, but we may venture to say that the scarce information (compared to the number of relevant documents from previous years) may be the result of the retention of existing documents or of a large-scale destruction of sources that took place in the following years. The next year, however, marked a great leap in both the quality and quantity of the available documentation. On 7 January 1987, the Hungarian Ministry of Interior received an enciphered telegram of outstanding importance from Bucharest, which was also the first ever to be passed to Hungarian party leader János Kádár on the issue on Romanian intelligence activity against Hungary: "We have been informed by a social contact from the Central Committee of the Romanian Communist Party of Romania of a resolution that had been made in the CC of the RCP to defame the Hungarian state and party leadership, and especially comrade János Kádár, before the Hungarian people and the entire socialist community." In terms of Hungarian domestic policy, internal tension was to be incited either by direct or indirect means, while internationally Romania aspired to discredit the Hungarians in the Soviet Union, before Gorbachev, emphasizing that Hungary gave grounds to antisocialist forces due to its far-fetched openness to the West. Other charges against Hungary included that nationalism was on the increase and that Hungarians wanted Transylvania first, but later may turn against the

Soviet Union as well. The Hungarian economic model was to be considered merely a Trojan horse in and against the socialist community. All these abominations had been supported by the West. According to Bucharest, "Poland and Hungary are the weak links in the Socialist bloc, and the GDR, Czechoslovakia and Romania are the only loyal Marxist and truly Communist countries." As for operations in Hungary, Romania planned to continue infiltration into important state and party functions, with the aim of collecting information and exerting influence.[50]

The Romanian move came as an answer to what experts and researchers refer to as a dividing line in the Hungarian–Romanian conflict: in November 1986, after years of anticipation, the three-volume *History of Transylvania*, edited by Minister of Culture Béla Köpeczi, was published in Budapest.[51] The extraordinary interest in and demand for the work (within a few months, one hundred thousand copies had been sold of the nearly two-thousand-page opus) were fuelled by the social solidarity with the "Transylvanian cause." Following the afore-cited internal order, in the spring of 1987, the Romanian authorities launched a full-scale propaganda offensive with a view to defending the official Romanian opinion.

Through the documents of the Hungarian intelligence dating back to the end of the 1980s, one may gain a rare insight into the diplomatic warfare of two countries belonging to the same political-military alliance. From 1987 on, the Hungarian–Romanian opposition deepened: the freeze in the bilateral relations (apart from the inconclusive 1988 Arad summit, Hungary refused to have any high-level contact with the Ceaușescu regime), soon turned into a conflict taking place on the international stage, unfolding before the US Congress and the West European governments, within the UN organizations and at the Conference on Security and Cooperation in Europe (CSCE). It was only when Hungary chose to support the Yugoslavian and Canadian proposal on the national minorities at the CSCE in Vienna without prior consultation that participants started to sense a wind of change in the official Hungarian politics. The decision sparked ardent protests from the Romanian, Soviet, and Bulgarian representatives, since they believed that the Hungarians had betrayed the unity of the Socialist bloc.[52]

From 1987 onwards, the public emergence of the conflict between Romania and Hungary became a source of concern in Moscow. The Hungarian archival sources and the post-1989 Romanian eyewitness accounts seem to agree on a single albeit critical issue: the Soviet pessimism over Ceaușescu regarding the minority issue. As a Soviet diplomat explained to his Hungarian colleague in March 1987, Gorbachev found the irrationally harsh Romanian nationality policy even more disturbing than Ceaușescu's uneasiness with the task of implementing reforms, because the first move exposed the Soviet bloc as a whole to Western criticism and further undermined the internal cohesion of the socialist camp.[53]

To win over the international public, the Hungarian diplomacy and state security emphasized Romania's responsibility in the escalation, and an increasing number of their partners expressed their agreement. In May 1987, Karl Stipsicz, the influential editor of the programme *Eastern Studio* on the Austrian state television ORF and a "loyal critic" of the Hungarian People's Republic, presented the Austrian media's stand on the conflict to his Hungarian intelligence contact. He explained that "as for the Hungarian–Romanian conflict over Transylvania, the Austrian media is interested in documenting the changes in the bilateral relations of the two countries. They will basically support the Hungarian position not because of the suppression of the Hungarian ethnicity in Transylvania, but because they have a strong aversion to the Romanian domestic policy."[54] The Romanians were not idle, either: in early May an intelligence report revealed that the Romanian church delegation visiting New York had held a press conference at the UN. The participants claimed that in Romania people had the right to freedom of religion, the state did not interfere with the affairs of the churches, and the presumed atrocities against religious citizens were based on nothing but biased accounts. Chief rabbi Moses Rosen explained that the Romanian Jews were free to practice their religion and any other rights, and were free to emigrate.[55]

The strong lobbying was necessary indeed, as in the spring of 1987 a proposal was once again made in the Congress to withdraw Romania's MFN status that had been granted since 1975.[56] The United States was concerned that Ceaușescu, who had until then been a maverick politician, would again turn to the Soviet Union for support if the West denied it. However, on 26 June, the Congress accepted the proposal of the State Department and decided not to prolong Romania's MFN status. According to Hungarian intelligence reports, the Hungarian lobbyists played a crucial role in the Congress developing a negative stance toward Romania, especially during the preliminary committee hearings where such experts as Juliana Pilon and George Schöpflin perorated.[57] The Hungarian emigration celebrated the Romanian failure as the greatest victory of the previous decades.

Based on the Hungarian intelligence, one may conclude that the Hungarian leadership, faced with grave internal political and economic challenges, had been reluctant to consistently engage in the conflict with Romania, although an increasing number of signs indicated that the passive and long-suffering Hungarian minority had reached their breaking point. Following the November 1987 worker uprising in Brașov, it had become clear that the Hungarian wait-and-see attitude that merely resorted to collecting information was no longer tenable. On 17 November 1987, the Hungarian intelligence station in Bucharest sent an excellent report on the events in Brașov that broke out on the day of the local elections.[58] In spite of the report, the official Hungarian media were forbidden to make mention of the uprising, and they could only give a short announcement three weeks later based on the official Romanian communication. The Hungarian censorship over the Romanian events and the mindless protection of Ceaușescu's dictatorship caused public uproar, since people had got a line on the events via non-official sources as well. This outrage would also greatly contribute to the ultimate erosion of the legitimacy of the Kádár regime.

Ceaușescu and Perestroika: An Entangled Story

This chapter has provided new evidence on the complex network of external contraints that contributed to making the Romanian reception of Gorbachev's perestroika unlikely though not impossible. Ceaușescu's refusal to implement any Moscow-sponsored reforms showed his fundamental misinterpretation of the evolving geopolitical trends of the 1980s. The Romanian leader overestimated the Western willingness to help him consolidate the ailing economy of his country, and underestimated the negative impact of the nationality issue over the global image of his regime. When the external constraints forced Ceaușescu to turn back to his senior ally, Romania's position had dramatically changed in relation to the previous decade. As Mircea Stănescu noted in his study on the Soviet–Romanian relationships in the late 1980s, Ceaușescu and his surrogates had to realize that with the end of the Cold War in sight, Romania had lost its room for maneuver as mediator between the West and the Soviet Union.[59]

Internal factors played an important role, too. Unlike most communist parties in Eastern Europe, internal conflict never took place between "orthodox" and "liberal" factions within the Romanian Communist Party or its predecessor, the Romanian Workers' Party. Those who were dissatisfied with Ceaușescu's personality cult did not attempt to modernize the system, but contrived palace revolutions based on the models of the interwar political machinations that had occurred in Romania, or the military putsch that had overthrown Marshal Antonescu in August 1944. Ceaușescu's potential opponents were marginalized in the 1970s, when the entire Romanian Communist Party apparatus operated under the supervision of Nicolae and Elena Ceaușescu. Opposition activity among Romania's intelligentsia remained confined to a few individual exceptions, and this also prevented the internal reception of perestroika and glasnost.

One has also to consider that distrust of the Soviet Union and of "Russians" had been a deeply shared feeling among the prominent members of Ceaușescu's inner circle since the 1960s. It was no coincidence that it was not until 13 November 1989, just after the fall of the Berlin Wall and on the eve of what would have been the last party congress, that Ceaușescu broke his public silence over the last taboo topic in Soviet–Romanian relations: the territories lost to the USSR after 1944 of Bessarabia and Northern Bukovina. At a meeting of the Political Executive Committee, Ceaușescu started speaking about the necessity to discuss "soon" the territorial issues with the USSR, and reminded his audience that the present situation was a direct consequence of the unlawful Ribbentrop–Molotov pact. Ceaușescu reiterated his views one week later, speaking to the much larger audience of the party congress.

Interestingly enough, this outburst was not apparently followed by any diplomatic move. Ceaușescu came back to the "business as usual" approach on 4 December 1989 in Moscow, when he avoided mentioning territorial issues or historical claims during his last meeting with Gorbachev, and according to the minutes, he focused attention on foreign policy and the future of the Bloc. Ceaușescu considered that every tool should be deployed to preserve the unity of the socialist bloc, and considered the failure of Károly Grósz in Hungary and Marshal Jaruselski in Poland a clear sign that only closer cooperation among socialist countries could avoid a catastrophe. He even urged Gorbachev to take a more active stance, and argued in favor of a congress of communist parties to be held at the beginning of 1990, stimulating the subtly ironic answer of the Soviet leader: "You'll be still alive on January 9th!"[60]

In the second half of the 1980s, Ceaușescu's rule came under attack from both the West and the Soviet Union. The long-lasting involution of the Romanian communist regime was the logical consequence of rational human choices and not the outcome of an external conspiracy, as the national-communist narrative has long suggested. But as long as the extreme personalization of the Ceaușescu regime was coupled with growing paranoia and forcible suppression of internal debate, its brutal showdown in December 1989 became the inevitable outcome of a political suicide.

Stefano Bottoni, PhD in Modern and Contemporary History (University of Bologna, 2005), is Senior Lecturer in History of Eastern Europe at the University of Florence. Between 2009 and 2019, he was senior fellow at the Research Centre for the Humanities of the Hungarian Academy of Sciences. His main fields of interest include the political and social history of Eastern Europe under the socialist regimes. In 2006, he served as expert member of the Romanian Presidential Commission in charge of the historical examination of the past communist regime. He has taken part in several international research projects, including "Schleichwege": Inoffizielle Begegnungen und Kontakte sozialistischer Staatsbürger 1956–1989 (Volkswagen Stiftung, 2007–2008), and Physical Violence in State Socialism (Zentrum für Zeithistorische Forschung, 2012–2014). In 2015, he was a fellow at Imre Kertész Kolleg in Jena. Between 2016 and 2019, he has been a research team member in the HORIZON 2020 winner project Cultural Opposition—Understanding the Cultural Heritage of Dissent in the Former Socialist Countries (COURAGE), coordinated by the Research Centre for the Humanities of the Hungarian Academy of Sciences. His publications include the recent *Long Awaited West: Eastern Europe since 1944* (Indiana University Press, 2017), and *Stalin's Legacy in Romania: The Hungarian Autonomous Region, 1952–1960* (Lexington Books, Harvard Cold War Book Series, 2018), as well as various research articles in peer-reviewed journals.

Notes

1. Verdery, *National Ideology under Socialism*; Tismaneanu, *Stalinism for All Seasons*.
2. See Buga, *Pe muchie de cuțit*.
3. Burakowski, *Dictatura*, 320–25. Even more succint on this issue is the multiauthored biography of Ceaușescu by Betea, Mihai, and Țiu, *Viața lui Ceaușescu*, 142–44.
4. More details in Bottoni, "Unrequited Love?"
5. Marculescu, "Captive Romania," 389.
6. Nelson, "Charisma, Control, and Coercion," 5.
7. Herbstritt, *Entzweite Freunde*, 432–33.
8. Ban, "Neoliberalism in Translation," 184.
9. International Monetary Fund (IMF) Archives, Washington, DC. Executive Board Meeting EBM/81/91, 15 June 1981, 3–29.
10. National Archives (NA), London, Foreign and Commonwealth Office (FCO) 28/4571. Economic assistance to Romania 1981; NA FCO 28/5065. Romania and the International Monetary Fund (IMF): debt rescheduling; NA Treasury 439/35. International Monetary Fund: Romania 1982. Relevant files in the UK National Archives have been declassified until December 31, 1984 at the time when this research has been conducted (September 2016).
11. Statement by Mr. Polak, NA Treasury 439/35. IMF/Romania 81/112.
12. Visit of Martin Williamson to Bucharest 25–29 January 1982, NA Treasury 439/35. British Embassy to Treasury, 1 February 1982.

13. Arhivele Naționale ale României (ANR), Bucharest, fond 2733—Anneli Ute Gabanyi, dosar 546, f. 69. Commerce 1983–1984. IMF requirements.
14. "Romania and the Western Trade: Problems and Perspectives." Romanian SR/20, 31 December 1983, ANR, fond 2733, dosar 546, f. 74.
15. Philip McKearney to FCO, NA, FCO 28/6354. Bucharest Embassy, Foreign Relations Department, 19 January 1984.
16. See this cable with instructions of the British Government to the UK Delegation to the IMF: "Encourage Romanian authorities to implement further structural reforms, so as to improve effectiveness of adjustment measures already taken and to permit more efficient allocation of resources. These steps are necessary to achieve viable economic performance, thereby enabling Romania to meet committments, both drawn and as yet undisbursed, as they fall due. ... Reforms introduced in programme since 1981 were welcome first step but unfortunate that their effectiveness has been reduced by decision to hold domestic prices stable ... Structural decision not to proceed at present with new Fund programme regrettable. Danger of weakening committment to reform process, which could undermine progress of past two years and further threaten viability of economic performance, when continued vigilance of external account is required." FCO to UK Delegation to IMF/IMRD Washington, NA, FCO 28/6534. Romania–IMF 1984. London, 6 September 1984.
17. Correspondence and Memos 1988–1989, Romania: Recent Development, IMF Archives, EURAI Romania, Memorandum for Files. 22 November 1989.
18. Dannenbaum, "International Monetary Fund and Eastern Europe," 108–9.
19. The Hungarian minority issue increasingly jeopardized US–Romania relations during the late Ceaușescu period. See detail in Harrington and Courtney, *Tweaking the Nose*, 501–20.
20. Bradley Graham, "U.S. Envoy Quits, Charges Policy Coddles Romania," *The Washington Post*, 15 May 1985; Funderburk, *Pinstripes and Reds*.
21. On this lobby organization, see Ludanyi, "Hungarian Lobbying Efforts." The archive of the organzation, which represents an outstanding source for the study of ethnic advocacy in the late Cold War period, was digitized in 2015–16 and will soon be put at the disposal of interested scholars.
22. More details in the self-biography of the Republican congressman Frank Wolf, the most active supporter of HHRF activity on human rights in Romania before 1989: Wolf and Morse, *Prisoner of Conscience*, 29–41.
23. The research was conducted in the National Archives (NARA) at College Park, Washington DC in November 2014, on National Estimate Intelligence files declassified and digitized through the CIA Records Search Tool (CREST System).
24. Pacepa, "The Defector's Story."
25. NARA, Record Group 263: Records of the Central Intelligence Agency. Geimer to Casey, 25 November 1985. NARA CIA-MDP8700539R001602350001-1.
26. Burakowski, *Dictatura*, 326.
27. NARA, Record Group 263. Romania: Rumours about Gorbachev's Meddling. Assistant National Intelligence Officer for Europe to the Director of CIA. 8 April 1986. CIA-RDP87R00529R000100060043-1.
28. NARA, Record Group 263. Background Paper. Eastern Europe: State of Societies, 22 September 1986. CIA-RDP86TO1017R000404270001-3.
29. Govrin, *Relațiile*, 118.
30. Herbstritt, *Entzweite Freunde*, 434–37.
31. RFE Situation Report, 29 May 1987. Vlad Socor, "The Soviet Presence in Romanian Industry," 19–23. The original document is stored at the Open Society Archives in Budapest: http://catalog.osaarchivum.org/catalog/osa:42f1e041-1f37-4269-b21d-bf559 1a09352 (last accessed 14 October 2016).

32. Siani-Davies, *The Romanian Revolution*, 48–49.
33. Chernayev, *My Six Years*, 15.
34. Ibid., 62.
35. Govrin, *Relațiile*, 110.
36. Burakowski, *Dictatura*, 333.
37. Ibid., 334.
38. Hungarian Press of Transylvania, Release No. 69/1987 Marosvásárhely (Tîrgu Mureș), Bucharest, 4 June 1987. "Gorbachev Met with a Transylvanian-Hungarian Dissident Leader." http://www.hhrf.org/dokumentumtar/irott/hpt/1987.069.pdf (last accessed 22 October 2016).
39. Hungarian Press of Transylvania/Erdélyi Magyar Hírügynökség, 71/1987. Bucharest, 15 June 1987. "Megerősítést nyert a Gorbacsov és Király Károly közötti bukaresti találkozás ténye." http://www.hhrf.org/dokumentumtar/irott/emh/1987.071.pdf (last accessed 22 October 2016).
40. This notion was put forward after 1989 by Romanian authors linked to the former security services (Radu Tinu, Ion Cristoiu, Alex-Mihai Stoenescu), legitimated in the domestic discourse by mainstream scholars (see Scurtu, *Revoluția română*), then internationally vehiculated by the controversial US-born intelligence analyst Larry L. Watts: Watts, *With Friends Like These*; and idem, *Extorting Peace*. Most of these conspiracy theories have been consistently debunked by professional scholarship. See Siani-Davies, *Romanian Revolution of December 1989*; and Cesereanu, *Decembrie '89*.
41. According to the 1989 yearly report prepared by the Békés county police department, 5,817 Romanian citizens asked for asylum during that year in the respective border sections alone, and approximately one-tenth of applications were rejected due to security concerns. Müller and Takács, *Szigorúan titkos '89*, 188–89.
42. Details in Bottoni, "Zögernde Spione," 9–37.
43. Állambiztonsági Szolgálatok Történeti Levéltára (ÁBTL), Budapest. Fond 1.11.4. T-III/85, 409. doboz, 79–85. BM III/II. Csoportfőnökség (Directory of Counterintelligence). Information on Romania. Bucharest, 19 April 1985.
44. ÁBTL 1.11.4. T-III/85, 409. doboz, 98. The Resignation of US Ambassador David Funderburk. Madrid, 20 May 1985.
45. ÁBTL 1.11.4. T-III/85, 409. doboz, 41. Plans of the Transylvanian World Federation. São Paulo, 21 October 1985.
46. ÁBTL 1.11.4. T-III/85, 409. doboz, 8–15. US Congressional Record—Senate. 1 November 1985.
47. ÁBTL 1.11.4. T-III/85, 409. doboz, 17. Declaration of László Hámos, President of the Hungarian Human Rights Foundation. New York, 18 December 1985.
48. ÁBTL 1.11.4. T-III/85, 409. doboz, 3. The US State Secretary's Talks in Bucharest. Budapest, 27 December 1985.
49. ÁBTL 1.11.4. T-III/85, 409. doboz, 48. On the Ethnic Issue in Transylvania. Vienna, 27 September 1985.
50. ÁBTL 1.11.4. T-III/86, 476. doboz, 227. Intelligence Report. Highest Priority. Bucharest, 7 January 1987.
51. See Mevius, "Defending," 569–606.
52. ÁBTL 1.11.4. BX-IV/1987/1. 490. doboz, 34. Reactions to the Hungarian Proposal at the CSCE meeting in Vienna. Belgrade, 2 March 1987.
53. ÁBTL 1.11.4. T-III/87, 476. doboz, 223. From our Chief Officer in Bucharest. 17 March 1987.
54. ÁBTL 1.11.4. BX-IV/1987/1. 490. doboz, 18. The Austrian Media and the Transylvanian Issue. Vienna, 27 March 1987.
55. ÁBTL 1.11.4. BX-IV/1987/1. 490. doboz, 9. The US Activities of the Romanian Clergy Delegates. New York, 5 May 1987.

56. For the escalation of the diplomatic conflict between the United States and Romania, see Kirk and Raceanu, *Romania versus the United States*, 110–204.
57. ÁBTL 1.11.4. T-III/87, 476. doboz, 120. Romania and the MFN Clause. Budapest, 18 June 1987.
58. ÁBTL 1.11.4. T-III/87, 476. doboz, 115. Information on the Brașov Riots. Bucharest, 15 November 1987.
59. Stănescu, "Relațiile româno-sovietice," 24.
60. Betea, "Ultima vizită."

Bibliography

Ban, Cornel. "Neoliberalism in Translation: Economic Ideas and Reforms in Spain and Romania," PhD dissertation, University of Maryland, 2011.

Betea, Lavinia, Florin-Răzvan Mihai, and Ilarion Țiu. "Ultima vizită a lui Nicolae Ceaușescu la Moscova I–II," *Sfera Politicii*, Vol. 142 (2009), 82–88; and *Sfera Politicii*, Vol. 143 (2010), 86–92.

———. *Viața lui Ceaușescu, Vol. 3 — Tiranul*, Târgoviște, 2012.

Bottoni, Stefano. "Unrequited Love? The Romanian Communist Party and the EEC in the 1960s and 1970s," in *Kommunismus und Europa: Vorstellungen und Politik europäischer kommunistischer Parteien im Kalten Krieg*, ed. Francesco Di Palma and Wolfgang Mueller, Paderborn, 2016, 118–36.

———. "Zögernde Spione: Die ungarische Staatssicherheit und Rumänien 1975–1989," *Halbjahresschrift für Südosteuropäische Geschichte, Literatur und Politik*, Vol. 25, No. 1/2 (2013), 9–37.

Buga, Vasile. *Pe muchie de cuțit: Relațiile româno-sovietice 1965–1989*, Bucharest, 2013.

Burakowski, Adam. *Dictatura lui Nicolae Ceaușescu 1965–1989: Geniul Carpaților*, Iași, 2011.

Cesereanu, Ruxandra. *Decembrie '89: Deconstrucția unei revoluții*, Iași, 2009.

Chernayev, S. Anatoly. *My Six Years With Gorbachev*, University Park, PA, 2000.

Dannenbaum, Anne H. "The International Monetary Fund and Eastern Europe: The Politics of Economic Stabilization and Reform," PhD dissertation, Yale University, CT, 1989.

Funderburk, David. *Pinstripes and Reds: An American Ambassador Caught between the State Department and the Romanian Communists, 1981–1985*, Washington, DC, 1987.

Govrin, Yosef. *Relațiile israelo-române la sfârșitul epocii Ceaușescu*, Cluj-Napoca, 2007.

Harrington, Joseph F., and Bruce J. Courtney. *Tweaking the Nose of the Russians: Fifty Years of American–Romanian Relations, 1940–1990*, Boulder, CO, 1991.

Herbstritt, Georg. *Entzweite Freunde: Rumänien, die Securitate und die DDR-Staatssicherheit 1950 bis 1989*, Göttingen, 2016.

Kirk, Roger, and Raceanu, Mircea. *Romania versus the United States: Diplomacy of the Absurd, 1985–1989*, New York, 1994.

Ludanyi, Andrew. "Hungarian Lobbying Efforts for the Human Rights of Minorities in Rumania: The CHRR/HHRF as a Case Study," *Hungarian Studies*, Vol. 6, No. 1 (1990), 77–90.

Marculescu, Corina. "Captive Romania: Police Terror and Ideological Masquerade under Communist Rule," *East European Quarterly*, Vol. 41, No. 4 (2008), 383–406.

Mevius, Martin. "Defending 'Historical and Political Interests': Romanian–Hungarian Historical Disputes and the History of Transylvania," in *Hungary and Romania beyond National Narratives: Comparisons and Entanglements*, ed. Anders E. B. Blomqvist, Constantin Iordachi and Balázs Trencsényi, Bern, 2013.

Müller, Rolf, and Takács, Tibor (eds). *Szigorúan titkos '89: A magyar állambiztonsági szervek munkabeszámolói*, Budapest, 2010.

Nelson, Daniel. "Charisma, Control, and Coercion: The Dilemma of Communist Leadership," *Comparative Politics*, Vol. 27, No. 1 (1984), 1–13.

Pacepa, Ion Mihai. "The Defector's Story," *The Washingtonian*, Vol. 21, No. 3 (December 1985), 168–83.

Scurtu, Ioan. *Revoluția română din decembrie 1989 în context internațional*, Bucharest, 2006.

Siani-Davies, Peter. *The Romanian Revolution of December 1989*, Ithaca, NY, 2005.

Stănescu, Mircea. "Relațiile româno-sovietice de la Masa rotundă poloneză până la căderea comunismului în Europa de Est," in *Sfârșitul regimelor comuniste: Cauze, desfășurare, consecințe*, ed. Cosmin Budeancă and Florentina Olteanu, Cluj-Napoca, 2011.

Tismaneanu, Vladimir. *Stalinism for All Seasons: A Political History of Romanian Communism*, Berkeley, CA, 2003.

Verdery, Katherine. *National Ideology under Socialism: Identity and Cultural Politics in Ceaușescu's Romania*, Berkeley, CA, 1995.

Watts, Larry L. *Extorting Peace: Romania, the Clash within the Warsaw Pact and the End of the Cold War*, Bucharest, 2013.

_____. *With Friends Like These: The Soviet Bloc's Clandestine War against Romania*, Bucharest, 2010.

Wolf, Frank, and Anne Morse. *Prisoner of Conscience: One Man's Crusade for Global Human and Religious Rights*, Grands Rapids, MI, 2011.

Part II

Western Europe

Chapter 8

Parallel Destinies
The Italian Communist Party and Perestroika

Aldo Agosti

When, on 11 March 1985, Mikhail Gorbachev became secretary general of the CPSU, the Italian Communist Party (PCI) was going through a difficult period of transition.[1] It was still unquestionably the strongest communist party of the capitalist world: it claimed 1.6 million members, a figure uncomparable with any other European communist party, and could rely on a still significant electoral support. The spectacular outcome of the European elections in 1984, in which the PCI received 34 percent of the votes (for the first and only time outrunning the DC), had certainly been helped by the emotional wave aroused by the circumstances of its leader's death: Enrico Berlinguer had collapsed during a party meeting, witnessing his unconditional and unselfish devotion to the cause. Yet, the party had already obtained a sound 30 percent in the general elections of the previous year. Moreover, it enjoyed an undisputed international prestige, and had played a major role in starting a dialogue between European social democracies and the communist block. Yet, some alarming signs were emerging. Politically, the PCI was at a stalemate. After the 1979 elections, the strategy of the so-called "historic compromise" (i.e., the attempt to revive Italian democracy's founding coalition, by rallying not only the Socialists but also the Christian Democrats), had seriously worn out, even more so because the international situation had removed any glimmer of hope for a possible communist participation in the government. At the beginning of the 1980s, the PCI lost the central position it had been occupying for some years; it was politically isolated and was losing members.

Notes for this chapter begin on page 198.

As had already happened at the end of the previous decade, it was at first on the ground of international relations that it seemed able to react. The break with the USSR became deeper. The party, with its large majority, had not hesitated to condemn the Soviet invasion of Afghanistan. In December 1981 the enforcement of martial law in Poland led Berlinguer to openly recognize that the "driving force" of the October revolution and the socialist system as a whole was exhausted. The PCI increasingly tended to conceive and to represent itself much more as a part of the multifarious European Left than as a member of the communist political family.

Within the Italian political system, however, the party tried to recover—though with the necessary updating—many features of an identity that had partly faded away. The goal was still the one it had set itself in the mid-1970s: a social and political alternative to capitalism, to be pursued through a series of democratic reforms.

In November 1980, an extraordinary session of the Party Executive rejected any further collaboration with Christian Democracy, and proposed a rather vague "democratic alternative." The party tried to renew and make stronger its bond with the working class. As early as September 1980 it had mobilized all its energies in a harsh conflict between the unions and the FIAT management in Turin, which ended in a serious defeat for the workers. Later on, in 1984, it put all its weight behind defending the *scala mobile* (an index of wages to inflation, agreed in 1975), and went so far as to promote a 1985 referendum aiming to cancel the law reducing its effects. It ended in another honorable defeat, but a defeat anyway.

On the other hand, the PCI strongly opposed the installation of Cruise and Pershing missiles in Italy, and in fact was the most important and effective component of the countrywide pro-peace movement. This did not mean a mere realignment to the positions of the Soviet Union in the style of the 1950s, but helped to corroborate an "internationalist" identity which still appealed to its rank and file. Last but not least, the party strongly stressed its thorough diversity from the current behaviors of the Italian political system and its ruling parties, which were already showing many signs of degeneration and corruption. Nevertheless, the PCI, in its efforts to act as an effective force for change, kept coming up against a wide range of obstacles.

Italian society was shaken by a process of deep and radical change, and the system of ideological and cultural references offered by the PCI was not as attactive as it had been ten years before. With its "border" identity, belonging on one side to the communist movement and on the other practically sharing the values and goals of European social democracy, the PCI finally cumulated the effects of the crisis of both. Its appeal to intelletctuals, which had been considerable in the mid-1970s, had gradually weakened. Marxism, even Gramsci's Marxism, was no longer sufficient to answer all the questions of post-industrial society, nor could its hybridization with other ideological approaches restore a strong identity to the party. After the revival of the 1970s, the membership was again declining, with a rhythm of thirty to forty thousand losses per year. This reflected the structural changes happening in Italian society: the working class, which despite opening to other social strata had always represented the hardcore of the party, was irremediably shrinking. The party influence upon youth was also sharply declining: no more than 3 percent of its members were aged under twenty-five, whereas the number of those over fifty and/or retired was increasing.

Alessandro Natta, who had replaced Berlinguer as the PCI secretary, was an elederly and respected leader who embodied the continuity of the historical Togliattian leadership. He had the merit of supporting a more open discussion within the party and did nothing to brake the irreversible estrangement of the PCI from a communist movement whose unity had become mere appearance. Yet the impression the party was giving outside its ranks was that of an organization too uncertain in its choices, and too slow in adjusting to the tumultuous changes of the international as well as of the domestic situation. In such a context, the change in the CPSU leadership represented an unhoped-for help for getting out of a deadlock.

Among the communist parties still enjoying some influence, the PCI was doubtless the one to bet on the perestroika with the firmest belief. In France, the PCF, after some initial enthusiasm, looked at Gorbacev's reforms with growing mistrust. In Spain, the PCE was mainly concerned with its inner crisis, which had started in the early 1980s, and most of all aimed to define its identity within a new political framework, Izquierda Unida; thus it was not always so interested in what happened in the Soviet Union, with each of its different factions trying to maintain the support of Moscow. The Portuguese Communist Party (PCP), which had always marked its distance from Eurocommunism, had been lukewarm toward perestroika since the beginning, and finally expressed its open support for the anti-Gorbachev coup attempt in Moscow in August 1991.

The PCI, by contrast, had long since taken its distance from "real socialism" of the Soviet brand, whose image, with its increasing features of an illiberal, senescent gerontocracy, had lost any charm, even among its rank and file. However, the USSR was still important as a symbol, and a change in the politics of its leadership could still represent a significant chance for the Italian party. On the one hand, a more flexible approach in their foreign relations would help to stop the "new Cold War," and create the conditions for softening or cancelling the veto opposed to the PCI entering the Italian goverment; on the other, the introduction of economic and political reforms in the Soviet system would prove that the PCI's criticisms of "real socialism" had been well founded. So Gorbachev's nomination as secretary general aroused considerable expectations, and his first moves were followed with the utmost attention, both in foreign and domestic politics.

As to the former, the Italian communists had gradually, since 1968, stopped aligning themselves unconditionally with every single move of Soviet foreign policy, but had not stopped justifying it on most occasions, laying the heaviest responsibilities for the "new Cold War" on the United States and their European allies. No wonder, then, that as soon as it became clear that the deep political and ideological revision of the Soviet leadership concerned first of all international relations, the PCI was ready to support it. It was soon pointed out that Gorbachev's *novoe myslenie*, or "New Thinking" in international affairs, went far beyond the principles of peaceful coexistence between states with different social systems, and implied the idea of "mutual interdependence" (*vsaimosavisimost'*) in order to tackle the big issue of collective security for mankind itself. Every single move through which Gorbachev tried to put his thinking into practice was strongly supported by the PCI: the announcement of a unilateral moratorium on nuclear explosions; the new openings to Europe and China; the detailed plan for the elimination of all nuclear weapons by the year 2000; the new organic proposal forwarded by the Warsaw Pact in order to reduce conventianal weapons in Europe; and the proposal brought to the October 1986 Reykjavik summit in which Moscow fully accepted Reagan's Zero Solution if the USA would abandon the anti-missile umbrella SDI, or at least confine the research to the laboratory. The finally unsuccessful outcome of the Reykjavik summit, however, was not merely presented as a failure due to American stiffness, but as the first step of a still viable route, in which the Soviet Union too "should prove further suppleness and awareness by avoiding unconvincing linkages between the issue of euromissiles and that of strategic arms and SDI."[2] The further steps of Gorbachev's foreign policy—his signature on the Washington agreement suppressing the intermediate missiles; the resumption of new negotiations aiming to reduce both Soviet and American nuclear forces, which would finally result in the START agreement of July 1991; and the desire for a serious reduction of conventional weapons—were all warmly cheered by Italian communists. And even warmer was their approval for the gradual but more and more evident disengagement of the USSR from its support to socialist regimes in Eastern Europe. Even the direct agreement with Kohl about German reunification in 1990 was seen as a realistic and far-sighted measure. In a word, the PCI left the Cold War climate behind considerably earlier than the Cold War itself was actually over.

At the same time, the PCI clearly understood how strict the bond was that linked Soviet foreign policy with the attempt to start economic and politcal reform inside the country: "The shutting of the country in itself, its autarkic impermeableness, are functional to a policy of sharp counter-positions. On the contrary, a radical 'detente' inevitably implies a wide opening of the country to external ideas, and shifts ideological competition itself onto a totally different plan."[3] The tightness of the connection between the two aspects had been clear since the beginnng. Generally speaking, going through the party press—particulary its daily, *L'Unità*, and its weekly, *Rinascita*—one can say that the emphasis was much more on international politics in Gorbachev's first year of Secretariat, while after Spring 1986 domestic politics had the same and sometimes even more stress placed on them.

The first comments of *L'Unità*, the PCI daily, about the nominantion of the new CPSU secretary were those of two authorative journalists, Giuseppe Boffa and Adriano Guerra, who had, at different times, been correspondents from Moscow. Incidentally, another general remark needs to be made here: during the whole period 1985–1990, the analysis of perestroika and its domestic and international consequences was mainly the work of these two journalists: militant journalists, indeed, but both high-end intellectuals and experienced interpreters of Soviet reality. Later, from 1988 on, their analysis was often supported, especially on *Rinascita*, by historians (mostly young Italian researchers, but also important foreign historians),[4] and by "insiders" favorable to Gorbachev's experiment.[5] In any case, there is a clear imbalance between the wide coverage the communist press assured to perestroika and the much more limited attention paid to it by the leading organs of the party.[6] The number of meetings of the latter to discuss the changes occurring in the USSR was small: and they mostly concerned the relations between the two parties, generally before or shortly after the visits of PCI delegations to Moscow.

The first comment of Adriano Guerra to Gorbachev's election stressed that it had been reached "through a hard phase of inner confrontations," and was a new step of "great, maybe even upsetting, significance to life in the USSR": a step that "aimed to break the complex and delicate system of balances which, from 1975 onward, seemed to doom the leadership into immobility."[7] On his hand, Boffa esteemed it was the expression of "a strong thrust to change, a widespread but still hardly articulated wish for renewal in the different fields of economy, habits and political life,"[8] which was felt in various areas of Soviet society.

It was soon clear that the new Soviet secretary too had a special care and consideration for the Italian Communist Party: after Cernenko's funeral, Gorbachev decided that the first European communist leader he would meet would be the PCI secretary, Alessandro Natta. A few days later, Natta extensively reported to the Party Executive about a conversation with Gorbachev that had lasted much longer than planned. He dwelt on the clearly "different style" of behavior of the new secretary, and then resumed his impressions: "There are aspects in the Soviet events that are hard to interpret ... What kind of discussion are they having? What are the relationships in the Political Bureau? In Soviet society? What chance has Gorbachev to win with his 'dynamism'? ... We can expect some changes and some dynamism, but we are aware how complicated the questions of CPSU and USSR are, because of the reasons we know. Trust and cautiousness together, then." [9]

During 1985, the comments of the Italian communist press were constantly inspired to this twofold standard. "The general situation ... is evidently still conditioned by the weight of Brezhnev's heritage which Andropov, notwithstanding its initial dynamism, could not begin upon,"[10] Guerra wrote in April. Better than anybody else, the correspondent of *L'Unità* in Moscow, Giulietto Chiesa, made himself conspicuous for his acuteness in reading every sign, both of discontinuity with the past and of the persistent immobilism or resistance provided by the mechanisms of power.

At the end of January 1986, on the eve of the 27th Congress of the CPSU, a PCI delegation again met again Gorbachev, this time flanked by Zagladin, vice-head of the CPSU international department. The Soviet leader insisted on the opposition he expected from the "international communist movement" regarding the dangers of "space militarization": a question unresolved by the summit between Reagan and Gorbachev in Geneva two months earlier. Natta shared the concern about this danger, but made it clear that "the PCI neither is nor feels to be a part of the international communist movement, which does not exist any longer in the traditional meaning of the definition, and whose refoundation, besides being impossible, would imply serious damages." Gorbachev admitted that on this point there were "different ideas," but confirmed he wished to reinforce the ties with the PCI. A few days later, Natta reported about this conversation in very positive terms to the Party Executive. He said he saw in Gorbachev's attitude "a big attempt of *captatio benevolentiae*," with the purpose of smoothing away the divergences between the two parties, though "from a somehow ptolemaic point of view" that continued to hold the USSR and its party in the centre; but he referred positively to its new openings at the international level, with an increased attention on European social democracies. He also said he had the impression that "there is in Gorbachev—I don't know whether in somebody else beyond him—a search for a new dynamism to impress Soviet society, albeit with a certain amount of cautiousness in order to avoid unleashing uncontrollable processes." The conclusion remained circumspect: "We should not expect immediate changes, nor radical reforms in economic and political structures. We must not take for granted the realized decisive progress and innovations."[11]

The discussion that followed the secretary's introduction expressed a general satisfaction with the outcome of the meeting, but also showed the different nuances that now existed about the loyalty towards the Soviet Union. On the one hand, Armando Cossutta, the last spokesman in the Party Executive of those who had criticized the so-called "snatch" of 1981 and, as he said, always thought that "the potentialities of USSR were soothed but not exhausted," stressed that "the still existing different appraisals should not hinder the cooperation between two big forces such as the CPSU and ourselves ... in the struggle for peace, against 'star wars,' for detente, etc." On the other hand, Giorgio Napolitano, the leader who was closest to European social democracies, warned about giving the party a sense of "a not idyllic discussion": "No way back to the old kind of relationship: it is impossible to assume the previous ideological unity and common engagement, as if an international communist movement of which we are integrated and disciplined members still existed."[12]

The 27th Congress of the CPSU, which opened shortly afterwards, was followed by the PCI with the utmost attention. The comparison with the 20th Congress was often mentioned in its press.[13] An important leader such as Paolo Bufalini (who had been very close to Berlinguer, often accompanying him to the Moscow meetings which had seen the highest peak of tension between the CPSU and the PCI) did not hesitate to assert that the turn impressed by Gorbachev, though "measured and quiet," went deeper than the one realized by Khrushchev, "perhaps just because times are now more than ripe and there is even a serious delay." He appreciated the way the secretary's report had urged to "raise initiative, interest and the widest participation of citizens in the productive process, decision making, and social and economic control." Yet, he significantly pointed out that "the big question of political rights and civil liberties, which have to be granted by a socialist regime,"[14] was still open for the PCI.

In the following months the new Soviet leadership had to cope with the dramatic effects of the catastrophe at the Chernobyl nuclear power station, which finally resulted in accelerating the glasnost that Gorbachev had invoked at the 27th Congress, but probably delayed the impulse toward reforms. The Italian communist press at first commented very cautiously about the initial reticence of the Soviet media[15]: it was clear that reforms met an even stronger opposition than expected, and Chiesa, in Moscow, was always extremely punctual in catching it. "The perestroika ... for which Gorbachev has called party and state upper cadres, finds it diffucult to march forward; on the contrary, it is producing signs of veritable rejection."[16] Chiesa himself, who evidently had access to important sources in the milieus of the CPSU secretary, published on 7 October wide excerpts from Gorbachev's speech of 19 June to the writers, which the *Pravda* had only hastily mentioned. It was a harsh denouncement of the tough resistance the line approved by the 27th Congress was encountering daily in the party apparatus.[17] If any doubt remained, this iniative of its daily proved that the PCI did not mean to hide or minimize the strife in the CPSU, and chose to align itself with the renewers, even if it was aware that the road would not be easy.

A confirmation of this clear-cut choice was given in December 1986, when Sacharov's liberation from confinement received the warmest approval from Giuseppe Boffa, who stressed its general importance as "a sign of an authentic will of renewal, which has now invaded the sphere of politics and, as such, acquired a remarkably symbolic significance, both inside the USSR and beyond its borders."[18] It was a development the PCI had warmly supported since the end of the 27th Congress: if during the first year of the new leadership the impulse to reforms had apparently concerned mostly the economic field, during 1986 the Italian party credited Gorbachev with "the awareness that the push of renewal had to be brought further, and extended to the whole area of relations between power and society."[19] Evidence of this trend was to be found in "the new atmosphere spreading in cultural life of the country," to which the communist press paid particular attention from 1987 onwards, with many surveys and reportages. The issue of political democratization of the country, yet, remained the most burning one. The PCI, maybe with the purpose of not exposing itself in a too direct way, chose to deal with it by giving the floor to a well-known spokesman of the Prague Spring, Ždenek Mlynar. Mlynar had been a close friend of Gorbachev when both were studying at Moscow University, and had been secretary of the Communist Party of Czechoslovakia from 1968 to 1970, until he was expelled after the end of Prague Spring. A founder of Charta 77, he had been removed from its post in the Prague National Museum, and had gone into exile to Austria, where he directed a research project on the crisis of the Soviet-type systems. Between November and December 1986, *Rinascita* published as many as five long articles of his: the central assumption was that the Soviet system was reformable, but that only its democratization would allow it to realize an effective economic reform. On the other hand, one could not expect, in the short term, an overthrow of the one-party system, which could only be effected from inside the party. Only by acknowledging the minority the right to exist was it possible to start "the overcoming of a petrified ideology, which could no longer function as an instrument of knowledge of the Soviet reality today."[20]

Although there were criticisms of this "centralizing vision"[21] of a possible democratic change, the Plenum of the CPSU Central Committee on 27–28 January 1987 was interpreted by the Italian communists as a very important step forward, at least in the direction foretold by Mlynar. "It is a turn wider and deeper than the one Gorbachev had effected at the 27th Congress. Impressive for the frankness of its analysis, the secretary's report left no blind areas," was Giulietto Chiesa's comment.[22] And Boffa echoed him one day later: "The real novelty is that the hard campaign for reforms launched about one year ago is going as far as to touch the essential problems for a desirable and necessary change: those concerning the functioning of the political system." Boffa thought that the most important novelties were the opening to "a real electoral system, namely one where there is a chance to choose from among different candidacies," and "the necessary supremacy of elected assemblies over executive organs and their apparatus, which had become the veritable holders of power."[23]

Achille Occhetto, who was co-ordinator of the PCI Secretariat and would become a few months later vice-secretary, also stressed as new and very important "Gorbachev's steadfast intention to plan the whole reform focusing the issue of the relationship between democracy and socialism, with a rather radical criticisim of the past." Yet, to the question asked by the interviewer ("But can these reform goals lead to what the Italian communists mean when they speak of a full spreading out of political democracy in actual society?"), he significantly replied keeping his distance: "Frankly, I think there is a fundamental difference between our concept of political democracy and the way we conceive the relationship between political democracy and society on one hand, and the Soviet vision on the other. Our hypothesis of a socialist society has been and still is very different from the one we can foresee and define in the Soviet Union."[24]

In any case, the PCI attitude towards perestroika remained very positive, and the hope in its success was apparently untouched. On 20 May 1987, *L'Unità* published a long conversation with Gorbachev, interviewed by the daily editor, Gerardo Chiaromonte: the questions and answers, though both expressed in rather diplomatic terms, touched all the grounds on which the new experience was developing, and revealed a substantial identity of views. At this moment, however, the attention of

Italian communists understandably focused on the next general election in their country, which resulted in a clear loss of votes for the PCI. No special attention was then paid to the CPSU Plenum, which took place at the end of June, even though Giulietto Chiesa, from Moscow, deemed it to be a victory of Gorbachev, who had "imposed his road map, breaking the second serious attempt of the conservative groups (after the one effected just before the January Plenum) to stop or delay the famous perestroika."[25] Only some months later, however, at the end of October, did the mood become different. If until then the path of Soviet leadership toward reforms had been presented by the communist press as a path bristling with obstacles, even though every step had been seen as a step forward, now certitudes were becoming less assured.

Chiesa himself, in a booklet annexed to *L'Unità* on the 70th anniversary of the October revolution, whose significant title was *If Gorbachev wins*, did not hide his concerns: the economic reforms announced by the June Plenum had enforced the "socialist self-management," devolving more power to the factory level and enhancing the autonomy of entreprise managers. But the problem of reforming central planning organs had not been solved, and its solution had been delayed. Gorbachev had not yielded on the connection between economic reform and political democratization: no perestroika could be accomplished without democracy, and no real democratization could take place without a deep economic, social and cultural perestroika. Nevertheless, this project was far from being supported by the ruling classes "in their widest meaning of groups and layers occupying the vital points of the party and the administration." Gorbachev and the reformers now needed not a "revolution from above," but a deep upheaval. And this was the most difficult knot to untie. Such an upheaval should be realized through an instrument, the party, "which was partly overwhelmed by the revolution it should lead, and partly itself the obstacle to overcome." Inner resistance was stubborn, at such a point that Chiesa clearly spoke of "a Vendé which is organizing," and stressed that faraway from power strongholds, sunk in the deep streams of history, the wide masses remained hard to be shaken in a short time."[26]

When the Yeltsin affair came on the scene in September–October 1987, and the Moscow party secretary, not without sparing criticisms to Gorbachev's glorification, resigned from the Politburo for the alleged slowness of perestroika, the Italian communist press dealt cautiously with the matter. It was again Ždenek Mlynar's turn to comment on it in very general and somehow abstract terms. He believed that "a real capacity of effecting compromises ... could be showed when a minority spokesman was not compelled to go away, provided he was allowed to remain a member of the political group which, as such, has decided on compromise"; but then he realistically concluded that "it would be ingenuous to assume today that struggles within the Soviet political apparatus develop for the sake of abstract principles and not of the real interests of the different groups, and about their positions of power."[27]

Only a few months later, Adriano Guerra would mention—deeming them to be now obsolete—the "very serious divisions and misunderstandings" that had by then split the front of reformers. A veiled criticism was expressed of Gorbachev's too cautious behavior: in order to contain the conservative attack, he had finally chosen a "struggle on two fronts," against "the adventurism of the impatients and the dogmatism of conservatives."[28]

The 70th anniversary of the October revolution was an occasion for the PCI for rethinking to far-reaching horizons its bond with the communist tradition, and also for carrying on its analysis of recent developments in Soviet policy. The latter aspect was examined in the *L'Unità* booklet mentioned above, while *Rinascita* devoted a whole issue of its cultural supplement *Il Contemporaneo* to a lengthy and deep discussion among historians, journalists, and philosophers.[29]

Meanwhile a new journey of a PCI delegation to Moscow had taken place. Giorgio Napolitano reported about it at the Party Executive meeting of 22 October, making some remarks that look significant even through the essential recapitulation of the minutes. Although making some reservations ("One feels the weight of a historical reconstruction subject to mediations and balancings ... One feels the weight of ideological references that do not correspond to the new thinking of the USSR foreign policy"), and showing awareness of "persistent resistances to perestroika," Napolitano appreciated "the liveliness of a cultural discussion," which he did not hesitate to describe as "sensational."[30]

After 1988, the PCI looked at perestroika with ever-increasing intensity. While the announcement of Soviet withdrawal from Afghanistan cleared up the international horizon, the Nagorno Karabakh crisis for the first time shed full light on the centrifugal forces acting in the USSR republics. This was a source of constant concern for the Italian communist press: Guerra suspected a plan by "Soviet conservatives ... to strand perestroika on the rocks of national questions," but at the same time he rejected as "unacceptable the methods (military interventions) and rhetorics (such as 'the Soviet people') of the past."[31]

L'Unità and *Rinascita* constantly reported the conflict between Gorbachev's reformers and the conservatives, who were clearly rallying around Ligacëv. The strife was openly brought to light when, on 13 March 1988, *Sovietskaja Rossija* published an article by Nina Andreeva, a chemistry lecturer at a Leningrad technological institute. While not attacking perestroika directly, Andreeva complained about a new and unhealthy emphasis on terror and repression in discussion of Soviet history, and warned not to forget the great outcomes of the Stalin years. Her article was published with the knowledge and support of Ligacëv,[32] just when Gorbachev was leaving on a foreign trip. The fact that it went unanswered for three weeks led many people to believe it represented a new official line. However, on 5 April a detailed contribution from Aleksandr Yakovlev, one of Gorbachev's closest associates, rebutted point by point this "anti-perestroika manifesto," and convinced a majority of the Politburo to align itself. The Italian communist press apparently considered the episode as a victory for Gorbachev. But Guerra warned that the battle had only just begun, and that the supporters of perestroika as a "revolution" (it was probably the first time that he used that term) had to reckon not only with an underhand resistance inside the party, but with the risks of an economic situation that had not improved, and a number of social forces hostile to change. What he found astonishing was that "the discussion had caught fire again with such virulence on issues about which a definite line seemed to have been acquired long ago."[33]

Meanwhile, another PCI delegation had met Gorbachev in Moscow at the end of March, and had been impressed by the speeding up in the revision of his European policy. He had embraced the idea of a "European common home," renounced "the international communist movement" as an actor of change, and shifted stress on the tasks of the whole European Left.[34] But the challenge Gorbachev was facing in domestic affairs, which apparently remained in the background during the meeting, was no less crucial. On the eve of the 19th CPSU Conference, it was again Guerra who clearly exposed in *Rinascita* the stakes in the clash between conservatives and reformers. While the formers aimed for a mere rationalization of the system, the latter could no longer be satisfied with such a result, even if their reluctance to admit pluripartism was understandble: "It is not enough ... to assure democracy inside the party: democratization must regard the whole society, both by modifying the nature and role of the old structures and fostering the rising of new organs ... The task of assuring the development of democracy and promoting the 'socialist rule of law' cannot be delayed to the future."[35]

The 19th Conference (29 June – 2 July 1988) was doubtless a crucial moment in the perestroika, and probably marked the zentith in the hopes of its supporters, parrticularly the Italian communists. The resolutions that were approved traced the profile of an institutionl reform: a new popularly elected People's Congress was to be partly elected through universal suffrage, partly composed of representatives elected by the social organizations. The People's Congress would elect the Supreme Soviet and its president by secret ballot. Although in contradictory terms, the reform enacted the separation of functions between state and party. An institutional mechanism for succession in power was established for the first time, and the permanence in elective duties limited to two consecutives terms. Political democratization, which the PCI had always deemed to be inseparable from economic reforms, moved its first real steps forward, and the country was preparing for an electoral campaign it had never experienced before.

The Italian communist press followed the conference sessions with unprecedented participation, and welcomed enthustiastically what was perceived as an irreversible turn. Even more than the political significance of its resolutions, it stressed the novelty represented by an authentically free discussion. A survey of the *L'Unità* headlines gives the measure of the impact: *Not a rite, a true confrontation*, was on the front of the daily on 30 June; *From now on everybody is freer*, wrote Giulietto Chiesa on 3 July, the day after the end of the conference; while the reportage of another correspondent was titled *Soviet, Constitution, Elections: The delegates discover the pleasure of voting*. The same day the leading article by Renzo Foa, the deputy editor, expressed the party's satisfaction with a finally overflowing glasnost:

> How many decades have we to go back to find a public duel as the one performed from the tribune on Friday by Eltsin and Gorbachev? And voting: with favorable, not favorable, and abstaining? And the reported squabbles between some delegates and Gorbachev himself? ... A long-term revolution is taking shape in several directions, uprooting ancient dogmas and useless certitudes, in a discussion that touched the one-party axiom (it would have been impossible to hear something similar, until yesterday, from the Kremlin tribune), with political confrontations whose meaning goes beyond the USSR borders.[36]

Many questions, of course, remained unanswered and there was still a long way to go.[37] Between July and September, in two successive Plenums of the Central Committee, Gorbachev impressed a resolute acceleration to the turn decided by the 19th Conference. Resistance opposed by the conservative group against reforming apparatus and redistributing functions within the Secretariat pushed him to a strongest; the most dramatic he had been called to cope with up to that moment. The September Plenum knocked out Gromyko, one of the last representatives of Brezhnevism, though he had been the guarantee of the 1985 turn, and ratified Gorbachev's nomination to the presidency of the Supreme Soviet. The role of Gorbachev's main competitor in the new leadership, Ligacëv, was also clearly downsized. These measures, method reservations excepted, were commented on by the PCI press in a realistic way.

Guerra interpreted them as measures "aiming to set in motion again perestroika, which, unlike glasnost, had so far encountered more difficulties than effective results."[38] Antonio Rubbi, at the time one of the most influent leaders of the PCI international department, hoped that—precisely for the sake of glasnost—the Soviet leaders would soon give "a limpid and exhaustive explanation" about their conflict and their choices, but he too was ready to justify them because "it was necessary to give the reformist policy of Soviet society the push and the determination that had so far been missing, thereby braking and hindering [perestroika] by wearying comprises."[39] This was all the more urgent because several emergencies were impending: the food crisis, which could not be resolved without a "revolution in the countryside," an electoral and constitutional reform promoting a true representation of civil society in local administrations, and most of all what Rubbi called "the delicate nationalities problems."[40]

These problems had not ceased to come to the fore throughout the year, both with the conflict between Armenia and Azerbaijan (which had caused casualties in October), and with the situation in the Baltic republics and Belorussia, where the "popular fronts" calling for the autonomy of local nationalities were confronting "internationalist committees" in defense of Russian minorities. The PCI press had never lost sight of the issue, sometimes even mildly criticizing the CPSU leadership actions.[41] Giulietto Chiesa later defined the Nagorno-Karabakh crisis as "the moment of highest hesitation and confusion showed by Gorbachev since his seizure of power."[42] *Perestrojka in the storm of nationalisms* was the title of an article publsihed on 3 December by *Rinascita*, in which Adraiano Guerra showed all his concern. Besides non-Russian nationalisms, Guerra warned not to forget great-Russian nationalism, "with its chauvinst programs and racist slogans." He suspected that—since the battle for perestroika was "far from conclusion"—someone could try to "use one nationalist gust or another in order to stop the new course."

Meanwhile the relations between the PCI and CPSU continued to develop in full syntony. Indeed, a note of Antonio Rubbi of 11 January 1989, written after a journey to Moscow, did express some reservations about "the confusion and uncertainty on the way to follow" that the Soviet party was showing towards European social democracies, while maintaining on the contrary "a strong and prevailing relation with the communist parties, even the smallest and most insignificant ones." On the other hand, Rubbi reported the opinion of Anatolij Cernjaev, one of Gorbachev's closest associates in the international department of the party. Cernjaev had expressed the Soviet gratitude to the PCI for having voiced, ten years ahead of time, "ideas, opinions, and criticisms which had been fully confirmed by facts," and for the unconditional support for reforms in the USSR. As Silvio Pons has remarked, "the Soviet leader stressed the international sense and mission of perestroika as opposed to its serious domestic difficulties: a stress bound to find an attentive hearing among Italian communists."[43]

It was in such a climate that Gorbachev and the newly elected PCI secretary met for the first time in Moscow on 28 February 1989. Occhetto reported at the Party Executive a few days later, in very appreciative terms, "five hours of a very free political discussion, that had confirmed the convergence of two reformist experiences: perestroika on the one hand and the PCI new course on the other." Gorbachev had declared that "the most difficult and dangerous moment for perestroika" would impend when "the conflict bursts out with millions of small and middle apparatchiks." He had also listened to Occhetto's exposition about the PCI new course "with authentic political interest for the true intertwining between a strong reformism, our concept of the state and the purpose of reforming it, an original road to socialism, and an integral democratization." Occhetto pointed out he had asked for no *imprimatur*, but remarked that it was interesting "to shed light on and stress the coincidence of political lines, and the appreciation showed for the policy of a communist party such ours."[44]

Since 1989, faced with the speeding up of a controlled evolution towards political pluralism in East European countries that both Occhetto and Gorbachev had hoped for, the Italian communist press focused its attention mainly on this issue. On the other hand, the PCI was obviously concentrating on the question of its inner transformation, which had been started at its 18th Congress. The new statute did not contain references to socialism, and even less to workers' internationalism, and the principle of democratic centralism had disappeared. The inner divergences, which would lead a year later to the party split, remained under the surface, but did already exist. Nevertheless, perestroika still occupied an important place on its horizons. The multiplying difficulties originated by the centrifugal forces and the persistent tensions between nationalities raised increasing concern, as did — even more so — the economic situation. *Rinascita* voiced the latter in an article by a British scholar, Julian Cooper, who spoke of a vicious circle between the progress of reforms and the worsening goods distribution. Cooper's advice was peremptory: "The leadeship must be aware that any loosening of the reformist tension as a consequence of the unavoidable difficulties of transition could mean the death not only of the economic reform, but of the whole attempt of restructuring the building of Soviet socialism."[45]

The elections of the People's Congress, held on 26 March, marked a break and a turning point in Soviet political life. In many constituencies where different candidates competed, particularly in Moscow and Leningrad, those supported by the CPSU were defeated. The Italian communist press welcomed this result as a sign of a promising evolution. It was, for *L'Unità*, "a political earthquake," a "historical vote" canceling "the myth according to which Soviet people would still need a 'democratic apprenticeship.'" It was now clear "that change was the goal not only of a scant group of intellectuals, entrenched around the reform-minded leaders of the party, but was demanded by the whole people."[46]

The enthusiasm of *L'Unità* correspondents were shared without hesitation by one of the major party leaders, at the time head of the international department, Giorgio Napolitano, who spoke of "a new democratic beginning, not only from above, but from below," and interpreted the electoral outcome as an unambiguous message: "A reform of the political system becomes more than ever a priority, and can rely on a wide consensus, on a popular demand broader and stronger than anyone could foresee."[47]

After the March elections, and the hopes they raised, the attention of the press concentrated on another issue, maybe the hardest and most complicated one: the relation between perestroika and the countries of the socialist camp. The PCI unconditionally appreciated Gorbachev's renouncement to any interference in the changes that had begun in most East European countries. On the other hand, its detachment from historical communism was accelerated by the ruthless repression of student protests unleashed by the Chinese regime in Tiananmen Square. On 4 June, Occhetto sent a message to the Chinese leaders, expressing the indignation and harshest condemnation of Italian communists. He stated that "nothing common exists between us and those who make themselves responsible for the kind of crimes occurring in China," and confirmed that "for the PCI the ends of socialism can never be separated from the values of democracy and freedom."[48]

In the following months, the PCI welcomed the so-called "velvet revolutions" in Eastern Europe, still hoping that the democratic process would not completely erase the ideals of socialism and allow to conciliate them with full civil rights and liberties. After the collapse of the Berlin Wall had sanctioned the historical defeat of communism in Europe, a successful outcome of the self-reform of the socialist system in the USSR was probably the only existing chance of keeping the PCI at least partially linked with its ideal roots. This was the context of Gorbachev's first visit to Italy, which took place a few weeks later. The prestige he enjoyed in the country was still high, as witnessed by the homage paid to him by another prestigious personage: Nilde Iotti, former partner of Togliatti and president of the Chamber of Deputies.[49] The meeting between Gorbachev and Occhetto took place on 30 November, two weeks after the "turn" the PCI secretary had announced: the PCI would be transformed into a progressive left-wing party, leaving behind communist tradition even by dropping its own name.

The Party Executive of 14 November had been introduced by a secretary's report revealing the dramatic moment the party was facing. It was time to become aware, Occhetto said, that what had happened in Berlin was "the catalyst, both upsetting and symbolic," of a process that had "crumbled a world to pieces" and sanctioned "the overcoming of socialism as an ideology," while asserting the priority of democratization and of world governance of global issues. One had to face an incontrovertible fact: "The historical process we come from, which has its political definition in the October Leninist choice, has to reckon today with an upheaval presenting all the features of a historical crisis."[50] After a long and passionate debate, the report had been approved by a large majoirty, but the tension remained high in the party in view of the next Congress, the 19th, which was called on 7 March 1990 and where opposite motions would confront each other.

Therefore, the conversation between the two secretaries coincided with a delicate moment. Reporting to the press, Occhetto wanted to stress that Gorbachev had confirmed "his very warm and strong appreciation" of the historical role played by the PCI, "with its renovating policy at the national and international level." He added that he had been able "to notice a deep trust, that is that Gorbachev esteems we are acting in the best way."[51] So the meeting came to take a twofold meaning: "a legitimization of Occhetto's turn in the conflict now dividing the party; and most of all its association with a process of radical reform of communism, the leadeship of which was in Gorbachev's hands."[52]

Yet, the course of political reforms in the USSR was following an uncertain and contradictory path, and the opinion of Italian communists was beginning to show some signs of skepticism. During the first months of 1990, the comments of *Rinascita*, which meanwhile had changed its format and partly its editorial board, seemed to reproduce a well-known cliché, alternating a denounciation of difficulties (particularly about the restlessness of the Union republics and the economic crisis)[53] with a renewed hope in reformist initiatives. The abolition of the CPSU political monopoly established by Article 6 of the Constitution—sanctioned by the Plenum of 6–9 February—even spoke of "February revolution."[54] But in the following weeks trust began to crack. Perestroika, up to then conceived as a unitary phenomenon, was becoming too complex and contradictory to be taken in at a glance. The desired opening to "pluralism within a one-party system," considered unavoidable for some time, was bringing unexpected protagonists to the fore: not only the ones who had long since been perceived of as dangerous, such as the tendencies of great-Russian nationalism embodied by the Pamjat movement,[55] but also—among forces favorable to change—tendencies not easy to classify,[56] such as those represented in the different wings of the "Democratic Platform."[57]

The new CPSU Congress, the 28th, was now approaching: it should complete a contrasted path, rewarded in March with the law on land and the one on property, while Gorbachev had been elected president for five years. Even the most expert PCI "sovietologists" tried hard to decipher the geography of different tendencies, and were very cautious in making foresights. On the whole, their sympathy still went to Gorbachev, deemed to be the most trustable guarantee to accomplish the reforms he had started. Eltsin was sometimes regarded with suspicion, "for the ambiguity of his populism veined of references to the national rebirth of Russia."[58] But a prudence often bordering on skepticism was now embraced, even by those who—like Adriano Guerra and Giuseppe Boffa, for biographic and generational reasons—had grown up with the idea of the Soviet Union as a model, even though imperfect, of socialist society and had supported perestroika with genuine conviction. An even more disenchanted attitude belonged to a new and totally "lay" generation of non-militant scholars, though close to the communist area, such as Silvio Pons, Fabio Bettanin, Maria Ferretti, and Sergio Bertolissi. In a booklet distributed with *L'Unità* a few days before the 28th Congress, Pons believed that "the prospect of a clash and a split [was] very likely."[59] Guerra too did not exclude it, but remarked that although "the CPSU was at the same time the promoter and the designed victim of the change ... the chance of relaunching or stopping perestroika still remained in its hands."[60]

The outcome of the Congress apparently left the way open to different solutions; and at first, the prevailing idea among Italian communists was that Gorbachev had taken adavantage of its conclusions. Moreover, Giulietto Chiesa had no doubts that it was for him "a victory, perhaps the most impressive and determinant of the whole five years of perestroika," since it had "reached most of its purposes, if not all of them," forcing Ligacëv to abandon the camp and placing all his most convinced supporters in the presidency or in the government."[61] With some more prudence, Boffa esteemed that "Gorbachev had not made concessions on any essential point. On the contrary, he has confirmed and strengthened his theories with coherence and determination."[62] In any case, both the analysts were aware that the Soviet leadership was facing a crucial passage, whose outcome could not be taken for granted. "A phase is now opening which—it is not difficult to foresee—will be highly dramatic at the political, social and national level. It would be ingenuous to think that it could be overcome without paying a hard price in suffering and victims," Chiesa wrote. And Boffa echoed him, voicing—prophetically— even more concern: "The bet is very serious and represents the essential dilemma of all Soviet policy: either a rebirth of the country on new foundations, or the disintegration of a great power on which depends the balance of global relations": in other words, "the alternative [is] between a better world and the unleashing of egoisms for which we all would pay an exceptionally high price."

Altogether, however, the great hopes in perestroika were somewhat tarnished, and the almost unconditional trust set in Gorbachev began to be tempered by some doubts. On 19 October 1990, the USSR Supreme Soviet approved, after six weeks of high tensions, his plan of economic reform. In analysing this delicate passage on the PCI weekly, Maria Ferretti leaked out several reservations about the "tacticism" that had inspired Gorbachev's action, and took a substantially equidistant position when describing the contrast that had developed between party, government and "democratic" or "Left opposition," as she qualified the one led by Eltsin and the mayors of Moscow and Leningrad.[63]

Indeed, the PCI attention was now entirely focused on the very lively internal debate preceding the congress called for February 1991—a debate in which an increasing distance could be seen between a majority ready to relinquish the communist tradition by changing the name of the party itself, and the minority aiming for its "refoundation."

The last meeting of Occhetto and Gorbachev as secretaries of their respective parties took place in this context. On 15 November, Occhetto again explained to his interlocutor the sense of his project, in terms intending not to hurt too much the susceptibility of those who, in his party, were feeling the dropping of communist identity as a danger: "We need a new Left, a new Left culture. We want to go beyond both communist and social democratic traditions. We don't propose to pass from one to the other."[64] Gorbachev expressed his full consent: "Both we and you are following similar ways, though within complete autonomy and responsability of each part."[65] On 21 November, Occhetto reported this opinion to the foreign affairs commission of his party: "Actually, he thinks that if we succeed in going beyond the actual, difficult transitional phase, we will accomplish a historic venture that will revitalize the idea of an authentic democratic socialism."[66]

At the end of 1990, with a peculiar coincidence of destinies, the PCI and perestroika were both approaching the final stretch of their parallel courses—the former: softer and quicker; the latter: rougher and more dramatically. Nearly thirty years later, it is quite evident that such a hope was a deception.

Aldo Agosti is honorary professor of Contemporary History at Turin University, Italy, where he taught from 1973 to 2008. He is author of several books, mainly concerning the history of the socialist and communist movements, both Italian and international. Among his works are: *La Terza Internazionale: Storia documentaria*, Rome, Editori Riuniti, 3 vols, 1974–1979; *Togliatti*, Turin, UTET, 1996, 2nd edition 2003 (English translation IB Tauris, London, 2008); *Bandiere rosse: Un profilo storico dei comunismi europei*, Rome, Editori Riuniti, 1999; *Storia del PCI*, Rome and Bari, Laterza, 2000; *Il partito provvisorio: Storia del Psiup nel lungo Sessantotto italiano*, Roma and Bari, Laterza, 2013. He has edited *Enciclopedia della sinistra europea*, Rome, Editori Riuniti, 2000. Several of his works have been translated into English, German, French, Spanish, Portuguese, Japanese, and Hungarian. He is co-editor of *Passato e Presente*, one of the main Italian journals of Contemporary History.

Notes

1. The best general survey of Italian political and social history of the 1980s in English is Paul Ginsborg's, *Italy and its discontents 1980-2001: Family, Civil Society, State*, London, 2001. See also eds E. Jones and G. Pasquino, *Oxford Handbook of Italian Politics*, Oxford, 2015, esp. parts III and IV. An accurate investigation of the history of PCI in the decade 1980–1990 is still missing, except for its final phase: David Kertzer, *Politics and Symbols: The Italian Communist Party and the Fall of Communism*, New Haven and London, 1998; Guido Liguori, *La morte del PCI*, Rome, 2009. Its international aspects are discussed in: Silvio Pons, *Berlinguer e la fine del comunismo*, Turin, 2006 and Michele Di Donato, *I comunisti e la sinistra europea. Il PCI e i rapporti con le socialdemocrazie (1964-1984)*, Rome, 2015.
2. Giorgio Napolitano, "Dopo Reykjavik non si può solo attendere," *Rinascita*, 20 December 1986.
3. This was the opinion of Giulietto Chiesa, "Irrompe la seconda rivoluzione," in *Se vince Gorbacëv*, 73–74, but the same appraisals may be found in all the Italian communist press since summer 1985.
4. Notably, Stephen F. Cohen, Robert Daniels, Alexander Rabynowich, and Julian Cooper.
5. The most constant presence was that of Roy Medvedev, the dissident historian who had published a history of Stalinism translated into Italian, and who in 1989 was elected to the People's Congress of Deputies.
6. "We do not so far have a party seat where we can discuss in-depth Gorbachev's policy—so remarked Giorgio Napolitano, one of the PCI leaders more sensible to international questions. So we have not really discussed the questions of USSR reforms or the reform of socialism, which are strictly intertwinned with the ones of a new system

of international relations": Verbale, 22 October 1987, Fondazione Istituto Gramsci, Archivio del Partito Comunista (from now on FIG, APC), Direzione.
7. Adriano Guerra, "Attesa nel mondo: che cosa c'è dietro il suo stile," *L'Unità*, 12 March 1985.
8. Giuseppe Boffa, "Un'altra generazione con antichi problemi," *L'Unità*, 12 March 1985.
9. Verbale della Direzione del 20 marzo 1985, FIG, APC.
10. Guerra, "Nel giardino di Gorbacëv," *Rinascita*, 13 April 1985.
11. Verbale della Direzione, FIG, APC, 4 February 1986.
12. Ibid.
13. Giuseppe Chiarante, "Il congresso di Krusciov e quello di Gorbacëv," *Rinascita*, 8 February 1986.
14. Paolo Bufalini, "Quella famosa 'spinta propulsiva,'" *L'Unità*, 27 February 1986.
15. Chiarante, "Popoli e governi dopo Chernobyl," *Rinascita*, 17 May 1986; Carlo Bernardini, "Non si può minimizzare Chernobyl," ibid.; Chiesa, "Il domani nucleare dell'Unione Sovietica," *Rinascita*, 2 August 1986.
16. Chiesa, "Vogliono bloccare il cambiamento," *L'Unità*, 24 July 1986.
17. Chiesa, "Trapela discorso segreto di Gorbacëv. 'I nemici del nostro rinnovamento,'" *L'Unità*, 7 October 1986.
18. Boffa, "Gli 'strappi' di Gorbacëv," *L'Unità*, 20 December 1986.
19. Guerra, "Il fronte rinnovatore di Michail Gorbacëv," *Rinascita*, 8 March 1986.
20. Ždenek Mlynar, "L'ostacolo del partito-Stato," *Rinascita*, 22 November 1986.
21. Fabio Bettanin, "I limiti della rivoluzione dall'alto," *Rinascita*, 20 December 1986.
22. Chiesa, "Più avanzano i cambiamenti, più sorgono le resistenze," *L'Unità*, 28 January 1987.
23. Boffa, "Una sfida di lunga lena," *L'Unità*, 29 January 1987.
24. Achille Occhetto, "La novità che mi colpì," *L'Unità*, 28 January 1987.
25. Chiesa, "Gorbacëv rilancia le riforme e sfida i conservatori," *L'Unità*, 26 June 1987.
26. Chiesa, "Irrompe la seconda rivoluzione," *Se vince Gorbacëv*, cit., 77.
27. Mlynar, "Mosca dopo Eltsin," *Rinascita*, 21 November 1987.
28. Guerra, "Il duello di Mosca," *Rinascita*, 7 May 1988.
29. "L'Ottobre di Gorbacëv," *Rinascita*, 7 November 1987, with fourteen contributions by Italian and foreign experts.
30. Verbale della Direzione, FIG, APC, 22 October 1987.
31. Chiesa, "Protesta degli armeni in URSS," *L'Unità*, 24 February 1988; Guerra, "La perestroika alla prova delle nazionalità," *Rinascita*, 12 March 1988; Guerra, "Gorbacëv e il protagonismo delle nazioni sovietiche," *Rinascita*, 26 March 1988.
32. Chiesa, "Storia segreta del manifesto anti-Gorbacëv," *L'Unità*, 23 May 1988. The journalist was able to compare the first version of Andreeva's writing with the article published in the journal: it was a rougher and more aggressive defense of Stalinism. According to Chiesa, Ligacëv and his associates had edulcorated it in order to utilize it in a subtler attack against perestroika.
33. Guerra, "Il duello di Mosca," cit.
34. Silvio Pons, "L'invenzione del 'post-comunismo': Gorbacëv e il Partito comunista italiano," *Ricerche di storia politica*, No. 1 (2008), 28–29.
35. Guerra, "Le chiavi della perestrojka," *Rinascita*, 25 June 1988.
36. Renzo Foa, "Finita un'idea e una pratica di socialismo," *L'Unità*, 3 July 1988.
37. This was remarked with different nuances by Guerra, "Mosca. La svolta," *Rinascita*, 9 July 1988, and Mlynar, "Ma l'URSS come cambierà?", *Rinascita*, 23 July 1988.
38. Guerra, "E Gorbacëv rilancia," *Rinascita*, 15 October 1988.
39. Antonio Rubbi, "I tre ostacoli della perestrojka," *Rinascita*, 15 October 1988.
40. Ibid.

41. "Perestroika raised demands that the leadership was not able to satisfy, and probably not fully understand. Perestroika split forces that until a short time ago looked firmly united under the banner of fighting corruption in the Soviet republic." Bettanin, "Il groviglio armeno," *Rinascita*, 8 October 1988.
42. Chiesa and Medvedev, *La rivoluzione di Gorbacëv*, 273–74.
43. Pons, "L'invenzione del 'post-comunismo,'" 31–32.
44. Ibid.
45. Julian Cooper, "La prova più dura per Gorbacëv," *Rinascita*, 11 March 1989.
46. Sergio Sergi, "Valanga di voti per Boris Eltsin: Un terremoto politico scuote l'URSS," *L'Unità*, 28 March 1989; Chiesa, "Il sapore della democrazia," ibid.
47. Napolitano, "In URSS un nuovo inizio democratico," *L'Unità*, 29 March 1989. Giuseppe Vacca likewise observed that "the image of passiveness and 'conservatism' of Soviet society had been downsized," *Rinascita*, 8 April 1989.
48. Documenti politici del PCI dal XVIII al XIX Congresso, Rome, 1990, 97.
49. "A man who puts in question the structure of his country and therefore the alliance system pivoting upon it; who is developing, in these hard but exalting years, a policy compelling everyone not only to overcome preconceived narrow mindedness and distrust, but also to wonder about the possible world and peoples' destiny." Nilde Iotti, "Profezie di tempi felici," *L'Unità*, 2 December 1989.
50. The report was published in *L'Unità*, 15 November 1989, under the heading *Un nuovo inizio davanti a noi*.
51. Fabrizio Rondolino, "Un abbraccio, poi il lungo colloquio," *L'Unità*, 1 December 1989.
52. Pons, "L'invenzione del 'post-comunismo,'" 34.
53. On 11 February, *Rinascita* published "La notte della perestrojka" (The night of perestroika), an article by Victor Gaiduk, a Russian Italianist who occasionally wrote in the weekly. The text opened with an ominous sentence: "The walls demolished by perestroika are crumbling down on Gorbachev's head."
54. Guerra, "E Gorbacëv cambia tutto," *Rinascita*, 18 February 1990.
55. Guerra, "Voglia di zar, il sogno revanscista del ritorno della grande Russia di Pamjat," *Rinascita*, 3 June 1989.
56. It was not uncommon, however, for the Italian communist press to use the terms "right" and "left" in order to characterize respectively the positions of those more reluctant to accept the dismantling of the Soviet party-state and those more favorable to it. So Ligacev became the spokesman of the Right, Eltsin of the Left, and Gorbachev was identified with the Center.
57. Guerra, "Enigmi di Mosca. Il successo dei radicali mette in difficoltà Gorbacev: Interrogativi sui reali rapporti di forza," *Rinascita*, 1 April 1990.
58. Maria Ferretti, "Laboratorio Russia," *Rinascita*, 20 May 1990.
59. Pons, "Il PCUS senza monopolio," in *Vita o fine della perestrojka*, Rome, 1990, 17.
60. Guerra, "Le scelte più difficili," *Rinascita*, 8 July 1990.
61. Chiesa, "Gorbacëv: due anni di tempo per vincere la sfida del consenso," *L'Unità*, 15 July 1990.
62. Boffa, "Quel che ho visto a Mosca," *L'Unità*, 19 July 1990.
63. Ferretti, "Gorbacëv naviga a vista," *Rinascita*, 4 November 1990.
64. Quoted in Pons, "L'invenzione del 'post-comunismo,'" 35.
65. Nota di Giuseppe Boffa su incontro con Gorbacev, FIG, APC, 15 November 1990.
66. Commissione Esteri del CC. 1990, mf. 9012, FIG, APC.

Bibliography

Boffa, Giuseppe. *Dall'URSS alla Russia: Storia di una crisi non finita (1964–1994)*, Rome, 1995.
_____. *Memorie dal comunismo*, Florence, 1998.
Chiesa, Giulietto, and Roy Medvedev. *L'Urss che cambia*, Rome, 1987.
Chiesa, Giulietto. *Se vince Gorbaciov: Storia, immagini documenti riflessioni nel 70° della rivoluzione d'ottobre*, Rome, 1987.
_____. *La rivoluzione di Gorbacëv: Cronaca della perestrojka*, Milan, 1990.
Di Donato, Michele. *I comunisti e la sinistra europea: Il PCI e i rapporti con le socialdemocrazie (1964–1984)*, Rome, 2015.
Ginsborg, Paul. *Italy and its Discontents 1980–2001: Family, Civil Society, State*, New York, 2006.
Guerra, Adriano (ed.). *L'Ottantanove di Gorbaciov*, Rome, 1989.
_____. *URSS. Perché è crollata: Analisi sulla fine di un impero*, Rome, 2001.
Jones, Eric, and Gianfranco Pasquino (eds). *Oxford Handbook of Italian Politics*, Oxford, 2015.
Kertzer, David. *Politics and Symbols: The Italian Communist Party and the Fall of Communism*, New Haven, CT, 1998.
Liguori, Guido. *La morte del PCI*, Rome, 2009.
Pons, Silvio. *Berlinguer e la fine del comunismo*, Turin, 2006.
_____. "L'invenzione del 'post-comunismo': Gorbacëv e il Partito comunista italiano," *Ricerche di storia politica*, 2008, n.1.
Ricchini, Carlo, Eugenio Manca, Luisa Melograni, and Sergio Sergi (eds). *Se vince Gorbacëv: Storia, immagini, documenti, riflessioni nel 70° della rivoluzione d'Ottobre*, Rome, 1987.
Romano, Sergio, *La Russia in bilico*, Bologna, 1989.
Shore, Chris. *Italian Communism: The Escape from Leninism. An Anthropological Perspective*, London, 1990.

Chapter 9

"I Felt as If I Were Faced with a French Honecker"
The French Communist Party Confronted with a World Falling Apart (1985–1991)

Dominique Andolfatto

At the end of the 1980s, Mikhail Gorbachev met Georges Marchais,[1] the general secretary of the PCF (Parti communiste français, i.e., French Communist Party), leader of one of the most important Western communist parties. After the meeting with Marchais, Andrei Gratchev, Gorbachev's political advisor, remarked: "I felt as if I were faced with a French Honecker. He didn't listen to what we told him. The new direction taken by Moscow didn't seem to interest him."[2]

Fundamentally, confronted with Gorbachev's reforms, the PCF leaders expressed a lot of skepticism.[3] Initially, they seemed interested but it became rapidly clear that they were, in fact, quite critical of the Soviet government's policies. Then in 1989, when the Eastern Bloc regimes were collapsing one after the other, they remained perfectly silent, and simply took note of the events. They were especially quiet when popular protest was increasing in East Germany. Again, in October of that year, at the celebration of the 40th anniversary of the GDR (German Democratic Republic), the PCF delegate remained mute, as if everything was normal, as if the GDR had a sustainable future.[4] At the end of 1989, the French party leadership made absolutely no comment when the Ceaușescu regime collapsed in Romania. However, it is a fact that some leaders of the French party, in particular Georges Marchais, did used go to Romania for their summer holidays, and often met Nicolae Ceaușescu, the general secretary of the Romanian Communist Party, discussing political issues and international relations with him. The French communist leaders also

---

Notes for this chapter begin on page 212.

used to go hunting with Eastern Bloc leaders. This tradition inspired Enki Bilal, a French comic strip artist, to create *The Hunting Party*,[5] which became a success in France, in 1983.

Finally, in 1991, the PCF leaders—like the French president François Mitterrand[6] himself—considered the coup d'état that had just taken place in the USSR as an act of "realpolitik." However, the attitude of the PCF leadership toward this important event remained very ambiguous to say the least.

In this chapter, I would like to consider the PCF faced with the following events: political change in Gorbachev's USSR; Soviet foreign policy in the 1980s; and the coup d'état of 1991 in Moscow. I will attempt to analyze the attitude of the French party to each them.

The PCF and Political Change in Gorbachev's USSR

What was the attitude of the PCF toward the reforms that took place in the USSR—Glasnost, Perestroika, new international policy—in the 1980s?

At first, the French party seemed to be enthusiastic about these developments in the Soviet Union. Its leaders explained that it was a "second communist revolution."[7] This apparently naive analysis was simply a way of avoiding considering the more fundamental reasons for the social and economic disorder in the USSR that justified Gorbachev's policy. The French party had only a historical and ideological approach toward these changes. It did not want to face up to Soviet realities in the 1980s, and so its understanding of the USSR was quite dated. For a long time, French communist leaders only spoke about routines, inertia, legacies of the past (pre-1917), and ethnic questions; these had characterized Russia and also the USSR itself, and explained the need for the economic and political reforms under Gorbachev. Furthermore, in 1987, the PCF certainly did not want to hear Yeltsin's criticisms of the Soviet system.[8] As the Communist Party's general secretary in Moscow, he had on several occasions sharply denounced bureaucracy and the blockage it created in Soviet society. He went on to criticize the *nomenklatura*, its privileges and corruption.

Above all, the PCF leaders knew that Gorbachev did not share their historical or ideological analysis. Roland Leroy, who was deputy in the PCF, stated that the general secretary of the Communist Party of the USSR (CPSU) had rejected the argument of a "second revolution" in a discussion they had had together. Gorbachev explained that Perestroika was not "a revolution within the Revolution"—that had taken place in

1917. His reforms were only necessary to prevent the failure of the whole communist system. Revolution was no longer on the agenda.⁹

Gradually, the PCF became more neutral and even critical towards the Soviet leader, explaining that his reforms only concerned the USSR and could not possibly apply to other communist states. They were certainly not an example to be emulated by other countries (or other communist parties). French communists tried not to get involved with the Soviet reforms, and in any case they did not want to support them.

The PCF also became worried because it did not share Gorbachev's analysis of the systemic crisis, or the need for change in the USSR. For the French party, the main reason for the Soviet crisis remained historical, and was, strangely enough, Stalinism and its legacy. Furthermore, for French communists, the reasons for Soviet economic difficulties dated back to the nineteenth century. According to the French communist leaders, the economic backwardness of Russia (and, afterwards, the Soviet Union) had on the one hand brought about the October Revolution, and on the other, had created the very problems Gorbachev was struggling with at that time. More fundamentally, the PCF was afraid that the Leninist basis of the Soviet regime would collapse.¹⁰ However, Gorbachev saw things quite differently. His analysis was not historical, nor ideological, but realistic. He referred to "errors" of the Soviet system.¹¹ For him, Stalinism itself, or the past, was not the problem. This one was more structural and due to current issues. That brought the Soviet system into question, and explained Perestroika and Glasnost. Gorbachev also expected a great renewal of the CPSU. However, for the French communist leaders, the Soviet party only had one problem: the relationship between the party and the people. So, for them, it simply came down to a problem of communication.¹²

In fact, the PCF's approach remained theoretical whereas Gorbachev's attitude was more realistic and practical. The French party refused to bring the Soviet political system into question, but only suggested some technical adaptations. The PCF also showed great concern about the "Yeltsin affair" when it came to light, in 1987. Boris Yeltsin denounced the administrative obstructions to Gorbachev's reforms and the deficiencies inherent in them. The PCF did not at all understand this public discussion of Gorbachev's reforms. For the French party, this kind of debate was unthinkable under a communist regime. To them, it looked like there was serious disorder in the USSR. Therefore, Perestroika would soon be seen as a deviation from the USSR's habitual Leninist policy line. Thus, the PCF adopted the same conservative position towards Gorbachev as that of several other communist parties, such as those in Czechoslovakia, Romania, Vietnam, Cuba and East Germany.¹³

Georges Marchais was also disappointed by the political changes taking place in Poland and then likewise in Hungary.[14] Similarly, in the summer of 1989, *L'Humanité*, the official organ of the PCF, was very critical of Lech Walesa, chairperson of the independent trade union "Solidarity," who had been negotiating the composition of the first democratic government Poland had seen for a very long time.[15] Then the French general secretary seemed very doubtful about the opening of the Iron Curtain in Hungary in September 1989, and he apparently ignored the scenes of thousands of East German citizens rushing to the West. In October 1989, the same conservative attitude, and blindness, characterized *L'Humanité* when the newspaper published a tribute to the Chinese Communist Party, for the 40th anniversary of the Chinese revolution. The article did not contain a single reference to the bloody repression of demonstrations in China earlier that spring. In June 1989, the French party Politburo did denounce "the criminal repression in Peking,"[16] but for the French communist leaders, despite such events, the communist world was still strong, and nothing could endanger it.

That discourse was intended for public opinion because, within the party, leaders and activists were afraid of any change whatsoever. They seemed to be scared that communism was coming to an end. This can appear paradoxical because, between 1974 and 1977, it had experimented with democratic developments, even if they were debatable. For example, it had removed the objective of "the dictatorship of the proletariat" from its official party program (1976). Along with the Italian, Spanish and other Western communist parties, it had also officially joined Eurocommunism.[17] This meant it could be an autonomous way to socialism compared to that of the Soviet Communist Party. The French party was also critical of the regime in the USSR, particularly of the Goulag, and advocated more respect for human rights and liberty.[18] Nevertheless, this political line was not clear. There was a sort of double think or a double talk in the party. The political scientist Jean Baudouin has clearly shown the contradictions of the PCF in the late 1970s.[19] The PCF also remained critical towards Soviet dissidents. Then, at the end of this period, it purged a number of its members, especially its Federation of Paris. The more critical and democratic militants, including some intellectuals and young members, were either excluded or put under severe moral pressure.[20] The French general secretary still approved, in January 1980, the Soviet invasion of Afghanistan. Despite a beginning to an ideological renewal in the 1970s, the leadership of the PCF remained unchanged for a long time. A same generation of activists, under the control of the charismatic Georges Marchais, led the party from the 1960s to the 1990s.[21] However, the party lost many of its members and voters from the end of the 1970s on (see figures 9.1 and 9.2).

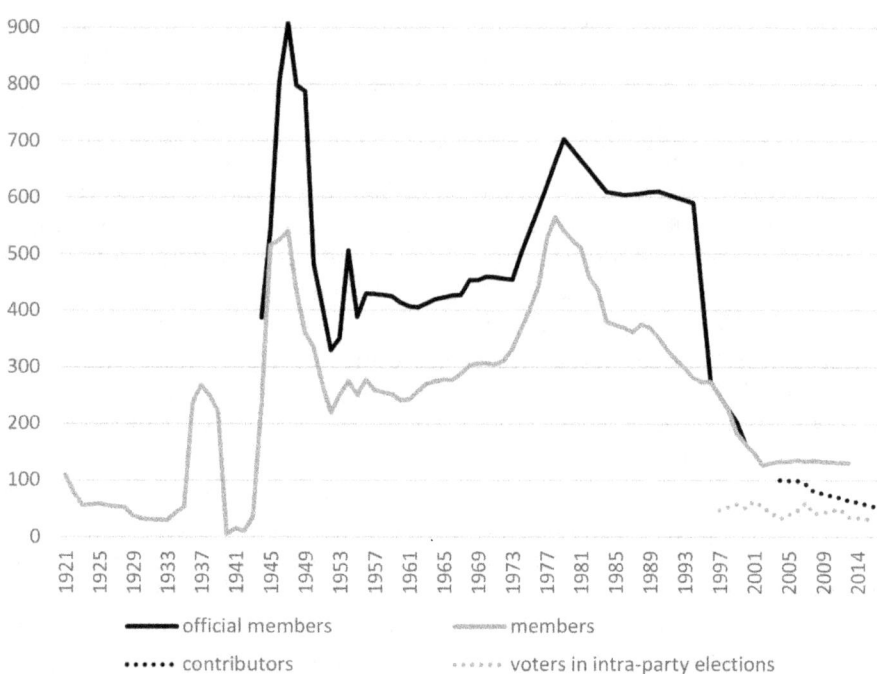

Figure 9.1 Membership of the PCF. The scale is expressed in thousands of members. Sources: PCF, D. Andolfatto, R. Martelli.

That changed the nature of the party. Having been at the center of French politics for a long time, it now became a minority party. Officially, 1989 was a turning point for the PCF, but this had actually taken place earlier, when the party began to lose more and more of its supporters.

At the end of September 1989, Georges Marchais and several members of the Politburo went to Moscow and met with Mikhail Gorbachev. The two leaders needed to agree on a common political perspective. Despite their apparently similar objectives, their reports of this meeting were quite different from one another. This lack of convergence revealed a wide gap in the understanding and analysis of the political situation on the part of both parties. For the French communists, Perestroika represented an important step toward Socialism and its "great potential," whereas the Soviets saw Perestroika as being the result of "miscalculations regarding economic, political and ideological activities."[22]

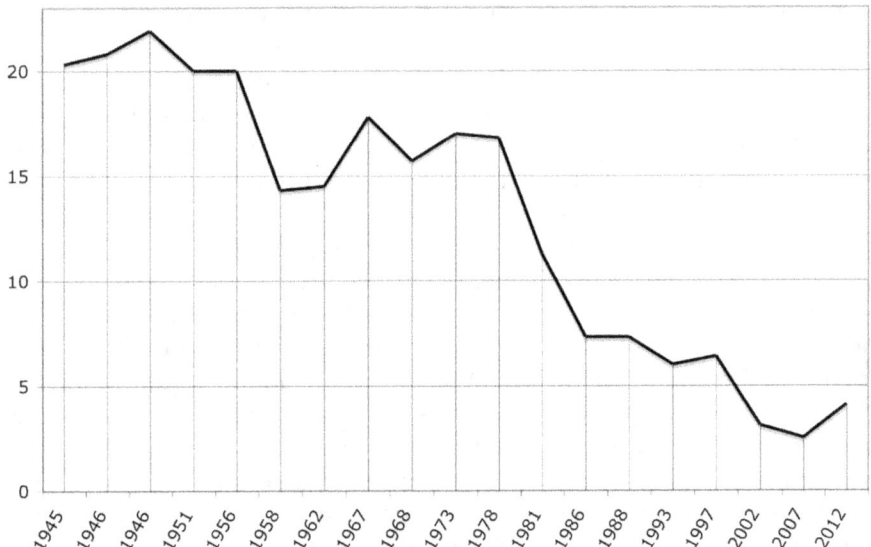

Figure 9.2 Communist votes in French legislative elections (1945–2012). Data in percentages of registered voters. In 2012, the PCF became a member of the Left Front (Front de gauche) which is led by Jean-Luc Mélenchon, a former leader of the Socialist Party (PS). Sources: PCF, D. Andofatto.

The PCF and Gorbachev's Foreign Policy

What was the attitude of the French Communist Party towards Gorbachev's foreign policy when the Berlin Wall came down?

Like many other political organizations, the PCF was incapable of imagining such an event. Many militants had been blinded to East German realities because they admired the GDR so much. For instance, in October 1989, *L'Humanité* celebrated the 40th anniversary of the founding of the GDR.[23] The article remained very positive about this political regime. It reminded readers of the political and economic reasons that had justified the building of the Berlin Wall in 1961. It asserted that young East Germans now had, in 1989, a secure future, and maintained that the situation in East Germany was quite "normal." However, the newspaper also condemned West Germany's attempt to destabilize the GDR. Of course, *L'Humanité* explained that the westward migration of East German citizens was due to Bonn's political maneuvering. For the newspaper, this meant the Cold War was still in progress. But a popular demand for political participation and economic changes was seen as being quite inconceivable.

However, the *L'Humanité* journalist also quoted Gorbachev's speech in Berlin for this celebration, and tried to understand the new policy of the USSR. Even Marie-George Buffet,[24] who represented the French party at the GDR anniversary celebration, did not say anything about the demonstrations and disorder going on in East Germany at that time. Some years later, in a book, she said that she regretted not having reacted to these events in the autumn of 1989.[25]

What exactly did Gorbachev say according to *L'Humanité*? Here are two extracts: "The choice of models of political development belongs to each sovereign country"; "German questions are resolved in Berlin, not in Moscow."[26] As we can see, Gorbachev broke with Brezhnev's theory of limited sovereignty. Despite these quotations in the French communist newspaper, the PCF officially chose not to comment on that subject. Clearly, the party preferred not to see the changes that were taking place, but some French communist leaders—or former leaders—demanded renewal in the party's political line. For Anicet Le Pors and Charles Fiterman, former communist ministers under President François Mitterrand, Perestroika should have had some effect on the PCF.[27] However, Georges Marchais's only reaction to all of this was to say that he was confident in the future of communism and East European regimes.

Speaking on the radio, just a few days before the Berlin Wall came down, Marchais repeated that socialism had achieved important accomplishments in Eastern Europe and in the USSR.[28] These countries were only experiencing "growing pains" or short-term problems. In his opinion, the political and economic system of East European countries remained strong. In short, the PCF did not understand the need for deep changes, such as those wished for by Gorbachev.

Marchais had already put forward the same arguments when had visited the USSR in 1987. In a speech given at the Kremlin, he spoke about the significant gains made by socialism.[29] The PCF essentially expressed a high degree of loyalty towards the Soviet system; nevertheless, Marchais remained reserved with regards to Gorbachev's policies. Quite a number of documents (intra-party ones, articles in communist press) reveal the significant amount of support that French party activists gave to East European regimes, particularly that of the GDR. Indeed, many French communists felt a strong bond with East Germany, and networks of communist militants (in communist municipalities or trade unions) frequently organized exchanges with them.

In January 1988, *L'Humanité* reflected the emotion within the PCF during the first official state visit to France of Erich Honecker, the general secretary of the Socialist Unity Party in the GDR. The newspaper spoke about the "fraternal atmosphere" during the Marchais–Honecker meeting.[30] However, the PCF regretted the criticisms made during the visit by the rest of the French media, who focused their criticisms on the Berlin Wall. In the same article, *L'Humanité* went as far as to say that the Wall was already open for "thousands of people"—which was surprising and confusing (at the beginning of 1988).[31]

Suddenly, on 10 November 1989, the PCF leadership stated it was satisfied with the opening up of the Berlin Wall. They even said they had been waiting for this event for a long time![32] For the political scientist Lilly Marcou, the PCF leadership was in fact deceitful and dishonest because no one in the party had ever mentioned this subject before (apart from arguing that the Wall was no longer an uncrossable border, as it said above).[33] A few years later, in one of his books, Roland Leroy, former editor of *L'Humanité*,[34] referred to the "gap" that existed between Gorbachev and the French Communist Party.[35] For him, the French communists were even more faithful to the Soviet model than Gorbachev himself or the other Soviet leaders.[36] As we have already seen, in a conversation with Gorbachev, Leroy had suggested presenting Perestroika as a new revolutionary objective, in order to create a new "October." However, for Gorbachev, his policy was no longer intended to bring about a new revolution. For him, revolution belonged to the past. That proves that French communists and Gorbachev were not on the same wavelength. The PCF looked to the past and old-fashioned ideological conformity, whereas Gorbachev was trying to create a future for the USSR (and a new way of thinking). For the French communists, it seemed impossible to escape from history and ideology. For Gorbachev, the ship was sinking, and so the situation required urgent action, a new method, results.[37]

In 1990, despite the fall of Eastern regimes, the PCF remained confident in the future of socialism. During its 27th Congress, the French party proclaimed "this failure (i.e., the failure of communist regimes) is not the failure of socialism."[38] For the PCF, it meant some Eastern Bloc states had actually toppled, but communism itself had not been affected—the ideal was still preserved. Again, the PCF explained that the fall of these regimes was due to historical factors. It strongly criticized the leaders of these states and their bureaucratic and corrupt systems. In fact, French communist leaders had had frequent meetings with these state executives, and they had never criticized them before.

The PCF and the Coup d'État of 1991 in the USSR

Finally, the PCF seemed to hope that Gorbachev would fall from power. It is interesting to consider its attitude, which is surprising but logical, when the coup d'état took place in August 1991.

First of all, *L'Humanité* and the CGT[39] newspapers (*Le Peuple* and *La Vie ouvrière*)[40] were worried about the economic crisis and the rise of nationalism in the USSR. Several articles dealing with former communist regimes and the USSR spoke of "disenchantment," "unemployment," "economic difficulties," "social discontent," "poverty," "social stress," and "unbridled capitalism."[41] Three days before the coup d'état in the USSR, *Révolution*, a French communist magazine, published an article about the crisis in the Soviet Union. The argument was close to the one that the putschists developed a few days later: criticizing economic reforms, the increase in criminality, immorality, authoritarian government and the loss of sovereignty of the USSR.[42]

On 20 August 1991, while the media everywhere were covering the coup d'état in the USSR, *L'Humanité* never even mentioned the word. It only said that there was a lot of uncertainty in Russian society and that people were worried.[43] Yet, in a declaration, the PCF said that this event (which it did not qualify) marked the end of Perestroika.[44] The party leadership also spoke about the failure of Perestroika, underlining the mistakes made by this policy for the Soviet economy. It connected these failings with the rising nationalism in Russia. So "the revolution within the revolution," as some French communists had initially perceived Perestroika, became a profound failure. In the end, the PCF hastened to make a negative assessment of the Perestroika experiment. It appeared to be relieved to be able to bring this chapter to a close.

Moreover, the French party acknowledged Gorbachev's fall, only regretting the conditions in which his removal had taken place. We can say that Gorbachev's demise liberated the PCF, enabling it to put the blame on him. Up until then, its criticism was only implicit. According to the testimony of a member of the Politburo of the PCF, this event did not "break any hearts in the party."[45]

In addition, several leaders of the French party knew Guennadi Ianaiev, who, after the coup d'état, became the head of state—though in fact only for three days. However, we do not really know if they actually appreciated him. For example, Henri Krasucki, the general secretary of the CGT, knew him well, because Ianaiev had been president of the Soviet trade unions.[46] He asked his colleagues in the French Politburo not to condemn the new power in Moscow.

Actually, the PCF did not want to disagree with the putsch, but it did not want to approve of it either. For the party, this event put a full stop to Perestroika. That was a positive point in the PCF's opinion, because Perestroika had opened up the way to wild capitalism, which was of course very far from the spirit of communist revolution. In a way, the French president, François Mitterrand, shared this analysis. With a realist view of international relations, he quickly noted the change of the power in the USSR, and he recognized it as fact.

After the failure of Ianaiev's government, *L'Humanité*—and the PCF leadership—modified their point of view.[47] The French leadership confessed that it was divided over the coup d'état. Two of its members— Charles Fiterman and Guy Hermier[48]—challenged the party's attitude toward this major event and would have preferred the party to formally condemn it, but Georges Marchais stubbornly stuck by his guns and he refused to change his point of view. The general secretary only referred to "the failure of ... capitalism."[49] He, along with a lot of French communists—activists or not—refused to admit the end of a "world." The ideological project of the party had to remain intact because the enemy was, more than ever, capitalism. However, as Martin Malia wrote, "the collapse of all European communist regimes in 1989–1991 is significant for this particular political system."[50] Nevertheless, for the PCF leadership, that was no longer the problem.

Even though, in 1991, the French party mainly followed its leaders, not all of its members shared this position. Afterward, some communist press journalists denounced the leadership's refusal to condemn the coup d'état.[51] They also criticized their poor analysis of Perestroika and the party's refusal to take into consideration the aspiration for freedom and democracy in Eastern Europe and Russia.

Finally, the French Communist Party was deliberately blind to all the events that caused the bringing down of the Iron Curtain in 1989 and the fall of the USSR in 1991. For it, the world could only change in the way the communists had been led to think it would. In fact, this blindness gradually explained the gap between the PCF and society. In the 1980s, the gap had widened and the party neared collapse: it had lost a considerable number of its members (officially more than 80 percent, but, in fact, probably more; see Figure 9.1).

Even if during the 1950s the PCF was the leading political party in France in terms of membership and voters, and the major opposition party against De Gaulle in the 1960s (at the beginning of the Fifth Republic), it had to face many new challenges from the 1970s on. However, it failed to adapt to the new political and social environment. It locked itself into its certainties, its way of thinking, and its vision of the world. The party did not understand—or did not want to understand—the changes that took place in Eastern Europe at the end of the 1980s, nor the people's longing for democracy and real change in society. Faced with Gorbachev's reforms, the PCF's reaction was one of the most "conservative" when compared to other Western and even some Eastern communist parties. This attitude is paradoxical to say the least, because in the 1970s it had claimed to be modern and democratic, under the guise of Eurocommunism. In fact, it had remained very ambiguous towards this project. The party seemed to practice "double game." The same ambiguity toward Gorbachev and Perestroika became more and more reinforced over several years. Even though the PCF did not support Gorbachev's policies for dogmatic reasons, its own decline could not be stopped.

Dominique Andolfatto is professor of political science at the University of Burgundy (France). He has published *PCF: mutation ou liquidation* (Le Rocher, 2005); and, with Alexandra Goujon, *Les partis politique, atelier de la démocratie* (Ed. de l'Université de Bruxelles, 2016). He works also on industrial relations.

Notes

The principal source of this chapter is a book published in 2005: Dominique Andolfatto, *PCF: mutation ou liquidation*, Paris and Monaco. The author thanks David Palmer, who helped him to translate this chapter into English.

1. Deputy general secretary (1969–1972), then general secretary of the PCF (1972–1993); member of the National Assembly (1973–1997); member of the European Parliament (1979–1989).
2. Quoted by Hofnung, *Georges Marchais*, 377–78.
3. See Hofnung, *Georges Marchais*; Le Pors, *Pendant la mue*, 118; moreover, my interview with Bernard Frédérick in 2004, former correspondent of *L'Humanité* in Moscow (at the end of the 1980s).
4. Buffet, *Un peu de courage!*, 101.
5. Bilal and Christin, *Partie de chasse* [The hunting party].
6. President of the French Republic (1981–1995), former first secretary of the French Socialist Party (PS), which is a social democratic party.
7. See Rey, "La gauche française," 152; Streiff, *La dynamique Gorbachev*, 238 ; Roland Leroy, "Editorial," *L'Humanité*, 11 November 1989; and Leroy, *La quête du bonheur*, 38, 41, 64.
8. Interview with Bernard Frédérick in 2004 (see note 3).
9. See Leroy, *La quête du Bonheur*; and Andolfatto, *PCF*, 87.
10. See Hayoz, *L'étreinte soviétique*, 293–94, 328.
11. Quoted by *Le Monde*, 14 November 1987.
12. See *L'Humanité*, 23 and 27 September 1989.
13. See Gratchev, *Le mystère Gorbachev*, 252–53.

14. See Marchais, "L'avenir appartient au socialisme."
15. See *L'Humanité*, 10, 14 and 15 August 1989.
16. At first, the general secretary only spoke of "highly regrettable" events in China (*Le Monde*, 7 June 1989).
17. The Japanese Communist Party had also joined this movement.
18. See Branko Lazitch, "Les étapes de la tension," 572. See also Staar, *Yearbook* 1977, 152–53; 1978, 138. We can also find a moderate criticism of the USSR in Adler et al., *L'URSS et nous*.
19. Baudoin, "Le PCF." See also Lecoeur, *Le PCF*.
20. See Henri Fiszbin, *Les bouches s'ouvrent*.
21. See Hincker, "Le groupe dirigeant," 70–79.
22. *L'Humanité*, 23 and 25 September 1989.
23. *L'Humanité*, 7 October 1989.
24. Buffet became the new general secretary of the PCF in 2001 (to 2008), following after Georges Marchais (1972–1993) and Robert Hue (1993–2001).
25. Buffet, *Un peu de courage!*.
26. *L'Humanité*, 7 October 1989.
27. The title of minister Le Pors's book is particulary significant for the PCF in the 1980s : *Pendant la mue, le serpent est aveugle* (op. cit., note 4) —i.e., During molting, the snake is blind.
28. Interview of Georges Marchais on RTL. See *L'Humanité*, 16 October 1989.
29. *L'Humanité*, 5 November 1987.
30. *L'Humanité*, 11 January 1988. See also *L'Humanité*, 7 and 8 January 1988.
31. A book published by the party in 1985 was prudently more critical of the GDR; see Laveau, *La RDA*, 218, 260. Yet its arguments were not incorporated into the party line.
32. *L'Humanité*, 11 November 1989.
33. Marcou, *Le Monde*, 17 November 1989.
34. He was also the deputy of the PCF.
35. Leroy, *La quête du Bonheur*.
36. Interview with Roland Leroy (2004).
37. Ibid.
38. "Résolutions. XXVIIe congrès du PCF," *Cahiers du communisme* (January–Febuary 1991), 335.
39. The CGT (*Confédération générale du Travail*, i.e., General Confederation of Labour) is one of the major French trade unions. Until the end of the 1990s, it was close to the PCF and their communist ideology.
40. "The People" and "The Worker's Life."
41. See *Le Peuple*, 29 November 1990, 13–21; *La Vie ouvrière*, 16–22 April 1990, 26–29; 30 September – 7 October 1990, 19–22; 31 December 1990 – 6 January 1991, 26–28; 17–23 June 1991, 26–29; 24–30 June 1991, 26–28; and 1–7 July 1991, 20–23.
42. *Révolution*, 16 August 1991. See also Streiff, *Ex-URSS*, 10; and Andolfatto, *PCF*, 105–6.
43. *L'Humanité*, 20 August 1991.
44. Ibid.
45. Interview with Roland Leroy (2004). Three other members of the PCF Politburo were also interviewed: Robert Hue, Francette Lazard, and Pierre Zarka.
46. For example, Henri Krasucki met Guennadi Ianaiev during the 18th Congress of the Central Council of the Trade Unions of the USSR in 1987. See *Le Peuple*, 26 March 1987, 27–31. As leader of the French young communists, Pierre Zarka also met Ianaiev when he was leading the Komsomol (Soviet youth movement).
47. See *L'Humanité*, 27 August 1991.
48. Member of the National Assembly, 1978–2001 (elected in Marseilles).

49. *L'Humanité*, 27 August 1991.
50. Malia, *La tragédie soviétique*, 600.
51. See *Libération*, 11 September 1991.

Bibliography

Adler, Alexandre, et al. *L'URSS et nous*, Paris, 1978.
Andolfatto, Dominique, and Stéphane Courtois. "France: The Collapse of the House of Communism," in *Communist and Post-Communist Parties in Europe*, ed. Uwe Backes and Patrick Moreau, Göttingen, 2008, 87–132.
Andolfatto, Dominique, and Fabienne Greffet. "Effondrement soviétique et déclin du PCF," in *Sortir du communisme, changer d'époque: Retour sur la chute du mur de Berlin*, ed. Stéphane Courtois, Paris, 2011, 617–36.
_____. "Le PCF comme objet de science politique," in *Les partis politiques: nouveaux regards*, ed. François Audigier, David Colon, and Frédéric Fogacci, Brussels, 2012, 409–26.
_____. *PCF: de la mutation à la liquidation*, Paris, 2005.
Baudoin, Jean. "Le PCF et le 'socialisme aux couleurs de la France': Evolution et contradictions du communisme français. 1968–1978." Doctoral dissertation in political science, University of Rennes, 1978.
Bilal, Enki, and Pierre Christin. *Partie de chasse*, Paris, 1983.
Boia, Lucain. *La Roumaine, un pays aux frontières de l'Europe*, Paris, 2003.
Buffet, Marie-George. *Un peu de courage! Entretiens avec Kathleen Evin, Pierre Laurent, Bernard Coches, Michel Cool*, Paris, 2004.
Courtois, Stéphane, and Marc Lazar. *Histoire du Parti communiste français*, Paris, 2000.
Courtois, Stéphane, et al. *Le livre noir du communism*, Paris, 1997.
Fiszbin, Henri. *Les bouches s'ouvrent: Une crise dans le Parti communiste*, Paris, 1980.
Furet, François. *Le passé d'une illusion: Essai sur l'idée communiste au 20e siècle*, Paris, 1995.
Gorbachev, Mikhail. *Mémoires*, Paris, 1997.
Gratchev, Andrei. *Le mystère Gorbachev: La terre et le destin*, Paris, 2001.
Hayoz, Nicolas. *L'étreinte soviétique*, Geneva, 1997.
Hincker, François. *Le parti communiste au carrefour: Essai sur quinze ans de son histoire, 1965–1981*, Paris, 1981.
Hofnung, Thomas. *Georges Marchais: L'inconnu du Parti communiste français*, Paris, 2001.
Laveau, Paul. *La RDA au quotidien*, Paris, 1985.
Lazar, Marc. *Le communisme, une passion française*, Paris, 2002.
Lazitch, Branko. "Les étapes de la tension entre le Parti communiste français et le Parti communiste soviétique," *Est et Ouest*, 1–15 May 1976.
Le Pors, Anciet. *Pendant la mue, le serpent est aveugle*, Paris, 1993.
Leroy, Roland. *La quête du bonheur*, Paris, 1995.
Malia, Martin. *La tragédie soviétique*, Paris, 1999.
Marchais, Georges. "L'avenir appartient au socialisme pas au capitalism," *Cahiers du communisme*, No. 10 (October 1989).

_____. *Le défi démocratique*, Paris, 1973.
_____. *Démocratie*, Paris, 1990.
Martelli, Roger. *Prendre sa carte 1920–2009: Données nouvelles sur les effectifs du PCF*, Paris-Saint-Denis, 2010.
_____. *Le rouge et le bleu*, Paris, 1995.
Rey, Marie Pierre. "Le gauche française et la perestroika," *Communisme*, No. 76/77 (2003/4), 141–68.
Robrieux, Philippe. *Histoire intérieure du Parti communiste*, Paris, 1982.
Staar, Richard F. (ed.). *Yearbook on International Communist Affairs*, Stanford University, CA, 1977/78.
Streiff, Gérard. *La dynamique Gorbachev*, Paris, 1986.
_____. *Jean Kanapa (1921–1978): Une singulière histoire du PCF*, Paris, 2001.
_____. "Du marxisme au darwinisme: Où va l'URSS?," *Révolution*, No. 598 (16 August 1991).
_____. *Ex-URSS: Un nouveau tiers monde*, Paris, 1992.

Chapter 10

A Dialogue of the Deaf
The CPGB and the SED during the Gorbachev Era, 1985–1990

Stefan Berger and Norman LaPorte

Even those familiar with the German Democratic Republic (GDR) in Britain, but who did not belong to the British Left, found it impossible to tell apart the political attitudes within the Communist Party of Great Britain (CPGB) toward "really existing socialism." As an undergraduate student of East German literature in the late 1980s, the now prominent journalist Anne McElvoy spent her year abroad at the Humboldt University in East Berlin. Yet her familiarity with university life behind the Berlin Wall did not stop her perceiving Jack Berlin as a "hardliner,"[1] when, for his part, Berlin had complained to the general secretary of the CPGB, Gordon McLennan, about party leaders on lecture tours of the GDR reinforcing Socialist Unity Party (SED) "comrades' distorted image of a Dickensian Britain."[2] This illustrates how difficult it was even for informed observers to delineate the ideological positions of British communists and their attitude toward "really existing socialism" in the final years of its existence.

In fact, the CPGB leadership welcomed Gorbachev and his program of reforms from the outset. According to the journalist and historian of the party, Francis Beckett—who interviewed a large number of leading British communists—the relationship between Gorbachev and Gordon McLennan was "excellent." McLennan had worked behind the scenes to encourage Gorbachev to visit Britain in December 1984 and, after the Soviet leader had held talks with Prime Minister Margret Thatcher, he went on to meet McLennan, giving him a sympathetic hearing and

---

Notes for this chapter begin on page 230.

reassuring him of Soviet support in the troubles threatening to split the British party.³ Among the strongest supporters of "reform" in the CPGB, the so-called Eurocommunists, many considered Gorbachev to be an ally. In the words of the long-time secretary of the Britain–GDR Society (BGS), Sheila Taylor, "Gorbachev was adopting policies that we had been promoting for some years in Britain and Western Europe generally."⁴ What she had in mind was a wholesale endorsement of democratic reform in Soviet Russia. She was not alone in these views. However, a significant minority of hardliners had long opposed the process of reform in the CPGB, even if their pro-Soviet orientation ensured continued expressions of support for glasnost and perestroika under Gorbachev.⁵ Notably, it was only the ultra-hardline New Communist Party (NCP), which had grown out of a party split over the issue of reform in 1977, that voiced hostility towards Gorbachev—and support for East Berlin's variant of "really existing socialism."⁶ But within the British party, the ultra-orthodox hardliners were increasingly outnumbered by the Eurocommunists, who set the tone in the party from the 1980s onward. In this sense the party was, from a Soviet perspective, reformist *avant la lettre*.

East Berlin's hostility to Gorbachev's reform agenda is well known. Like in the Soviet Union before Gorbachev took power, the SED had become a rigid gerontocracy. The party's general secretary, Erich Honecker, saw himself as a guardian of Marxist–Leninist orthodoxy, with its roots in his activism during the Weimar Republic.⁷ Caught in a triangular relationship with Bonn and Moscow, there was a rationale to Honecker's intransigence. If Gorbachev ended the universalism of the Soviet model, then the GDR's fragile legitimacy as a nation-state would be threatened. Recent research even shows how Honecker developed bilateral relations with China in a policy aiming to engage Deng Xiao Ping as a counterweight to Gorbachev—one effect of which was East Berlin's support for the crushing of the student movement in Tiananmen Square in 1989.⁸

Despite these differences, however, the leadership of the SED and the CPGB wanted to maintain, and even further develop, relations between "brother parties" in the name of "proletarian internationalism." British Eurocommunists had a wide range of contacts and connections with the GDR and, while criticizing the regime's lack of democratic rights, praised its social and economic "achievements." Importantly, too, those Eurocommunists who had the closest contacts with East Germany believed that Gorbachev's reforms in the Soviet Union offered the GDR a "historic opportunity" to democratize, while remaining aware that the SED leadership comprised unreformed Stalinists.⁹ They continued to be critical friends of the GDR, and hoped that a new generation of reform-minded communists would lead the GDR in the direction taken by Gorbachev. The CPGB's hardliners also looked to East Berlin, not merely for political solidarity, but to help fund their daily newspaper, the *Morning Star*. East Berlin, for its part, aimed to influence the CPGB in a manner that would move the party to reverse its "neo-revisionism" and return to old-style Marxism–Leninism. Graham Taylor, a Eurocommunist who had developed long-standing relations with the GDR, voiced concerns about East Berlin's machinations in London,[10] as did Gerry Pocock, the reform-minded head of the CPGB's International Department in a letter to his counterpart in East Germany.[11]

Nevertheless, a common commitment to "proletarian internationalism" held these two dissimilar sister parties together in a common cause against global capitalism. In what follows, we will, first of all, provide some historical context, as the reception of Gorbachev in the CPGB is impossible to understand without accounting for the rise of Eurocommunism among a new generation of communists—a development that was perceived with great skepticism by East Berlin's hardliners. Secondly, we will examine Gorbachev's impact on the CPGB and contrast this with developments in the SED. In doing so, we will detail how (their deep ideological differences apart) the CPGB remained, by and large, a loyal ally of the SED and of "really existing socialism" behind the Iron Curtain.

The Rise of Eurocommunism in the CPGB

Up until the fall of communism, the SED and CPGB leaderships continued to show a fond nostalgia for their historical links. Thus, for example, Gordon McLennan talked proudly of how these contacts and connections dated back to the years of Ernst Thälmann.[12] However, McLennan's words brushed aside some serious disagreements that had characterized the two parties' relationship during the Cold War. Admittedly, the parties had become closer during the German Communist Party's period of exile in Britain during World War II. Then, in 1946, the CPGB had been the only force in British politics to welcome the foundation of the SED and, three years later, the GDR. In the 1950s and early 1960s, the CPGB stood at the forefront of East Berlin's campaign for diplomatic recognition in Britain, and, in public at least, did not oppose the military suppression of Hungarian "reform communism" in 1956 or—of more direct bearing on inter-party relations—the construction of the Berlin Wall in 1961.[13] But a much more openly critical friendship emerged after the Soviet-led invasion of Czechoslovakia in 1968, despite the party's reliance on "Moscow's

Gold" to pay the salaries of full-time staff and its wide range of publications.[14] As events played out, admittedly, John Gollan—the party's general secretary—stated in the *Morning Star* that, "We [the CPGB] will never be found in the company of anti-Soviet forces in this country."[15] But a Stasi report of an Executive Committee meeting, which had been called to discuss these events, detailed how behind the scenes all but one of those present had spoken against the use of military force in Czechoslovakia.[16]

In broad outline, the loudest voices placing critical distance been British communism and Soviet-styled "really existing socialism" belonged to a new, post-1956 generation of party activists, who were often university educated, receptive to the analyses of the "New Left" and strongly influenced by Gramscian ideas.[17] Against the backdrop of Britain's declining industrial economy, the policy prescription of the Eurocommunists was increasingly to ally the party with the new social movements—notably the women's movement, gay liberation, and student politics—in order to forge a "broad alliance" of all those oppressed by capitalism, culturally as well as at the point of production.[18] In this, they were opposed by the party's "workerist" wing, which remained focused on class politics and could point to an upsurge in industrial militancy; their main base of support was among more staunchly pro-Soviet communist trade unionists.[19]

Developments in the CPGB were monitored by the SED with some trepidation. The East Germans received detailed reports on the "ideological deviation" of individuals and groupings in the CPGB, which were compiled by the Stasi, the Central Committee's International Relations Department, and the GDR embassy in London.[20] In the mid-1970s, tensions between the two parties burst into the open when the Eurocommunists demonstrated outside the East German Embassy in London after the imprisonment of Rudolf Bahro, a dissident intellectual who had published his book, *Die Alternative*, in West Germany.[21] Then, at the turn of the decade, the CPGB leadership's public disavowal of the Soviet invasion of Afghanistan and of the imposition of martial law in Poland worsened relations with East Berlin and the party's own hardliners.[22] Yet, domestic political developments arguably proved to be the source of deepest acrimony—above all, how to respond to the Conservative governments that dominated the 1980s under Margret Thatcher. The party's now feuding factions lined up behind rival party publications, the *Morning Star* and *Marxism Today*; and both of them reached out to supporters in the Labour Party, which was also deeply divided over how to respond to Thatcherism. The "traditionalists" looked to the Bennites and pro-Soviet sections of the Labour Party, while the Eurocommunists forged links with the "reform" wing of the party, which was close to Neil Kinnock.[23]

Marxism Today, which reached a readership far beyond the narrow confines of British communists in the 1980s, had been edited by Martin Jacques since 1977. The journal's advocates included the party's student organizer, Dave Cook; Beatrix Campbell and Judith Hunt who were members of the party's Woman's Advisory Committee; Chris Myant, a party journalist; and Monty Johnson, a party intellectual and polyglot who was an expert on "socialist democracy."[24] For the most part, their intellectual roots were in the New Left milieu, which infused university politics, and had been crucial in gestating Eurocommunist positions.[25] Jacques, who held a doctorate from Cambridge, had lectured in economics at Bristol University before taking a significant cut in his salary to become a full-time party editor. Critical of the Soviet Union's invasion of Czechoslovakia in 1968, in domestic politics he came increasingly to question the validity of class-based politics, and in the pages of *Marxism Today* promoted Gramscian and poststructuralist analyses that departed a long way from Marxism–Leninism.[26] If Jacques stood at one end of an increasingly divergent spectrum of British communism, Tony Chater stood far closer to the other.[27] Chater was also an academic with a doctorate in chemistry from Queen Mary and Westfield College, University of London. On becoming a full-time party official in 1969, he ran the CPGB's Press and Publicity Department before succeeding George Matthews as editor of the *Morning Star* in 1974. It was in this role that Chater played a leading role in the feud with the Eurocommunists around *Marxism Today* who, from the early 1980s, had won the backing of the "party loyalists" in the leadership around Gordon McLennan. The spectrum of support for class-based politics included influential trade union leaders such as Ken Gill, the general secretary of the Technical, Administrative and Supervisory Union, which was usually known by its acronym TASS, miners' leader Mick McGahey, and the party's grassroots union officials. This section of the party also drew support from the resolutely pro-Soviet "Straight Left" faction under Fergus Nicholson, whose background in radical student politics reminds us that these party divisions did not reflect a neat sociological rupture—unlike the SED's reports suggested. The de facto faction's strong support from pro-Soviet sections of the Labour Party—for example, the Members of the European Parliament (MEPs) Alf Lomas and James Lamond and the Member of Parliament (MP) William Wilson—also reminds us of the blurred party-political lines in this milieu. Lomas, Lamond and Wilson had all taken a strong interest in the GDR, and could agree with the *Straight Left* lead article commemorating the regime's anniversary in 1979: "A Hard but Glorious 30 Years."[28]

These tensions within the CPGB were intensified in 1982 when *Marxism Today* published Tony Lane's criticism of industrial policy, including an attack on the alleged corruption of communist shop stewards. When Gordon McLennan intervened to prevent the *Morning Star* publishing the hardliners' response, a battle for control of the party's daily newspaper ensued, which ended in defeat for the leadership. For historical reasons, the *Morning Star* was legally owned by the People's Press Printing Society (PPPS), and when a vote was forced, it led to the party leadership losing to the newspaper's shareholders—who comprised rank-and-file activists.[29] From then onward, the leadership grouping around McLennan increasingly allied itself to the Eurocommunists, including the outriders of reform who edited *Marxism Today*. Not even the 1984/85 miners' strike—which received financial support from Moscow and East Berlin—could preserve party unity.[30]

The party split came at a high cost for the CPGB. Not only did the party lose high-profile trade union leaders—such as Ken Gill, the long-standing general secretary of TASS who sat on the TUC's General Council and chaired the 1984 TUC annual congress—it also lost many of its foot soldiers in industrial branches, above all among local union officials, who supported the *Morning Star*.[31] By the summer of 1985, barely six months after McLennan had met Gorbachev in London, key figures on the party's traditionalist wing had been expelled. Ironically, these "purges" were carried out using "democratic centralism"—an inheritance from the Stalin era.[32] Ideological reform had been imposed on a divided party, which began to disintegrate in the second half of the 1980s, at exactly the same time as Gorbachev was beginning the reform process in the Soviet Union.[33]

The CPGB and "Really Existing Socialism" during the Gorbachev Era

The Eurocommunists and the "loyalists" in the party leadership comprised the staunchest supporters of Gorbachev's reforms in the CPGB. In the second half of the 1980s there was an endless string of articles, speeches and memoranda that testify to this support, which at times was tinged with insinuations that the Soviet reformers had themselves been motivated by Western reform communism, or that, at the very least, Western communist parties had embarked on communist reformism before the Soviet Union. In a letter from communist activist Graham Taylor to MacLennan in February 1987, he stated: "It seemed to our meeting that Gorbachev was bringing a breath of fresh air into our movement, was validating the position taken by our party over the last ten years or so, and was likely to reunite the world communist movement in, perhaps, a very short space of time."[34] Similarly, in a paper given to the Executive Committee in 1987, Monty Johnson welcomed the Gorbachev reforms, but did not see them as a model for the British party, which was already much further advanced in its democratic renewal and in seeking a realignment of political forces on the Left. Johnson wrote: "We should welcome and publicize further developments in Soviet society under Gorbachev, which can certainly help to develop a more positive perception of socialism, but [it] should not be presented as a model for Britain. The socialism we propagate should incorporate democratic, pluralist, internationalist, humanist, feminist, and ecological elements drawn from the best traditions and conceptions of the British labour and democratic movement, of which we should be seen as an integral part."[35]

MacLennan and Pocock attended the Communist Party of the Soviet Union (CPSU) Congress in 1986, and the British fraternal delegates reported back in glowing terms about the reforms being undertaken in the Soviet Union.[36] In April 1988, another delegation from the CPGB held talks in Moscow with key advisors of Gorbachev, Dobrynin, and Zagladin, and also reported back very favorably on the reforms undertaken in the Soviet Union.[37] One year later, when Gorbachev visited Britain in 1989, he again met with the CPGB leadership at the embassy in London. The mainstream British press at the time, however, was more interested in the decline of communism in Britain than in any questions of how these reforms might revive the fortunes of the international communist movement. An article in *The Times*, for example, noted how the party had a mere 6,700 members and was run from a shabby little office in Smithfield Market. It compared the success of Thatcher's policies with the utter failure of British communism.[38]

For a very long time, the internal debates in the CPGB had focused on perspectives for renewal. Gorbachev's glasnost was seen as confirmation that there were many different roads communists could travel, depending on their respective political circumstances, and that they had to look for new allies on the Left. According to the minutes of the Political Committee of the CPGB in January 1987, the leadership agreed that: "As a party we take this opportunity to welcome wholeheartedly this process of renewal. The modernization of the USSR and the increased openness of its society can only be of great benefit to the Soviet people."[39] As Monty Johnston wrote in 1987: "[A]n increasing number of CPs have been searching for new forms of internationalism respecting diversity of views and practices, and embracing not only CPs but also a wide range of socialist, democratic and national liberation movements."[40] Johnson, who collected a large range of articles on Gorbachev's reforms, not only in English but also in Russian, Italian, French, and German, showed himself deeply convinced that the renewal of communism in the Soviet Union would spark a reversal of communist fortunes around the globe.[41] Time and again, the supporters of Gorbachev reaffirmed their belief that the economic reforms could only be successful if they were accompanied by more openness and democracy.[42] Yet, at times, the enthusiasm of British communists, such as Monty Johnson, for pluralist democracy could also draw criticism from the Soviet Union. So, for example, a member of the CPSU, Alexey P. Kozlov, wrote a letter to the editors of *Marxism Today* in 1985, in which he criticized Johnson for failing to understand the achievements of "really existing socialism" in the Soviet Union, and applying Western democratic theory to a country wholly unsuited to such ideas.[43]

When the velvet revolutions swept communist regimes from power across Eastern Europe, an emergency resolution at the 41st Congress of the CPGB reaffirmed the party's support for a democratic socialism. Welcoming Gorbachev's policies of non-intervention in Eastern Europe, and contrasting them positively with the Chinese communists' crackdown in Tiananmen Square, the resolution stated: "There is a need for speedy moves to [ensure] a thoroughgoing political reform, separation of party and state, and a pluralism of views and proposals that can be openly discussed, publicized and campaigned for, including elections. This has long been the policy of our party. Socialism must mean the fullest expansion of an active participatory democracy."[44]

The SED's position in 1989 was very much the mirror opposite to that of the CPGB. Three years earlier, East German communists had not even been invited to send fraternal delegates to the CPGB's 39th Extraordinary Party Congress. Yet the SED sent observers whose reports were compiled for the Politburo. They noted that the Tory's election victory in 1983 had made the situation in the CPGB—as well as in the Labour Party—much worse, intensifying the ongoing feud over how to oppose Thatcherism's attacks on trade unions, public sector workers, the privatization of nationalized industries, and high levels of unemployment. The SED's diagnosis of the situation, however, looked to traditional communist means: "The CPGB's problems arise from the neglect of fundamental Marxist–Leninist positions. This prevents the preservation of party unity, and has led to the expulsion of genuine Marxist–Leninist elements."[45] The SED's response was to promote party "unity," which they understood as supporting the "hardliners" being readmitted to the CPGB and, if possible, dominating it.[46]

In order to work toward these ends, the SED pursued a strategy of dialogue and deepening fraternal relations with its British "brother party." As the CPGB leadership, including the head of the International Department, Gerry Pocock, actively supported fraternal relations, the

SED was pushing at an open door. East Berlin's assumption was that most Eurocommunists were ignorant of "really existing socialism," and thus a lack of exposure to the GDR was at the root of the problem. This "analysis" even applied to the outrider of reform, Martin Jacques, who was to be sounded out about visiting East Germany in 1987. At the very least, the SED could point to his readiness to continue meeting with visiting East Germans in London.[47] SED officials stressed that contacts with Eurocommunists had to be used to bring them back onto the road of ideological orthodoxy, including "socialist democracy" and the planned economy, as well as a wholesale endorsement of the achievements of communist Eastern Europe.[48] If this did not convince the CPGB leadership of the error of their ways, then the SED could at least summarize fraternal relations in 1988 as "positive" and "improving," with regular delegations at leadership level crossing the "Iron Curtain" in the thawing Cold War.[49]

However, maintaining contacts and connection with all of the various British communist groupings meant that the SED's relations with British hardliners contravened repeated assurances given to the CPGB leadership that it would only maintain relations with the official (i.e., Moscow sanctioned) party. A report from 1986 detailed the wide range of the SED's ongoing contacts and connections with leaders of expelled party groupings, above all the *Morning Star*'s Management Committee under Tony Chater and the "Communist Campaign Group" (CCG), which operated out of an office in the newspaper's premises after 1985. One leading figure in the CCG was Mike Hicks, who subsequently became the first general secretary of the split-off Communist Party of Britain (CPB) in 1988. What amounted to a network of hardliners maintained strong links with the Bennite and pro-Soviet sections of the Labour Party and sympathetic trade union leaders. The initial aim was to work for a change of leadership, policy, and the readmittance of those who had been expelled. However, the outcome of the CPGB's 1987 Congress was a disappointment for them, and led to the formation of the CPB the following year.[50] The SED also continued to foster contacts with "Straight Left," who again broke promises given to the CPGB's International Department not to do so.[51] All of these contacts with hardline dissident communists in Britain indicated the value that the SED attached to strengthening orthodoxy in the CPGB, thereby opposing the Eurocommunist euphoria for Gorbachev's reforms.

In early 1986, Gerry Pocock met with his East German counterparts to discuss the leadership's loss of control of the *Morning Star* and the recent extraordinary party congress, which had confirmed a series of expulsions of hardliners. His main message was that these "sectarian" groupings has been expelled for a breach of party discipline, and that the *Morning Star* no longer represented the official position of the party majority. For this reason, Pocock insisted the SED should cut off its financial lifeline to the newspaper by terminating its long-standing subscription and transferring its allegiances to the new official party journal, *Seven Days*. East Berlin, however, was reluctant to do so.[52] The *Morning Star* remained a reliable ally. From the SED's perspective, it was the only "traditional daily newspaper of the British workers' movement [that] promotes the correct policy against Thatcherism and supports the trade unions, the peace policy of the socialist states, and the development of really existing socialism."[53] By contrast, Chris Myant, the editor of *Seven Days*, published unwelcome criticism of "really existing socialism" while providing very positive coverage of Gorbachev's reforms. Consequently, East Berlin was highly reluctant to have it sold from kiosks and stocked in libraries in the GDR at a time when Soviet publications—most famously *Sputnik*—had already been proscribed for addressing unwelcome issues in communist history. SED officials portrayed Myant as a typical British revisionist who was "anti-Soviet" and had little understanding of the "historic mission" of the proletariat, the character of revolutionary socialism, or the achievements of "really existing socialism."[54]

Despite repeated pleas from Pocock and McLennan for the SED to break off its contacts with communist hardliners in Britain, the SED continued as before, while offering an equivocal denial: "The SED does not intervene in the internal affairs of its British brother party." Conspicuously, however, East Berlin added its "regret that the CPGB's divisions weakened its campaigning for socialism."[55] It is, therefore, not surprising that on a visit to Britain during the summer of 1986, Frank Teutschbein, a member of the Central Committee, held talks with Tony Chater about the SED's continued financial support for the *Morning Star*.[56] Finally, however, the leadership of the CPGB succeeded in winning the support of the CPSU to intervene in order to restrain East Berlin. Hermann Axen, the SED's chief ideologist, was informed by Moscow that: "After consultation with the Central Committee of the CPSU, the SED's relationship to the former central organ of the CPGB is to be changed. There is, at the very least, to be a discussion with the editor-in-chief of the *Morning Star* in order to move him to end his attacks on the leadership of the CPGB in the newspaper, and to contribute to the unity of the communist movement in Britain."[57]

From this point onward, there is a noticeable shift in the language used in the SED's reports, with the hardliners being criticized for their "sectarian" views and their unwillingness to restore "unity" within the British communist movement.[58] However, contacts with the *Morning Star* were by no means abandoned. Instead, they now ran through staff at SED's central organ, *Neues Deutschland*, rather than the Central Committee's Department for International Relations. *Neues Deutschland* personnel met with Tony Chater and others on the fringes of media events in East Berlin.⁵⁹ These backchannels continued despite Pocock writing to his counterparts in East Berlin, including the irate demand that Erich Honecker should be made aware that the CCG had set up a network of *Morning Star* supporters inside the party, which was functioning as an opposition to official policy.⁶⁰

The *Morning Star* affair sheds a stark light on the fragmentation of the wider political culture of the British Left in the late 1980s. In June 1988, as the newspaper published articles by MPs and MEPs on the Bennite Left of the Labour Party and by trade unionists, Gordon McLennan told Werner Felfe, who worked for the SED's International Relations Department, that "Tony Benn lives in a world which has long gone." The general secretary of the CPGB even asked Felfe to use his contacts to exert a moderating influence on Benn and his supporters in the British labour movement.⁶¹ The reformers in the CPGB had moved decidedly to the right of the Bennite Left in the Labour Party.

In 1988, the CCG and its network of supporters of the *Morning Star* finally moved to "re-found" the communist party on the basis of Marxist–Leninist principles. The SED monitored these events and collected literature published by both the CPGB and the new CPB.⁶² Two of the seventeen British citizens living in the GDR as their main residence—John Tarver, who was at the Party University in Potsdam, and John Manning, who taught English as a foreign language—also wrote unsolicited letters to the SED's International Department emphasizing the merits of the CPB's return to Marxist–Leninist principles.⁶³ According to Jack Berlin, this was representative of the hardline views taken by many British teachers of English in the GDR.⁶⁴ Nevertheless, all the documentary evidence points to the SED trying to avoid the formation of a new, hardline communist party. However, the extent of East Berlin's contacts with hardliners was no secret in the CPGB and led to persistent rumors of East Berlin's machinations to actually split the party, rather than "merely" to attempt to influence its political direction. Graham Taylor, who organized summer schools for teachers in the GDR during the late 1980s, had been warned by friends in East Germany that the embassy was using its contacts to split the CPGB.⁶⁵ Sheila Taylor, a leading light in the Britain–GDR Society, had already heard similar threats by embassy officials in the late 1970s. More significantly, she soon found herself in conflict with her East German partner organization, the *Liga für Völkerfreundschaft*. As a university-educated Eurocommunist, her endorsement of the GDR's social and economic "achievements" came with open criticism of the lack of "freedom and democracy" in the "socialist states"—while firmly believing that the regime could democratize. This prompted East Berlin to try to sideline the Eurocommunists who ran the BGS. With the explicit aim of forcing Sheila Taylor out of office, her salary was axed. But, after a period of acting as an honorary secretary, she was replaced by other Eurocommunists—first Kathy Vanovitch (1981) and then Jack Berlin (1981–89). In the early 1980s, the SED tried to increase the role of pro-Soviet hardliners on the BGS's Executive Committee. Behind the scenes, East Berlin backed Gordon Schaffer, John Kotz, and James Lamond, all of whom were members of the pro-Soviet wing of the Labour Party, and thus free of the Eurocommunists' unwelcome political criticisms. When this too failed, there was an attempt to "regionalize" the society to eclipse the influence of the London-dominated Eurocommunist leadership, using the embassy rather than the society as the organizational hub.[66] In the second half of the 1980s, when the SED became increasingly anxious about *Westkontakte,* Sheila Taylor was prevented from entering East Berlin. Both occasions, in 1985 and 1987, were subsequently explained as "administrative errors," although—to her subsequent horror—the Stasi were investigating alleged links with MI5. Taylor's own account of events emphasizes her personal contacts with the Sussex-based academic Barbara Einhorn, who was involved with European Nuclear Disarmament, the multilateral inter-bloc anti-nuclear movement with links in East and West Germany.[67] Ironically, Sheila Taylor was working at the time for Berolina Travel, the London-based GDR travel agency.[68]

Despite all of these tensions, the Eurocommunists continued to be the driving force facilitating a surprisingly wide range of contacts and connections with the GDR. However, in 1986, confrontation came into the open between Eurocommunists and hardliners on a CPGB Teachers' Group study visit to East Germany. After hardliners attacked the Eurocommunists' outspoken support of Gorbachev's reforms, the CPGB insisted on a formal meeting with the SED leadership; the outcome was passing the leadership of the organizing committee to the Eurocommunists' Graham Taylor and Pat Allen in order to prevent any facilitation of international links between British hardliners and East Berlin. Yet, thereafter, the summer schools took on a new lease of life and ran—with adverts in *Marxism Today*—until 1990.[69] The hardline views of both East German and visiting British lecturers at the Party University were well known in party circles.[70] But the incident finally allowed Gerry Pocock to reach agreement with his counterpart Günter Sieber: from now on, the selection of all delegates attending summer schools in the GDR had to be in consultation with the CPGB leadership.[71] This warmed relations considerably.⁷² For his part, Graham Taylor wrote a short history of the summer schools in the CPGB's newsletter, which underscored the need for solidarity with East Germany.⁷³ Despite serious differences of opinion, not least over their support for Gorbachev's reforms in the Soviet Union, "proletarian internationalism" held both sides together—right up until the dying moments of the GDR.

Paradoxically, it was British Eurocommunists, especially those in the BGS, who remained the GDR's earliest and most enduring supporters, maintaining their "critical friendship" until the very end. At a celebration in London marking the GDR's 40th anniversary, an official statement from Ambassador Mitdank was read out, proclaiming: "The GDR has arrived. It has become an advanced industrial economy testifying to the vitality of socialism. It ranks today among the ten leading industrial countries of the world."⁷⁴ The assembled group believed this, and could not accept that German socialism was in its death throes. Sheila Taylor went on national television and radio to insist that the refugees streaming into the Federal Republic were only going "to visit the West, not to defect," and that "democratic renewal" remained possible.⁷⁵ Her views were typical of this small group of British communists, who had tried—very much against the odds—to show a more humane side of the GDR to a largely uninterested and understandably dismissive British public.⁷⁶ Reform communists in Britain increasingly saw themselves as democratic socialists who supported what they perceived as Gorbachev's democratizing reforms in the Soviet Union and who felt vindicated by those reforms.

When the CPGB's Congress met in 1989 to discuss the manifesto for "New Times"—a document highlighting the transition from communism to democratic socialism—the delegates were confronted by the events unfolding in the "socialist states" of Eastern Europe. Many of the delegates saw 1989 as an opportunity to relive 1968—only now with Gorbachev welcoming "reform communism" in place of Brezhnev, who had sent the tanks in to crush it. These hopes reflected the desire in the party—now divested of its own neo-Stalinists—for a viable and democratic socialist alternative to capitalism. In Willie Thompson's view, "Communist Party members could not have escaped the awareness that in maintaining fraternal relations with East European regimes and defending their essence in spite of particular criticisms, they had put themselves on the wrong side of history." This was a painful recognition. One new recruit at a Glasgow branch meeting, which was devoted to these events, felt that he was intruding on "private grief."⁷⁷ Having loyally supported Soviet communism for so long, it was difficult to let go of the illusion that it could be reformed; but Gorbachev had been hope's last gasp. None other than Eric

Hobsbawm had welcomed the arrival of Gorbachev as a representative of "our type of socialism," who offered a "glimmer of hope" that socialism with a "human face" might just about be possible still. Yet he too conceded that this flicker of "proletarian internationalism" was "the last relic of the spirit of world revolution" that had been set alight by the October Revolution of 1917.[78]

The CPGB and the End of an Era

Long before Gorbachev came to power in the Soviet Union, the CPGB had embarked on the road to reform of orthodox Marxism–Leninism. The party's program "The British Road to Socialism," which was first published in 1951 and abandoned in 1985, contained what the SED regarded as the heresy of "revisionism" from the outset—and this criticism had become acute by the 1970s.[79] In particular, the Soviet suppression of the Hungarian anti-communist rising of 1956 brought about a membership exodus in the CPGB.[80] Yet, after the suppression of the "Prague Spring" in 1968, many communists who had been critical of the Soviet military intervention stayed, and in the following years incrementally pushed the CPGB toward reform in the hope that this would allow a deeper implantation in British society.[81] What remains under-researched and in need of further study are any concrete personal links between both reform-minded and orthodox British communists with their counterparts in the Soviet Union. The CPGB archives that we have consulted for the preparation of this chapter do not give much away here, and perhaps it is simply the case that these contacts were not all that developed. After all, the British party was one of the smaller Western communist parties, and the Soviet leaders could look elsewhere, notably Italy, for inspiration if they were reform-minded, and perhaps France, if they were less so.[82]

Yet, as this chapter has argued, British reform-oriented communists never broke with "really existing socialism." They retained a position of "critical friendship" and, ultimately, a loyalty rooted in a strong internationalist tradition and a firm belief in a common enmity toward capitalism. A clean break with their common heritage always threatened to unravel a communist identity—as happened shortly after the fall of the Soviet Union in 1991, when the party voted to dissolve itself.[83] This helps to explain the enthusiasm among reform communists for Gorbachev's pursuit of perestroika and glasnost, seeing it as a belated affirmation of their own long-standing agenda, even heralding a communist renaissance.[84] Not only did the end of "Moscow's Gold" dry up the CPGB's coffers,[85] but the end of a seeming Soviet alternative to capitalism desiccated its sense of political purpose. The CPGB thus dissolved into the broader British democratic Left.[86] Nina Temple, the last general secretary of the CPGB, speaking at its final congress, told those gathered in the hall: "'We must recognize that the era of communist parties is at an end. Our own party cannot be revived by nostalgia, discredited ideologies, [or] rosy views of history."[87] The reform communism that large sections of the CPGB had championed fell with the fall of Gorbachev and his attempt to reform Soviet Russia.

Stefan Berger has been, since 2011, Professor of Social History and director of the Institute for Social Movements at the Ruhr University Bochum. He also is serving as the chairman of the History of the Ruhr Foundation. Since 2016 he has been honorary professor at Cardiff University in the UK. Previously he held the position of professor of Modern German and Comparative European History at the University of Manchester.

Norman LaPorte is an independent researcher. He has published widely on German communism, including *The German Communist Party in Saxony, 1924–33* (Peter Lang, 2003) and, with Stefan Berger, *Friendly Enemies: Britain and the GDR, 1949–1990* (Berghahn Books, 2010). His most recent publication, edited with Ralf Hoffrogge, is *Weimar Communism as Mass Movement* (Lawrence and Wishart, 2017). He is co-founding editor of the journal *Twentieth Century Communism*.

Notes

1. McElvoy, *Saddled Cow*, 172–74.
2. Jack Berlin to Gordon McLennan, 16 April 1986, in Labour History Archive, Manchester (LHAM), CPAM, CP/Cent/Int/15/03.
3. Beckett, *Enemy Within*, 212.
4. Sheila Taylor, "Reply to Authors' Email Questionnaire," October 2015.
5. Thompson, *Good Old Cause*, 201.
6. Paul Markowski, Information 87/1977 für das Politbüro, 14.7.1977, in Stiftung Archiv der Parteien und Massenorganisationen der DDR im Bundesarchiv (SAPMO-BArch), DY 30/IV/B 2/20/31, Bl. 5. Interview with Dieter Müller, September 2001. Müller met with various British hardliners, including those from split-off groupings, in his role as a lecturer at the Party University in Potsdam.
7. See Epstein, *Last Revolutionaries*, 16–18; Sabrow, *Erich Honecker*.
8. For a detailed account of this relationship, see Chen, "Defying Moscow."
9. Graham Taylor, "Reply to Authors' Email Questionnaire," October 2015.
10. Ibid.
11. Informationen zu Gesprächen mit Genosse Pocock, 29.1.1986, in SAPMO-BArch, DY 30/12865, Bl. 105.

12. 'Bericht über den Aufenthalt einer Delegation des ZK der SED unter Leitung von Roland Bauer, Mitglied des ZK, auf Einladung der KPGB vom 1. Bis 8.12.1986,' in SAPMO-BArch DY 30/12866, Bl. 78–80.
13. Berger and LaPorte, *Friendly Enemies*, 46–55, 97–99.
14. Andrews, *Endgames and New Times*, 168.
15. *Morning Star*, 26 August 1968; see also the articles in *Marxism Today*, September 1968.
16. 'Einzel-Information über die Haltung der kommunistischen Parteien Österreichs, Großbritanniens, Italiens und Norwegens zur Ereignissen in der CSSR,' 19 October 1968, in Stasi Archive, MfS HVA 136, Bl. 140.
17. Andrews, *Endgames and New Times*, 92–95, 172.
18. For a wider account of Eurocommunism, see Plotke, *Politics of Eurocommunism*; Callaghan, "Endgame," 172.
19. For wide-ranging discussion of these developments, see Morgan, Cohen and Flinn, *Communists and British Society*, 228–29; Andrews, *Endgames and News Times*, 151–52; Green, *Britain's Communists*, 282–87; Kenny, "Communism and the New Left"; Andrews, "Young Turks and Old Guards."
20. The Stasi and the International Department of the Central Committee of the SED reported regularly about the growing influence of intellectuals and members of a younger generation who were university educated and middle class. There were exceptions to the rule, such as Pete Carter, a former builder who had risen through the party ranks after joining the Young Communist League. See, for example, the documentation in Stasi Archive, MfS HVA, 78; Information über die Situation in der Kommunistischen Partei Großbritanniens, Nr.415/79 [undated: 1979], in Stasi Archive, MfS HVA 78, 10–11. SAPMO-BArch, SAPMO-BArch, DY 30/J IV/2/2/1711.
21. Information für das Politbüro, Nr.5/1979. Betrifft: Veröffentlichungen im "Morning Star" und Haltung der KPGBs, in SAPMO-BArch, DY 30/J IV/2/20/78, Bl. 3.
22. Berger and LaPorte, "Great Britain."
23. Thompson, *Good Old Cause*, 198–200.
24. In 1979, Johnson had published a seminal article calling for an end to the falsification of communist history by party historians, and for a more self-critical approach that would allow discussion of previous mistakes made by the communist movement. See Johnson, "What Kind of Communist Party History."
25. Andrews, *Endgames and New Times*, 79; Thompson, *Good Old Cause*, 183–84; Beckett, *Enemy Within*, 199; Green, *Britain's Communists*, 220, 283.
26. For an interesting discussion of these developments, see Harris, "Marxism Today." (last accessed 1 November 2016); Andrews, *Endgame and New Times*, 53–54, 57, 145, 160–62, 165, 169, 194, 203–6; Thompson, *Good Old Cause*, 165, 176.
27. For a wider discussion, see Seifert and Sibley, *Revolutionary Communist*, 171–72, 174; Andrews, *Endgames and New Times*, 189; Thompson, *Good Old Cause*, 173–74, 177, 183–87.
28. See the reports and collection of materials in: Bericht über den Aufenthalt des Genossen Frank Teutschbein von 30.7 bis 7.8.1986 in Großbritannien, 11 August 1986, in SAPMO-BArch, DY 30/12865, Bl.207ff; see also Thompson, *Good Old Cause*, 181–82, 197, 205–6.
29. For a non-communist summary of these events, see R. Morris, "Victory for Communist Hardliners," *The Times*, 12 June 1985.
30. Berger and LaPorte, "Official Anti-Communism," 156–58; Ackers, "Gramsci at the Miners' Strike."
31. Thompson, *Good Old Cause*, 197–98.
32. Bericht über den Aufenthalt des Genossen Frank Teutschbein von 30.7 bis 7.8.1986 in Großbritannien, 11 August 1986, in SAPMO-BArch, DY 30/12865, Bl. 209–10.
33. Beckett, *Enemy Within*, 190–92; Thompson, *Good Old Cause*, 191–99.
34. Graham Taylor to Gordon McLennan, 8 February 1987, in LHAM, CP/CENT/PC/16/18.

35. Monty Johnson, "The Communist Party, Marxism and Future Perspectives" [1987], in LHAM, CP/CENT/EC/23/05.
36. Gerry Pocock, "The Soviet Congress Marks Turning Point" [1986], supplement to *News & Views*, copy in LHAM, CP/CENT/INT/42/01.
37. See Political Committee Minutes of the meetings held on 11 March, 9 May, and 18 July 1988 in LHAM, CP/CENT/PC/17/04 and 05.
38. "British party has its day, but not at home," *The Times*, 8 April 1989.
39. Meeting of the Political Committee, 6 January 1987, in LHAM, CP/CENT/PC/16/17.
40. Monty Johnson, "Internationalism and the Autonomy of Communist Parties" [manuscript], paper given to the Round Table '87: Socialism, Nations, International Cooperation, in LHAM, CP/CENT/INT/51/04.
41. Monty Johnson, "Gorbachev Sets Out to Reverse Declining Trend," *7 Days*, 1 March 1986, copy in LHAM, CP/IND/JOHN/7/4/1.
42. Gerry Pocock, Discussion on 27th Congress CPSU, 26 April 1986, in LHAM, CP/CENT/INT/42/01.
43. Alexey P. Kozlov to *Marxism Today* editorial board, March 1985, in LHAM, CP/IND/JOHN/7/4/2.
44. *News and Views*, December 1989, copy in LHAM, CP/CENT/CONG/23/14.
45. Information über das Vereinigte Königreich von Großbritannien und Nordirland [1986], DY 30/12866, Bl. 20.
46. Graham Taylor, "Das andere Potsdamer Abkommen" [1987], in SAPMO-BArch, DY 30/12866, Bl. 89.
47. Bericht über den Aufenthalt des Genossen Frank Teutschbein von 30.7 bis 7.8.1986 in Großbritannien, 11 August 1986, in SAPMO-BArch, DY 30/12865, Bl. 214.
48. Ibid.
49. R. Bauer to H. Axen, 10 December 1986, in SAPMO-BArch, DY 30/12866, Bl. 75.
50. Beckett, *Enemy Within*, 211. For a report to the SED leadership, see Bericht über den Aufenthalt des Genossen Frank Teutschbein von 30.7 bis 7.8.1986 in Großbritannien, 11 August 1986, in SAPMO-BArch, DY 30/12865, Bl. 210-11.
51. Information für das Politbüro. Betrifft: Außerordentlicher 39. Parteitag der KP Großbritanniens, 12 June 1985, in SAPMO-BArch, DY 30/11533, Bl. 279–85.
52. Informationen zu Gesprächen mit Genosse Pocock, 29 January 1986, in SAPMO-BArch, DY 30/12865, Bl. 102–3.
53. [Günter] Sieber an [Hermann] Axen, 31 December 1986, in SAPMO-BArch, DY 30/12866, Bl. 73–74.
54. Paul Markowski, "Information 22/76 für das Politburo. Betrifft: Entwurf eines neuen Parteiprogramms der KPGBs, Berlin 18.2.1977," in SAPMO-BArch, DY 30/IV/B 2/20/31.
55. Konzeption für die Gespräche mit Genossen Gerry Pocock, Mitglied der Abteilung Internationale Verbindungen des Exekutivkomitees des KP Großbritanniens, 9 January 1986, in SAPMO-BArch, DY 30/12865, Bl. 92.
56. Bericht über den Aufenthalt des Genossen Frank Teutschbein von 30.7 bis 7.8.1986 in Großbritannien, 11 August 1986, in SAPMO-BArch, DY 30/12865, Bl. 214.
57. R. Bauer an Hermann Axen, 10 December 1986, in SAPMO-BArch, DY 30/12866, Bl. 77.
58. Bericht über den Aufenthalt des Genossen Frank Teutschbein von 30.7 bis 7.8.1986 in Großbritannien, 11 August 1986, in SAPMO-BArch, DY 30/12865, Bl. 81–82.
59. [Günter] Sieber an [Hermann] Axen, 31 December 86, in SAPMO-BArch, DY 30/12866, Bl. 74.
60. Vermerk über ein Gespräch zwischen Werner Felfe, Mitglied des Politbüros und Sekrtär des ZK der SED, und Gordon McLennan, Generalsekretär des ZK der KP Großbritanniens, 23 June 1988, in SAPMO-BArch, DY30/12866, Bl. 85.
61. Ibid., Bl. 85–86.

62. For copies of the CPGB's *News and Views* and CPB discussion documents, including a congress held in April 1988 at the North London Polytechnic, see SAPMO-BArch, DY 30/12868.
63. John Tarver to the International Relations Department, Socialist Unity Party of Germany, 9 May 1988, DY 30/12868, Bl. 66; John Manning an der Redaktion "Fremdspracheenunterricht," 4 October 1988, in ibid., Bl. 115.
64. Jack Berlin to Gordon McLennan, 16 April 1986, in LHAM, CPAM, CP/Cent/Int/15/03.
65. Graham Taylor, "Reply to Authors' Email Questionnaire," October 2015.
66. Interview with Sheila Taylor, 29 August 2005. Her views are confirmed by the extensive documentation in SAPMO-BArch, DY 13/3120.
67. For her response, see Sheila Taylor to GDR Ambassador, 2 April 1987, in LHAM, CP/Cent/Int/15/03.
68. Taylor, "View from the Inside," 315–17. For a wider study of this relationship, see Golz, *Verordnete Freundschaft*, esp. 212–14.
69. Taylor, "View from the Inside," 327.
70. Interview with Dieter Müller, September 2001.
71. Statement by Gerry Pocock, 17 December 1987, in DY 30/12866, Bl. 2.
72. Stand der Beziehungen SED-KPGB [1987], in SAPMO-BArch, DY 30/12866, Bl. 43.
73. Taylor, "The Other Potsdam Agreement," *News and Views*, October 1987, copy CP/CENT/CONG/23/08.
74. J. Mitdank, "A Message from the Ambassador of the GDR," in 40th Anniversary of the GDR: Souvenir Programme of the Britain–GDR Society [1989], copy in possession of authors.
75. Taylor, "View from the Inside," 328–29.
76. Berger and LaPorte, *Friendly Enemies*, 289–95.
77. Thompson, *Good Old Cause*, 204–5, and note 13.
78. Hobsbawm, *Interesting Times*, 278.
79. For SED comment on the CPGB's policies, see Glees, *The Stasi Files*, 69, 128–29.
80. For an interesting study of 1956, the definitive moment precipitating reform in the international communist movement, see Haig, "Gorizian Heretics," 8–39.
81. For a valuable overview, see Thompson, *Ideologies in the Age of Extremes*, 214–16; Andrews, *Endgame and New Times*, 92–94.
82. See the respective chapters in this volume.
83. Robinson, "New Times, New Politics."
84. See, for example, the views of reform-oriented communist John Bloomfield, in Bloomfield, "Introduction."
85. Granlund, "Moscow Gold."
86. Willie Thompson, "End of Our History: The Terminus of the CPGB," *Our History* (July 1992), 3–6.
87. M. Horsnell, "Class Warriors Fold Away Tattered Red Flag," *The Times*, 23 November 1991.

Bibliography

Ackers, Peter. "Gramsci at the Miners' Strike: Remembering the 1984–1985 Eurocommunist Alternative Industrial Relations Strategy," *Labour History*, No. 2 (1985), 151–72.

Andrews, Geoff. *Endgames and New Times: The Final Years of British Communism, 1964–1991*, London, 2004.

———. "Young Turks and Old Guards: Intellectuals and the CP Leadership in the 1970s," in *Opening the Books: Essays on the Social and Cultural History of the British Communist Party*, ed. Geoff Andrew, Nina Fishman, and Kevin Morgan, London, 1995, 225–50.
Beckett, Francis. *The Enemy Within: The Rise and Fall of the British Communist Party*, London, 1995.
Berger, Stefan, and Norman LaPorte. "Great Britain: Between Avoiding Cold War and Supporting Free Trade Unionism," in *Solidarity with Solidarity: Western Trade Unions and the Polish Crisis, 1980–1982*, ed. Idesbald Goddeeris, Plymouth, 2010, 129–58.
———. "Official Anti-Communism and What Lay Beneath: The British Trade Unions and the 'Other Germany,' 1949–1989," in *The Other Germany: Perceptions and Influences in British–East German Relations, 1945–1990*, ed. idem, Augsburg, 2005, 141–58.
———. *Friendly Enemies: Britain and the GDR, 1949–1990*, Oxford, 2010.
Bloomfield, John. "Introduction," in *The Soviet Revolution: Perestroika and the Making of Socialism*, ed. idem, London, 1989, 7–16.
Callaghan, John. "Endgame," in *Western European Communists and the Collapse of Communism*, ed. D.S. Bell, Oxford, 1993, 121–38.
Chen, Zhong Z. "Defying Moscow, Engaging Beijing: The German Democratic Republic's Relations with the People's Republic of China, 1980–1989," PhD dissertation, London School of Economics, 2014.
Epstein, Catherine. *The Last Revolutionaries: German Communists and their Century*, Cambridge, MA, 2003.
Glees, Anthony. *The Stasi Files: East Germany's Secret Operations against Britain*, London, 2003.
Golz, Hans-Georg. *Verordnete Freundschaft: Das Wirken der Freundschaftsgesellschaft DDR-Großbritannien und der Britain–GDR Society—Möglichkeiten und Grenzen*, Leipzig, 2004.
Granlund, Chris. "Moscow Gold: You Bought the Magazine Now Play the Game," *Marxism Today* (December 1991), 32–33.
Green, John. *Britain's Communists: The Untold Story*, London, 2014.
Haig, Fiona. "Gorizian Heretics of 1956: Euro-communism Starts Here?", *Twentieth Century Communism* No. 9 (2015), 8–39.
Harris, John. "Marxism Today: The Forgotten Visionaries Whose Ideas Could Save Labour," *The Guardian* (online version), 29 September 2015. Retrieved 1 November 2016 from https://www.theguardian.com/politics/2015/sep/29/marxism-today-forgotten-visionaries-whose-ideas-could-save-labour.
Hobsbawm, Eric. *Interesting Times: A Twentieth-Century Life*, London, 2002.
Johnson, Monty. "What Kind of Communist Party History," *Our History*, No. 4 (1979), 5–9.
Kenny, Michael. "Communism and the New Left," in *Opening the Books*, ed. Geoff Andrews, Nina Fishman, and Kevin Morgan, Boulder, CO, 195–209.
McElvoy, Anne. *The Saddled Cow: East Germany's Life and Legacy*, London, 1992.
Morgan, Kevin, Gidon Cohen and Andrew Flinn. *Communists and British Society, 1920–1991*, London, 2007.

Plotke, David. *The Politics of Eurocommunism: Socialism in Transition*, Boston, MA, 1999.
Robinson, Emily. "New Times, New Politics: History and Memory during the Final Years of the CPGB," *British Politics*, No. 4 (2011), 453–78.
Sabrow, Martin. *Erich Honecker: Das Leben davor, 1912–1945*, Munich, 2016.
Seifert, Roger, and Tom Sibley. *Revolutionary Communist at Work: A Political Biography of Bert Ramelson*, London, 2011.
Taylor, Sheila. "A View from the Inside," in *The Other Germany: Perceptions and Influences in British–East German Relations, 1945–1990*, ed. Stefan Berger and Norman LaPorte, Augsburg, 2005, 315–30.
Thompson, Willie. *The Good Old Cause: British Communism 1920–1999*, London, 1992.
_____. *Ideologies in the Age of Extremes: Liberalism, Conservativism, Communism and Fascism 1914–91*, London, 2011.

Chapter 11

Premature Perestroika
The Dutch Communist Party and Gorbachev

Gerrit Voerman

The reaction of the Communist Party of the Netherlands (CPN) to glasnost and perestroika, the reforms with which Mikhail Gorbachev as secretary of the Communist Party of the Soviet Union (CPSU) surprised the world after his coming to power in March 1985, was in essence "déjà vu." Basically, the CPN believed that it itself had gone through a process of reconstruction in the early 1980s in a way that anticipated the reforms initiated in the Soviet Union, although, of course, the scale and setting were completely different. Because of its premature renovation, the CPN assigned itself a position in the modernizing avant garde of the international communist movement.

In this chapter, the response of the CPN to the reforms of Gorbachev will be described.[1] Some attention, however, has to be paid first to the metamorphosis the Dutch party underwent at the beginning of the 1980s, especially with reference to its international standpoint and its reappraisal of Leninism and "really existing socialism." The changes that came about in this area were determinant in the attitude the CPN adopted later. In addition, the somewhat ambivalent reactions to the downfall of East European socialism within the CPN will be discussed. Although the Dutch communists had already decided in principle on cooperation with the Radical Party (PPR) and the Pacifist Socialist Party (PSP) within the framework of a new environmental political formation called "Groen Links" (Green Left), the tearing down of the Iron Curtain certainly contributed to the decision to merge completely

---

Notes for this chapter begin on page 251.

with the PPR and PSP in Green Left, and to dissolve the CPN in June 1991.

Hence, before describing the modernized CPN of the 1980s, its existence as an orthodox communist party and in particular its less orthodox relation to the Soviet Union must be examined.[2] From the early 1960s to the mid-1970s, the CPN was one of the byways of the international communist movement. During this period, the party distanced itself from Moscow's leading role within world communism (although it did not dissociate itself from Soviet theory and practice), and later on the CPN would boast of this "autonomous" position and describe itself as "pioneering."

The Orthodox CPN

The history of the CPN stretches back to before the Russian Revolution. In the Netherlands, the split between reformists and orthodox revolutionary Marxists within the labor movement had already taken place in 1909. This gave the CPN a certain independence when the Communist International was set up. However, Moscow quickly gained control of the Dutch Communist Party, and, like every other party, it had been "bolshevized" by the late 1920s.[3] In the following decade it became Stalinized: the party identified fully with the Soviet Union, its organization was highly centralized, it banned dissenting opinions, and was guided by an omnipotent leader. This leader, from 1938 until 1977, was party secretary Paul de Groot, who dictated the political line of the CPN and monopolized the relations with its sister parties, and especially the CPSU.[4]

After World War II, the CPN returned to legality as a political satellite of the Soviet Union, and during the Cold War the party completely associated with Moscow.[5] In international affairs, the CPN espoused the so-called "theory of the two camps," accusing the capitalist camp, led by the United States, of preparing a third World War. Only through the efforts of the (by nature) peaceful socialist camp headed by Moscow, said the CPN, could this be avoided. In this "battle for peace," the CPN took part in "indissoluble solidarity with the Soviet Union," according to the party's draft declaration of principles (the definite version has never been determined). Not only because of its international role but also its social system, the Soviet Union was held to be a radiant example. The CPN reassured its adherents that the victory of socialism in the Soviet Union was attended "with the birth of a new type of human being ... namely Socialist man, who as a priority believes the welfare of the community to be a precondition of his personal welfare." All these triumphs were attributed to Stalin, who was praised as "the greatest reformer of society, teacher and statesman who has ever led progressive humanity."[6]

De-Stalinization, which was started in 1956 by Khrushchev's secret speech, shocked the Dutch Communists.[7] The CPN executive announced that Stalin had made some mistakes, but it remained nevertheless very favorable about its Soviet mentor. Yet the party leadership regretted that it had defended the personality cult to the Dutch public, and stated that it would never again "stand against internal events in other countries if these fell outside of its area of knowledge."[8] Non-interference in other parties (confirmed by the 18th Congress of the CPN in October 1956) was a prelude to the concept of "autonomy" to which the CPN was converted in the early 1960s. The concept of "polycentrism," developed by Palmiro Togliatti, the leader of the Italian Communist Party (PCI), however, was strongly criticized by the CPN: the leading role of the Soviet Union was not in question. In fact, the CPN was *plus royaliste que le roi*—that is to say, more Stalinist than Moscow itself. The introduction of the idea of "non-interference" seemed to be dictated only by repugnance at Khrushchev's unmasking of Stalin, and was an excuse for the party not to have to face the problem of de-Stalinization. In this way, party secretary De Groot was able to avoid a debate about his powerful and dominant position within the CPN.

The CPN as International Outsider

In the 1960s, the CPN was estranged from the Soviet Union because of the conflict between Moscow and Peking. In summer 1963, after the breakdown of the negotiations between the two communist powers, De Groot declared the "autonomy" of the CPN within the international communist movement. The impulse behind this came from the possible rupture of the special relations between the Dutch communists and the pro-Chinese Indonesian Communist Party, which could come about because of the Sino–Soviet dispute. Both parties had been engaged for decades in a common struggle against the Dutch colonial system. On the ideological differences between Khrushchev and Mao, De Groot stated that the conflict was essentially "about economic issues, about the balance of power within the Socialist camp and within the international communist movement." From then on, the CPN would be "responsible to the working population of the Netherlands only ... Our international activities are only useful if they are made subservient to our primary tasks."[9]

Nevertheless, the CPN stuck to its view that the socialist countries as such—including the Soviet Union—were the only factors promoting global peace, and declared therefore that "the expansion of the Soviet sphere of influence was a historic step forward."[10] Moreover, the CPN did not turn pro-Chinese; the emerging Maoist tendency within the party was expelled overnight, as was a small pro-Soviet group. Moscow was held responsible for the schism in the international movement and, in consequence, relations of the CPN with the Soviet Union worsened. International communist meetings were attended either by a low-ranking delegation or not at all; contacts with sister parties were placed on the back burner. In 1967, the Dutch party did not celebrate the sixtieth anniversary of the Russian Revolution and, one year later, the armed intervention of the Warsaw Pact in Czechoslovakia was strongly condemned as a "shameful violation of Leninist principles."[11]

The Eurocommunist Curse

After a short period of détente with Moscow around 1970, Dutch communists' xenophobia continued: the CPN isolated itself and was vigilant against "hostile interventions."[12] However, it kept aloof not just from orthodox communist parties such as the CPSU, but also from the "Eurocommunist" Italian, French, and Spanish parties, which were trying to modernize.[13] The CPN not only perceived them as "revisionist," but also suspected they would create a new European framework with a new (Italian) "center"—which was regarded as a threat to its "autonomous" position. However, the CPN boasted that it had introduced the concept of "autonomy" in the international communist movement long before Eurocommunists were claiming a greater degree of independence from Moscow.

In the mid-1970s, this position of self-chosen isolation started to change: slowly but surely the CPN made its entry onto the international scene, coming closer to Moscow again. In June 1976 it took part in the conference of European communist parties in East Berlin, and supported the resolution in which the "autonomy" and "independence" of all parties was defended.[14] The importance the conference attached to the concept of "autonomy" as one of the basic rules of mutual relations within the international communist movement was regarded as a victory by the CPN.[15] Sticking to this principle, the Dutch refused to take a stand in the dispute between the Eurocommunist parties on the one hand and the Moscow-orientated orthodox ones on the other. In practice, the CPN praised the "international peace-loving policy" of the Soviet Union, but also condemned "reactionary interference in the internal affairs of the Socialist countries."[16]

Renewal of the CPN

This temporary public courtship of the CPN with the CPSU did not bring electoral good fortune. On the contrary, in May 1977, just after an unexpected visit of the party leadership to Moscow, the CPN lost five out of its seven parliamentary seats. Instead of participation in government, which the party had aimed for, Dutch communism became politically marginalized. After some time, however, the electoral defeat ushered in a period of profound ideological change.[17] First the party shook off its Stalinist coat and went on to renounce its Leninist heritage: "Leninism" was abolished, both as a theory and as an organizational model. At the same time, the emerging new social movements managed a hold onto the CPN. In the course of the 1980s, an entirely new party made its appearance, which eventually merged into the new political formation Green Left at the end of the decade.[18] In this landslide, the traditional view of the socialist countries changed profoundly, and the principle of the "two camps" also perished. Paradoxically, since the East Berlin conference in 1976 and the party congress in 1978, the CPN in parallel intensified contacts with its sister parties, including those in Eastern Europe and the Soviet Union.[19]

The CPN's metamorphosis was preceded by a change in the social composition of its membership.[20] Within the communist membership, industrial workers were replaced by members of the "new middle class," who were promoting new, post-materialist demands like equality between women and men, environmental protection, and democratization, and were less attached to the Soviet Union. The young newcomers initially conformed to the rules and traditions of the Stalinist party, but after the disastrous parliamentary elections in 1977, intellectuals and (later) feminists rebelled against the Stalinist cadres and demanded more freedom of discussion and ideological renewal.[21] The strife between the orthodox wing and the renovators ended in a victory for the latter. Under the pressure of the combined opposition of intellectuals and feminist members, Leninist ideology was thrown overboard in 1984; the abolition of the Leninist principle of democratic centralism followed five years later.

The new era was ushered in at the 26th Congress of January 1978. Here the strategic concept of the "coalitions formation" was unfolded. Communists, socialists, progressive Christians and others were urged to link up to form an alternative to the center-right governing coalition. Apart from parties, all kinds of social organizations were invited to contribute to this so-called "democratic power formation." Apart from these strategic changes, a new ideological program was announced in which the CPN would map out the "Dutch road to socialism."

Although the CPN seemed to adopt a different tone, it initially remained Marxist–Leninist, which also became manifest in its attitude toward the socialist countries. In accordance with its "autonomous position," the CPN declared its unwillingness to defend everything happening in Eastern Europe, but at the same time it condemned "the reactionary interference in the internal affairs of the socialist countries." The party admitted that there were "unsolved problems," "contradictions in the internal development" and "common difficulties" in the Eastern bloc, but also stated that "no party had the right to interfere in another party's affairs."[22]

The CPN also remained committed to the orthodox "theory of the two camps," in which the United States was escalating the arms race, whereas the Soviet Union was not only pursuing a policy of détente but was also the power supporting the masses struggling for peace. Hence, "the socialist countries are indispensable allies of the Dutch working class in the struggle against the dangers of the arms race."[23] At the beginning of the 1980s, this Moscow-dominated stand was still predominant within the CPN: the bracketing of the Soviet Union with the United States as jointly responsible for the arms race was rejected. Any analysis that put the Soviet Union and the United States on a par ignored all distinctions between "bellicose" capitalism and "peace-loving" socialism, according to the CPN;[24] therefore the peace movement in the Netherlands and elsewhere had to oppose Washington, and not Moscow.

Changes in International Policy

Within a few years, however, the CPN had changed this "theory of the two camps" precisely for the traditionally abused "theory of the superpowers." Although this volte-face in its international position was part of the general metamorphosis the Dutch party was experiencing, two factors in particular played a role. In the first place were events that took place in the late 1970s and early 1980s, such as the Soviet invasion of Afghanistan, the military coup in Poland, and the war between Vietnam and China. Then there was the success of the peace movement in the Netherlands, the one the CPN had initiated, and which led to a kind of merger with the more significant, broader and less radical peace movement. At the same time, the CPN itself was drawn in a more "neutral" direction.

In August 1977, the CPN started a wide campaign against the introduction of the neutron bomb by the United States, which, apart from its direct aim, was also intended to improve the morale of the communist rank and file after the electoral disaster. The anti-American objective of the campaign was of course fully in line with Moscow's international policy; no wonder the CPN's campaign was supported financially by the CPSU and the Socialist Unity Party of Germany (Sozialistische Einheitspartei Deutschlands, SED), the ruling party in the German Democratic Republic.[25] The campaign proved to be a success; within nine months the communists had collected more than a million signatures. This improved the prestige of the CPN within the international communist movement and contributed to the breaking of its isolation. Moreover, the Dutch Parliament spoke against the N-bomb. The communist leadership decided to extend the campaign to the arms race as a whole; the 27th Congress of the CPN of June 1980 made the "struggle for peace" a priority. The "Stop the N-bomb, Stop the Arms Race" committee took part in the developing broader peace movement in the early 1980s and campaigned against the stationing of American Pershing IIs and cruise missiles in the Netherlands in the first place, but the Soviet SS-20s were also criticized. Of course, the leadership of "Stop the N-bomb" could not do less without isolating itself and losing its gains; hence, in this respect, it made concessions in order to participate in the broader peace movement.

Criticism of Soviet nuclear armament was facilitated by the change in the international position of the CPN in the early 1980s. The unshakable faith in the "peaceableness" of the socialist block[26] was damaged firstly by the Soviet invasion of Afghanistan in December 1979. The invasion was indirectly and cautiously denounced after some weeks of silence. The chair of the communist group in the Dutch parliament, Marcus Bakker, described the "one-sided military" Soviet way of acting as "an ill-fated decision," though in the last resort the United States was held responsible.[27] The credibility of "really existing socialism" received a severer blow from the military coup d'état in Poland. Immediately after General Wojciech Jaruzelski had seized power in December 1981, the coup and the subsequent repression of the non-communist trade union Solidarność (Solidarity) were condemned by the CPN "unconditionally and unequivocally."[28] The involvement of the CPSU in a neighboring country was also rejected as "an intervention in Polish affairs." In an explanation, Jaap Wolff, the director of the scientific bureau of the CPN, repudiated the argument that the Polish military had to intervene in order to protect the safety of the Warsaw Pact as a whole. His party rejected the idea that "the interests of the blocs—and within these, those of the strongest powers—are decisive."[29]

Thus, in the early 1980s, the CPN gradually abandoned the dogma of the socialist bloc as its natural ally in the "anti-imperialist" struggle. In fact, socialism as a mobilizing theme was replaced by the peace movement. This simultaneous emancipation and revaluation was partly the result of the relative success of the communist campaign against the N-bomb and the rise of the broader peace movement in which the communists participated. The CPN argued that the concept of "mutual deterrence" and the maintenance of the balance of power between both superpowers had not resulted in a lasting peace; henceforth the mass struggle for peace in the capitalist world was held to be decisive. However, the view of both the Soviet Union and the United States as joint instigators of the arms race and dominators of their "blocs" was contested within the CPN. The orthodox wing argued that the ideological disorientation of the party had resulted in the integration of "Stop the N-bomb" into the "pacifist, neutralist, and classless" peace movement; only a return to class consciousness in international affairs could open a new perspective. The "objectively" positive anti-imperialist contribution of the Soviet Union and the partition of the world into two camps had to be accepted.[30] Yet at the 28th Congress of the CPN in November 1982, the orthodox wing suffered a heavy defeat. The congress no longer endorsed the Soviet Union as an "automatic and natural ally in the struggle against the arms race."[31] The party recognized that the existence of two hostile political-military blocs, one under the leadership of the United States and the other headed by the Soviet Union, had induced the arms spiral (although the CPN still saw the United States as the engine of the arms race). In order to halt escalation, both blocs, NATO and the Warsaw Pact, had to be dissolved.

Building on the congress resolution that had put the peace struggle at the top of the agenda, the CPN started a diplomatic offensive within the international communist and left-wing movement. Despite all political and ideological differences, the party maintained and further built on friendly relations with its sister parties elsewhere, focusing on peace and disarmament, and the exchange of information and experiences.[32] This policy of consultations was consistent with its domestic coalition strategy: the CPN had contacts not only with ecologist movements elsewhere, and with Polish Solidarity and the informal civic movement in Czechoslovakia, Charta 77, but also with the CPSU and other orthodox communist parties. The CPSU leadership in its turn was interested in the CPN because of the hesitations the Dutch government manifested about stationing American missiles in the Netherlands. In these contacts, the CPN did not shy away from raising sensitive issues. When a Dutch communist delegation visited Moscow at the end of 1984, they made no secret to their Soviet interlocutors of their reservations with regard to the concept of military parity between East and West: the CPN advocated nothing less than the dissolution of the blocs. In discussions with the CPSU, the Dutch party chair Elly Izeboud stated that they "did not believe the SS-20s [nuclear missiles of the Soviet Union] to be a contribution to Dutch safety."[33] Despite the change of line and the open criticisms, some members of the renovating wing in the CPN believed that the party was still too Moscow-minded and broke away (like Member of Parliament Gijs Schreuders).

Criticism of the One-Party System

The emancipation of the CPN from international Soviet policy was accompanied by dissociation from the sociopolitical system of the Soviet Union. This criticism of the one-party system was also a part of the CPN's transformation. In this process of detachment, the Polish military coup d'état by General Jaruzelski was again a catalyst. The intervention of the Polish military had demonstrated the "bankruptcy of the authoritarian statist model of socialism."[34] According to the CPN in its denunciation, the Polish Communist Party had blocked a real renovating popular movement, demonstrating the failure of the one-party system at the same time. In the eyes of the renovating CPN, democracy started from power sharing and coalitions. Restoration of all democratic rights in Poland was demanded, including the freedom of trade unions.

In the wake of the Polish events, the monolithic and totalitarian structures in Eastern Europe increasingly became the subject of criticism, which focused on the monopoly of power by a small group within the apparatus of party and state. At the same time, the CPN attached greater value to the unfolding new social movements in the Netherlands, such as women's liberation, environmental, anti-nuclear and peace movements as partners within the hoped-for coalitions. Correspondingly, the dissident political groups in Eastern Europe that had taken a stand against the socialist regimes came into the Dutch party's view—not only as possible alternatives to the one-party state, but also as possible allies against the division of Europe into two blocs. This development culminated at the 28th Congress of the CPN in November 1982. The party expressed its sympathy with "the democratic opposition movements in East European countries" such as Solidarity and Charta 77, and decided "not to maintain relations with the Polish and Czechoslovak communist parties in the circumstances."[35]

The New "Marxist–Feminist" Party Program of 1984

The criticism of the international position of the Soviet Union by the CPN and its related verdict on the domestic affairs in the "Socialist motherland"—in fact, a violation of the principle of non-intervention, which was part of the doctrine of autonomy so much cherished by the Dutch communists—were laid down in an entirely new declaration of principles which was ratified by the extraordinary party congress of February 1984. In this declaration, the CPN not only distanced itself from the pretentious Leninist concept of the communist party as the vanguard of the working class and its leading role—the justification of the one-party state—but also exchanged Leninism as an ideology for feminism as one of its "sources of inspiration." Although Marxism survived, the idea of "class struggle" as the sole motor of history was abandoned. Instead of the basic clash between capital and labor, the declaration recognized the existence of various other "contradictions," such as the ones between the genders, man and nature, North and South, and hetero- and homosexuality. The CPN declared that it was "opposed to the mixing of the policy of the state with religion or a specific ideology, and rejected the identification of state with party." The party supported the multi-party system as being "essential to a democratic way of decision making. Within socialism, constitutional rights ... have to be guaranteed to every party, whatever their social views."[36]

In the new declaration of principles, there was no laudatory reference to the Soviet Union. The CPN still accepted the antithesis between West and East, but it did not side with one of the protagonists. Instead it committed itself to a "new socialist internationalism," which was aimed at the dissolution of the international blocs. In the party's program, Moscow and Washington were again held jointly responsible for the arms race, although it was thrust upon the socialist countries, which had "overestimated the role of military force within international relations and underestimated the consequences of military might on the attractiveness and development of socialism."[37] Democratic renovating movements within "really existing socialism" were pressured by the authorities, who were manipulating the perception of an imperialist threat. The CPN again expressed its support for these dissident democratic groups in Eastern Europe.

Immediately after the party congress, the conservative wing proceeded to found the League of Communists of the Netherlands (Verbond van Communisten in Nederland: VCN). An orthodox manifesto was drawn up, based on rigid Marxist–Leninist principles such as the leading role of the communist party, a positive view of "really existing socialism," and unconditional loyalty to the Soviet Union as the "fortress of peace and progress."[38] The CPN was charged with "revisionism and defeatism," because it had underestimated the power of the socialist countries in the "anti-imperialist battle." Orthodox party members who would later play a dominant role in the VCN asserted that by denying the class character of the struggle for peace, and by seeing Moscow and Washington as similar superpowers, the CPN had slid down to "neutralism, anti-Sovietism and opportunism."[39] Hence, as a result of the CPN's politics, the position of the United States and NATO was objectively strengthened.

Perestroika before the Word

By the mid-1980s, the CPN had been completely transformed. Its traditional concept of the communist avant garde had been abandoned, the multiparty system had been embraced, democratic centralism had been repudiated, and the party had been remodeled into a "democratic and feminist organization"[40] in which pluralism, respect for minority opinions, and open decision-making processes were guaranteed. It was not so surprising that the reforms introduced by CPSU general secretary, Mikhail Gorbachev, which can be placed under the labels of glasnost and perestroika, were well received within the CPN. In late 1985, the first positive remarks could be read in the party's publications. In the following years, both the changes in the international policy of the Soviet Union and the domestic process of renovation, in which rigid bureaucratic centralism apparently made way for more democracy, were welcomed.

After a period in which the orthodox communist parties elsewhere were scornful of the renewal of the CPN, the Dutch communists now saw prospects for their rehabilitation. Former chairman Henk Hoekstra, for instance, recalled the skepticism when talking to East European officials about the transformation of the CPN in the early 1980s. Now he was justified. "It cannot be denied that issues that we have put on the agenda were very relevant and are nowadays central problems everywhere—in the CPSU and other Communist Parties."[41] According to Hoekstra,[42] the CPN had made the running in the international communist movement by putting these vexing questions on the agenda. His successor as party chair, Izeboud, shared his opinion: "The problems that are on the agenda in the Soviet Union ... do not sound unfamiliar to us. They have been the subject of discussions in the CPN." According to her, these were essential issues related to contemporary communist politics. "This is confirmed by what is happening in the Soviet Union right now."[43]

Apart from this somewhat pretentious notion of having been one of the pioneers of the modern international communist movement, the CPN claimed to have exercised some influence on Gorbachev's change of the Soviet Union's international policy, especially the abandonment of its objective of strategic nuclear parity with the United States. With his strategy of de-escalation, Gorbachev had rejected the search for parity of military power between the two superpowers, at least as the CPN saw it. This renunciation of the reliance on increasing armaments in order to maintain peace was regarded as a "'Copernican revolution' in the political-military way of thinking" of a superpower.[44] Now Gorbachev had tried to stop the war of attrition by offering fundamental concessions in order to reduce arms, despite efforts by the United States' president, Ronald Reagan, to step up the race again by announcing the deployment of Euromissiles and the Strategic Defense Initiative (SDI).

When the United States and the Soviet Union agreed to halt the arms race, the CPN considered itself one of the pacemakers in the communist world. It took it for granted that conversations that had been held with the CPSU in previous years had contributed somewhat to this change of direction. Wolff, the official representative of the CPN at the 27th Congress of the CPSU, argued that "the discussions, the sometimes critical dialogue the CPN has had with the CPSU, have had a positive influence."[45] In his party's view, the underlying factor behind Moscow's transformation in foreign policy was the growing awareness within the Soviet leadership that the imperialist United States could not be stopped without the support of the peace movement of the capitalist countries. The Kremlin's analysis was believed to be a recognition of the stand that the CPN had taken for years: in order to establish a strong peace movement, Dutch communists had not been willing to subordinate the struggle for peace to the "class struggle," and had criticized the Western as well as the Eastern contribution to the nuclear arms race. By exceeding narrow class bounds, the coalitions for peace could be broadened to the full. At that time, this strategy had not been appreciated in orthodox communist circles, according to Jan de Boo, the CPN's international secretary, but in retrospect the CPN had advocated political initiatives "that now are taken by the Soviet Union on a large scale."[46]

The Latent Socialist Ideal

Despite the renovation of the CPN, its distance from the Soviet Union and the subsequent departure of the orthodox wing, a basic and also traditional affinity with the "socialist motherland" had still not fully disappeared within the party. In welcoming Gorbachev, some within the CPN nourished hopes that Soviet communism might be able to renew itself. Members of the old guard cherished these expectations. The party's *éminence grise* Bakker, for instance, asked himself whether "communism might again become a fascinating ideal ... because of this large socialist state, the Soviet Union?"⁴⁷ Others also hoped that Gorbachev's efforts to add democracy to the "really existing socialist system" might increase the political appeal of socialist ideology. Remarkably, opinion about the Soviet Union became more positive again within the party as a whole, even though Moscow seemed to have been definitively "eradicated as a source of inspiration within the CPN" in the previous years.⁴⁸

The main reason for a revaluation of the Soviet Union was that despite all the criticisms, the CPN still believed the Soviet socioeconomic system to be essentially socialist. An open-minded, fundamental, and critical analysis of the sociopolitical structure of the "really existing socialist" countries had never been undertaken, despite the party's ideological renovation. Its traditional outlook on the Soviet Union in this sense was demonstrated very clearly at the seventieth celebration of the October Revolution in 1987, when a special issue of the theoretical magazine of the CPN was dedicated to the "first successful Socialist revolution." Moreover, at the international celebration in Moscow in November, the CPN wished "much success in the building of socialism."⁴⁹ Soviet society was "socialist," for better or for worse; for the CPN the formal possession of the means of production by the community was apparently a sufficient basis for socialism.

As a consequence of this partial revaluation of the Soviet Union within the CPN, a rapprochement appeared to be under way between the renovating and orthodox currents of Dutch communism. The CPN believed that Gorbachev's reforms were in line with the party's own policy in the early 1980s. The VCN, which had followed Moscow slavishly, hailed the political changes under Gorbachev as a proof of the renovating capacities of Leninism. In the eyes of the orthodox communists who had broken away, a rendezvous in Red Square with their former opponents within the party was conceivable. Yet despite their insistence, the CPN was not willing to even consider a reunion.

Instead of merging with the orthodox communists, the CPN—which had not been represented in the Second Chamber since the elections of 1986—entered in a Green Left electoral coalition with Radicals (PPR) and Pacifist Socialists (PSP) in 1989.⁵⁰ At the parliamentary elections, under the banner Green Left, these parties—together with a small progressive Christian party and representatives of new social movements—took 6 out of 150 seats, which was 3 more than the component parts had acquired separately in the previous elections in 1986. Dutch communists re-entered the Second Chamber after an absence of three years. After the elections, the organizational development of Green Left was continued at the expense of the independence of the participating parties, and in November 1990, a new party, using the same Green Left name, was officially founded.

This party tried to combine ecological, "green" demands aimed at environmental protection with traditional left-wing "red" issues, like a just income distribution. The "old" parties all dissolved themselves in 1991, including the CPN, on 15 June. During the 1990s, the former communists, in an ideological and political respect, gradually changed from red to green within their new eco-socialist organizational environment. By the beginning of the twenty-first century, there was hardly any trace of a communist legacy in Green Left.[51]

Disintegration of Eastern Europe in 1989

Partly because of the hopes that were entertained for the possible appearance of a revitalized socialism of high moral standing as the result of glasnost and perestroika, the revolutions behind the Iron Curtain at the end of 1989 were a cold shower for the CPN. Of course, the Dutch communists were pleased with the disintegration of the first of the two political blocks in Europe, which was consistent with their international objectives.[52] They desired not only the dissolution of the Warsaw Pact, but also of NATO—however, NATO had no intention at all of doing so. Even more disappointing, or even shocking, was the awareness of how "really existing socialism" and one-party states had *really* functioned; the break-up of the Warsaw Pact shed a harsh light on the way socialism had operated in practice, revealing moral bankruptcy.

When this was discussed within the party executive, some members maintained that the CPN was not touched by the revelations; as it had already long distanced itself from the Stalinist party model, introduced internal democracy, and condemned the invasions of the Warsaw Pact in Czechoslovakia and the Soviet Union in Afghanistan. Others, however, used the terms "identity crisis" and "disillusion." Because the CPN had always stuck to the dogma that East European societies were still socialist in a certain way, the party was hit very hard by the destruction of the Iron Curtain. Ina Brouwer, the last chair of the communist group in the Dutch parliament, wrote shortly after the events in February 1990: "What do you mean, socialism? Just a short time ago, the October Revolution of 1917 produced a worthy successor in the Revolution of 1989, which deposed the ruling communist parties or compelled them to abdicate."[53] Socialism turned out not to have been a guarantee against unemployment, poverty, environmental destruction and so on, but appeared to have been a facade to hide corruption and abuse of power. This was not, of course, completely unsuspected—but the bare truth that was revealed went far beyond what had been imagined.

Within the CPN, a debate started in 1990 about the practice of socialism, in which fundamental questions were not evaded. The concept of the "communist vanguard" in particular was identified behind the East European abuses and the besmirching of elevated socialist ideals. Yet the CPN's fundamental affinity with the East European social systems (despite all its criticisms), was not questioned during these discussions. Avoiding this painful self-analysis, the CPN turned away from the East European socialist variant. It was losing an illusion but not abandoning its ideals, as the party executive made clear at the beginning of 1991, a few months before the congress was going to decide about the dissolution of the CPN:

> The objective of the CPN was the accomplishment of a Socialist Netherlands in a democratic way and by forming coalitions. This aspiration was seriously hampered in the course of time by errors and abuses in the countries that called themselves socialist. And although in the early 1960s the CPN, as one of the first communist parties, had opted for an autonomous course, the image of "really existing socialism" has always haunted the CPN, despite clear statements of the party with respect to important events, such as the Russian invasions of Czechoslovakia in 1968 and Afghanistan in 1979, the Polish coup in 1981, and the bloody repression of the democratic people's movement in China in 1989. The fact that systems have existed in the world that called themselves Socialist, and which are bankrupt politically and morally, is no reason for the CPN to abandon its ideals, although it has to be recognized that the crisis within the East European countries was far deeper than had been assumed in the past, and that the basis for socialist ideas has been narrowed considerably because of this crisis.[54]

The End of Dutch Communism

The history of the relations of the CPN with the Soviet Union is paradoxical. In the "autonomous" phase in the 1960s and early 1970s, the CPN had hardly any contacts with Moscow but followed in the ideological tracks of the CPSU. In the 1980s, the CPN gave up Marxist–Leninist orthodoxy and drifted away from the Soviet Union, but at the same time, contacts became more frequent than in the period after the Cold War. The traditional concept of socialism as a peace-loving global force could not withstand the drive to renovation within the CPN after around 1980. Yet the idea that the societies behind the Iron Curtain were in essence socialist, though in a rudimentary form, survived the ideological and organizational transformation of the Dutch party, and formed the link between the orthodox and the modernist phase in the relations with Moscow.

The fraternal thread between the CPN and the CPSU was cut by the fall of communism in Eastern Europe in 1989. Just before, the affinity with the Soviet Union had become stronger again because of Gorbachev's reforms, in which the CPN recognized some of its own ideas. The impending end of the party-state and the new era of détente gave rise to hopes of a socialist renaissance. Yet after the downfall of East European socialism, the party could not maintain the myth of "really existing socialism" any longer, and turned away.

Thus in 1990, the CPN merged into Green Left; one year later it dissolved itself. Its route to this new political formation, however, was traced out some time before 1989, though the speed of the merger—and the corresponding decision to dissolve the party—was accelerated by the fall of the Berlin Wall. As in the beginning when the CPN was not the consequence of the Russian Revolution of 1917 (the existing revolutionary Marxist party merely changed its name), so in the end the death of the party was not caused by the East European revolution of 1989 alone. Above all, the dissolution of the CPN was the product of an "autonomous" development, which—viewed in retrospect—was ushered in by the "premature perestroika" that Dutch communism went through in the early 1980s.

Gerrit Voerman has a PhD in history from the University of Groningen, the Netherlands, on the Communist Party of the Netherlands (CPN) and its relationship with the Communist International (1919–1930). He is historian and director of the Documentation Centre Dutch Political Parties, and professor of Development and Functioning of the Dutch and European Party System at the University of Groningen. He has published widely in (inter)national journals and edited volumes on the CPN, and also more generally on Dutch political parties, especially on party history and identity, organization and membership, and candidate selection. Since 2008, he has served as editor of a series on the political parties in the Netherlands. With Paul Lucardie, he published *Populisten in de Polder* (Boom, 2012).

Notes

1. This contribution is an updated and somewhat extended version of G. Voerman, "Premature Perestroika: The Dutch Communist Party and Gorbachev," in *Western European Communists and the Collapse of Communism*, ed. D.S. Bell, London, 1993, 157–71; which in turn is based on G. Voerman, "Perestroika avant-la-lettre: De CPN en de hervormingen van Gorbatsjov," in *Jaarboek 1992 Documentatiecentrum Nederlandse*

Politieke Partijen, ed. G. Voerman, Groningen, 1993, 99–118. Used with permission from Berg Publishers, an imprint of Bloomsbury Publishing plc.
2. Voerman, "Relationship between the Dutch and Russian Communists."
3. Voerman, "From Lenin's Comrades in Arms."
4. Stam, De CPN en haar buitenlandse kameraden; Stutje, De man die de weg wees.
5. Verrips, Dwars, duivels en dromend.
6. CPN, De weg naar socialistisch Nederland.
7. Stam, De CPN en haar buitenlandse kameraden, 39–69.
8. CPN, "Resolutie over het twintigste congres van de CPSU," 311.
9. De Jonge, Het communisme in Nederland, 145–46.
10. Hellema, "De dilemma's van Jalta," 203.
11. De Jonge, Het communisme in Nederland, 154.
12. CPN, "Resolutie van het 24ste congres," 333.
13. Stam, De CPN en haar buitenlandse kameraden, 409–10.
14. CPN, "Voor vrede, veiligheid," 186–205.
15. Stam, De CPN en haar buitenlandse kameraden, 405.
16. CPN, "Delegaties CPN–CPSU spraken over gevaren."
17. Voerman, "Away with All Your Superstitions!"
18. Voerman, "The Netherlands: Losing Colours, Turning Green."
19. De Boo, "De internationale bagage."
20. Voerman, "Away with All Your Superstitions!" 467–72.
21. Fennema, "The End of Dutch Communism?"
22. CPN, Stellingen van het partijbestuur, 34–35.
23. Ibid., 35–36.
24. Bakker, "Spanning en verantwoordelijkheid," 45.
25. Horstmeier, "Stop de Neutronenbom!"
26. CPN, De weg naar socialistisch Nederland, 10.
27. Bakker, "Spanning en verantwoordelijkheid," 45.
28. CPN, "Verklaring van het dagelijks bestuur."
29. Wolff, "Tragedie in Polen."
30. CPN, "Verslag diskussiegroep"; de Leeuwe, "Een kritiek op de hoofdlijnen," 233.
31. CPN, "Resolutie CPN-congres," 42.
32. CPN, "Internationale contacten"; Stam, De CPN en haar buitenlandse kameraden, 437.
33. Izeboud, "Een open debat is nodig"; van Hoek, "Den Haag—Moskou balans?"
34. Benschop, "Bonapartistisch socialisme?", 120.
35. CPN, "Resolutie CPN-congres," 43.
36. CPN, Machtsvorming voor een socialistisch Nederland, 32, 12, and 72.
37. Ibid., 20–22.
38. Dammen, "Hereniging van communisten."
39. Dammen and Meertens, "De Lange Mars naar het Winterpaleis."
40. CPN, Machtsvorming voor een socialistisch Nederland, 16.
41. Hoekstra, "Diepgaande veranderingen," 204.
42. Hoekstra, "Bouwstenen voor de toekomst," 265.
43. Izeboud, "Nieuwe vormen en gedachten," 158; see also idem, "Vernieuwingslijn CPSU verdient steun."
44. Molenaar, "De kernbom en het "nieuwe denken," 426; Hoekstra, "Diepgaande veranderingen," 206.
45. Wolff, "Indrukken van het CPSU-congres," 125.
46. De Boo, "Keerpunt in de wapenwedloop," 212.
47. Bakker, "Idealen," 194.
48. Hellema, "Internationale politiek en de crisis van links," 300.
49. CPN, "Begroeting en discussiebijdrage," 54.

50. Voerman, "The Netherlands: Losing Colours, Turning Green."
51. Lucardie and Voerman, "Organisational and Ideological Development of Green Left."
52. De Vries, "CPN-bestuur besprak veranderingen in Europa."
53. Brouwer, "Het socialisme als poldermodel?", 19.
54. CPN, "Discussienota over de wijze van voortbestaan van de CPN."

Bibliography

Bakker, M. "Idealen," *Politiek en Cultuur*, Vol. 47 (1987), 191–98.
_____. "Spanning en verantwoordelijkheid," *Politiek en Cultuur*, Vol. 40, No. 2 (1980), 41–49.
Benschop, A. "Bonapartistisch socialisme? Stellingen over de gemilitariseerde partijdictatuur in Polen," *Komma: tijdschrift voor Politiek en Sociaal Onderzoek*, Vol. 3, No. 1 (1982), 119–49.
Boo, J. de. "De internationale bagage van de CPN," *CPN-ledenkrant*, Vol. 1, No. 3 (1982), 5.
_____. "Keerpunt in de wapenwedloop," *Politiek en Cultuur*, Vol. 47, No. 5 (1987), 209–16.
Brouwer, I. "Het socialisme als poldermodel?" *Politiek en Cultuur*, Vol. 50, No. 1 (1990), 19–24.
Communist Party of the Netherlands (CPN). "Begroeting en discussiebijdrage," *Politiek en Cultuur*, Vol. 48, No. 1 (1988), 53–56.
_____. "Delegaties CPN–CPSU spraken over gevaren bewapeningswedloop," *Politiek en Cultuur*, Vol. 37, No. 3 (1977), 139–41.
_____. "Discussienota over de wijze van voortbestaan van de CPN," *CPN-Ledenkrant*, Vol. 10, congreseditie (1991), 3.
_____. "Internationale contacten," *CPN-ledenkrant*, Vol. 1, No. 5 (1982), 1.
_____. *Machtsvorming voor een socialistisch Nederland: partijprogram van de CPN*, Amsterdam, 1984.
_____. "Resolutie CPN-congres," *Politiek en Cultuur*, Vol. 43, No. 1 (1983), 41–46.
_____. "Resolutie over het twintigste congres van de CPSU," *Politiek en Cultuur*, Vol. 15, No. 5 (1956), 309–11.
_____. "Resolutie van het 24ste congres van de CPN," *Politiek en Cultuur*, Vol. 32, No. 6/7 (1972), 316–33.
_____. *Stellingen van het partijbestuur van de CPN voor het 26ste congres*, Amsterdam, 1977.
_____. "Verklaring van het dagelijks bestuur," *Politiek en Cultuur*, Vol. 42, No. 2 (1982), 79.
_____. "Verslag diskussiegroep 'internationale politiek'," *CPN-ledenkrant*, Vol. 1, No. 5 (1982), 4.
_____. "Voor vrede, veiligheid, samenwerking en sociale vooruitgang in Europa," *Politiek en Cultuur*, Vol. 36, No. 4 (1976), 186–205.
_____. *De weg naar socialistisch Nederland*, Amsterdam, 1952.
Dammen, R. "Hereniging van communisten op basis van Marxisme-Leninisme," *Manifest*, (2 June 1987), 4–5.

Dammen, R., and L. Meertens. "De Lange Mars naar het Winterpaleis," *Manifest* (October 1983), 1.
Fennema, Meindert. "The End of Dutch Communism? The Communist Party of the Netherlands," in *Communist Parties in Western Europe: Decline or Adaptation?*, ed. M. Waller and M. Fennema, Oxford, 1988, 158–78.
Hellema, D. "De dilemma's van Jalta," *Politiek en Cultuur*, Vol. 45, No. 6 (1985), 201–4.
_____. "Internationale politiek en de crisis van links," *Politiek en Cultuur*, Vol. 47, No. 6 (1987), 296–300.
Hoek, van T. "Den Haag—Moskou balans?," *CPN-ledenkrant*, Vol. 4, No. 9 (1985), 2.
Hoekstra, H. "Bouwstenen voor de toekomst," *Politiek en Cultuur*, Vol. 48, No. 5 (1988), 263–73.
_____. "Diepgaande veranderingen vanuit hun eigen visie beoordelen," *Politiek en Cultuur*, Vol. 47, No. 4/5 (1987), 199–208.
Horstmeier, C. "Stop de Neutronenbom! The Last Mass Action of the CPN and the Moscow—Berlin—Amsterdam Triangle," in *Three Centuries of Russian–Dutch Relations*, ed. C. Horstmeier et al., Groningen, 1997, 65–77.
Izeboud, E. "Een open debat is nodig," *CPN-ledenkrant*, Vol. 4, No. 1 (1985), 2.
_____. "Nieuwe vormen en gedachten," *Politiek en Cultuur*, Vol. 47, No. 4 (1987), 153–62.
_____. "Vernieuwingslijn CPSU verdient steun," *CPN-ledenkrant*, Vol. 6, No. 3 (1987), 7.
Jonge, A.A. de. *Het communisme in Nederland: de geschiedenis van een politieke partij*, Den Haag, 1972.
Leeuwe, J. de. "Een kritiek op de hoofdlijnen van het ontwerpprogram van de CPN," *Politiek en Cultuur*, Vol. 42, No. 6 (1982), 227–34.
Lucardie, P., and G. Voerman. "The Organisational and Ideological Development of Green Left," in *The Crisis of Communism and Party Change: The Evolution of West European Communist and Post-communist Parties*, ed. J. Botella and L. Ramiro, Barcelona, 2003, 155–75.
Molenaar, L. "De kernbom en het 'nieuwe denken'," *Politiek en Cultuur*, Vol. 48, No. 6 (1988), 407–26.
Stam, A. *De CPN en haar buitenlandse kameraden*, Soesterberg, 2004.
Stutje, J.W. *De man die de weg wees: Leven en werk van Paul de Groot 1899–1986*, Amsterdam, 2000.
Verrips, G. *Dwars, duivels en dromend: De geschiedenis van de CPN 1938–1991*, Amsterdam, 1995.
Voerman, G. "'Away with All Your Superstitions!': The End of Communism in the Netherlands," *Journal of Communist Studies and Transition Politics*, Vol. 7, No. 4 (1991), 460–76.
_____. "From Lenin's Comrades in Arms to 'Dutch Donkeys': The Communist Party in the Netherlands and the Comintern in the 1920s," in *International Communism and the Communist International 1919–43*, ed. T. Rees and A. Thorpe, Manchester, 1998, 127–42.
_____. "The Netherlands: Losing Colours, Turning Green," in *The Green Challenge: The Development of Green Parties in Europe*, ed. D. Richardson and C. Rootes, London, 1995, 109–27.

_____. "The Relationship between the Dutch and Russian Communists, 1909–1991," in *Three Centuries of Russian–Dutch Relations*, ed. C. Horstmeier et al., Groningen, 1997, 58–64.

Vries, I. de. "CPN-bestuur besprak veranderingen in Europa," *CPN-ledenkrant*, Vol. 9, No. 1 (1990), 1–2.

Wolff, J. "Indrukken van het CPSU-congres: versnelling en vernieuwing vereist," *Politiek en Cultuur*, Vol. 46, No. 3 (1986), 123–29.

_____. "Tragedie in Polen," *Politiek en Cultuur*, Vol. 42, No. 2 (1982), 41–46.

Chapter 12

Perestroika and the Greek Left

Andreas Stergiou

Introduction

Like in many countries, Greek communism underwent a crisis in the 1980s. This was the result of both internal and external developments. The first existential challenge emanated from the rise of the idiosyncratic Greek socialism, marked by the founding of the Greek Socialist Party (Panhellenic Socialist Movement, PASOK) in 1974. Within a short period after the fall of the military junta, it managed to establish its hegemony over an increasingly Left electorate, and achieved a comfortable victory in the 1981 elections. The second development that shook Greek Left parties resulted from Mikhail Gorbachev's liberalization programs, which caught the Greek communists, Eurocommunists and orthodox ones by surprise. The initial ideological and political factional infighting caused by the Perestroika and Glasnost spirit was followed by a unification process among the main Left parties. This ended up in an electoral alliance and, due to some extraordinary post-electoral constellation, in participation in a transitional government together with the Greek right-wing party in 1989, staging a Greek version of the "historic compromise." The collapse of communism in Europe, however, tested the leftist unity experiment, which fell apart two years later when the orthodox Greek Communist Party (KKE) split off from the alliance, condemned Perestroika, and reaffirmed the validity of its link with the bygone Stalinist Soviet model.

Notes for this chapter begin on page 272.

This chapter tries to shed light on this political development, which has sealed the course of the Greek communist movement to this day. So far, this is the first comprehensive analysis on the issue. Moreover, given the restrictive policy that the KKE has been following toward its archive, it is the first to draw on some scarce empirical information from interviews (with two former general secretaries of the KKE, Charilaos Florakis and Grigoris Farakos), archives and previous researches the author has conducted on the history of the Greek Communist Party.

The Political and Ideological Evolution of the Greek Left

Due to Greece's geographical and intellectual isolation from Europe and its specific social structure, the labor movement remained embryonic in this country for a long time. Thus, the emergence of a communist party coincided largely with the task of creating a labor movement. As was the case in many countries, the first Greek Communist Party came into existence a short time after the October Revolution in 1918 with the name SEKE (Socialist Labor Party of Greece). In November 1924, the party was renamed the Communist Party of Greece (KKE) and adopted the principles of the Third International. This marks the beginning of party's bolshevization, as Democratic Centralism very soon became the exclusive and sacrosanct organizational principle. From then on, its turbulent history decisively shaped the profile of the party and its political-ideological identity, as well as its functional-organizational theory and practice. The ideological dimension of party's tactics resulted from the fact that the Soviet Union was identified as the true and utmost expresser of Marxism–Leninism and communist society, and also from the fact that the KKE relied for decades on help from the Soviet Union and other communist countries in order to resist persecution by the Greek state. As a consequence, the Moscow-inspired third principle of proletarian internationalism in particular gradually turned out to be almost the only important rule by which the Greek communist movement had to abide.[1]

Therefore, its theoretical assumptions have been an unreflective application of imported foreign models, either from the Second International in the very early period or from Comintern, Cominform or other later Soviet-dominated political institutions. Throughout its history, its dependence on foreign theory and models has gone hand in hand with an inability to formulate a viable perspective of its own. Furthermore, the party failed to integrate itself into Greek society by refusing to formulate a realistic and viable perspective for social change, and nor did it offer an alternative to the bourgeois parties. On the contrary, its visions and views were mostly dogmatic reflections of official Soviet ideological patterns.

Beyond that, the specific political culture of Greece, especially the clientelistic system prevailing in the country, prevented the penetration of communist or socialist ideas into the lower social strata. Indeed, the entanglement between state, political parties, and family-owned business made meritocratic promotion difficult for those outside of this entangled network. The rise of a self-sufficient and enlightened bourgeois class was, in particular, hampered by these conditions. Greek civil society has traditionally been weak—the product of Greece's history of clientelism, aggravated by the postwar period's restrictive atmosphere in which any form of political organization from below was suspect. Interest groups, which before 1974 tended to be controlled by the state, have subsequently been colonized by the established political parties.[2]

Political parties were family businesses to a great extent, while the party in power not only dominated the highest rank of the bureaucracy, as is normal and proper in a democracy, but the middle and lower ranks too.[3] The combination of clientelism, anti-communism (which appeared almost simultaneously with communism in Greece), and the all-pervasive state resulted in the effective blurring of class cleavages, mainly through the development of vertical clientelistic networks.[4]

Moreover, KKE's early bolshevization in the 1920s and 1930s deprived Greek communists of their independence, rendering it a tool of Soviet foreign policy, a propagandist for foreign models of social change, and a spokesman for dogmatic Soviet Marxism. KKE's perspective on socialism can be condensed into what the party ritually called in almost every party document: "the defense of the contribution of socialist construction in the USSR, in general of socialist construction during the twentieth century and its unique achievements." In KKE's analysis, the East European countries were without doubt realizing socialism; Soviet bloc policies were supported without question, and the USSR Communist Party's leaders hailed as great revolutionary figures.[5]

Furthermore, and in line with most West European communist parties during the Cold War,[6] the Greek communist party perceived its essential task as being the protection of the heartland of the revolution and the interests of the Soviet Union. Thus, it rigorously interpreted the world as split between the capitalist/imperialist forces on one side, and the peace forces (that were the pro-Soviet forces) on the other. There was no room in this simplistic divide for either an intermediary or for partial allegiances. The corollary was that all of the international organizations, institutions or bodies (e.g., European Economic Community, European Council) were included in this Manichean view.[7]

In 1968, the Communist Party of Greece split into a Moscow-orientated, orthodox Marxist–Leninist wing (KKE) and a Eurocommunist wing (KKE Interior). The origins of the split lay in the different positions taken on KKE's political direction and organizational strategy respectively by the party cadres who operated illegally inside Greece and those in exile in Eastern Europe.

After Greece's transition to democracy in 1974 and the consequent legalization of communist parties, the 'orthodox' and the Eurocommunist fractions followed divergent political and policy positions, and established themselves as two mutually independent communist parties: KKE, the old valuable brand name with considerable resonance among communist voters, and the new "KKE Interior," which cultivated relations with the West European parties. In 1975, KKE Interior and the Spanish Communist Party issued a joint declaration adopting the main Eurocommunist ideological positions. Nevertheless, after a provisory joint electoral venture with the United Democratic Left Party led by Elias Eliou, in the general elections of 1974 both of them claimed to represent the true interests of the communist movement.[8]

The year 1976 marked the definite split between the two communist rivals, as the Eurocommunists organized their first party congress in Athens, which was boycotted by the pro-Soviet parties. Their program advocated parliamentary democracy, a pluralistic model of socialism based on the particular and specific conditions of the country, and the strengthening of civil liberties, as well as maximum cohesion between the people and the armed forces.[9] Very important for the outcome of the legitimation struggle between the two fractions was the East Berlin Conference of European Communist Parties in June 1976, from which the KKE Interior was excluded, and the KKE therefore appeared as representative of all Greek communists.[10]

The Revisionists, on the other side, moved away from orthodox Leninism, opted for a "Renewal of the Left," and supported a parliamentary regime, a mixed economy, the concept of socialism with a human face, and Greece's accession to the EEC. They broke ties with the Communist Party of the Soviet Union (CPSU) and established bonds with parties such as the Italian Communist Party (PCI), thereby adopting a Eurocommunist perspective.[11]

The orthodox communists, however, thanks to their superior organization and financial resources as well as Eastern bloc financial[12] and political assistance, managed to retain their grip on the loyalty of a sizeable portion of Greece's industrial proletariat, and were much more successful in electoral terms as they consistently secured a much higher percentage of votes (around 10 percent until the end of the 1980s) than the revisionists, who were permanently struggling for their political survival. The average increase in its electoral base and a stable relational distance from other parties of the political spectrum lent the party an established and historically distinct place in Greek society and politics. The specific political education and culture of the traditional Greek communist voters, supporters, cadres, and stalwarts, in particular their allegiance to the orthodox Marxist–Leninist worldviews expressed by the orthodox Communist Party, were important reasons for their limited political attractiveness.[13]

The Moscow-oriented communists' dominance over the Greek Left electorate consolidated in the 1980s. It was not only vindicated in the various elections but also reflected in the organizational field. Their estimated average membership in the 1980s was 40,000 to 70,000, whereas the Eurocommunists' membership was estimated at less than 10,000.[14]

According to other sources,[15] by the time of its 11th Congress (1982), it numbered 73,000 members, of which 32.8 percent were workers, 14.5 percent salaried employees, 18.11 percent farmers, 9.7 percent shopkeepers and artisans, and 12.3 percent liberal professions and the intelligentsia. In all, 22.3 percent of the members were women.

KKE's well-shaped and effective organization network was structured along traditional communist party lines, with party cells emerging in villages, factories, and other collectives in selected parts of the cities. The hierarchical structure of the party is broken down to the Politburo (the most powerful organ of the party), the Central Committee (which appoints the Politburo) and the Party Congress. Over time, the party has also had branch organizations, which operate within the labor and trade unions, professional organizations, and the workers' centers. A key element of the party organization has been the so-called "aktivs"—small party groups in neighborhoods, small towns and villages. KKE's electoral strongholds were the predominantly industrial areas of Athens, Volos, Piraeus, Salonika, and Patras, due to the party's attractiveness among the working class. However, the orthodox Greek communists failed to achieve any significant advances among the rural or middle-class strata.[16]

On the other side, KKE Interior's only redeeming factor was its broad influence in cities, in the intellectual and artistic world, and among citizens aged 18 to 34 with a relatively high income and good education.[17] Paradoxically, in contrast to their negligible political echo in Greek society, stands the Greek Eurocommunist theoretical contribution to the Western Marxist community. KKE Interior's key intellectual, Nikos Poulatzas, was one of the most widely read social theorists of the 1970s in Europe, North America, and Latin America, and his analyses—the theorization of the capitalist state, in particular—were repeatedly utilized to formulate a democratic road toward socialism. Although Poulantzas died in 1979, his intellectual legacy permeated the Greek leftist political culture in the following decades.

The 1980s turned out to be very challenging for both parties. In contrast to other European countries, in which this period was characterized by the cultural dominance of the "New Right," Greek politics was overwhelmed by the rise of the Greek Socialist Party (PASOK), which came to power in October 1981 at the very heavy expense of the Left parties. In fact, the socialists adopted all those elements from the popular leftwing ideology that addressed the petit bourgeois sensitivities of national sovereignty and independence, but did not have any connection with the Soviet Union or Soviet Marxist model. In this way, PASOK managed to present itself as seemingly advantageous compared to all the political parties lying in the political landscape between the conservative and communist spectrum, which were mostly identified with the hardliners. Furthermore, PASOK could ride the waves of radicalism dating from the early 1960s, and the resistance movement that developed during the years of the military dictatorship, 1967–1974.[18]

The Reverberations of Gorbachev's Reform Policies in Greece

Mikhail Gorbachev's liberalization programs caught the Greek communists by surprise. In fact, even the confession that the revered decades-long system should be reformed from grass roots was reason enough to irritate Greek communists. The Greek comrades viewed the renewed examination of Soviet history askance, especially the exploration of Stalin's repressive policies and the rehabilitation of victims like Nikolai Bukharin, who had championed policies similar to those of Gorbachev.

Hitherto, the orthodox Communist Party's obvious and persistent subservience toward the Soviet Union was more of an asset than a liability in attracting support and closing ranks. Loyalty to the Soviet Union, "the motherland of socialism," was an article of faith, the yardstick against which "true" revolutionaries should be measured. At the same time, it was clearly an obstacle to its expansion.[19] Moreover, in world affairs, the Soviet Union has to this day been perceived as "a world peace guarantor," leading some to an unquestioning support of Moscow's foreign policies, such as their interventions in Hungary, Czechoslovakia, and Afghanistan, the imposition of martial law in Poland, and their attitude to NATO and the European Community.

Officially, the KKE first began dealing with Gorbachev's reform policies in 1987, at the 12th Congress, at which the leadership tentatively proposed the idea of a qualitative change in the party. A year earlier, on

3 November 1986, a meeting lasting three hours took place in Moscow between the KKE's general secretary, Charilaos Florakis, and Mikhail Gorbachev, earning front page coverage in all the Greek newspapers. Greek society interpreted the event as an expression of Moscow's approval of KKE's tactics in Greek political life, and of the importance that Gorbachev attached to the Greek party, at a time when so many other West European communist parties had fallen out of favor with the Soviet Communist party.[20]

Indeed, the 12th Congress conveyed the impression that the party was in favor of glasnost and perestroika. Although some orthodox communists might have looked skeptically at the landslide reforms in the Soviet Union, they did not dare to question them, and hence no coherent opposition to the dominant party-views emerged. The incumbent general secretary, Charilaos Florakis, was re-elected, and no organizational or programmatic changes took place. The resolutions adopted by the 27th Congress of the CPSU (Perestroika, Glasnost) were cherished as an acceleration of the social and economic transformation toward the construction of socialism.[21] A slight Perestroika influence could be gleaned from the party's call for the construction of a coalition of left-wing and progressive forces on the basis of a common program, with the aim of precipitating a change in the country.[22]

Nevertheless, there were at that time many signs indicating that the KKE seemed to be entering into a phase of liberalization, following Moscow's lead. For the first time, some young up-and-coming party cadres began criticizing past Soviet policies. Indeed, inspired by Perestroika, a large section of the younger cadres of the KKE began to search for a new direction that would involve internal democratization, programmatic renewal, and an opening to new issues, such as the environment and gender equality, a direction the KKE Interior had already taken some time before.[23]

However, it took almost two years for this liberalization wind to effect alterations within the KKE party organization and hierarchy. At the July 1989 plenum, the party unanimously elected a new general secretary, the widely respected editor-in-chief of the party newspaper *Rizospastis*, Grigoris Farakos. His elevation to the highest KKE office marked the first such election in the party's history that had not been imposed by the Communist Party of the USSR. Farakos was known for his admiration of Western Europe's communist parties, whose culture and structure he believed the KKE should emulate. Nevertheless, without the support of the party's top leadership, and a without power base of his own beyond mainly obedient apparatchik, it was unrealistic and naive to think that he could transform the KKE from the rigidly Stalinist institution it had been into a modern political party for a democratic society.²⁴ Therefore, Grigoris Farakos was also the only general secretary in the history of the party who had limited access to the party finances and the party archive.²⁵

The Perestroika renewal spirit had serious effects on the Greek Left's political architecture as well. The first party affected by the Perestroika spirit was the Greek Eurocommunist one. As the KKE Interior's moderate socialist ideas had been mostly embraced by their rival PASOK in the previous years, there were practically no Leftist voters to whom the reformists could appeal. This was reflected in the party's waning electoral performance, which ranged between 1.3 and 2.7 percent. At the 4th Congress of the KKE Interior in 1986, it became obvious that the political course the party had followed hitherto was not satisfying anybody.

Just a few months after the congress, the Eurocommunists were dissolved, splitting into two parties. The more moderate, reformist wing allied with various out-parliamentarian left-wing ecology, feminism-oriented groups, and held a new congress in April 1987 which was attended by approximately eight hundred delegates. The delegates decided to found a new party, the "Greek Left" (Elliniki Aristera, EAR), which took a critical symbolic and political turn by dropping its "Communist" name, as well as fundamental doctrines of Marxism–Leninism, such as proletarian internationalism, democratic centralism, and dictatorship of the proletariat. In this manner, it was signaled that the target group of the new party was not the communist Left spectrum but the political center that had hitherto been occupied by the socialists. About half of the members of the KKE Interior, however, and the party's communist youth organization, the EKON Rigas Feraios, refused to embrace EAR's new moderate political identity, preferring to stick to the Marxist–Leninist tenets, thereby maintaining the symbolic communist name.²⁶ The most influential figures in the SYRIZA-party and government 2015–2019 belonged to this faction.

An immediate impact of Gorbachev's differentiated approach to the Western capitalist countries was the tentative shift in the Moscow-friendly KKE's fierce anti-European course. Greek communists' relationship to the European Economic Community had traditionally been a very divisive issue between the Eurocommunists and the orthodox communists.²⁷ Greece had been closely linked with the EEC since 9 July 1961, when an agreement establishing an association between the EEC and Greece was signed. This agreement established the closest relations that any country had ever had with the Community, and was designed to pave the way to Greece's full membership. After the fall of the military junta in 1974, the Greek state undertook serious efforts for a full membership. The Greek candidacy, although accepted in principle by the member states, was in fact cautiously received. The initial examination of the Greek application by the Commission reflected increasing worries in the Community framework emanating from political and economic considerations.[28] Eventually, in 1981, after twenty years and hard negotiations, Greece became the tenth member of the European Community.

At the time of Greece's accession to the European Economic Community, the Greek Communist Party was banned, while its leaders and a large number of its members and cadres went into exile in the Eastern bloc countries. From the first moment on, the Greek communists—in line with the Kremlin's stance on Greece's membership of the EEC[29]—declared a merciless and unrelenting war against European integration.[30]

From that time on, all government measures on either socioeconomic or foreign policy matters were addressed by the KKE leadership with public announcements about the destructive nature of the European Community. The polemic was usually followed by demands for the immediate dissociation of Greece from the EC, and the fostering of Greece's economic relations with COMECON (Council for Mutual Economic Assistance) as a counterpart to the "monopoly capitalist European Community." In their analysis, the European Community and the Single Market solely constituted a field of inter-imperialist, inter-capitalist rivalry between the European, Japanese and US "Big Capital." In line with the Soviet analysis, the orthodox communist party approached European integration in terms of Lenin's theory of imperialism. As Greece was a peripheral country, its accession to the European Community precipitated its transformation into an object of exploitation by the West European metropolitan monopolies and predator multinationals.

Accordingly, the pro-Moscow KKE emphasized not only issues built around Marxism–Leninism but also the potentially more beneficial—in electoral terms—issue of Greece entering the international division of labor on unfavorable terms. The orthodox communists believed that given the existence at that time of an international relations landscape and Greece's special geographic position, Greece would only really develop in the interests of the workers if outside of the European Community. Specifically, agricultural production and medium-sized enterprises would be driven—because of the European single market competition—either to catastrophe or to submission to the international monopolies. Therefore, the KKE leadership was consequently accusing conservative and socialist governments, with regard to their stance on the European Community, of "subjecting the country's as well as the people's fortunes to the forces of dependence on Big Capital and the supranational authorities of the European Community."[31]

The KKE Interior, on the contrary, under the influence of Eurocommunism, cultivated an alternative approach to the European

Community. In its own analysis, Europe was in the process of evolving from an organization of the monopolies into a Europe of the working people. The "progressive forces" across Europe could cooperate to accelerate this process, and achieve the democratic socialist transformation of Europe far away from the Soviet socialist model. The progress of Greece's integration was irreversible, and it was imperative to adapt to the new situation opened up through Greece's participation in the European Community. The Eurocommunist's main political assumption was that the road to democratic socialism in Greece, which had become the ultimate objective of KKE Interior, was identical to the European road to socialism. The peoples and countries participating in the European Community would, through the same rationale, gradually gain autonomy from the international imperialist center, and would thus begin to differentiate themselves socially toward a socialist transformation. In this sense, the European Community would become ipso facto the objective field of the class struggle.[32] The fact, however, that the general mood in Greece was against the European Community was at the same time in favor of the anti-EEC parties like KKE and PASOK, seems to be a significant factor that Greece was the only West-European country in which the pro-Soviet communists were considerably stronger than the Eurocommunists.[33]

The year 1988, however, marked a caesura in the EC–Greek Left relationship. In that year the KKE's political bureau published the *Propositions on the European Internal Market ahead of 1992*, or the "Red Book," which responded to the predictions of the European Commission's White Book concerning the likely impact of the 1992 EU integration process stage. Under the influence of the recent agreements between the European Community and the Eastern Bloc (EC–CMEA relations), which was supported by the party in this publication as the starting point of a new road toward the creation of a Europe of people, peace and cooperation, Greek communists were compelled to modify their hitherto negative stance toward the EC. Thus, the "Red Book" admitted that many of the economic problems Greece was facing could not be blamed on the EC, as they would have arisen anyway as a result of the intensifying internationalization of the country's economy. Hence, the time had come for all progressive forces to join together to address within the EC framework the challenges deriving from this competitive internal market. The party further declared its willingness to cooperate with parties that did not support the country's withdrawal from the Community, hinting that the EC issue should no longer form an obstacle to the unification of the Greek communist Left.[34]

This publication was followed by statements from other parties on some examples of positive European Community legislation allegedly reflecting the achievements of the popular movement in this interstate organization, such as combating environmental pollution and establishing educational exchange programs. Temporarily, many were under the misleading impression that the party was finally underway in becoming pro-European, depicted in the press as a "delayed idyll" between the KKE and the European Community.[35]

The most serious effect of Perestroika on the Greek Left scene, however, was the creation in February 1989 of the so-called Alliance of the Left and Progress (Synaspismos tis Aristeras kai tis Proodou).[36] By the end of the 1980s, domestic political developments were favorable to a rapprochement between the fragmented Left forces in Greece. The socialists were accused of serious scandals, which involved party funding from illicit sources and revealed the extensive clientelistic linkages between business interests and politics, which had been built up under PASOK's eight-year rule. Under the imperatives of the impending electoral contest, an array of consultations and deliberations within the Left spectrum began aiming at providing an alternative rallying point for the Left, which could enable the Left parties to reclaim their lost constituency from the PASOK.

Indeed, in December 1988, the KKE opted for an alliance with other left-wing forces, notably the Greek Left (EAR), but also other splinter left-wing groups. In the same month, Greek Left and the KKE signed a common report, which had been very carefully prepared in the previous months, analyzing the current turbulent political situation and politically justifying this venturesome alliance with the much-hated revisionists of former times. The report, jointly written by Mimis Androulakis and Giannis Dragasakis of the KKE and Grigoris Giannaros and Dimitrios Papadimoulis of the Greek Left, and published in the KKE's party newspaper *Rizospastis* on 8 December 1988, underlined the crucial repercussions of Perestroika and Glasnost on world politics, thereby laying down the foundations for a new approach to the state, market, and society. Taking into account the KKE's traditional political culture, it is quite impressive—and simultaneously indicative of the changes the at least one part of the party had experienced—that KKE leadership consented to a text that contained numerous references to democracy. A typical example is the linkage between socialism and democracy: "The struggle for democracy is not a road toward the socialism but the road of the socialism."

In fact, after nearly twenty years of bickering, orthodox and revisionist communist rivals joined forces again, even though this was inspired primarily by electoral considerations and tactics. The coalition of the Left, formed with great expectations of becoming a reliable political alternative to an inflexible bipolar political system dominated by the conservatives and the socialists, proved to be fragile. In the critical June 1989 elections, held after a steady stream of revelations of high-level corruption and chronic maladministration by the socialists, Synaspismos garnered 13.1 percent of the votes, which was well below the expectations of its leaders. Synaspismos found itself at the center of the political maneuvering that followed the failure of both PASOK and the conservative New Democracy party to win a parliamentary majority.

Since the Cold War, Greece's electoral laws had always been designed with the aim of excluding the communist Left from government participation. As the third major party, the leaders of Synaspismos took the historical decision to ally with the right-wing New Democracy party and to participate in an interim government. Consequently, for the first time since 1944, government participation by the communist Left no longer appeared to threaten the whole political system. In this respect, Greek Left followed the example of the other Southern European communist parties in their efforts to achieve legitimacy in the context of consolidated democratic regimes, and to secure themselves a suitable political role within their respective systems. On the other side, however, it was a strategic move in the contest for hegemony in the Left electorate rather against its main political rival, the PASOK. The formation of the Tzannetakis coalition, nevertheless, precipitated a number of resignations and the final split with the hardline youth wing, KNE, which had been disaffected since the contraction of the formal alliance with EAR.[37]

However, this move turned out to be very costly for both parties of the radical Left. As the political division between Left and Right, which goes back to the Civil War (1946–49), remained deeply embedded in Greek political culture, Leftist voters did not appreciate the decision of the Left parties' leaderships to engage in government cooperation with right-wing parties.[38] The following general elections, in 1989 and 1990, showed that a substantial proportion of the voters who had supported Synaspismos just four months before did not approve of it and defected from the party, casting their vote for PASOK instead. The party's share of the vote fell by approximately 20 percentage points. Synaspismos's alliance with the conservatives, who were still hosting cadres with farright political perceptions and ideology, remained out of harmony with the country's historical conditions and the collective memory as it had been formed by the Socialists over the preceding years. A big part of Synaspismos's electorate feared a restoration of some regime like the one they had been compelled to live under before PASOK's rise to power.[39] PASOK's effective demonizing of the political Right in preceding years had borne fruit, enabling it to vastly capitalize on the vulnerable electoral basis of the KKE, particularly that section with the most sensitive anti-rightist reflexes.[40]

Perestroika as a Crisis Catalyst in the Greek Left Spectrum

The fall of the Berlin Wall in combination with the disappointment resulting from the marginal success the "Greek compromise experiment" had had, raised daunting challenges for the Greek communists. Like everywhere else in Europe, the collapse of the Soviet bloc triggered a big crisis within the Greek communist movement between two factions, who for the first time in the history of Greek communism were expressing their contentious views in public (television, radio, newspapers) and not only in the KKE party newspaper *Rizospastis*.

On the one side stood the younger generation, who were endeavoring to modernize the party. It appealed mainly to the "Polytechnic generation," who provided the resistance movement against the military dictatorship of 1967–1974. It was confronted by the traditionalists, consisting mainly of the older members of the Central Committee and the Politburo, as well as some members of the 1960s generation who were negatively disposed against those modernization attempts. The Left's identity in the new era was the subject of the debate, as many began questioning the archetypal image of monolithic communism and the basic norms of democratic centralism, referring to the demise of the centralist regimes and the breakdown of the planned economy.

On the other side, the traditionalists regarded Gorbachev and his reforms as the greatest single negative factor in the process that had brought about the demise of the socialist regimes, accusing him of being the only leader in the history of mankind to abolish his own state. In the same trajectory, those who had promoted Perestroika and Glasnost had in fact betrayed the most sacrosanct principles of world communism, democratic centralism, dictatorship of the proletariat, and the absolute and unquestioned supremacy of the Communist Party as a preemptive means against all anti-revolutionary tendencies. By contrast, the reformist view considered Perestroika as a serious attempt at a democratic reform and a modernization of the socialist society and revolution. It also perceived Gorbachev's policies as the only possible way out of the crisis for the Soviet Union, and as precursors of a new socialist development not necessarily controlled by Gorbachev. As a consequence, the Greek communists had to formulate a wholly different party conception, tactics, and strategy.[41]

The more the time passed by, the more the fronts between modernizers and hardliners hardened. The crucial battle took place at the party's 13th

Congress, in February 1991, where the first real debate on Gorbachev's reforms was also carried out. The crisis within the party culminated in summer 1990, when the draft proposal for the 13th Congress was revealed, proposed by a Central Committee that was mostly change-oriented, causing a furor in the ranks of the party members. For first time in the party's history, the so-called construction process of socialism in Eastern Europe was criticized, though it was repeatedly praised for its anti-imperialistic nature and its contribution to the betterment of mankind. The criticism evolved around the democratic deficiencies and the one-dimensional and obstinate clinging to the Soviet pattern as a ubiquitous socialist model that should be put into practice in other countries at any cost. As a result, it was further mentioned, local peculiarities and special needs of the various countries were ignored so that bureaucratic deformations emerged, which slowed down the scientific and social development of the socialist countries. Moreover, the draft proposal acclaimed the Perestroika experiment, labeling it an innovating force for the modernization of socialist societies. The text could not sustain the reactions, and was dismissed a few months later. Although the final text adopted in the congress was far away from the submitted proposal, the party officially abandoned the position of withdrawal from the European Community, and vindicated the strengthening of the alliance over party members.[42]

At the same time, beside the ideological confrontation, another, more practical bitter feud for the organizational control of the party was being carried out. The overwhelming part of the party leadership was in favor of radical ideological and organization renewal, in the way the other European communist parties were undertaking this at that time. However, the district organizations and middle-class members and cadres were in general beset by mistrust against innovations due to the ideological and political education that had long been instilled into them. Thus, they were permanently under the strong impression of being prosecuted by the class enemy, who was lurking to capture the party of the working class. They looked askance at the proposals for a radical modernization of the party, and were reluctant to accept any abrupt changes in the modus operandi of the communist movement. Eventually, the race for supremacy in the Central Committee went in favor of the hardliners. Out of the 111 members elected to the new Central Committee at the 13th Congress in February 1991, 60 belonged to the hardliner fraction. They did not hesitate to install a new hardline party general secretary, Aleka Papariga, who turned out to be a loyal guard of the old and obsolete party structure and culture, at a time when the West European parties had begun emulating new democratic structures.[43]

Consequently, the KKE crisis spilled over to the Coalition of the Left and Progress, causing its breakup in the summer of 1991. Following the election of Aleka Papariga as the new general secretary, the KKE announced its withdrawal from the Coalition of the Left and Progress. Those forty-five members of the Central Committee who declared their willingness to remain in the alliance were expelled from the party. In turn, the modernizers, led by Maria Damanaki, resigned from the KKE and pledged their loyalty to Synapismos, which established itself as a new, moderate, European-integration-friendly party.[44]

As Ole Smith in his authoritative analysis of 1993 noted,[45] the debate on Perestroika clearly demonstrated that the problem of Gorbachev's reforms and more or less evident political goals were of central importance for the unity of the KKE. The two tendencies in the KKE, which have to a great extent been generated by differing appraisals of Eastern Europe's tumultuous political and social developments, could not coexist in a party that was still dominated by Stalinist views of party discipline. It was obvious that unity would sooner or later be achieved, either by a gradual opening-up of the party or by a clean break.

Moreover, it is important to mention that the split between hardliners and modernizers/reformers reflected a historical schism as well as serious generational and social cleavages within the party that even the perestroika effect could not bridge. Hardliners were primarily older in age (and had typically spent much of their lives as political exiles in Eastern Europe and the Soviet Union), whereas reformers were younger, having joined the KKE after 1974, when the party was legal.[46] Hardliners also came mostly from the ranks of the trade unions, whereas reformers mostly had a rather intellectual profile. Lastly, hardliners tended to have an emotionally charged set of memories shaped by the Civil War, whereas reformers tended to be motivated by more strategic concerns.[47]

The split followed suit within the European Parliament as well, in the political alliance of Communist and Allies Group founded in 1973 and divided in July 1989 into two groups, the Left Unity Group and the European United Left. The KKE joined the first Euroskeptical one, which comprised members from the French Communist Party, the Portuguese Communist Party and the Workers' Party of Ireland. The Greek MEPs who, after the split of Synaspismos, granted their allegiance to the new Synaspismos party, preferred the European United Left group, with members from the Danish Socialist People's Party, the Italian Communist Party, and the United Left of Spain.[48]

In the following months, the orthodox communists—or more precisely, what was left of them—gradually retreated to their own political and ideological universe, consisting of glorious memories of the socialist revolution rather than the developments in the postcommunist world. In August 1991 they fully supported the failed coup in the USSR.

At a new extraordinary congress in December 1991 (the fourteenth in the history of the party) the party recalled most of the adopted resolutions of the 13th Congress, and reaffirmed the validity of the Marxist–Leninist principles of democratic centralism and proletarian internationalism as unalienable rules to abide by. Unanimously the delegates rejected the reforms that had emanated from Perestroika and Glasnost in the USSR, accusing Gorbachev of betraying Perestroika and socialism, thereby causing the collapse of the USSR and Eastern Europe's socialist regimes. (It is important to mention that in the following years the term "collapse" was dismissed as a bourgeois anti-revolutionary term, and replaced by the term "overthrow," deliberately hinting at political actions that amount to coups d'état and conspiracies.) They also argued that the USSR had not collapsed primarily due to its structural flaws but because "counterrevolutionary" forces inside the CPSU had deviated from Stalinism and drifted gradually into capitalism. In their appraisal, the policy of Perestroika had initially appeared as a method of renewal and restructuring of socialism in order to master existing economic and social problems. However, quite soon its true counterrevolutionary face was revealed, undermining fundamental pillars of socialist society. The true incentive of these reforms was the transitional transfer of the means of production to private ownership, starting with the agrarian economy and with the clear intention of extending it to all sectors. Furthermore, Greece's orthodox communists estimated that there was something like a secret plan, forged by the leading core of the CPSU, which was consciously promoting the restoration of capitalism, and that aimed at eliminating social ownership of the means of production, abolishing socialist planning as well as dismantling the system of delivery and distribution of consumer goods and services. Using the same rationale, it was of paramount importance that the CPSU abandoned its leading role in Soviet society to enable the emergence of an opposition that was openly propagandizing a rapid return to capitalism.[49]

After the collapse of the Soviet Union, the KKE retreated into a navel-gazing process by upholding a *sui generis* dogmatism, as if the period of Perestroika had never existed. This political-ideological dogmatism embodied a narrow-minded, almost obsessive vilification of the Synaspismos Party. Three official texts published by the Central Committee of the KKE in March 1995, with the title "Considerations about the Factors Leading to the Overthrow of the Socialist System in Europe," and in February 2009 (also adopted by the 18th Congress of the party) with the title "Assessments and Conclusions on Socialist Construction during the Twentieth Century, Focusing on the USSR: KKE's Perception on Socialism," mark the still official party appraisal of Perestroika. In both texts, Perestroika is seen as the main negative factor that sparked off the process leading to the entire collapse of the socialist countries and to "victory of the counterrevolution and of capitalist restoration." In the latter publication it states: "In the 1980s, the party gradually lost its revolutionary guiding character and, as a result, counterrevolutionary forces were able to dominate the party and the government." In a third publication, dated 1999 and titled "The Restoration of Capitalism and its International Repercussions," is more or less repeated what had already been pointed out in previous congress resolutions:

> The policy of "Perestroika" quite soon began to reveal its true counterrevolutionary face, as the specification and practical application of the initial slogans took on the content of "reforms" and measures that affected and tended to reverse crucial and fundamental sectors of the socialist society, at the level of both the political system and the economy ... It has been revealed as a policy for exporting the counterrevolution through measures and options that abolish proletarian internationalism as well as fraternal, equal relationships within the framework of the socialist division of labor.

Andreas Stergiou is associate professor at the Department of Economics, University of Thessaly, specializing in European Institutions and International Relations, and teaching fellow at the Open University of Greece. He has studied history and political science in Greece, Germany, and the United States. He has published in French, English, Greek, German, and Portuguese.

Notes

The transliteration system used in this chapter is available on the website of the Library of Congress: http://www.loc.gov/catdir/cpso/romanization/greek.pdf (last accessed 8 April 2019).

1. Zapantis, *Greek–Soviet Relations*, 29–52; Richter, "Greek Communist Party"; Kontis et al., *Soviet Union and the Balkans*.
2. Mavrogordatos, *Between Pityokamptes and Prokroustes*.
3. Tsoukalas, *Social Development and State*.
4. Lyrintzis, "Political Parties in Post-Junta Greece," 102–3.
5. Nefeloudis, *The Reasons for the Misery*, 365–67; Lymperios, *The Communist Movement*, 95–107.
6. Bell, "Western Communist Parties," 222–23.
7. Mavroidis, *The Two Faces of the History*.

8. Zachos, "Greek Road to Socialism or Revisionism?"; Koutoulas, "Self-governance and Internationalism"; Beveratos, "Who is Responsible for the Split in the Party?".
9. Dimitriou, *Profoundly*, 363–65.
10. KKE, *Conference of the Communist Parties of Europe*, 129–35.
11. Dagkas and Leontiadis, *The Party Archive*, 221–26; Kyrkos, *Subversively: Past and Future*, 196–98.
12. A considerable part of the party's assets came from the financial kickbacks they received for initiating the honoring of state contracts by East bloc firms. Participation in handling these commissions was mostly by companies that were close to the party. These included the Greek–Soviet Transorient Shipping and Trading Company, with its headquarters in Piraeus, which carried out maintenance on Soviet ships in Greek shipyards; and the party's tourist agency, Lev Tours, which organized tourism in Eastern Europe. See Stergiou, "Kommunistische Realpolitik," 238–39.
13. Stergiou, "Die Linke in Griechenland," 159–60.
14. It is still extremely difficult to find accurate data and statistics on the Greek Communist Party, as it has consistently refused to place such figures, as well as its archives, in the public domain. A quite reliable but ideologically motivated source is the reports written by George Kousoulas on the Greek Communist Left for the period 1975–1991, published by the Hoover Institution Press in the *Yearbook on International Communist Affairs*.
15. Kitsikis, "Populism, Eurocommunism and the KKE," 107.
16. Lyrintzis, "Political Parties in Post-Junta Greece," 115.
17. Mpalampanidis, *Eurocommunism*, 185.
18. Kapetanyannis, "Greek Communists," 91.
19. Kapetanyannis, "The Left in the 1980s," 83.
20. Kitsikis, "Populism, Eurocommunism and the KKE," 108.
21. KKE, *Central Committee's Propositions ahead of the 12th Congress*, 8–10.
22. Ibid., 91–111.
23. Tsakatika and Eleftheriou, "The Radical Left's Turn," 3.
24. Iatrides, "Witness to History," 40.
25. Personal communication with Farakos, Athens, April 1999.
26. Dimitriou, *Profoundly*, 397–400; Elliniki Aristera, *The New Left Party*.
27. Giataganas, *Europe and the Left*, 231–247.
28. Rizas, *The Rise of the Left*, 68.
29. Archive of the Greek Foreign Ministry, Central Department, Folder 62, Sub-Folder 2/1 and 10/2, and Folder 63, Sub-Folder 7: "Telegrams of the Greek Ambassador in Moscow to Athens about the heavy reactions of the Soviet press to Greece's accession treaty with the European Community (May and June 1961)."
30. KKE, *Official Documents*, 654.
31. KKE, *10th Congress of the KKE*, 14–15; KKE, *From the 10th to the 11th Congress*, 49–50; KKE, *Posts of the Central Committee of the KKE for the 12th Congress*, 13–14, 33.
32. Moshonas, "A Disputed Partnership," 389–413; Karras, *Ideology and Policy*, 123–124, 205–206; Timmermann, "Griechenlands Eurokommunisten," 14–17.
33. Leonhard, *Eurocommunism*, 270–71.
34. KKE, *Propositions on the European Internal Market ahead of 1992*; Alavanos, *Notes on the political Left in Europe*, 15–33.
35. Verney, "New Red Book of the KKE."; Giataganas, *Europe and the Left*, 233.
36. Marantzidis, "Communistes et postocommunistes," 101.
37. Verney, "Between Coalition and One-Party Government," 131–34; Bosco and Gaspar, "Four Actors in Search of a Role," 329.
38. Tsakatika and Eleftheriou, "The Radical Left's Turn," 4.
39. PASOK's reaction to the coalition confirmed the divisive nature of Greek politics at that time, as it repeatedly portrayed it as an "unholy alliance" and a betrayal by the

Synaspismos of solidarity on the Left. Not accidentally, the coalition tried to counterbalance this "Civil War spirit" by introducing a "Law to Lift the Consequences of the Civil War" that were still valid. This basically repealed the remaining legislation discriminating against Resistance and Civil War participants (pensions, and the removal of Civil War offences from the criminal record). The old appellation of "Brigands' War" still in use in textbooks and in Army publications was replaced by the term "Civil War" as a symbolic act on this "national reconciliation." However, when the government decided to celebrate the 40th anniversary of the Civil War's official end, on 29 August 1989, by burning all the police files from the postwar period, there was an outcry against it. The fact that this deed was denounced as an act of historical vandalism, turning it into one of this government's more controversial acts, speaks volumes for the political and historical wounds that determined political and electoral behavior at the time. Pridham and Verney, "The Coalitions of 1989–90," 59.
40. Kapetanyannis, "The Left in the 1980s: Too Little, Too Late," 90.
41. Smith, "The Impact of Gorbachev on the Greek Communists," 226–30.
42. KKE, *From the 12th to the 13th Congress*, 11–16 and 20–25.
43. Farakos, *Witnesses to History and Thoughts*, 336–51.
44. Synaspismos was the main forerunner of current SYRIZA governing party, founded in 2004 as a coalition of left-wing and radical Left parties. In contrast to Synaspismos's full Euro-friendly course, SYRIZA presented many Euroskeptic tendencies.
45. Smith, "The Greek Communist Party in the Post-Gorbachev Era," 89.
46. According to Charilaos Florakis, general secretary of the Greek Communist Party from 1973 until 1989, the fact that those cadres had not been compelled to act under illegal circumstances, accounted for their limited proletarian conscience and their opportunist behavior (Personal communication, Athens, April 1999).
47. Marantzides and Kalyvas, "Two Paths of the Greek Communist Movement," 21.
48. Bell, "Western Communist Parties," 226.
49. KKE, *Central Committee's Propositions ahead of the 14th Congress*, 15–20; KKE, *14th Congress of the KKE*, 109–25.

Bibliography

Archival Sources

Archive of the Greek Foreign Ministry

Secondary Sources

Alavanos, Alekos. *Simeioseis gia tin Aristera stin Evropi* [Notes on the political Left in Europe]. Athens,1988.
Bell, David. "Western Communist Parties and the European Union," in *Political Parties in the European Union*, ed. J. Gaffney, London, 1996.
Beveratos, Stelios. *Poioi einai oi diaspastes* [Who is responsible for the split in the party?], Athens, 1975.
Bosco, Anna, and Carlos Gaspar. "Four Actors in Search of a Role: The Southern European Communist Parties," in *Parties, Politics and Democracy in the New Southern Europe*, ed. Nikiforos Diamandouros and Richard Gunther, Baltimore, MD, 2001, 329–387.

Dagkas, A., and G. Leontiadis. *To Kommatiko Archeio: Dadromes, emblokes: To «archeio toy KKE esoterikou» kai I andidikia tou KKE me tous epaggelmaties istorikous* [The party archive: History, stalemates: The KKE interior archive and KKE's clash with the historians], Thessaloniki, 2009.

Dimitriou, Panos. *Ek vatheon: Chroniko mias Zois kai mias epochis* [Profoundly: Memoire of a life and an era], Athens, 1997.

Elliniki Aristera (EAR) [Greek Left] (ed.). *To neo komma tis aristeras, Programmatiki Diakirixi, Katastatikes Arches, Diadikasies Idrytikou Synedriou* [The New Left Party: Founding Declaration, Statute, Founding Congress Proceedings], Athens, 1987.

Farakos, Grigoris. *Martyries kai Stochasmoi 1941–1991* [Witnesses to history and thoughts, 1941–1991], Athens, 1993.

Giataganas, X., *I Evropi kai I Aristera* [Europe and the Left], Athens, 1990.

Iatrides, John. "Witness to History: Grigoris Farakos and the Greek Communist Movement," in *Grigoris Farakos: Diadromes stin Istoria* [Grigoris Farakos: Flashback to history], ed. Grigoris Psallidas, Corfu, 2011, 25–41.

Kapetanyannis, Vassilis. "Greek Communists: Dilemmas and Opportunities Following the Local Elections," *Journal of Communist Studies*, Vol. 3, No. 1 (1987), 90–95.

_____. "The Left in the 1980s: Too Little, Too Late," in *Greece 1981–1989: The Populist Decade*, ed. Richard Clogg, New York, 1993, 78–93.

Karras, Stavros. *Ideologia kai Politiki sto KKE Esoterikou* [Ideology and policy in the KKE interior), Athens, 1978.

Kitsikis, Dimitri. "Populism, Eurocommunism and the KKE," in *Communist Parties in Western Europe: Decline or Adaptation?*, ed. Michael Waller and Meindert Fennema, Oxford, 1998, 96–113.

KKE (ed.). *I diaskepsi ton Kommounistikon Kommaton tis Evropis* [The Conference of the Communist Parties of Europe], Athens, 1976.

_____. *To Dekato Synedrio tou KKE* [The 10th Congress of the KKE], Athens, 1978.

_____. *Apo to Dekato sto Entekato Synderio tou KKE* [From the 10th to the 11th Congress of the KKE], Athens, 1982.

_____. "Theseis tis Kentrikis Epitropis tou KKE gia to Dodekato Synedrio" [Central Committee's propositions ahead of the 12th Congress], Athens, 1987.

_____. "Oi Theseis tou KKE gia tin eniaia esoteriki agora kai to 1992" [KKE's propositions on the European internal market ahead of 1992], https://21aristera.wordpress.com (last accessed on 15 July 2016), Athens, 1988.

_____. "Apo to dedekato sto dekatotrito synedrio" [From the 12th to the 13th Congress], Athens, 1990.

_____. "Theseis tis Kentrikis Epitropis tou KKE gia to dekatotetarto synedrio" [Central Committee's propositions ahead of the 14th Congress], Athens, 1991.

_____. "Dekatotetarto Synedrio tou KKE" [14th Congress of the KKE], Athens, 1992.

_____. *Skepseis gia tous paragontes pou odigisan stin anatropi tou sosialistikou sistimatos stin Evropi* [Considerations about the factors leading to the overthrow of the socialist system in Europe], Athens, 1995.

_____. "Episima Keimena" [Official Party documents], Vol. 8, covering the period 1958–1961, Athens, 1997.

_____. "The Restoration of Capitalism and Its International Repercussions," http://interold.kke.gr/TheSocial/MARCH1999/march19997to9/index.html (last accessed on 20 July 2016), 1999.

_____. "Eisigisi tis Kentrikis Epitropis: Ektimiseis kai Symperasmata apo ti Sosialistiki Oikodomisi ston Eikosto aiona me epikentro tin ESSD. I antilipsi tou KKE gia to Sosialismo" [Central Committee's proposition ahead of the 18th PartyCongress: Assessments and conclusions on socialist construction during the twentieth century, focusing on the USSR: KKE's perception on socialism], Athens, 2009.

Kontis, V., et al. *Sovietiki Enosi kai Valkania stis dekaeties 1950–1960. Syllogi Eggrafon* [Soviet Union and the Balkans in the 1950s and 1960s. Documents Collection], Thessaloniki, 2003.

Kousoulas, George. *Greece, Yearbook on International Communist Affairs*, Stanford, CA, 1975–1991.

Koutoulas, Panagos. "Aftoteleia kai Diethnismos" [Self-governance and internationalism], *Kommounistiki Epitheorisi*, Vol. 6 (1975), 21–29.

Kyrkos, Leonidas. *Anatreptika: Parelthon kai Mellon* [Subversively: Past and future], Athens, 1995.

Leonhard, Wolfang. *Eurocommunism: Challenge for East and West*, New York, 1978.

Lymperios, Theodoros. *To kommounistiko Kinima stin Ellada* [The communist movement in Greece], Vol. I, Athens, 2005.

Lyrintzis, Christos. "Political Parties in Post-Junta Greece: A Case of 'Bureaucratic Clientelism'," *West European Politics*, Vol. 7, No. 2 (1984), 99–118.

Marantzides, Nikos "Communistes et postocommunistes en Greece 1991–2013," in *Communisme en Europe 1989–2014: L'eternel retour des communistes*, ed. Stephane Courtois and Patrick Moreau, Paris, 2014, 99–118.

Marantzides, Nikos, and Stathis Kalyvas. "The Two Paths of the Greek Communist Movement, 1985–2001," in *The Crisis of Communism and Party Change: The Evolution of West European Communist and Post-Communist Parties*, ed. Joan Bottela and Luis Ramiro, Barcelona, 2003, 11–36.

Mavrogordatos, George. *Metaxi Pitiokampti kai Prokrousti. Oi Epaggelmatikes Organoseis sti Simerini Ellada* [Between Pityokamptes and Prokroustes: Interest groups in today's Greece], Athens, 1988.

Mavroidis, Lefteris. *Oi dyo opseis tis istorias* [The two faces of the history], Athens, 1997.

Moshonas, Andreas. "A Disputed Partnership: The Political Debate on the Greek Accession to the European Community," PhD dissertation, Queen's University, Kingston, Canada, 1982.

Mpalampanidis, Giannis. *Evrokommounismos: Apo tin Kommounistiki sti rizospastiki evropaiki aristera* [Eurocommunism: From the communists to the radical European Left], Athens, 2015.

Nefeloudis, Pavlos. *Stis piges tis kakodaimonias: Ta vathitera aitia tis Diaspasis tou KKE 1918-1968. Episima Keimena kai Prosopikes Martyries* [The reasons for the misery: The real causes of the KKE split, 1918–1968. Official texts and personal witnesses], Athens, 1974.

Pridham, Geoffrey, and Susannah Verney. "The Coalitions of 1989–90 in Greece: Inter-party Relations and Democratic Consolidation," *West European Politics*, Vol. 14, No. 4 (1991), 42–69.

Richter, Heinz. "The Greek Communist Party and the Communist International," *Jahrbuch für Historische Kommunismusforschung*, Vol. 8 (2002), 111–40.

Rizas, Sotiris. *The Rise of the Left in Southern Europe: Anglo-American Responses*, London, 2012.

Smith, Ole. "The Greek Communist Party in the Post-Gorbachev Era," in *Western European Communists and the Collapse of Communism*, ed. David Bell, Oxford, 1993, 87–100.

———. "The Impact of Gorbachev on the Greek Communists," in *The Southeastern Yearbook 1991*, Athens, 1992.

Stergiou, Andreas. "Kommunistische Realpolitik: das bizarre Verhältnis der SED zur Kommounistikó Kómma Elládas 1968–1989," in *Bruderparteien jenseits des Eisernen Vorhangs: Die Beziehungen der SED zu den kommunistischen Parteien West- und Südeuropas (1968–1989)*, ed. Arnd Bauerkämper and Francesco Di Palma, Berlin, 2011, 226–240.

———. "Die Linke in Griechenland: Ein historischer Überblick von ihrer Entstehung bis zu den Maiwahlen 2012," *The International Newsletter of Communist Studies*, Vol. 18 (2012), 152–68.

Timmermann, Heinz. "Griechenlands 'Eurokommunisten': Anmerkungen zum Programm und Profil der Inlands-KP," *Berichte des Bundesinstituts für ostwissenschaftliche und internationale Studien*, Vol. 17, Cologne, 1984, 1–22.

Tsakatika, Myrto, and Costas Eleftheriou. "The Radical Left's Turn toward Civil Society in Greece: One Strategy, Two Paths," *South European Society and Politics* (peer-reviewed online journal), Vol. 18 (2013), 81–89.

Tsoukalas, Konstantinos. *Koinoniki Anaptixi kai Kratos* [Social development and state], 5th edition, Athens, 1993.

Verney, Susannah. "Between Coalition and One-Party Government: The Greek Elections of November 1989 and April 1990," *West European Politics*, Vol. 13, No. 4 (1990), 131–38.

———. "The New Red Book of the KKE: The Renewal That Never Was," *Journal of Communist Studies*, Vol. 4, No. 4 (1988), 170–73.

Zachos, Thanasis. "Ellinikos Dromos pros to Sosialismo I Anatherotismos?" [Greek road to socialism or revisionism?], *Kommounistiki Epitheorisi*, Vol. 1 (1975), 13–23.

Zapantis, Andreas. *Ellinosovietikes Scheseis 1917–1941* [Greek–Soviet relations, 1917–1941], Athens, 1989.

Chapter 13

The Austrian Communists and Perestroika

Maximilian Graf

Introduction

In order to understand the attitude of the Austrian communists to Perestroika, one has to have a thorough understanding of the party's history after World War II. The first two postwar decades, and, in fact, even later years, reflect how the Austrian Communist Party (Kommunistische Partei Österreichs, KPÖ) had been shaped by its interwar leadership, and by those leaders who had been in exile in Moscow during the war. It is equally important to know how the KPÖ positioned itself within the world communist movement over time. Before going into detail on the historical background explaining the party's positioning towards Perestroika, some information on the difficulties that historians have to face when dealing with the KPÖ is necessary. First, historiography on Austrian communism is in many cases a field of study of its own rather than a helpful tool for further research. Except for the interwar period and the first postwar decade, when Austria was under quadripartite Allied control and occupation, there are hardly any studies written by historians who are not in some way affiliated with the KPÖ.[1]

The second major problem is the lack of primary sources originating from the party itself. There is no party archive comparable to the communist parties of the Eastern bloc or the well-organized party archives of larger West European communist parties like the Italian Communist

---

Notes for this chapter begin on page 292.

Party or, to a lesser degree, the French Communist Party.[2] To fill this gap one has always to rely on the papers and memoirs of party members who were later expelled,[3] and archival sources of other communist parties who documented the policy of the Austrian communists, and wrote minutes about their conversations with Austrian "comrades."[4] However, when dealing with the politics of the KPÖ in the Perestroika period, in many cases the analysis has to be based on published materials of the Austrian communists. Most of the post-1960s documents are still in the private possession of former actors or their descendants. Without being affiliated with the KPÖ, it is usually still very hard to contact former party members or their relatives, and even harder to access private archives. However, by analyzing the theoretical journal of the KPÖ named *Weg und Ziel* and the party's daily *Volksstimme*, one can make a judgment about the official stance of the Austrian communists. Additionally, memoirs and other accounts by former KPÖ politicians and, most importantly, sources of other communist parties, reveal their true positioning in regard to Perestroika. In this respect, the sources of the East German Sozialistische Einheitspartei Deutschlands (SED) are of special importance.

Against the historical background that formed and shaped the already extremely small KPÖ of the late 1980s, the party's attitude to Perestroika is relatively simple to explain. Therefore, a concise introductory round-journey through the KPÖ's post-1945 history is necessary. From the end of World War II up until the early 1980s, one can identify three different phases. First, the Stalinist era of the postwar decade that continued to shape the party for some time; second, the short "Eurocommunist" phase of the 1960s, admired in the West, but massively opposed by orthodox party members and many so-called fraternal parties in the East and the West; third, the "normalized" KPÖ of the 1970s and 1980s. All phases were somehow equally important in creating what was little more than a sectarian movement—especially in the domestic theatre.[5]

The Austrian Communists after 1945: A Journey from Moscow via "Austro-Eurocommunism" to East Berlin?

Despite its remarkable merits in the resistance of 1933–1945,[6] in retrospect, the decade from 1945 to 1955 was the most successful period in the history of the KPÖ. The party was represented in the Austrian parliament from 1945 to 1959 and from 1947 even in governmental responsibility. Nevertheless, the KPÖ never achieved more than 5 percent of the overall votes, and remained an outcast of Austrian politics. Lacking the tradition of a workers' party, and burdened by its close relationship to the

Soviet occupation power, detested by a vast majority of Austrians, the KPÖ never managed to gain a significant voter base. In the first postwar decade, the KPÖ was a clear-cut Stalinist party.[7] It joined the condemnation of Tito,[8] praised the brutal Sovietization of Eastern Europe, publicly justified the show trials, and ruthlessly participated in every reversal of Soviet policy.[9] After the signing of the Austrian State Treaty in 1955,[10] as well as the disillusioning effects of Nikita Khrushchev's secret speech at the 20th Congress of the CPSU and his crackdown on the Hungarian uprising in 1956, the KPÖ lost about one-third of its membership. Criticism within the party arose, but these discussions were aborted in favor of the unity of the party.[11] Indeed, the development in the neighboring "people's democracies" made it even harder to promote "socialism" on the domestic scene. At the next elections in 1959, the KPÖ lost its last members of parliament, and marginalization on the domestic political level continued. However, in the 1960s, some enlightened officials of the Austrian communists became "masterminds" of early "Eurocommunist" ideas.[12] Against the backdrop of the Stalinist socialization of the leaders, as well as of the party's rank and file, this development seems somehow surprising and already implies the reason why the "Austro-Eurocommunist" experiment failed in the end.[13] Two remarkable characters shaped this phase, Ernst Fischer[14] and Franz Marek[15]—the former, by introducing public criticism of the situation in socialist states; the latter, due to his anticipation of "Eurocommunist" ideas that became popular in many West European communist parties during the 1970s.

At its 19th Congress in 1965, the KPÖ adopted a reformist program, which was to a large extent written by Marek and heavily influenced by the ideas of the Italian communist leader Palmiro Togliatti.[16] The congress brought about the long overdue generational change in the leadership: Franz Muhri replaced Johann Koplenig as the party's chairman, and suddenly reform-minded functionaries dominated the Politburo. Additionally, the reformist wing controlled the party media. This constituted the setting for an atmosphere in which an open discussion of reformist ideas was possible—not only within the KPÖ, but also on a European scale. In 1966, Marek organized a conference of West European communist parties. His introductory presentation forestalled most of the "Eurocommunist" ideas of the 1970s. However, the shape of the party media and its international appearance did not correspond to the internal situation of the KPÖ. Those who could have backed this course in a standoff with orthodoxy had left the party a decade earlier as a consequence of 1956. Instead, the "Austro-Eurocommunist" experiment was attacked and fought not only from within the party, but notably by the East European state parties—first and foremost, the SED.[17]

Since the reformers held strong positions in the Politburo and in the party media, in 1968 the KPÖ publicly welcomed "Socialism with a human face." Internally, conflicts on the appraisal of the Czechoslovakian reforms aggravated. The KPÖ officially condemned the crackdown on the "Prague Spring" by the Warsaw Pact powers. This was a result of the composition of the KPÖ leadership and the wait-and-see attitude adopted by the anti-reformists. The positioning of the Austrian communists led to open conflict with the socialist bloc. Immediately after the invasion, the orthodox forces started to prepare for their final battle against the reformers, which they intended to take place at the party's 20th Congress in January 1969. For the sake of the unity of the party, Chairman Muhri, in cooperation with Secretary General Friedl Fürnberg, who in fact shaped the party most, forced the congress to abstain from outvoting the reformers; but as further developments showed, their position had dramatically weakened. The orthodox forces managed to expel Fischer and to crowd out of the party most of the reformers within a year. In 1971, the KPÖ finally took back its condemnation of the 1968 invasion, now calling it a "bitter necessity."[18] Thereafter, the KPÖ returned to an entirely Muscovite line. On "Eurocommunism" the party took a negative stance.[19] Those who had crowded out the KPÖ reformers still feared possible influences or a return of reformist ideas propagated by larger West European parties in the 1970s.[20] During the Polish crisis of the early 1980s, the Austrian communists were among the fiercest critics of the United Workers' Party. Party media harshly attacked the Polish leadership and—like the SED[21]— the KPÖ seemed to have been in favor of an intervention in order to end what they called a "counterrevolution."[22] In the end, it welcomed martial law and the prohibition of Solidarność (Solidarity), however, doubts about the future developments remained.[23] At the same time, the various "peace movements" were of imminent importance for West European communist parties, even for the KPÖ. Despite being overrepresented in the rather small Austrian peace movement,[24] the Austrian communists played hardly any political role.[25] Due to the fact that two-thirds of the party members were aged sixty or older, Eastern observers even considered the extinction of the KPÖ within a decade to be a possibility.[26]

Nevertheless, despite being in continuous decrease and keeping a hardline stance on international issues, in 1982 the KPÖ adopted a new party program called "Socialism in Austria's Colors." In this, it was put straight that "every path to socialism can only be a democratic one." However, the entirely uncritical attitude toward the Soviet Union and the socialist states had not changed.[27] In his memoirs, Chairman Franz Muhri conceded that "embellishment" was the main weakness of the new program.[28] In fact, this way of positioning was the fundament of the post-1971 KPÖ. It guaranteed good relations with the Eastern bloc parties, first and foremost the SED. With the falling apart of everything that the KPÖ had praised for almost two decades, it had to deal with the resulting multifaceted consequences. This process accelerated after Mikhail Gorbachev came to power in the Soviet Union in 1985.

The KPÖ and Perestroika

Interestingly enough, there is a "scientific" study on the KPÖ's reception of Perestroika, which was approved as a doctoral dissertation at the University of Vienna. The author Philipp Wimmer, son of the former chief ideologist of the KPÖ Ernst Wimmer, based his analysis on articles published in the party's theoretical journal *Weg und Ziel* and on a few documents originating from his father's private archive.[29] Wimmer's study analyzes Perestroika from a dogmatic Marxist–Leninist perspective, hence the results are foreseeable. His approach aims at unmasking Perestroika as "revisionism" and in the end as "counterrevolutionary."[30] Even though it is questionable if twenty-first century academic standards should allow someone to receive a doctorate for such a study, because of the riches of otherwise unavailable sources and the reproduction of KPÖ articles at great length, Wimmer's study is useful for an analysis of the KPÖ position on Perestroika. Owing to his approach, Wimmer remains puzzled by the fact that the KPÖ ideologists did not come to his conclusions and abstained from publicly rejecting Perestroika. To him this fact is even more astonishing since most of the actors involved, back in the 1960s, had successfully fought the reformers—or as Wimmer names them, "revisionists"—within the KPÖ.[31] By analyzing these articles and documents from an unbiased perspective and against the background of the KPÖ's post-1945 history, this constitutes no surprise at all. Since its "normalization," the KPÖ abstained from criticizing the socialist states and the ruling communist parties. If criticism occurred, this criticism never exceeded the level on which the CPSU or the SED criticized certain developments or fraternal parties. According to this pattern, the KPÖ heavily criticized and even attacked the Polish party at the beginning of the 1980s, and in later years showed its disapproval of the Hungarian reform process;[32] however, any criticism of the CPSU remained a taboo. After Gorbachev's rise to power, communication hierarchies of the disparate communist world did not immediately change; hence, every Moscow announcement remained sacrosanct—even if it was contradictory to everything the party had hitherto stood for. This pattern holds true for the publicized opinions of the KPÖ, which only by the very end of the

1980s had slowly started to criticize certain developments in the Soviet Union; however, until the very end it abstained from openly criticizing the CPSU. In the case of developments that the KPÖ obviously disliked, the party media only reproduced the official Soviet news without commenting or discussing it further in *Weg und Ziel*.[33] Internally and in conversations with like-minded communist parties such as the SED, criticism was openly expressed. Since we only know a little about the internal discussions of the KPÖ leadership in the 1980s, the records of its meetings with fraternal parties are of top priority if we are to reach the core of the Austrian communists' perception of Perestroika. After these general remarks on the KPÖ's positioning, let us take a chronological look at how perceptions changed, and how they were publicized and communicated in the course of fraternal meetings.

When Gorbachev introduced his reforms, the KPÖ officially welcomed Perestroika. Chairman Muhri attended the 27th Congress of the CPSU in 1986, at which the new Soviet leader openly analyzed and criticized the contradictions and deformations in Soviet society. Impressed by the greater public interest in the proceedings of the congress, and the new hopes people cherished, he also noticed the prevailing doubts over whether there would be real changes this time. Back home his party declared full solidarity with Perestroika.[34] The 26th Congress of the KPÖ in spring 1987 confirmed this stance. However, in his conversation with the head of the SED delegation to the congress Walter Eberlein, Muhri clarified that the party's welcoming of the developments in the USSR did not mean neglecting to take account of the different conditions that existed in the various socialist countries. The KPÖ fully agreed if other parties did not schematically adopt the experiences of the CPSU. With regard to the "specific conditions" in East Germany, Muhri spoke of the GDR's remarkable advances in economic and technological matters.[35]

It is almost impossible to judge if Perestroika in its initial stages created hopes among ordinary party members and some functionaries, who may once again have sensed that the time was ripe for change. The effects that 1989 had on the KPÖ point in this direction. The institutionalized and personalized solidarity of the KPÖ leadership with the Soviet Union hindered it from openly criticizing Glasnost and Perestroika right from the start. As a matter of tradition, the old guard lauded everything that came from Moscow, but very soon the first dissonances loomed on the horizon. Interestingly enough, the de-ideologization of international politics pursued by Gorbachev in order to revive superpower détente, irritated the KPÖ the most.[36] This is even more surprising since the Austrian communists had used precisely the same rhetoric in justifying their position in the Austrian peace movement, but to orthodox communists de-ideologization was only justified if it aimed at delegitimizing the other superpower. In principle, the KPÖ officially welcomed the new criticism and self-criticism in the Soviet Union, but as it revealed more and more the chasm between reality and what was claimed to be Soviet reality, the party's leadership became anxious about how far this process would lead. However, by not distancing themselves from the reforms of Perestroika, the orthodox KPÖ ideologists contributed to unleashing hopes for change among the party's rank and file, not only in the Soviet bloc, but also within the Austrian party itself.

It is impossible to discuss the KPÖ's position on every step of Perestroika in detail. Hence, it makes sense to pick and portray one key document that illustrates best the attitude of the party's leadership. The record of the conversation between Franz Muhri and Erich Honecker that took place in the course of a visit by a KPÖ delegation to East Germany in late 1987 provides an in-depth insight, and shows how far the party leadership had already sided with the SED on the question of Perestroika. Besides the contents of their negotiations, the document is of special interest because of the time the meeting took place. By the end of 1987, the effects of Perestroika in the Soviet Union had become visible, even though not yet in full scale. At the same time, the severe repercussions of Gorbachev's reforms on the entire Soviet bloc were far less clear than they would become in 1988—and especially in 1989. Even though the SED had already started to clash with the CPSU,[37] the document provides us with quite a pure view on Muhri's and Honecker's perception of Perestroika. Later documents would tell us more about how the undesired and disliked effects of Perestroika were seen. Officially, the KPÖ still unconditionally supported Perestroika.[38] In accordance with the communication cultures of communist parties, Honecker formulated his critical remarks on Perestroika in a positive way, but unmistakably highlighted his reluctance to adopt these reforms in the GDR. Muhri immediately replied: "Regarding the restructuring in the Soviet Union, the KPÖ fully agrees with the SED."[39] In his own remarks on Perestroika, he stated:

> [The Austrian communists welcome] the goals of speeding up the development of socialist democracy as well as an offensive peace policy. However, we cannot show solidarity with all forms and measures earmarking the current development of the Soviet Union. Only practice will prove if they serve the right objectives. We fully agree with the new political thinking, but in our understanding a solution of big global problems has to be closely linked with the struggle for societal change.[40]

The Soviet economic reforms constituted a challenge to the KPÖ's propaganda, since to the public they seemed to prove the analyses of the "bourgeois media." The effects of the Hungarian economic reforms were considered to be even worse. Muhri spoke of a "contradictory process" that had started at the 27th Congress of the CPSU. After Soviet scientists and artists had openly expressed their critical opinion on "really existing socialism" during their stays in Austria, the KPÖ aimed at "blocking" their delegation from the party school of the Austrian communists. Muhri justified this with the problems it could cause for the KPÖ. In this regard, he voiced his "very consent" with the SED's harsh critique on the Soviet film *Repentance (Die Reue)*, which constituted a semi-allegorical critique on Stalinism. The chairman of the Austrian communists worried especially about possible repercussions for the situation in Austria if history was revised. He frankly admitted that the party would be in trouble if a reappraisal of the events of 1968 or Polish–Soviet relations were to take place.[41] In this regard, he was aptly right. With the hitherto official interpretations of Soviet and East European history revised, the KPÖ would immediately be back in the fractional struggles of the 1960s, the fundament of the post-1971 KPÖ being overthrown.

At the sixth plenum of the KPÖ Central Committee in December 1987, Ernst Wimmer reported on the current developments in the socialist countries. He was irritated by several recent statements by soviet scientists and artists, which in his view were "not only unaccustomed, half-baked, but un-Marxist, if not even anti-socialist." The problems in Poland, Yugoslavia, Hungary, and Romania were a result of the countries indebtedness, which impaired their capacity to act. However, it was still common sense not to report about these specific problems in the party's daily *Volksstimme*. As a counter-example to the disliked developments in the socialist bloc, he referred to East Germany and to a lesser degree to Czechoslovakia—two of the most rigid, but still seemingly stable regimes. Wimmer concluded his sobering analysis by stating that the acute problems of several socialist countries were anything but helpful for the KPÖ's struggle.[42]

At roughly the same time, the East German state security collected some information about the internal situation in the KPÖ, and it drew a dismal picture. The party was in continual contraction. The number of young members leaving the party increased, not least due to the "old comrades" who were more interested in keeping their positions than in the "class struggle" in Austria.[43] Additionally, the election campaign performances were considered weak and unenthusiastic. In conversations with former members of the KPÖ, the Stasi had learned that for some time the Austrian party had been "intestine cleaved" and decomposed. Those who had already left the party openly stated that in Austria there was no understanding of the actual political situation in East Germany;

for example, the travel restrictions, the sealed border guarded by armed soldiers and the only limited opening to the West continued to shape the public image of the East German regime in Austria. They had observed the recent developments in the socialist world with much interest. Unambiguously, they judged: "Gorbachev has sensed these developments. Now Poland and Hungary are following him. Those states are now pursuing a more flexible policy." While welcoming these reforms, the East German regime was seen rather negatively. Inflexible planning frustrated the workers and caused excessive bureaucracy and regulation. In their interpretation, there was no alternative to an opening-up of the rigid regime, not least because even the Soviet Union had become more flexible and more pluralistic. Economic reforms as pursued by Hungary seemed unavoidable too.[44] One of those who had been expelled from the KPÖ after 1968 was Leopold Spira. As editor of the *Wiener Tagebuch*, he had shown much interest in Perestroika right from the start; however, by that time he remained doubtful if this process would be successful. During a discussion on Austrian television he openly asked the Soviet foreign policy maker Valentin Falin why Perestroika was initiated so late. Gorbachev's reforms had started to show their effects on the Austrian party, but to the public they only became visible in 1989.[45]

In 1988, Muhri again visited the Soviet Union and was received by Gorbachev for a meeting that lasted for two hours. In their conversation, he renewed the KPÖ's solidarity with the "basic aims" of Perestroika. According to his memoirs, this relativizing statement aimed at stressing that the Austrian communists could not show solidarity with every step by the CPSU, since the KPÖ was unable to judge everything and did not consider every development right. We do not know if Gorbachev recognized what Muhri said, or if he cared about it at all. Muhri claims that at that very moment he did not yet anticipate the dire consequences of Perestroika. The Austrian delegation returned home in good spirits and with conviction of a "fundamental consensus" in the mutual views on the most decisive matters. One of the main concerns in his conversation with Gorbachev was not Perestroika, but the "Common European Home" and the Austrian communist's opposition to European integration. Against the background of the Austrian government's approaching decision to apply for membership of the European Community, Muhri hoped for Soviet support in prohibiting any such step.[46] In those very years, the KPÖ not only campaigned against European integration in Austria, but also engaged in forming a new West European internationalism opposing integration. Thereby the small Austrian party became one of the pioneers of the European Left, formed more than a decade later. In the end, the KPÖ's efforts bore no fruit. In July 1989, when the revolutions and transformation processes in Eastern Europe were already on their way, Austria officially applied for membership of the European Community. Later that year Gorbachev finally publicly confirmed that each country—neutral or not—had to decide for itself whether it wished to join the Community or not.[47] After an overwhelmingly positive plebiscite in 1994, Austria finally joined the European Union in 1995.

The KPÖ, the Revolutions of 1989, German Unification, and the End of the USSR

The KPÖ's leadership claimed that having removed "revisionism" and "dogmatism" from the party, it had already carried out its own Perestroika. However, re-emerging discussions within the party affected the further perception of Perestroika and the effects of Gorbachev's politics on East European regimes. While Perestroika was still praised officially in the late 1980s, the Hungarian reforms were increasingly criticized and any need for reform in the Austrian party was rejected. This created a paradoxical situation. Slowly, as in the 1960s, it seemed that at least two different parties existed within the KPÖ. However, this fact only surfaced when the die had already been cast in Eastern Europe. The reason for this was that despite opposing Gorbachev's reforms, the orthodox members and publicists of the KPÖ had abstained from officially criticizing Perestroika. Blind loyalty to the CPSU prevailed in the publicized opinion of the KPÖ. It was only after most of the communist regimes had been overthrown that the orthodox members of the KPÖ started to criticize the economic crisis in the Soviet Union explicitly and, in consequence the CPSU, which meanwhile had lost its power over a dissolving empire.[48] This flow of critique was not overwhelmingly present in the party's daily *Volksstimme* throughout the revolutionary year of 1989. Instead, in the first half of the year, the KPÖ's media chorus complained that Poland and Hungary were lost for the "cause of socialism." The massacre at Tiananmen Square in Beijing constituted a remarkable turning point in the party's official positioning. Not least due to massive public pressure, the party immediately and unanimously condemned the action taken by the Chinese regime,[49] even though among its leadership there was no consensus on this issue. Thereby, for the first time in almost twenty years, the KPÖ had taken a stance divergent from the SED. Hermann Axen instantly travelled to Vienna to clarify the situation.[50] However, in further consequence, the KPÖ could not elude the changes in the eroding Soviet bloc. In the end, the *Volksstimme* even welcomed the peaceful revolution in the GDR.[51] Yet, the fact that this process within less than a year led to

German unification was a "shock"[52] for the Austrian communists. On the occasion of the annual commemoration of the *"Anschluss"* (annexation) of Austria to the "Third Reich" on 12 March 1938, the party leadership sent a letter to the Austrian chancellor, Franz Vranitzky, criticizing the West German approach to unification and warning of a possible re-emergence of a "German Reich" potentially dominating Europe. Against the backdrop of Austria's experiences with German "expansionism" they called for a statement by the Austrian government demanding among other things the neutralization and far-reaching demilitarization of a united Germany. In connection with Austria's ambitions to join the European Community, the KPÖ feared an even stronger dependence of the Alpine republic on its big German neighbor.[53]

It was not only the Austrian communists' "German trauma" that let them oppose the dissolution of the East German state, formerly ruled by the SED. Another factor was the party's financial dependence on the SED. In retrospect, Muhri spoke of the *Preisgabe* (divulging)[54] of the GDR by Gorbachev. The provisions that companies of the Austrian communists had earned by participating in trade between Austria and the GDR had financed—at least in part—the KPÖ. Thus, the end of the SED regime caused the financial decline of the party. This process was later aggravated with the trials through which unified Germany successfully managed to sue for payment of money illegally transferred from the GDR in 1989/90.[55]

Not only did the provisions earned in economic relations with East Germany seep away, but the Moscow funds ran dry. From the end of 1989, many companies of West European communist parties faced severe problems and even the risk of bankruptcy. This was a direct consequence of the economic failure of Gorbachev's reforms. Facing an aggravating economic crisis, the Soviet Union stopped paying its debts to those companies of their fraternal parties. The situation only eased after a joint appeal by several party leaders to Gorbachev. To the Soviet Union, the sums in discussion were rather negligible, but to smaller European communist parties the profits of these companies were essential for their survival.[56] In mid-1991, the Soviet embassy in Vienna reported to Moscow that the cash flow into the party's register had severely decreased over the previous year. The main reason was the end of trade relations with Czechoslovakia, Poland, Bulgaria, and East Germany as well as rising Soviet debts. These developments made an abrupt restructuring of the KPÖ's oversized party apparatus necessary.[57] At this time, the party was already lost in transformation—a process initiated by the revolutions of 1989, and aggravated by the emerging financial problems.

When the bloody revolution in Romania sounded out the year 1989, the editorial staff of the *Volksstimme* openly confessed that due to their downplayed, hesitant, and uncritical reporting the daily paper had lost its credibility. Behind the scenes, there had been some simmering whenever the word "Romania" had come up, but in print "solidarity" with "despotism" had prevailed. For years, *Volksstimme* journalists had abstained from publishing critical articles, and had constantly reported according to the official line provided by the party leadership, not least because of their dependence with regard to employment. Now their professional lives lay in ruins.[58] This was a reflection of the situation of the entire party.

Those who were in favor of a gradual opening of the KPÖ in the direction of a less doctrinaire party of the political Left may even have felt relieved by the collapse of the socialist regimes and the loss of power by state parties that had been the guardians over the ideological stance of the KPÖ. Many of them left the party in the early 1990s after realizing that a complete renewal of the Austrian party was impossible. Due to the (re-)emerging of inner conflicts in 1989, and facing financial turbulences, the KPÖ restructured at their 27th Congress in January 1990. The co-chairpersons, Walter Silbermayr and Susanne Sohn, replaced chairman Muhri. The new leadership aimed at an opening of the KPÖ toward the broader Left. However, within a short period it turned out that this would ultimately put an end to the party's unity. The dwarfish party lost further members, who were disappointed by the first post-1989 revelations. The new leadership retired in March 1991, little more than a year after its election. The main struggle was about the future orientation of the KPÖ. A general opening to the less ideological Left beyond certain dogmata never became a party consensus.[59]

From the Soviet perspective, the situation of the KPÖ had worsened throughout the previous months. Since the "radical" positioning of the new leadership had faced severe opposition within the party, it had not succeeded in detaching the party from its "revolutionary character." In the end, not even the Viennese party organization had supported the Sohn–Silbermayr line. Instead, pressure from below had forced the tumbling KPÖ to hold an extraordinary party congress in mid-1991. To Soviet observers at the time, it was obvious that Walter Baier (who was elected chairman in 1994) would become the next leading figure of the Austrian communists.[60]

According to another report by the Soviet embassy in Vienna, it was not only the new leadership that faced opposition, but the old guard was also entirely discredited. The Soviet embassy spoke of years of "permanent instability." The KPÖ witnessed no public support or electoral success. Regarding the size of the party, the Soviets spoke of a maximum of eight thousand members—mostly retirees. Their judgment about Perestroika's influence on the KPÖ was unambiguous: Perestroika in the Soviet Union had aggravated the party's situation. The analysis of the Soviet diplomats in Vienna was that even though Glasnost was officially welcomed, it had rid the party membership of certain taboos resulting from a "fetishization" of inner-party discipline. Immediately, secrecy (with regard to the party finances) was put into question. Ordinary party members felt relieved from unconditional support of every step taken by the party's leadership. This laid the cornerstone for the re-evaluation of historical events like the Hitler–Stalin pact of 1939 or the crushing of the "Prague Spring" in 1968. Now the hitherto official party line that had been imposed, sometimes even decades ago, was revised. Against the background of the developments in Eastern Europe, especially in Czechoslovakia with the revision of 1968 in the course of the "velvet revolution," and the intensifying discussion about Stalinism, the hitherto unchallenged solidarity with the Soviet Union was put into question. The following inner-party backlash caused the retreat of the new leadership and the extraordinary party congress of 1991. Even though the Soviet embassy stated that the passion of the discussions had died down through the congress and led to a certain relaxation of inner-party life, it was obvious that it was too early to talk about overcoming the party crisis.[61]

Whilst those who left the KPÖ in 1989–1991 did not shed any tears over the collapse of the Soviet Union, the "old guard" had kept its own worldview. In Muhri's interpretation, the main reason for the collapse of the Soviet Union was the "failure of the party." However, its abolishment in 1991 went too far. On the failed coup against Gorbachev, the former KPÖ chairman opined that the actors aimed at "defending the Soviet constitution" and "preventing the destruction of the Union." In its aims, their action was not a coup at all—yet it was in the way it was carried out. Organized by a small minority and behind the backs of the party, government and people, in the end the result of their action was the opposite of their intentions. It paved the way for the "counter-coup" by Boris Yeltsin that led to the prohibition of the CPSU; and by destroying the organs of the Union it led to the end of the USSR. Not surprisingly, Muhri disliked the future developments in the Russian Federation.[62]

Due to Perestroika, history haunted the Austrian communists. Despite severe opposition from some parts of the KPÖ, one of the lasting results of Perestroika within the Austrian party was a wholehearted examination of Stalinism. This affected not only the party's own Stalinist years,[63] but also the fate of (mostly communist) Austrian victims of Stalinism in the Soviet Union. The KPÖ's initiatives toward the Soviet Union originated in the late 1980s, and Muhri himself had negotiated and corresponded with the responsible Soviet actors and institutions. Together with historians affiliated with the KPÖ, he and Baier continued these efforts in the newborn Russian Federation throughout the 1990s. The KPÖ's engagement in the early 1990s marked an important contribution to the clarification of the victims' fate, and the party quite successfully engaged in favor of their rehabilitation.[64]

Conclusion

In the end, Perestroika had driven the "normalized" KPÖ into its severest crisis since the 1960s, from which it never actually recovered. With the socialist bloc falling apart and losing its financial support, the Austrian party was downsized to what it had been in the interwar period: a minimum-size party without any domestic political relevance, even lacking sufficient funding from the world movement. The Austrian communists' fortune was closely linked to the self-inflicted decline of socialism and the Soviet Union. After World War II, the KPÖ had been a Stalinist party, and its Stalinist legacy had continued to shape the evolution of the Austrian communists for the decades to come. In the end, this even holds true for the fate of the "Austro-Eurocommunist" experiment. After a short period of reform communism, that can be regarded as a precursor of "Eurocommunism," the party returned to an entirely Muscovite stance. The dwarfish party became a close ally of the SED. As a financial (trans) actor between East and West, it managed to survive until the end of the Cold War. Critique on "really existing socialism," the CPSU or the SED was a taboo. On the emergence of Gorbachev's Perestroika, the KPÖ increasingly sided with the dogmatic East German communists, since it rightly feared the possible repercussions of Perestroika on the socialist bloc and on the Austrian party itself. Nevertheless, because of its personalized and institutionalized solidarity with the CPSU, the KPÖ held back with official criticism until the revolutions of 1989 had almost entirely and definitively swept away communist rule in Eastern and Central Europe. The effects of Perestroika and the end of communism in Europe, however, led not only to a further decline of the KPÖ but also brought back the internal divergences of the 1960s. To this day, the Austrian communists are still unable to overcome this status, one way or another. A general opening to the Left never became a party consensus. Regional centers are pursuing differing politics and holding highly diverging, sometimes even conflicting positions. The lasting result of the repercussions that Perestroika had on the KPÖ was its new (though not uncontested) dealing with Stalinism—the phenomenon that had shaped the KPÖ most throughout the Cold War.

Maximilian Graf (European University Institute, Florence) is a historian who specializes in Cold War studies and the history of communism. His most recent publications include a prizewinning book on Austrian–East German relations during the Cold War: *Österreich und die DDR 1949–1990: Politik und Wirtschaft im Schatten der deutschen Teilung* (ÖAW, 2016); the co-edited volume, *Europa und die deutsche Einheit: Beobachtungen, Entscheidungen und Folgen* (Vandenhoeck & Ruprecht, 2017); and the co-edited memoirs of the Austrian resistance fighter and reform communist, Franz Marek: *Beruf und Berufung Kommunist: Lebenserinnerungen und Schlüsseltexte* (Mandelbaum, 2017). In 2014 he was awarded the Karl von Vogelsang Prize—Austrian State Prize for the History of Social Sciences.

Notes

1. For an overview on the historiography on the KPÖ, see Mugrauer, "Die Kommunistische Partei Österreichs." For a first synthesis on Austrian communism in the interwar period, see McLoughlin, Leidinger and Moritz, *Kommunismus in Österreich*. For the official party history, see Historische Kommission, *Die Kommunistische Partei Österreichs*.
2. The *Zentrales Parteiarchiv der KPÖ*, Alfred-Klahr-Gesellschaft, Vienna, contains only limited information on the international relations of the Austrian communists.
3. The papers of Paul Frischauer, Josef Meisel, Egon Kodicek, Josef Lauscher, Fred Margulies, Leopold Spira and (in part) Ernst Fischer are situated in the archive of the *Österreichische Gesellschaft für Zeitgeschichte* that can be consulted in the library of the Department of Contemporary History of the University of Vienna. Further materials by Bruno Frei and Franz Marek can be found in the *Dokumentationsarchiv des Österreichischen Widerstandes*, and the literary remains of Ernst Fischer (containing a lot of correspondence) are part of the *Österreichisches Literaturarchiv* of the Austrian National Library.
4. For the topic in discussion, the East German sources on the KPÖ are very helpful: Stiftung Archiv der Parteien und Massenorganisation der ehemaligen DDR im Bundesarchiv Berlin (SAPMO-BArch). Of course, Russian archives are also of eminent importance. I am grateful to my colleagues of the Ludwig-Boltzmann-Institut für Kriegsfolgenforschung in Graz for granting me access to their copies from the Russian State Archive of Contemporary History (RGANI).
5. I have discussed this journey elsewhere in greater detail in Maximilian Graf, "Die KPÖ und Europa," 241–51.
6. Mugrauer, "Die KPÖ im Kampf"; Neugebauer, "Zur Struktur."
7. On the KPÖ in the period 1945–55, see Mueller, *Die sowjetische Besatzung*; idem, "Genosse Filippov"; idem, "Die gescheiterte Volksdemokratie"; Keller, "Die KPÖ 1945–1955"; Mugrauer, "Die Politik der KPÖ."
8. Mueller, "Soviet Policy, Political Parties"; Karner and Ruggenthaler, "Stalin, Tito."
9. Keller, "Die KPÖ und die Schauprozesse"; Graf, "The Austrian Communists."
10. On the Austrian State Treaty, see Stourzh, *Um Einheit und Freiheit*; Suppan, Stourzh and Mueller, *Der Österreichische Staatsvertrag*.
11. Mugrauer, "Zwischen Erschütterung."
12. Graf, "Frühstart des 'Eurokommunismus'?"

13. Spira, *Ein gescheiterter Versuch*.
14. On Fischer, see Kröhnke, *Ernst Fischer*; Baryli, *Zwischen Stalin und Kafka*; Fetz, *Ernst Fischer*.
15. On Marek, see Graf, "Franz Marek"; Graf and Knoll, *Franz Marek*.
16. *Beschlüsse des XIX. Parteitags der Kommunistischen Partei Österreichs 27. bis 30. Mai 1965*, Vienna, 1965, 3–18.
17. Graf, "The Rise and Fall." On the Vienna conference, see idem, "Frühstart des Eurokommunismus?" 223–26; and Ehmer, "KPÖ und SED."
18. Mugrauer, "Der 'Prager Frühling'"; and in greater detail, idem, "Oft setzte man sich über vernünftige Argumente hinweg."
19. Muhri, "Zur Diskussion."
20. Information Nr. 36/76 für das Politbüro, Betrifft: Arbeitsbesuch auf Einladung des Zentralkomitees der Kommunistischen Partei Österreichs in Wien, Berlin, 27. April 1976, gezeichnet Markowski, SAPMO-BArch, DY 30/13649 [Information for the SED Politburo on a visit to the KPÖ in Vienna, April 1976].
21. Kubina and Wilke, *Hart und kompromisslos durchgreifen*.
22. Priester, "Polen: die Krise geht weiter."
23. Janecek, "Polen: Das Ende der Solidarnosc."
24. On the Austrian peace movement, see Maislinger, "Friedensbewegung in einem neutralen Land." On the self-perception of the KPÖ, see Baier and Garscha, "Friedensbewegung—ein Faktor der Innenpolitik."
25. Auswertung des Plenums des ZK der KPÖ vom 10. und 11. Mai 1983, gezeichnet Beuthin, Wien, 13. Mai 1983, SAPMO-BArch, DY 30/13652 [SED assessment on the plenary session of the Central Committee of the KPÖ, May 1983].
26. Bericht über die Konsultation mit der Abteilung Internationale Verbindungen des ZK der Ungarischen Sozialistischen Arbeiterpartei, Berlin, 28. September 1977, SAPMO-BArch, DY 30/IV B 2/20/165, Bl. 290–99 [SED report on consultations with the international department of the Hungarian Socialist Worker's Party, September 1977].
27. *Sozialismus in Österreichs Farben: Programm der Kommunistischen Partei Österreichs*, Vienna, 1982.
28. Muhri, *Kein Ende der Geschichte*, 131.
29. Wimmer, "Die Rezeption der Ideologie."
30. For the Introduction, see ibid., 5–10.
31. Ibid., 268–76.
32. On the KPÖ's perception of transforming Hungary, see ibid., 77–79, 196–200.
33. Ibid., 94–116, 130–60.
34. Muhri, *Kein Ende der Geschichte*, 59–60.
35. Vermerk über ein Gespräch zwischen Genossen Werner Eberlein, Mitglied des Politbüros des ZK, und Genossen Franz Muhri, Vorsitzender der Kommunistischen Partei Österreichs, am 30. März 1987 in Wien, (=Anlage zu: Bericht über die Teilnahme einer Delegation des ZK der SED unter Leitung von Werner Eberlein, Mitglied des Politbüros, am 26. Parteitag der Kommunistischen Partei Österreichs (KPÖ) vom 27. bis 29. März 1987 in Wien, Berichterstatter W. Eberlein), in Arbeitsprotokoll der Sitzung des Politbüros des Zentralkomitees vom 7. April 1987 (= Protokoll Nr. 14/87), SAPMO-BArch, DY 30/J IV 2/2A/2998, Bl. 145–47 [Memcon Eberlein – Muhri, 30 March 1987].
36. Wimmer, "Die Rezeption der Ideologie," 84.
37. See the chapter by Hermann Wentker in this volume.
38. On 16 December 1987, the Central Committee of the KPÖ, at its sixth plenum, still spoke of "unconditional support for the principal line of Perestroika." See Wimmer, "Die Rezeption der Ideologie," 133.
39. Niederschrift über das Gespräch des Generalsekretärs des ZK der SED, Genossen Erich Honecker, mit dem Vorsitzenden der Kommunistischen Partei Österreichs, Genossen

Franz Muhri, am 30. November 1987, in: Arbeitsprotokoll der Sitzung des Politbüros des Zentralkomitees vom 8. Dezember 1987 (= Protokoll Nr. 49/87), SAPMO-BArch, DY 30/J IV 2/2A/3085, Bl. 136–60 [Stenographic records of the conversation Honecker – Muhri, 30 November 1987].
40. Ibid.
41. Ibid.
42. Information für das Politbüro über die 6. Tagung des ZK der KPÖ am 15. und 16. Dezember 1987, ausgearbeitet von Sieber, Berlin, 12. Januar 1988, SAPMO-BArch, DY 30/11573, Bl. 41–45 [Information for the SED Politburo on the meeting of the Central Committee of the KPÖ, December 1987].
43. Information der Hauptabteilung II zu Situation innerhalb der KPÖ, Berlin, 21. September 1987, Informations-Nr. 3538/87, Streng geheim, Archiv des Bundesbeauftragten für die Unterlagen des Staatsicherheitsdienstes der ehemaligen DDR (BStU), MfS, HA II, Nr. 34476, Bl. 57 [Information by the East German Ministry of State Security on the situation within the KPÖ, September 1987].
44. Information, Nr. 4180/87, Berlin, 13. November 1987, Streng geheim, BStU, MfS, ZAIG Nr. 6356, Bl. 2–3 [Information by the East German Ministry of State Security, November 1987].
45. Spira, *Kommunismus adieu*, 144–48.
46. Muhri, *Kein Ende der Geschichte*, 61–64.
47. Graf, "Die KPÖ und Europa," 255–59.
48. Wimmer, "Die Rezeption der Ideologie," 200–3.
49. "Muhri: Armee-Einsatz nicht gerechtfertigt. Mehrere tausend Tote in Peking," *Volksstimme*, 6 June 1989, 1, 4.
50. Vermerk über ein Gespräch zwischen Hermann Axen, Mitglied des Politbüros und Sekretär des ZK, und Walter Silbermayr, Mitglied des Politischen Büros und des Sekretariates des ZK der KP Österreichs, am 29. Juni 1989, gezeichnet Axen, Berlin, 30.6.1989, als Hausmitteilung übergeben an Honecker am 12. Juli 1989, SAPMO-BArch, DY 30/13651 [Memcon Axen – Silbermayr, 29 June 1989].
51. DDR-Bürger erlernen den aufrechten Gang, in *Volksstimme*, 5/6 November 1989, 1; Max Weidinger, Sie riefen: "Wir sind das Volk!", *Volksstimme*, 7 November 1989, 3.
52. Zur Reise von Gregor Gysi in die Republik Österreich (5. bis 8. Juni 1990), 11.06.1990, Archiv des Parteivorstands Die Linke [Report on Gysi's visit to Austria, June 1990].
53. Sohn and Silbermayr to Chancellor Franz Vranitzky, Vienna, 12 March 1990. Österreichisches Staatsarchiv, Archiv der Republik, Bundesministerium für Auswärtige Angelegenheiten, Sektion II-Pol 1990, GZ. 22.17.01/110-II.1/90.
54. Muhri, *Kein Ende der Geschichte*, 67.
55. Graf, "Parteifinanzierung oder Devisenerwirtschaftung?"; Seliger, "KPÖ-Firmen."
56. Über die Verschuldung sowjetischer Organisationen bei Firmen der Freunde, 12. Oktober 1990, RGANI, F. 5, op. 103, d. 650, 70–72 [Memorandum on Soviet debts at companies of fraternal parties, October 1990].
57. Bericht der sowjetischen Botschaft in Österreich über die Lage der KPÖ, 7. August 1991, RGANI, F. 5, op. 104, d. 470, 47–54 [Report by the Soviet embassy in Austria on the situation of the KPÖ, August 1991].
58. Fanta, *Arbeiter der Feder*, 49.
59. For a summary of this process, see Ehmer, "Die Kommunistische Partei Österreichs"; Baier, *Das kurze Jahrhundert*, 196–9, 204–8. Also, see Sohn, *Als der Kommunismus stürzte*; for a perspective opposing any reform, see Furch, *Das schwache Immunsystem*.
60. Aufzeichnung eines Gesprächs mit KPÖ-Mitgliedern. Aus dem Diensttagebuch des sowjetischen Botschaftsrats in Wien, V.S. Matlaš, 4. März 1991, RGANI, F. 5, op. 104, d. 70, p. 14–15 [Notes of a Soviet diplomat in Vienna on conversations with members of the KPÖ, March 1991].

61. Bericht der sowjetischen Botschaft in Österreich über die Lage der KPÖ, 7. August 1991, RGANI, F. 5, op. 104, d. 470, 47–54.
62. Muhri, *Kein Ende der Geschichte*, 69–73.
63. Bildungsreferat der KPÖ, *Spät, aber doch*.
64. Baier and Muhri, *Stalin und wir*.

Bibliography

Baier, Walter, and Winfried R. Garscha. "Friedensbewegung—ein Faktor der Innenpolitik: Breite Basisbewegung—Differenzierung in der SPÖ," *Weg und Ziel*, Vol. 40, No. 6 (1982), 205–8.

Baier, Walter. *Das kurze Jahrhundert: Kommunismus in Österreich. KPÖ 1918 bis 2008*, Vienna, 2009.

Baier, Walter, and Franz Muhri. *Stalin und wir: Stalinismus und die Rehabilitierung österreichischer Opfer*, ed. Bundesvorstand der KPÖ, Vienna, 2001.

Baryli, Stefan. *Zwischen Stalin und Kafka: Ernst Fischer von 1945 bis 1972*, Bonn, 2008.

Bildungsreferat der KPÖ (ed.). *Spät, aber doch: Materialien zum Thema "Stalinismus,"* Vienna, 1991.

Ehmer, Josef. "Die Kommunistische Partei Österreichs, Geschichte, soziales Profil, aktuelle Situation," in *Der Kommunismus in Westteuropa: Niedergang oder Mutation*, ed. Patrick Moreau, Marc Lazar and Gerhard Hirscher, Landsberg am Lech, 1998, 214–18.

_____. "KPÖ und SED: Ein ambivalentes Verhältnis," in *Von der Utopie zum Terror: Stalinismus-Analysen*, ed. Wolfgang Neugebauer, Vienna, 1994, 171–81.

Fanta, Maria Bianca. *Arbeiter der Feder: Die Journalistinnen und Journalisten des KPÖ-Zentralorgans "Österreichische Volksstimme" 1945–1956*, Graz, 2016.

Fetz, Bernhard (ed.). *Ernst Fischer: Texte und Materialien*, Vienna, 2000.

Furch, Bruno. *Das schwache Immunsystem: Historisch-kritischer Essay über den Niedergang der Kommunistischen Partei Österreichs und seine politischen Hauptursachen*, Vienna, 1995.

Graf, Maximilian. "The Austrian Communists and the Show Trials: The Unposed Question of Denunciation," in *Show Trials, Concentration and Labour Camps and the Fate of Political Refugees before and after World War II*, ed. Zoltán Maruzsa, Budapest, 2011, 87–93.

_____. "Franz Marek. Stalinist, Kritiker, Reformer, Ausgeschlossener," in *Dissidente Kommunisten: Das sowjetische Modell und seine Kritiker*, ed. Knud Andresen, Mario Kessler and Axel Schildt, Berlin, 2018, 107–134.

_____. "Frühstart des 'Eurokommunismus'? Das Experiment der KPÖ und die Konferenzen westeuropäischer KPs im Kontext der europäischen Reformkommunismen der Sechzigerjahre," in *Jahrbuch für historische Kommunismusforschung* (2017), 217–32.

_____. "Die KPÖ und Europa: Internationale Stellung und Europapolitik einer Kleinpartei (1945–heute)," in *Kommunismus und Europa: Europapolitik und -vorstellungen der europäischen kommunistischen Parteien 1945–1989*, ed. Francesco Di Palma and Wolfgang Mueller, Paderborn, 2016, 240–60.

———. "Parteifinanzierung oder Devisenerwirtschaftung? Zu den Wirtschaftsbeziehungen von KPÖ und SED, 1946–1989," in *Jahrbuch für historische Kommunismusforschung* (2014), 229–47.

———. "The Rise and Fall of 'Austro-Eurocommunism': On the 'Crisis' within the KPÖ and the Significance of East German Influence in the 1960s," *Journal of European Integration History*, Vol. 20, No. 2 (2014), 203–18.

Graf, Maximilian, and Sarah Knoll (eds). *Franz Marek, Beruf und Berufung Kommunist: Lebenserinnerungen und Schlüsseltexte*, Vienna, 2017.

Historische Kommission beim Zentralkomitee der KPÖ (ed.). *Die Kommunistische Partei Österreichs: Beiträge zu ihrer Geschichte*, Vienna, 1987.

Janecek, Otto. "Polen: Das Ende der 'Solidarnosc'," *Weg und Ziel*, Vol. 40, No. 12 (1982), 432–33.

Karner, Stefan, and Peter Ruggenthaler. "Stalin, Tito und die Österreichfrage: Zur Österreichpolitik des Kreml im Kontext der sowjetischen Jugoslawienpolitik 1945 bis 1949," in *Jahrbuch für historische Kommunismusforschung* (2008), 81–105.

Keller, Fritz. "Die KPÖ 1945–1955," in *Jahrbuch für historische Kommunismusforschung* (1994), 104–21.

———. "Die KPÖ und die Schauprozesse in Osteuropa 1948 bis 1953," in *"Ich habe den Tod verdient": Schauprozesse und politische Verfolgung in Mittel- und Osteuropa 1945–1956*, ed. Wolfgang Maderthaner, Hans Schafranek and Berthold Unfried, Vienna, 1991, 199–218.

Kröhnke, Karl. *Ernst Fischer oder Die Kunst der Koexistenz*, Frankfurt am Main, 1994.

Kubina, Michael, and Manfred Wilke. *"Hart und kompromisslos durchgreifen": Die SED contra Polen 1980/81. Geheimakten der SED-Führung über die Unterdrückung der polnischen Demokratiebewegung*, Berlin, 1995.

Maislinger, Andreas. "Friedensbewegung in einem neutralen Land: Zur neuen Friedensbewegung in Österreich," in *Medienmacht im Nord-Süd-Konflikt: Die Neue Internationale Informationsordnung*, ed. Reiner Steinweg and Jörg Becker, Frankfurt am Main, 1984, 392–415.

McLoughlin, Barry, Hannes Leidinger and Verena Moritz. *Kommunismus in Österreich 1918–1938*, Innsbruck, 2009.

Mueller, Wolfgang. "Genosse Filippov und seine österreichischen 'Freunde': Fallstudien zur 'Macht der Schwachen' im Verhältnis zwischen der KPdSU und einer Bruderpartei," in *Osteuropa vom Weltkrieg bis zur Wende*, ed. Wolfgang Mueller and Michael Portmann, Vienna, 2007, 133–60.

———. "Die gescheiterte Volksdemokratie: Zur Österreich-Politik von KPÖ und Sowjetunion 1945 bis 1955," in *Jahrbuch für Historische Kommunismusforschung* (2005), 141–70.

———. "Soviet Policy, Political Parties, and the Preparation for Communist Takeovers in Hungary, Germany, Austria, 1944–1946," *East European Politics and Societies*, Vol. 24 (2010), 90–115.

———. *Die sowjetische Besatzung in Österreich 1945–1955 und ihre politische Mission*, Vienna, 2005.

Mugrauer, Manfred. "Die Kommunistische Partei Österreichs: Zum Stand der Forschung über die Geschichte der KPÖ," in *Jahrbuch für historische Kommunismusforschung* (2013), 211–34.

_____. "Die KPÖ im Kampf gegen die austrofaschistische Diktatur," in *Das Dollfuß/ Schuschnigg-Regime 1933–1938: Vermessung eines Forschungsfeldes,* ed. Florian Wenninger and Lucile Dreidemy, Vienna, 2013, 41–68.

_____. "'Oft setzte man sich über vernünftige Argumente hinweg...': Die krisenhafte Entwicklung der KPÖ in den Jahren 1968 bis 1971," in ed. idem, *90 Jahre KPÖ,* 261–318.

_____. "Die Politik der KPÖ 1945 bis 1955/56," in *90 Jahre KPÖ: Studien zur Geschichte der Kommunistischen Partei Österreichs,* ed. Manfred Mugrauer, Vienna, 2009, 37–52.

_____. "Der 'Prager Frühling' und die Parteikrise der KPÖ," in *Prager Frühling: Das internationale Krisenjahr 1968, Vol. 1: Beiträge,* ed. Stefan Karner et al., Cologne, 2008, 1043–61.

_____. "Zwischen Erschütterung, neuer Offenheit und 'Normalisierung': Die KPÖ, der 20. Parteitag der KPdSU und die Ungarn-Krise 1956," in *Osteuropa,* ed. Wolfgang Mueller and Michael Portmann, Vienna, 257–97.

Muhri, Franz. "Zur Diskussion über den 'Eurokommunismus'," in *Eurokommunismus? Eine Sammlung von Stellungnahmen,* ed. Franz Muhri, Erwin Scharf and Ernst Wimmer, Vienna, 1978.

_____. *Kein Ende der Geschichte,* Vienna, 1995.

Neugebauer, Wolfgang. "Zur Struktur, Größe und Effizienz des kommunistischen Widerstands in Österreich 1938–1945," in *Zeithistoriker— Archivar—Aufklärer: Festschrift für Winfried R. Garscha,* ed. Claudia Kuretsidis-Haider and Christine Schindler, Vienna, 2017, 165–77.

Priester, Eva. "Polen: die Krise geht weiter. Reaktionäre Kräfte in der 'Solidarnosc' wollen die Konfrontation," *Weg und Ziel,* Vol. 39, No. 10 (1981), 353–54.

Seliger, Maren. "KPÖ-Firmen und Osthandel 1945–1989: Rahmenbedingungen und einige Aspekte der Außenhandelspraxis," in *"Zarte Bande": Österreich und die europäischen planwirtschaftlichen Länder* ["Delicate Relationships": Austria and Europe's Planned Economies], ed. Gertrude Enderle-Burcel, Dieter Stiefel and Alice Teichova, Innsbruck, 2006, 107–29.

Sohn, Susanne. *Als der Kommunismus stürzte und mir nichts mehr heilig war,* Vienna, 2017.

Spira, Leopold. *Ein gescheiterter Versuch: Der Austro-Eurokommunismus,* Vienna, 1979.

_____. *Kommunismus adieu: Eine ideologische Biographie,* Vienna, 1992.

Stourzh, Gerald. *Um Einheit und Freiheit: Staatsvertrag, Neutralität und das Ende der Ost-West-Besetzung Österreichs 1945–1955,* 5th edn, Vienna, 2005.

Suppan, Arnold, Gerald Stourzh and Wolfgang Mueller (eds). *Der Österreichische Staatsvertrag: Internationale Strategie, rechtliche Relevanz, nationale Identität,* Vienna, 2005.

Wimmer, Philip. "Die Rezeption der Ideologie der Perestroika durch die KPÖ von 1985 bis 1990: Anhand 'Weg und Ziel', der 'Monatsschrift für Theorie und Praxis des Marxismus-Leninismus'," PhD dissertation, University of Vienna, 2003.

Chapter 14

The Spanish Communist Party and Perestroika

Walther L. Bernecker

It may appear very strange, but in most books and articles about the Communist Party of Spain (Partido Comunista de España, PCE) the term "Perestroika" is not even mentioned—or, at the most, only tangentially. One reason may be that most of the histories of the PCE were written in the 1970s and 1980s, when the communists played a major role in Spanish politics, and were concentrating on the internal crisis and the political decline of the party. But more important is probably the fact that the leading Spanish communists were convinced that Perestroika was of no importance for them, because the changes in ideology and organization that occurred in the communist parties in the wake of Perestroika had already taken place in Spain a decade or more before. The question is whether this appreciation was correct, and how do we explain the critical development of the PCE in the decisive years of "transition" after Franco's death in 1975.

The PCE and Its Turn Away from the Soviet Union

In order to evaluate correctly the relationship between the Spanish communists and the Soviet Union in the years of Perestroika, one has to look back to at least the 1960s. Although, from the 1930s, the PCE had been absolutely loyal to the international communist movement controlled and directed by the Soviet Union, in the 1960s the PCE leaders became more

---

Notes for this chapter begin on page 319.

and more convinced that they had to break with the Marxist–Leninist ideology, and terminate the uncritical obedience to Stalinism, if they wanted to survive in a post-Franco Spain.[1] Already in 1967, the secretary general of the PCE, Santiago Carrillo, had said: "Nobody—not least the Communist Party—thinks today about making a Communist revolution. The country's alternative choices are the following: reactionary and fascist or democratic dictatorship." And in 1974, he said to Nicolás Franco that the PCE would collaborate in Spain "with every government that liberated the political prisoners, that granted a general amnesty, and that enabled political freedom."[2]

From the early 1950s on, Carrillo was increasingly convinced that the international situation had changed so much since the Civil War of 1936–39 that the policies and strategies of the PCE needed urgent adjustment. He agreed with Khrushchev at the 20th Congress of the Communist Party of the Soviet Union (CPSU) in early 1956 that Stalinism was an aberration in an otherwise healthy communist system. He also followed the Soviet line after the invasion of Hungary. In 1956, under Carrillo's direction, the Political Bureau of the PCE approved a call for National Reconciliation. This appeal represented an important break with the past, because it was the first step toward bridging the two camps that divided Spain. This change in the ideological and strategic dimension of Spanish communism was responding to a profound domestic imperative, but it was also due to the crisis of confidence and leadership in the Soviet Union since the death of Stalin, which had encouraged claims for national roads to socialism and for political and ideological independence from Moscow. On the other side, when in the early 1960s Fernando Claudín and Jorge Semprún presented a global critique of the PCE's policies, anticipating many "Eurocommunist" tenets, Carrillo engineered their expulsion.[3]

In contrast to the PCE's reaction to the Soviet invasion of Hungary 1956, the Spanish communists criticized the Warsaw Pact invasion of Czechoslovakia in August 1968, arguing that in this case socialism and the existing order were not in danger. From now on, the PCE demanded absolute autonomy and independence from Moscow. The communist Spanish leadership was convinced that the prospects for socialism in Spain were inextricably linked to the general fate of the European communist movement, and therefore a regional approach by the Left to the problems of socialism and democracy was vitally necessary.[4] The PCE became one of the most acerbic critics of the Soviet Union in the international communist movement, and the Soviets repeatedly manifested their growing concern with the Spanish communist efforts to devise a theoretical framework justifying their position of autonomy and independence. Events in the years after 1968 eroded more and more any lingering sense of loyalty that Carrillo and his closest associates still retained toward the Soviet Union.⁵

In the sequel of 1968, the PCE forged links with other communist parties at an international level. Party representatives met with delegations from different countries that shared the same desire to reduce their dependence on Moscow. In particular, relations with their Italian communist counterparts gathered momentum. At the same time, the PCE elaborated its own vision of a Spanish road to socialism—what some years later was called Eurocommunism. The PCE's differences with the Soviet leadership deepened as a result of the April 1974 Portuguese revolution. The PCE welcomed the events in Portugal at the outset, seeing in them a prelude to the offensive by the Left in Spain. But the euphoria quickly dissipated when the Portuguese Communist Party attached its fortunes to the most radical wing of the revolutionaries, and it soon became clear that the Portuguese communist vision of socialist society did not have much in common with the proclaimed Spanish road to socialism.⁶

In the final years of Francoism, when Carrillo was eager to project in the liberal and conservative European press an "open" image of his party, the PCE distanced itself more and more from the Soviet Union. The Spanish communists saw the necessity of collaborating with at least certain "progressive" elements of the Spanish bourgeoisie in order to have allies for the post-Franco era. Now, the PCE intensified the contacts with bankers, monarchists, and representatives of the Catholic hierarchy. These contacts were intensified even more after the assassination of Prime Minister Luis Carrero Blanco on 20 December 1973. At the same time, Central Committee member Manuel Azcárate published a paper about the international policy of the PCE, affirming that the fusion between the CPSU and the Soviet state made real democratic socialism in Russia impossible. The CPSU reacted very critically, accusing the PCE of being an enemy of the Soviet Union.⁷ But in Spain itself and in Western Europe, the turning away from the Soviet Union and its political-economic system helped the PCE to present itself as a serious, independent and responsible party on which the reformist Francoists had to count after Franco's death.

In the years following 1975, Spain became a representative Western democracy. In this phase, the so-called *Transición* (Transition), the Spanish communists, who had just been legalized in March 1977, after nearly forty years in exile and clandestinity, were of crucial importance for the reform process in Spain and the stabilization of the new Spanish democracy. The Communist Party renounced many of its Marxist–Leninist principles and integrated itself into the new parliamentary system.⁸ Already in 1977, Secretary General Santiago Carrillo published his programmatic manifesto *Eurocommunism and State*.⁹ The author soon became the leading exponent and representative of Eurocommunism, along with Enrico Berlinguer in Italy.

Carrillo's book was heavily criticized in the press of the Soviet Union. It appeared that by late summer 1977 an irrevocable split might develop between the CPSU and the Spanish communists. Then, in early September, the PCE announced that V. Pertsov, attached to the International Affairs Department of the Central Committee of the CPSU, had met with Carrillo and other Spanish communist leaders in an effort to reduce tensions between the two parties. Both sides, it would appear, had at least a temporary interest in resolving the dispute. Negotiations continued into the fall, with the final agreement that Carrillo would attend the sixtieth anniversary celebrations of the October 1917 Revolution in Moscow. But at the meeting itself, the Soviets did not permit Carrillo to speak, this would become an international affair.[10] A couple of weeks later, Carrillo traveled to the United States, and there he announced, somewhat surprisingly, that the Communist Party of Spain would say goodbye to Leninism at its next congress.[11]

Many party members were outraged when they heard this announcement. Although Leninism did not play a larger role in the practical work of the Spanish communists, the renouncement of Leninism was unacceptable for many traditional PCE members. What followed was a rich and lively pre-congress discussion in which many ideological, personal, and generational cleavages came up, all of which combined to create a serious PCE identity crisis.[12] But finally, Carrillo's theses were successful, and in 1978 the 9th PCE Congress defined the Communist Party as "Marxist, democratic, and revolutionary." From then on, the myth of the unity of the party was broken, and the debates that had led up to the congress were the first salvoes in what promised to be a long, drawn-out battle over the identity and policies of the PCE.

In July 1976, Carrillo had assisted at a conference of communist and labor parties in East Berlin. There, he expressed his compromise with a liberal and pluralistic vision of socialism, and he insisted on the idea that Europe's communists were not subject to any central authority or to international discipline. In the next months, the secretary general published again and again declarations in which he showed an image of the PCE as a party completely independent of Moscow, defined with a pluralistic model of socialist democracy, using only peaceful and democratic methods to reach its goals, and disposed to respect ideological and religious differences, and even negative results in free elections.

In his book *Eurocomunismo y Estado*, Carrillo sketched a theoretical framework that could serve as (what he called) the revolutionary model for developed capitalist countries. He argued basically that it was possible to combine socialism and democracy in the countries of Western Europe. With respect to the nature of the Soviet system, he stated that although the October 1917 Revolution had laid the structural foundation for socialism in the Soviet Union, in the ensuing years a bureaucratic stratum had emerged that prevented the democratization of political life in the country; therefore, he did not consider the Soviet Union to be a fully developed socialist country. Basically, he envisioned the eventual creation of a rival center (in Western Europe) that could show the Soviets the way to real socialism, to a "democratic workers' state."

The term "Eurocommunism" was centered around three key themes: the identity between socialism and democracy, independence from Moscow, and the belief that the transition to socialism could be achieved peacefully. Eurocommunism was characterized by theoretical inconsistencies, and the concessions to parliamentary democracy led many observers to question the communist identity of a party, the PCE, which espoused ideologically dubious Eurocommunism.[13] The Soviet reaction against Carrillo's book was tremendous. In the ideological Soviet review *Novoye Vremya* (New Times), several articles criticized Carrillo very harshly because he distanced himself so explicitly from Soviet communism. The Russians accused Carrillo of being the leader of a decidedly brutal campaign against the Soviet Union and the CPSU, and that he served the interests of imperialism and the forces of aggression and reaction. The division between Moscow and the PCE provoked international reactions, in Europe as well as in the United States.[14] The Russians were especially furious because Carrillo insisted in the prognosis that the success of democratic socialism in the communist parties of the Western world would have a huge impact in the Eastern bloc and foster many Prague Springs.

In November 1977, Jorge Semprún's *Autobiografía de Federico Sánchez* was published. In this book, Semprún remembered his activities in the 1950s and 1960s as organizer of the clandestine network of the PCE in Spain. Semprún argued that the adoption of the term "Eurocommunism" was merely tactical and of no value, because Carrillo continued leading the party with Stalinist methods. The accusation that Carrillo had systematically falsified his own history and the history of the PCE by creating a democratic image, and that in reality he was a loyal servant of the Kremlin, was typical of the political Right in Spain. But now, the accusation came from the Left, from a former member of the PCE Politburo. The impact of the book was enormous, and it massively hurt the credibility of the PCE. An significant section of the press interpreted the book in the sense that the Eurocommunist position of Carrillo did not reflect a democratic conviction, but rather opportunistic tactics. These discussions about Carrillo's Eurocommunist theses went on for a couple of years.

The legalization of the PCE in spring 1977 made it necessary to modify the party's statutes. From the text disappeared, for example, the concepts "proletarian internationalism" and the "fight to destroy capitalism." The legalization awakened many expectations that the Communist Party was likely to become the main standard-bearer for the Left in the nascent party system. But the reality was that the history of the PCE became a chronicle of frustrated hopes, electoral failures, internal conflicts, splits, purges, and desertions. Many factors contributed to the PCE's crisis and decline. First of all, the many years of clandestinity had ossified party structures, creating a rigid and authoritarian hierarchy, completely unsuited to the demands of life in a democratic context. Furthermore, the biographies of the main communist leaders like Santiago Carrillo and Dolores Ibárruri were linked in the minds of many Spaniards to memories of the Civil War, reinforcing their fear of communism instilled in them by Francoist propaganda. And finally, Carrillo had tried to impose a hierarchical and centralized party structure, which had led to bitter confrontations with the younger members.

In the decisive years of Transition in Spain, the communists failed in their intention to become the leading force in the Left political spectrum. The political hegemony on the Left was conquered by the socialists. When the PCE celebrated its sixtieth anniversary in 1980, the party was disappointed with its situation. It had lost its influence in the labor movement and in the Comisiones Obreras, the most influential trade union; at a local level, the communists could not exercise as much influence as they had expected. The communist influence in the organizations of the civil society increasingly evaporated. The party newspaper *Mundo Obrero* gradually lost its readership. The international context also worsened. The Soviet invasion of Afghanistan in 1980 had as a consequence an incrementation of the Cold War and, within the Spanish Communist Party, the emergence of a new pro-Soviet line, called from then on *afganos*. In addition, the developments in France, with the severe confrontations between socialists and communists, and in Italy, with the murder of Aldo Moro, made the continuation of Eurocommunism more and more difficult.[15]

By the end of the 1970s, the PCE therefore faced a deep crisis, proliferating several tendencies within the main and the regional communist parties. Against this backdrop, the official Spanish communist reaction to the December 1981 military coup in Poland was swift: the PCE secretariat issued a statement describing the Jaruzelski coup as "an act in open contradiction to the essentials of Socialism, Marxism and Leninism"; and a unanimous Central Committee insisted that "the failure of the Polish

Unified Workers' Party [could] only be explained as the failure of the Soviet Union in exporting its political and economic models to other countries, and [as] the failure of the attempt to maintain those models against wind and tide."[16] Subsequently, Carrillo flew to Yugoslavia and Italy. All in all, the PCE's rhetoric was "Eurocommunist," but behind the facade of Central Committee unanimity lay profound differences of opinion over the communists' international relationships and identity.

From the Communist Party of Spain to the United Left

Since Franco's death in November 1975, the history of the PCE was, despite some ups and downs, basically a chronicle of frustrated hopes, electoral failures, and internal conflicts—in short, a period of crisis and decline.[17] In these years, and after the bad results in the elections of June 1977, winning just under 10 percent of the votes, the Communist Party virtually disintegrated. Acrimonious internecine struggles within the leadership, a collapse in membership, and the loss of prestige amongst the intellectual elite, who had originally been drawn to the PCE by its opposition to Franco: all combined to leave the party on the verge of extinction. In the 1982 elections, its support fell to under 4 percent, while the Socialist Party won the absolute majority.[18]

The socialists' success in preempting what might have been the political space of Eurocommunism in Spain was partly due to the communists' evolution and campaign to the first free elections in June 1977. There was, for example, the openly pro-Soviet attitude of the 83-year-old president of the PCE, Dolores Ibárruri, on her return from exile in Moscow in early May 1977, which confronted *Pasionaria* with the official line of her party.[19] The Spanish communists had gone to great lengths in the years after 1968 to demonstrate their independence from the Soviet Union, and relations had deteriorated sharply. Carrillo had even questioned the degree to which the Soviet system was socialist—an unprecedented step for the secretary general of a communist party in Western Europe. Carrillo's statement implied that deep structural changes would be necessary in the Soviet Union before this country could claim the status of socialism.[20]

The bad electoral results of 1977 and the even worse ones of 1982 culminated in several conflicts within the PCE that led to a severe crisis in the party. First of all, there was a conflict concerning its organization. The transformation from a clandestine party based upon relatively autonomous cells to a centralized party based upon masses, and the return of the cadres from exile, led to polarization and bitterness on different levels of the organization. Secondly, there arose a social conflict: the generation of Civil War and clandestinity was opposed by the generation of late Francoism and Transition; and furthermore, a conflict arose between intellectuals and workers. Thirdly, it became a visibly ideological conflict. The concept "Eurocommunism" overarched many different tendencies: for example, the pro-Soviet *afganos*, the Leninists, and the social-democratic *renovadores* (renewers) all within the same party. And fourthly, a conflict could be observed between the center and the periphery, even within the party. The Basque and the Catalan federations asked for more organizational autonomy, and these federations had a certain affinity toward nationalist positions. But finally, it was the division between the Madrid-based PCE leadership and regional federations that truly shattered the communist movement.[21]

Another important reason for the party's collapse was the mismatch between the Eurocommunist rhetoric of openness and democracy, and the reality of rigid control as exercised by the PCE leadership. For Santiago Carrillo, democratic centralism was a defining characteristic of communism. Party discipline and loyalty were not negotiable, no matter what the rhetoric of Eurocommunism might suggest. To concede on this point would be to risk the very identity of the party. Eurocommunism, which had initially been seen as a way of achieving autonomy from Moscow and as a public acceptance of the principles of political pluralism, soon became a major source of dissent within the PCE. All these conflicts cumulated during the years 1980 and 1981, and led finally to the electoral debacle of October 1982. In the wake of this electoral disaster, the secretary general Santiago Carrillo, who had occupied this position since 1960, had to resign. He was followed by the Asturian mineworker Gerardo Iglesias. The huge problems that the PCE had in the early 1980s were due not only to the development of the Soviet Union and the crisis of legitimacy of the CPSU, but also and primarily with the disillusionment of the communist membership in Spain and Carrillo's autocratic measures within the party, when he was proclaiming at the same time his compromise with pluralistic socialism.[22]

When Gerardo Iglesias was elected secretary general of the PCE in 1982, he was eager to normalize relations with the Communist Party of the Soviet Union and those parties that were aligned with it, not least because he hoped this would undercut the pro-Soviet splinter groups. The CPSU had little sympathy for the PCE leadership, although if forced to choose, the Soviet party would have preferred Iglesias to Carrillo. In the following months the Soviets and their allies actively supported the creation of the pro-Soviet Partido Comunista de los Pueblos de España (PCPE), which was achieved by Ignacio Gallego in January 1984. Thereafter there were numerous official exchanges between the CPSU and the PCPE.[23]

During the following years, the ideological position of the PCE's former secretary general, Santiago Carrillo, was very contradictory. For some time, before and after his resignation as secretary general in 1982, he spoke frequently about international conspiracies against the Eurocommunist line, accusing the Soviet embassy of trying to destroy the party, or he expelled out of the party any members who were nostalgic for the dictatorship of the proletariat. On the other side, he suddenly cheered Lenin, praised the Soviet Union, and repeated that he had never been anti-Soviet.[24] At the same time—in the first half of the 1980s—the dramatic losses in electoral support and party affiliation were accompanied by a long series of ideological swings and confused programmatic declarations, which in the end alienated many followers—revolutionaries as well as reformists.[25]

After the 11th Congress of December 1983, the PCE re-elaborated his programmatic manifesto. Up to then, and even based on Eurocommunist strategy, the communists had considered themselves as the vanguard organization of the masses, and the political formation that had to lead the workers toward emancipation. In 1986, the party changed its autodenomination; it was from then on no longer "the gathering element of the people's organized avantgarde," but only another group among the forces that considered themselves "the totality of the leftist forces that, from different perspectives, want to change this society with progressive character."[26] Furthermore, the Spanish communists wanted to introduce some changes in their relationship with the Soviet Union. They still described themselves as "independent," but on the other hand they diminished the confrontation with the Soviet Union, basically because of two reasons: firstly, they saw the necessity of integrating Ignacio Gallego's pro-Soviet Partido Comunista de los Pueblos de España, which had separated from the PCE a couple of years before; and secondly, it was much easier to accept the positions of the Communist Party of the Soviet Union after Mikhail Gorbachev had assumed power and had relieved Boris Ponomiarow of his responsibilities for the relationship of the party with the "brethren parties."

In 1986, the internal disintegration of the PCE carried on. Secretary General Gerardo Iglesias was unsuccessful when he tried to reunify all the communist groups. First of all, he was not disposed to come to terms with Santiago Carrillo; and secondly, the confrontation continued with Ignacio Gallego, an "old school" and pro-Soviet leader who very much opposed the Soviet reform process under Gorbachev. Nevertheless, he seriously tried to bridge the deep divisions that had split the Spanish communists into various factions. Most of all, Iglesias realized in the mid-1980s that "traditional" communism was reaching the end of its historical cycle, and that it was time to create a new coalition that would encompass other progressive forces side by side with the PCE. It was the moment of birth, in the spring of 1986, of the Izquierda Unida (IU, "United Left").

Concurrently, Gorbachev's Perestroika was beginning to gather momentum in the Soviet Union, and the changes in that country probably had a certain influence on the creation of Izquierda Unida. But the really creative impulse for IU was provided by the referendum held in March 1986 to ratify Spain's membership of the North Atlantic Treaty Organization (NATO). The PCE retained a hegemonic position in IU. Arguing in electoral terms, the new political formation was not successful. The root of IU's problems was that the PCE was trying to present a renovated image, whilst at the same time it was reverting to its old traditional ways in order to bring about unity in the divided communist camp.

Simón Sánchez Montero, one of the leading communists in the PCE, writes in his memoirs that in 1986 he went to Moscow on behalf of his party to try to convince the Soviets that they should stop their financial help to Gallego's Partido Comunista de los Pueblos de España. He was able speak with Foreign Minister Shevardnadze, but finally his attempt failed. In any case, the memoirs are interesting because they contain a definition of Perestroika from one of the important PCE leaders:

> Why was I so enthusiastic with Perestroika? Because I saw in it a new policy of the Soviet Union, applicable to the other socialist countries, that pursued two fundamental objectives: [firstly], in the sector of foreign policy, in its relations with the United States and the other imperialistic powers, to finish the Cold War and to firmly establish, with guarantees, a world peace, independently of the ideological differences; and [secondly], in the sector of internal policy, to change radically the structure of the Soviet state, and to finish with the bureaucratic system, established by Stalin over many years ... I thought, and I go on thinking, that if Perestroika had been performed the way I have just described, the political, economic, social and cultural situation would have changed radically in the Soviet Union and in the socialist countries, and their development would have demonstrated in practice the superiority of the socialist system over the capitalist one. That would have been the best help that could have been given to the workers and the progressive forces in all the capitalist countries, and also in the countries of the Third World that are dominated and exploited by the most powerful capitalist countries ... On the other side, I have noticed that Gorbachev still believed that Marxism–Leninism was the work of Marx and Lenin, and not a creation of Stalin.[27]

The debate about the communist identity and the future of a Spanish communist party within the leftist project of Izquierda Unida in the times of Perestroika had already begun some years before, with the founding of IU in 1986. The central topic of this debate was the question of the relationship between the PCE and IU. One of the poles in this debate was formed by the so-called *renovadores* (renewers) within the communist party, and by some independent members of IU. From the beginning, they favored a separation from the communist tradition and an inclusion in the political bloc of the New Left. They believed that PCE should dissolve itself and merge with other political and social forces in the Izquierda Unida, and thus IU could constitute itself as a political party.[28] The opposite pole was formed by militants of the communist party, who from the beginning had contemplated Izquierda Unida as a mere electoral coalition that should be controlled by the PCE and that should be directed according to the tactical ideas of the party. In a certain way, this group was strengthened, at least in the beginning, by the reunification of the communist party with Gallego's Partido Comunista de los Pueblos de España, which had preserved many Leninist conceptions of party organization.

The IU majority, under the leadership of Julio Anguita, coordinator of the organization from 1988 on, was in favor of maintaining the PCE as a political organization and as a historical and ideological reference; but at the same time, Izquierda Unida should be developed beyond the status of an electoral coalition to a political-social movement with an autonomous identity, organization and program, and the PCE should display all its political activities in this movement. All the member organizations should hand over their sovereignty, at least partly, to the IU.

The loss of power of the communist state parties in Eastern Europe, the beginning of the dissolution of the Warsaw Pact, and the implosion of the Soviet Union at the end of the 1980s and the beginning of the 1990s, challenged all the communist parties to justify their existence. Although many of the European communist parties had dissociated themselves from Soviet-type socialism, to a certain degree the Soviet Union was still a historical point of reference for them. Even if Moscow was only a negative point of reference for their own democratic conception of a socialist society, the idea of a communist party without the center of a communist world movement was nearly unimaginable.

Furthermore, even if the *intelligenzija* of many Western communist parties had already dissociated themselves in the 1960s from the authoritarian variety of socialism, and had found new answers to the basic socialist conflict of the relationship between freedom and equality by the reception of democratic Marxist theoreticians like Antonio Gramsci, many militants at the core of the parties still had collective historical memories, desires, and emotional ties to the Soviet Union. These old loyalties could not be subordinated to the changes of the party line. For these groups of communist militants, the end of the East European socialism was a deeply traumatic experience that put in question their own political biography and the collective political biography of their respective communist party.

These and other conflictive lines had also existed in Izquierda Unida since its foundation. They only were enforced by what happened in 1989–1991. The debate increased dynamically after 1989, and the decisive period was before the 13th Congress of the PCE in 1991, which ended with a clear victory for the model of the majority around the then secretary general, Julio Anguita. But in the two regional federations of Catalonia and Valencia, the so-called social-democratic *renovadores* were successful. The regional federation of Valencia merged with the "Esquerra Unida" ("United Left" in Catalan) of this region and was registered as a new political party; and in Catalonia, the autonomous sister party "Partit Socialista Unificat de Catalunya" (PSUC, Unified Socialist Party of Catalonia) was marginalized, and all the competences were transferred to "Iniciativa per Catalunya" (Initiative for Catalonia), the Catalan variety of Izquierda Unida. In April 1990, the Iniciativa per Catalunya declared itself to be a socialist party, breaking therewith the communist tradition of the Civil War-PSUC.[29]

With Izquierda Unida, the PCE had inaugurated a process of transformation that made the party less vulnerable to the shock of 1989; nevertheless, it had to confront the question concerning the consequences. At the 6th National Conference of the PCE in April 1990, the Spanish communists debated the effects that the breakdown of the communist bloc would have on the future of the party. This debate was continued at the 13th Congress of the party, intensifying the process of reflection concerning the structure of the PCE. The result was the confirmation of the communist identity within the IU—but at a very high price: the departure of many defeated *renovadores* and an ideological polarization within the IU, that later led to the separation of the New Left (*Nueva Izquierda*).

The *renovadores* did not succeed. The PCE was not ready for a development *à la italiana*, and it did not accept its own dissolution, although it severely criticized the socialism existing until then in the East. Izquierda Unida should be the political project in which the Spanish communists would represent, together with other political and social forces, their political positions in the institutions of the state. And in this project, the PCE should operate first of all as a "collective intellectual" (*intelectual colectivo*), as an organization to discuss on all levels the political contents and programmatic positions. The implementation of these positions should be the task of Izquierda Unida. The new and rather complicated denomination "Partido Comunista de España de Izquierda Unida" reflected this plan. The secretary general of the PCE, Julio Anguita, described the place of the communist party within the IU with the words: "We are the instrument, not the aim." That meant that in the long run the PCE could be dissolved, when the social and political Left had consolidated itself.

The decisions taken by the 6th Conference of the PCE in April 1990 were of crucial importance for the future development of the communist party. Concerning the communist identity, the conference confirmed the validity of communist values and of the communist project. Concerning the character of the party, the PCE was defined as a reference point of communist identity, and as a space of theoretical reflection and political discussion. Concerning the party model, the conference planned the abolition of democratic centralism, the introduction of organized tendencies within the party, and the decentralization of the party structure. All these reforms would be conducive to the definite discarding of the Leninist model.

The discussions within the PCE continued also after the Conference of 1990. And the tensions in the communist organizations were intensified in 1991 after the failed coup in Moscow and the dissolution of the Communist Party of the Soviet Union. Now the "renewers" inside and outside the party demanded more intensely than ever the dissolution of the PCE and the transformation of the IU into a political party that breaks with the communist tradition. But the leadership of the PCE insisted on the model already discussed and decided at the 6th Conference: the continuation of the PCE within the IU. When in November 1991 the regional federation of Izquierda Unida in Valencia constituted itself as a political party, and the *renovadores* within the PCE sanctioned this decision, Julio Anguita abandoned his position as "General Coordinator" of the United Left, demonstrating with this spectacular step the deep division existing within the PCE and the IU.

Izquierda Unida was far from being a homogenous organization—quite the opposite. The 3rd Federal Assembly (*Asamblea Federal*) of IU in May 1992 continued the organizational and ideological debates of the previous years, and it became clear that two sharply differentiated tendencies existed within the IU. One was in favor of defining the IU as leftist and socialist, while the other defined itself as social democratic. The majority moved in a leftist direction; they rejected the Treaty of Maastricht, heavily criticized the Spanish and the international Social Democracy, practiced an anticapitalistic discourse, and initiated again a debate about republicanism. In total, Izquierda Unida drove ideologically to the Left—much more than the PCE had done in the previous decades. The ideological polarization within the IU had a vertical and a horizontal dimension. The opposition between the radical majority and the much more moderate *renovadores* of Nueva Izquierda were unbridgeable. Finally, in 1997, it led to the expulsion of Nueva Izquierda. Eleven years after the creation of Izquierda Unida, the polarization ended in a splitting of the federation.

In the second half of the 1980s, PCE members who were critical of their own party asked for a Perestroika for their own communist party—for an organizational and ideological renewal. The new PCE should be able to synthesize unity and plurality through great political interests; the idea of democratic centralism had to be modernized.[30] Secretary General Gerardo Iglesias confirmed in February 1988 that the PCE was "decidedly in favor" of Perestroika in the sense that it intended a "democratic profundization" of the party.[31]

The reformed PCE with its ideological openness was called in the press, after the founding of Izquierda Unida in 1986, the "Spanish variety of Perestroika." Ideologically, IU seemed to be somewhat undefined. Julio Anguita, the new secretary general of the PCE from 1988 on, hoped to attract new groups like socialists, feminists, ecologists, and other "progressive" orientations. The new leftist organization rejected actively dogmatic communist ideas.[32] And the great majority of Spanish communists were in favor of Gorbachev's Perestroika; most of them were even convinced that after the changes in the Soviet bloc, the trench that had separated communists and socialists from the 1920s onwards would be closed. At the same time, many communists looked at the socialists and social democrats in a much more benign way than formerly. Santiago Carrillo, the former PCE secretary general, thought that Perestroika would change the character of the Soviet Union, but that it would not demolish socialism. "The bureaucratic dictatorship will be substituted by a pluralistic socialist system, that is the idea of Gorbachev," he said, and that meant that "we will assist with a new impulse of socialism."[33]

After the founding of Izquierda Unida and the collapse of the Soviet bloc, the liberal-leftist review *Cambio 16* proclaimed: "*Solo hay una cosa clara: la perestroika triunfa en España*" (Only one thing is clear: Perestroika triumphs in Spain).[34] Looking at the Spanish and the Italian communist parties, it is striking that the two communist parties that had proclaimed the idea of a new occidentalized communism some years ago, independent from the Soviet Union—the basic idea of Eurocommunism—and that had criticized Stalinism long before the fall of the Berlin Wall, and even long before the proclamation of Perestroika in the Soviet Union, were the very first ones to disintegrate.

Summarizing, it is interesting to outline the main causes of the PCE's failure, and some of its consequences, so as to make clear that when Gorbachev set in motion the process of change in the Soviet Union, which would eventually uncover the profound sickness of Soviet communism, the PCE was already terminally ill, because the PCE had not been called into question until the dramatic events of 1989–1991. The party had undergone earlier a near fatal crisis in the late 1970s and the 1980s. This experience predates the general crisis of European communism by a decade. Among the many factors that contributed to the PCE's initial lack of success, and to its progressive decline, were the ossified party structures with a rigid and authoritarian hierarchy; the fact that the biographies of the exiled communist leaders who returned to Spain were linked in the minds of many Spaniards with memories of the Civil War; and that Eurocommunism soon became a major source of dissension within the PCE because this new form of communism never allowed the post-Franco winds of democratic change to reach the inner circle of party power. The antagonisms and confrontations that followed were to have disastrous consequences.[35]

The PCE and the Breakdown of the Soviet Bloc

When Julio Anguita was elected, in 1988, as secretary general of the PCE and general coordinator of Izquierda Unida, both organizations got a new direction and new dynamism. Anguita's new leadership symbolized a late victory for the radical factions that had been the losers in the debates of the decade before. And just in this historical moment, the Spanish communists had to deal with Perestroika and, somewhat later, with the breakdown of communism in the East European states. The PCE reacted with a twofold strategy, which was successful from the point of view of the communist party. Firstly, Anguita strengthened the project Izquierda Unida; but secondly, and at the same time, he impeded a dissolution of the PCE within the structures of IU and thereby made impossible the solution of a foundation outside the traditional communist lines. With the above-mentioned model Partido Comunista de España de Izquierda Unida, the communists continued the reform process that had begun in 1986, and they impeded a social-democratization of the IU project. The new political, organizational, and ideological orientation, which the PCE had begun by founding Izquierda Unida, was the defense line from where the Spanish communists could stop all the dangers and attacks against their political and ideological existence.[36]

It might be worth stating that nearly all the issues discussed in the PCE and in Izquierda Unida appeared to have little to do with changes gathering pace in the Soviet Union and in Eastern Europe at that time. At most, they were a distant echo. For example, the PCE's 12th Congress in 1988 was attended by seventy foreign delegations, but among them only three delegates were representatives of the Communist Party of the Soviet

Union, and they were only silent guests at a Spanish ceremony. Suffice it to say that in the eighty-page summary of Congress speeches, debates, and documents, the Soviet Union is mentioned just three times—and then only tangentially. In the PCE program for the forthcoming elections, references were made to various points of high international tension— Nicaragua, the Middle East, South Africa—but, surprising though it may seem, no mention was made of the changes in the Soviet Union and its satellite countries.[37] One year and a half later, Julio Anguita affirmed that the changes in the Eastern bloc affected primarily the communist parties of the East, and not so much those of the Western countries. To the Soviet ambassador in Spain, he said: "You are ideologically weak."[38] He was convinced that the stagnation in the communist countries and the exhaustion of the Soviet model had its origin in the existence of a single party, and that in Spain Perestroika had consisted in strengthening Izquierda Unida, without being necessary to dissolve the PCE.

While Julio Anguita was secretary general of the PCE, his main efforts concentrated on finding ways and means of guaranteeing the survival of the party. Initially, he saw the salvation for the PCE in a return to more traditional and dogmatic positions, to the Left of Gorbachev's Perestroika. His interpretation of the Soviet leader's views underlines this point. In an interview with a Spanish newspaper in March 1988, he said: "I have read Gorbachev in depth, not just his bestseller book, but also his reports, and what I find in them is a return to pure Leninism, with democracy, debate and discussion. Pure Leninism and Marxism."[39] And this was the direction in which Anguita tried to push the PCE in the initial stages of his leadership. His early radicalism was to include a Leninist view of the party and a revival of the Communist International. This attitude made possible the return to the PCE of Ignacio Gallego's Partido Comunista de los Pueblos de España, which had abandoned the PCE in 1983 in order to defend what this group considered to be the Marxist–Leninist inheritance of Spanish communism. Now, in January 1989, they were able to return, convinced that the party had regained its ideological purity.

Just as communism in Spain seemed, at the end of the 1980s, to be emerging from a protracted period of crisis, so communism in Eastern Europe entered its death throes. The impact of this on both the PCE and the IU was profound. By the end of 1989, unmistakable lines of division that had marked the first crisis of Spanish communism were beginning to reappear. Once again, the PCE was faced with three similar critical issues: the role of a communist party in what looked to be a postcommunist age; relations between the Madrid leadership and regional centers; and disputes over the party's structure and direction. And these concerns were now overlain by the wider issue of how the PCE related to Izquierda Unida.[40]

Anguita responded to all calls for reform by insisting on the need to maintain the PCE intact. But it was not clear what he understood to be a communist party in the 1990s, because the PCE seemed barely distinguishable from any other leftist catch-all political party. In the second Federal Assembly of Izquierda Unida, Anguita's line received a clear overall victory: closer links and electoral agreements with the PSOE were firmly rejected, and Izquierda Unida's full autonomy, with the PCE's continued dominance within it, was confirmed.

The breakdown of the communist bloc, and the beginning of the end of the Soviet Union, led to a loss of orientation at the base and in the leadership of many communist parties in Western countries. The central question was if, considering the historical development, a communist identity could be preserved. The answer was very different from case to case, and it depended on the programmatic, organizational, and ideological development of the respective party. In the Spanish case, the communist party was much less affected by the crisis of the international communist movement than in the French and the Italian cases, because the Spanish communists had dissociated themselves from the Soviet Union as early as 1968, with their critique of the communist intervention against the Prague Spring and their turn toward Eurocommunism. Founding Izquierda Unida as a coalition of different leftist parties in 1986, and changing its organization, its politics, and its ideology, the party had already made a profound change before 1989, and this change prevented the PCE from being identified with the communist parties of Eastern Europe, and falling into ruin. But, of course, the Communist Party of Spain also had an intense discussion about the perspectives of communist identity and the future of the party—and the majority were in favor of preserving the communist identity within the project Izquierda Unida.

The crisis and transformation of the Soviet bloc after 1989 shook the PCE much more than Perestroika had done. In many respects, the Spanish communists experienced a rapid transformation, similar—but less spectacular—to that of the Italian communists. The PCE/IU was overwhelmed by an ideological perplexity, and they remained insecure about the future of Gorbachev's Perestroika in Spain. Julián Ariza, a communist leader of the trade union Comisiones Obreras, deplored that Perestroika had begun too late in Spain, and that the communist reform movement was not oriented against communism, but rather against the evolution in the Soviet Union after World War II. The Spanish communists did not see themselves on the defensive because of the changes in Eastern Europe— quite the opposite. A considerable number of them were optimistic about the idea that the elimination of the negative models in the East would pave the way for a regeneration of the communist ideals. The only lesson that could be derived from the developments in Eastern Europe and that the Spanish communists had already understood many years ago, was the conviction that socialism could not be imposed without freedom, and that only with freedom could it survive. But ideologies, said Julio Anguita, cannot be discredited on the basis of their "perverse practical applications."[41]

Within Spanish communism the debate about the future of the communist parties after the breakdown of the socialist bloc was superimposed by the debate concerning the future character of the project Izquierda Unida. The background for this constellation was the autonomous developmental path taken by the PCE after its breach with the Soviet Union in 1968, and its ideological turn to Eurocommunism. The great crisis of the communist party at the beginning of the 1980s forced the Spanish communists to deal much earlier than other West European communist parties with the strategic, political, and organizational accommodation to the new realities. The result of this reorientation was the policy of convergence, which should unite in a bloc all the political and social forces that were in favor of a social change; and this policy of convergence should also unite the values of the labor movement with the alternative and postmaterialistic values of the new social movements; Izquierda Unida should become an organizational platform to implement this policy.

When the 6th Conference of the PCE took place in 1990, the Communist Party of Italy (PCI) had just initiated a process that ended one year later with its dissolution and the founding of a new Social Democratic Party. The decisions of the PCI were a tremendous challenge for the Spanish communists, because they had always observed Italian developments with enormous interest. A part of the PCE's leadership considered the Italian solution of the crisis as the only way to react to the challenges of 1989. This fraction around Nicolás Sartorius, the leader of the *renovadores*, contemplated the IU project as a process, whose end would be a new and modern party of the Left. And the development in Eastern Europe made this process even more urgent. But other *renovadores* had drawn a very different conclusion from the breakdown of the Soviet bloc. They proposed an approach to the Socialist Party (PSOE), or even integration with this party. These communist dissidents demanded the dissolution of the PCE and the integration of the militants in the PSOE.[42]

In 1990, Fernando Pérez Royo, then Member of the European Parliament for Izquierda Unida, presented an analysis of the consequences of the East European changes for the communist parties of Western Europe. In the Spanish case, he warned that the correct lessons should be drawn from what had happened in the Soviet bloc: "In the case of the PCE, on the basis of our traditional positions of critique of the so-called popular democracies and their most significant actuations in the international field (the invasions of Czechoslovakia and Afghanistan), there could be a temptation to think that this was enough, and that our past attitude of distance and independence will screen us against any harm coming from the cyclone of the East."[43] But, he added, the historical moment put the Spanish communists "in the necessity to revise urgently certain fundamental points of our strategic definition" (*delante de la necesidad de revisar con urgencia determinados puntos fundamentales de nuestra definición estratégica*). It was definitely not enough to distinguish between the ideals of equality, justice, and freedom—still alive—on one side, and the realities of societies that have come to the dead end of a degenerative process, already criticized by the Spanish communists many years ago. This type of distinction, he continued, was not so easy as it may appear:

> Firstly, because it is the perception itself of these ideals or, more exactly, of the Communist strategy for its realization, that is doubtless affected. Secondly, because the relations established by the PCE along its history—even recently—have not been limited to the field of ideals; rather, they have included—also in a critical way—more prosaic realities of the so-called "really existing socialism." It is enough to think on the references, in not so distant epochs, that were made to the communist family. And, more concretely, one can remember the influence of Breznevism upon the latest separations from the PCE—later reabsorbed through an extraordinary Congress. But it is necessary to call the attention upon the limited influence of the critique referring to the realities in Eastern Europe. Without citing the clumsy formula of the 'globally positive balance' (Marchais), it was said that in these countries there had been put the material basis of Socialism, and that the only thing that was missing was a political reform or revolution that had to introduce democracy and human rights. Nevertheless, when democracy comes, we are surprised that the first thing that make the masses, is to put in question the foundations themselves of the social and economic organizations.[44]

According to Pérez Royo, the Spanish communists had, in 1990, an important agenda of discussions. First of all, they had to clarify the identity of the party, throwing aside all the myths of the past and admitting that the communists were a reformist force amongst others, and that they had to restore the relationship with other reformist organizations. Secondly, they had to revise their pejorative judgment about social democracy, and accept the plurality existing on the Left. Thirdly, they had to make a unitarian effort to bring together progressive coalitions in order to change the society democratically. Finally, in the field of international policy, they must reconsider their attitude towards NATO. If in

1986 the opposition to an integration of Spain in NATO was justified, four years later, when the ideological and military blocs were disappearing, it was more important to strengthen the politics of disarmament and to revise military doctrines than to fight against NATO. Gorbachev himself had recommended studying the political contents of the two opposed alliances. And in the organizational sector, he pleaded for a strengthening of Izquierda Unida: "Izquierda Unida should be the privileged sphere in which to present and develop the major part of the ideological and strategic options, mentioned before. Firstly, that implies completing the organizational strengthening and the public presence of Izquierda Unida, and the transfer of sovereignty from the PCE and the other affected organizations."[45] Even the form of the traditional parties should be questioned, especially those on the Left. Izquierda Unida could be a very important tool with respect to this topic.

The demolition of the Berlin Wall, the collapse of the old communist regimes in Eastern Europe, the change of name and identity of the Communist Party of Italy, and, above all, the attempted coup d'état of August 1991 in the Soviet Union have added tremors to the already shaky foundations of the PCE. However, the official party line has been to pretend that all these events had little to do with the state of communism in Spain, because, they claimed, the PCE had for years been moving ahead of the Communist Party of the Soviet Union. Just a few days before the 19 August "coup," Julio Anguita stated publicly: "The PCE has nothing to learn from what is happening in the Soviet Union; if anything, Gorbachev should learn from us."[46] It was true that relations between the PCE and the CPSU had been less than cordial for some years, and Gorbachev had done little to improve them. When the Soviet leader paid an official visit to Spain in October 1990, he showed scant interest in either the PCE or the IU. In his public pronouncements while in Spain, Gorbachev did not make any reference to the PCE; in fact, the word "communism" was never mentioned, Gorbachev preferring to declare himself a socialist.

After the dramatic events of August 1991 in Moscow, which presaged the disintegration of the political hegemony of the Communist Party of the Soviet Union, some leading PCE militants immediately called for the party to be dissolved and replaced by a reconstituted Izquierda Unida in order to avoid the increasingly negative associations of the term "communism." Anguita, however, refused to countenance any such move, arguing instead that it was more important than ever that the PCE should survive. Anguita's response to the August crisis in the Soviet Union was based on his continued belief that developments in the Soviet Union were of no relevance to the PCE.[47]

The 13th PCE Congress, which took place in December 1991 in Madrid, was the first congress after the breakdown of the Soviet bloc. The main question of this congress was the justification of the existence of the PCE. The developments between 1989 and 1991 had fostered the irreconcilable ideological contrasts existing within the party. They ranged from the desire to dissolve it, to the will to strengthen its Leninist character. In view of the extremely polarized situation, and all the ideological and political differences, there was one decisive and overarching question: Should the PCE follow the example of the Partito Comunista d'Italia and dissolve itself, or should it continue as a party with a communist identity and in communist tradition? The dichotomy posed by this question had as a consequence that all the tendencies oriented themselves on this conflict line—with the result that the faction of the *renovadores* were opposed by a broad coalition between the majority sector and the orthodox wing. This majority agreed on the desire of not dissolving the party. The congress abolished the democratic centralism, and the whole party structure was decentralized. The regional federations became autonomous; the Central Committee was transformed into the "Comité Federal." With these new statutes, the PCE was no longer a communist party in the Leninist sense of the word.

Final Remarks

In the last years of the 1970s and the first ones of the 1980s, the Communist Party of Spain suffered several deep crises: it lost many members and voters, it was divided into different factions, and it was isolated from its social basis. The experience of this existential crisis led the PCE to implement, after 1982, a "policy of convergence" that was to lead to a new project of all the non-social democratic left forces in Spain, and that a couple of years later was known as the Spanish variety of Perestroika. The anti-NATO campaign of 1986 offered the communists the opportunity to transform the policy of convergence into a concrete political project. The result was Izquierda Unida. This new Left organization was successful in uniting the positions of the Marxist Left with the new social movements. In terms of organization, Izquierda Unida developed a new model of a social and political movement corresponding with its heterogeneity. With the project of Izquierda Unida, the communist party could stop its decline and convert the downward movement, at least for a while, into an upward movement.

It can be summarized that significant realignments took place on the Spanish Left before the collapse of communism in Eastern Europe and the Soviet Union. But the events in the Soviet bloc posed a number of issues that had a significant bearing on the future of the Left. Ideological redefinition raised fundamental questions as to the status of leftist ideology at the end of the 1980s. In Spain, the fifteen to twenty years since the mid-1970s saw what seemed to be a gradual draining of clearly identifiable ideological content in the programmatic positions of the Left. Both the PSOE and the PCE/IU moved a long way from their Marxist roots to arrive at a position where their aims seemed to have more in common with an ethical politics based on moral imperatives than with any teleological Marxist view.[48] The developments in the Soviet Union in the second half of the 1980s, and their repercussions throughout the communist movement, only helped to accelerate a process that was already well advanced inside the PCE. In this sense, Perestroika was not of crucial importance for the development of Spanish communism. When Perestroika displayed all its impact upon the state, party, and society in the Soviet Union with its far-reaching consequences, the PCE was already a moribund party. It did not die completely, but its future influence in the political panorama of Spain and upon Spanish politics was very limited.

Walther L. Bernecker is professor emeritus of modern and contemporary history at the Friedrich-Alexander University Erlangen-Nürnberg in Germany, where he taught from 1992 to 2014. Before that, he was professor at the universities of Augsburg, Bielefeld, Bern and Fribourg (Switzerland), Universidad Nacional Autónoma de México, and El Colegio de México. His main areas of investigation are Spain, Western Europe, and Latin America in the nineteenth and twentieth centuries. He has published widely about the political and socioeconomic history of Spain and Mexico. His works include, among others, *Spaniens Geschichte seit dem Bürgerkrieg*, Munich, 2018; *Das Franco-Regime in Spanien: Der Streit um einen chamäleonhaften Systemtypus*, Frankfurt am Main, 2016; *Memorias divididas*, Madrid, 1998; and *Die Handelskonquistadoren*, Stuttgart, 1988. Several of his works have been translated into English, Spanish, Chinese, and Russian.

Notes

1. On the history of the PCE, see Alba, *El Partido Comunista de España*; Baumer, *Kommunismus in Spanien*. For the party's official version, see Ibárruri et al., *Historia del Partido Comunista de España*. See also the overview of the PCE's history in the years of the post-Franco democracy by Mujal-León, "Decline and Fall of Spanish Communism."
2. Carrillo, *Nuevos enfoques a problemas de hoy*, 17–18 and 140–59.

3. See Semprún, *Autobiografía de Federico Sánchez*.
4. Mujal-León, *Communism and Political Change in Spain*, 103–31.
5. For the reaction of the Spanish communists to the Warsaw Pact invasion of Czeckoslovakia, see Höch, "Richtungsstreit im Untergrund"; Treglia, "La elección de la vía nacional."
6. For the political development in Portugal after 1974, see Hottinger, "Die kommunistische Partei Portugals"; and the last chapters in Bernecker and Pietschmann, *Geschichte Portugals*.
7. Azcárate, *Crisis del Eurocomunismo*, 66–71.
8. On the PCE during the Transition, see Mujal-León, *Communism and Political Change in Spain*.
9. Carrillo, *Eurocomunismo y Estado*; or the German translation: *"Eurokommunismus" und Staat*, Hamburg, 1977. For Carrillo's thoughts on Eurocommunism and the confrontation with the Soviet Union, see his memoirs: Carrillo, *Memorias*, esp. 661–72; for the ideological and political foundations of Eurocommunism in Spain, see Mujal-León, "Eurocommunism, Spanish Version."
10. Mujal-León, *Communism and Political Change in Spain*, 171.
11. Baumer, *Kommunismus in Spanien*, 171–227.
12. Mujal-León, *Communism and Political Change in Spain*, 174.
13. Heywood, "The Spanish Left."
14. Cf. Preston, *El zorro rojo*, 303–5.
15. Baumer, *Kommunismus in Spanien*.
16. *Mundo Obrero Semanal* (18–24 December 1982 and 1–8 January 1983), quoted in Mujal-León, *Communism and Political Change in Spain*, 219.
17. Amodia, "Requiem," esp. 59.
18. Heywood, "The Spanish Left," 59.
19. There exist several biographies of Dolores Ibárruri. See, e.g., Cruz, *Pasionaria*.
20. Mujal-León, *Communism and Political Change in Spain*, 163.
21. Baumer, *Kommunismus in Spanien*.
22. Preston, *El zorro rojo*.
23. On the PCPE and the discussion of the separation process, see Camiller, "Spain: The Survival of Socialism?"
24. Cf. "Carrillo defiende en Madrid a la Unión Soviética," *El País*, 3 October 1983, 13.
25. For the various crises of the PCE, cf. Vega and Errotera, *Los Herejes del PCE*; Vilar, *Por qué se ha destruido el PCE*; Morán, *Miseria y grandeza del Partido Comunista de España*. Especially for the crisis of the 1980s, see Botella, "Spanish Communism in Crisis."
26. "El PCE renueva su estrategia y acaba con la era Carrillo," *Cambio*, Vol. 16 (22 September 1986), 39.
27. Sánchez Montero, *Camino de Libertad*, 395–96.
28. See Baumer, *Kommunismus in Spanien*.
29. Ibid.
30. See Curiel, "Al PCE le falta una perestroika."
31. Manfred F. Schröder, "Spaniens KP sucht eine neue Führung," *Süddeutsche Zeitung*, 20 February 1988, 8.
32. See Manfred F. Schröder, "Spaniens unorthodoxe Kommunisten," *Süddeutsche Zeitung*, 16/17 December 1989, 12.
33. "La izquierda se unirá," *Cambio*, Vol. 16 (18 December 1989), 20.
34. "La crisis del Este," 12.
35. Amodia, "Requiem," passim.
36. Baumer, *Kommunismus in Spanien*, passim.
37. Amodia, "Requiem," 107–9.

38. Anguita, "El modelo soviético se ha agotado."
39. Interview in *El Independiente*, 26 March 1988, quoted in Amodia, "Requiem," 112.
40. Heywood, "The Spanish Left," 71.
41. "Spaniens Linke auf der Suche nach neuen Standorten," *Neue Zürcher Zeitung*, 27 February 1990, 5.
42. Baumer, *Kommunismus in Spanien*, passim.
43. Pérez Royo, "Abandonar el misticismo."
44. Ibid.
45. Ibid.
46. Interview in *Tribuna*, 12 August 1991, 25; quoted in Amodia, "Requiem," 116.
47. Heywood, "The Spanish Left," passim.
48. Heywood, "The Spanish Left," 82.

Bibliography

Alba, Victor. *El Partido Comunista de España*, Barcelona, 1979.
Amodia, José. "Requiem for the Spanish Communist Party," in *Western European Communists and the Collapse of Communism*, ed. S. Bell, Providence, RI, 1993, 101–19.
Anguita, Julio. "El modelo soviético se ha agotado," *El País*, 8 January 1990, 16.
Azcárate, Manuel. *Crisis del Eurocomunismo*, Barcelona, 1982.
Baumer, Andreas. *Kommunismus in Spanien: Die Partido Comunista de España—Widerstand, Krise und Anpassung (1970–2006)*, Baden-Baden, 2008.
Bernecker, Walther L., and Horst Pietschmann. *Geschichte Portugals, Vom Spätmittelalter bis zur Gegenwart*, Munich, 2001.
Botella, Juan. "Spanish Communism in Crisis: The Communist Party of Spain," in *Communist Parties in Western Europe: Decline or Adaptation?*, ed. M. Waller and M. Fennema, Oxford, 1988, 69–85.
Camiller, Patrick. "Spain: The Survival of Socialism?" in *Mapping the West European Left*, ed. P. Anderson and P. Camiller, London, 1994, 233–65.
Carrillo, Santiago. *Eurocomunismo y Estado*, Barcelona, 1977.
_____. *Memorias*, Barcelona, 1994.
_____. *Nuevos enfoques a problemas de hoy*, Paris, 1967.
Cruz, Rafael. *Pasionaria: Dolores Ibárruri. Historia y Símbolo*, Madrid, 1999.
Curiel, Enrique. "Al PCE le falta una perestroika," *Cambio*, Vol. 16 (1 February 1988), 28–29.
Heywood, Paul. "The Spanish Left: Towards a 'Common Home'?" in *West European Communist Parties after the Revolutions of 1989*, ed. M.J. Bull and P. Heywood, London, 1994, 56–89.
Höch, Rudolf. "Richtungsstreit im Untergrund: Die Kommunistische Partei Spaniens und ihr Verhältnis zur sowjetischen KP," *Frankfurter Hefte*, Vol. 27, No. 2 (1972), 81–84.
Hottinger, Arnold. "Die kommunistische Partei Portugals," in *Eurokommunismus: Die kommunistischen Parteien Frankreichs, Italiens, Spaniens und Portugals*, ed. Adolf Kimmel, Cologne, 1977, 258–59.
Ibárruri, Dolores, et al. *Historia del Partido Comunista de España*, Warsaw, 1960.

"La crisis del Este convulsiona al comunismo español," *Cambio*, Vol. 16 (18 December 1989), 10–20.
Molinero, Carme, and Pere Ysàs. *De la hegemonía a la autodestrucción: El Partido Comunista de España (1956–1982)*, Barcelona, 2017.
Morán, Gregorio. *Miseria y Grandeza del Partido Comunista de España*, Barcelona, 1985.
Mujal-León, Eusebio. *Communism and Political Change in Spain*, Bloomington, IN, 1983.
──────. "Decline and Fall of Spanish Communism," *Problems of Communism*, Vol. XXXV (March–April 1986), 1–27.
──────. "Eurocommunism, Spanish Version," in *Eurocommunism: The Ideological and Political-Theoretical Foundations*, ed. George Schwab, Westport, CT, 1981, 187–215.
Noveno Congreso del Partido Comunista de España. *Informes, debates, actas y documentos, Madrid 19–23 de abril de 1978*, Madrid, 1978.
Pérez Royo, Fernando. "Abandonar el misticismo," *El País, Temas de Nuestra Epoca*, 1 March 1990, 10–11.
Preston, Paul. *El zorro rojo: La vida de Santiago Carrillo*, Barcelona, 2013.
Sánchez Montero, Simón. *Camino de Libertad: Memorias*, Madrid, 1997.
Sánchez Rodríguez, Jesús. *Teoría y práctica democrática en el PCE (1956–1982)*, Madrid, 2004.
Semprún, Jorge. *Autobiografía de Federico Sánchez*, Barcelona, 1978.
Spieker, Manfred (ed.). *Der Eurokommunismus—Demokratie oder Diktatur?*, Stuttgart, 1979.
Steinkühler, Manfred (ed.). *Eurokommunismus im Widerspruch: Analyse und Dokumentation*, Cologne, 1977.
Timmermann, Heinz. *Eurokommunismus: Fakten—Analysen—Interviews*, Frankfurt am Main, 1978.
Treglia, Emanuele. "La elección de la vía nacional: La Primavera de Praga y la evolución política del PCE," *Historia del presente*, Vol. 16 (2010), 83–96.
Vega, Pablo, and Pablo Erroteta. *Los Herejes del PCE*, Barcelona, 1982.
Vilar, Sergio. *Por qué se ha destruido el PCE*, Barcelona, 1985.

Afterword

Gorbachev and the End of International Communism

Silvio Pons

From their different perspectives, the chapters in this volume demonstrate the devastating impact that Gorbachev had on international communism, leading by the end of the 1980s to its final dissolution. Gorbachev's reform approach implied the abandonment of the legacy of world revolution. His "new thinking" contradicted basic elements of traditional communist identity by embracing "humanistic socialism" and casting aside the "two camps" theory that had been at the heart of the USSR's Cold War outlook for decades. However, this did not mean erasing the universalist thinking rooted in the Revolution of 1917. Gorbachev behaved right to the last as a leader still committed to the socialist mission and devoted to construct a new legitimacy. Paradoxically, however, precisely for the purposes of accomplishing this, he had to concede that international communism was dead as a worldwide movement, and enter into dispute with most communist parties in both Europe and the Third World.

Initially, Gorbachev adopted a very cautious approach to relations with communist parties. It looked as if the domain of transnational communist relations was not a priority of his. Perestroika focused on re-creating the conditions for détente with the West and reshaping relations within the Soviet Bloc. Gorbachev's internationalist rhetoric was seen as old-fashioned not only by European social democrats, but also by the heirs of Eurocommunism, namely the Italian communists. However, it took him only one year to develop the conviction that while other political forces, such as social democrats and green movements, had found

---

Notes for this chapter begin on page 329.

their place in world affairs, communists had yet to redefine their own.[1] Despite Gorbachev's intention to avoid interfering in the domestic affairs of communist states and parties, Perestroika came to be extended into a vision that also regarded the other communist parties—whether ruling or non-ruling. The importance of such a shift must be properly understood. It basically meant focusing not only on the problem of stopping the decline of Soviet power, but also on the legitimacy of communism as a political culture of late twentieth-century modernity. The source of inspiration was the legacy of what we may call "reform communism"—a transnational set of ideas dating back to the post-Stalin change and to the Prague Spring.[2]

This is a point that historians have largely overlooked, either because they exclusively acknowledge Gorbachev's notion of returning to an imagined original Leninist purity (which was a trait of the generation of *shestidesyatniki*) or by simply referring to his convergence with social democratic languages (which was a consequence, and not a source, of his inspiration). We might well argue that the background to Gorbachev's thinking was more multifaceted than his formation as a post-Stalin communist and even the myth of the Prague Spring may suggest. For it also revealed influences from the 1970s and early 1980s related to visions of reform, human rights, and "third ways"—even if such a set of ideas obviously lacked any consistency and was marginal to the main course of communist experiences. During the 1970s, it was essentially left to Eurocommunists to convey those ideas, but even their excommunication could not entirely prevent them from exerting an influence in Eastern Europe and in the Soviet Union itself.

Connections were reactivated from 1985 onwards via those collaborators of Gorbachev who had been more perceptive of Western communism, particularly the only communist party that maintained mass roots in Europe, the Italian Communist Party. Limited as it was, this represented the only legacy within communist cultures that Gorbachev could take over from. In fact, his relationship with the Italian communists became stronger from mid-1987 onward, in parallel with the radicalization of his reform attempts, whereas he experienced increasingly icy relations with most of the other West European parties, and first of all the French Communist Party.[3]

The immediate consequence of fully adopting the prospect of reform was a very straightforward one. It no longer made sense to talk of a communist movement. The very notion of international communism had to be reframed in the context of progressive forces and cultures. By following such a vision, Gorbachev and his group came to radical conclusions, which went beyond any previous communist attempt at conceptualizing reform. Furthermore, the real state of the communist movement could only suggest a dismissive evaluation. Following a conversation with the PCI leader Alessandro Natta in March 1988, Gorbachev reported to the Politburo that he agreed with the Italians as to the "serious and dangerous backwardness of the concepts of many communist parties ... in particular the ones that are most loyal to us."[4] His close associate on international policy, Anatoly Chernyaev, maintained that defining a role for the communist movement was an unworkable plan, since the solution to global problems could not be the task of a revolutionary movement, and even less so now that its original vitality had been lost. After years of merely stagnant conservation, the time had come to wind up the international communist movement. In other words, not only was world revolution no longer on the agenda, but it should not be seen as the mission of communists embracing "humanistic socialism" if they wanted to play a credible role in global modernity.[5] The very notion of the "international communist movement" disappeared from Gorbachev's vocabulary as he referred to Europe as well as to the Third World.

However, such substantial change did not involve a break with universalism. It was, rather, an attempt to shift the foundations of communist legitimacy. Gorbachev's recurrent argument was that the decline of the Soviet Union in world affairs had to be avoided not only out of patriotic pride but also because it would put at risk the destiny of socialism itself. The abandonment of the idea of the leading state, and the repeated declarations of non-intervention in the affairs of other communist states in Central and Eastern Europe, did not at all imply that Gorbachev had given up on the socialist mission. He thought of the future of Eastern Europe as a group of countries that would maintain a basically socialist character regardless of their changes of government—and that would therefore preserve the heritage of a socialist community emancipated from geopolitical dominance but still connected to a reformed Soviet Union. His approach to the socialist countries was quite evidently contradictory, as he argued both that change had to mature autonomously in the satellite states, and that it was necessary to accomplish substantial change in the wake of Perestroika.[6]

Gorbachev's impact brought about a split between the supporters and opponents of reform in the communist world. However, these latter were much more numerous. By far the main reaction to Gorbachev's message from the communist parties was defensive and conservative. In Central and Eastern Europe, in the habit of perceiving restricted sovereignty as a protective umbrella for their regimes, the communist establishments mostly found the drive for liberalization and the professed renunciation of the use of force as a threat to their own existence—even if up until the end they were unable to understand that Gorbachev intended to drop the "Brezhnev doctrine." This was particularly the case with East Germany and Romania, but before 1989 none of the parties in power in Europe espoused Gorbachev's cause—not even Kádár or Tito's successors in Yugoslavia. A political will to follow the inspiration of Perestroika only emerged clearly in Hungary and Poland as late as 1989.[7]

In the West, the only important party to support Gorbachev was the PCI, whose partnership was founded on the acknowledgement that reform communism had to integrate its ideas and actions within the West European Left, and promote change in Eastern Europe. The PCI was by far the biggest Western communist party, but it had almost no followers in the communist movement. Other pro-Gorbachev parties represented quite limited forces—like the Communist Party of Great Britain, and the Greek Communist Party, KKE Interior.[8] Local conditions did much to explain the different attitudes that certain parties took toward Perestroika. For instance, the increasing divergence between the PCI and the PCF in this respect should be understood also in terms of their different national contexts. The French communists' decline as a social and electoral force proceeded much more quickly, whereas the Italian communists still maintained their hegemony over the Left, in spite of their worsening predicament.[9]

However, the transnational reaction to Perestroika looks much more significant than national diversities as a historical perspective. A transnational front of leaders and parties opposed to Gorbachev, spanning the boundaries between East and West, was in fact at work well before the fall of the Berlin Wall. Communists' ideological and emotional concern for the destiny of "really existing socialism" was not confined to the European party-states. It was crucial to all other communist parties. The Western communist front hostile to Perestroika was made up of marginal and sectarian parties with poor social roots in their own countries, which were interconnected with, and influenced by, the Eastern communist regimes. The attitudes shared among the Austrian and East German communists were in many ways typical in this respect.[10] When the PCF leader, Georges Marchais, declared in December 1988 that Perestroika only concerned the Soviet Union, he expressed an opinion shared by most of the remnants of European communism, from Portugal's Álvaro Cunhal to the leaders of the People's Alliance in Iceland, and Erich Honecker in East Germany.

We should not overlook the fact that the broad front of European communist opposition to Gorbachev could count on quite similar feelings and attitudes in Asia, Africa, and Latin America. Castro's rejection of Perestroika was widely upheld among communists from Vietnam to

Angola. Third World communists mostly saw Perestroika as a revisionist policy. Indeed, as the Soviets withdrew from Afghanistan and also from their former African partner countries, Gorbachev abandoned proletarian internationalism. He did so out of the conviction that the Soviet interventions in the Global South had failed and had helped to delegitimize socialism worldwide, having produced a legacy of violent methods and economic fiascos. The old, if controversial, link between the Soviet Union and Third-Worldist revolutionaries had been lost. On the other hand, even the end of the Sino–Soviet split and the re-establishment of official relations between Moscow and Beijing hardly made Perestroika acceptable to China. The bloody repression at Tiananmen Square in June 1989 — soon after Gorbachev's visit to Beijing — provided a potential template for the European communist establishments. Gorbachev's commitment to non-violent means and the declining self-confidence of the communist regimes prevented such a tragic scenario from playing out in Europe.[11]

In 1989, Gorbachev's ruling group did not appear to have any remaining illusions about communism's global role. However, they continued to work for radical and peaceful change, which, in their view, could only emerge in Europe. Chernyaev noted that one of Gorbachev's merits was to have made clear the irreversible demise of the "myths" of the international communist movement, the socialist model in Central and Eastern Europe, and the role of communist parties in Western Europe.[12] In less than a year, the former communist movement, or what was left of it, exploded as parties dissolved, transformed their own identity, or stayed in power by increasingly changing their means of legitimation. The post-1989 scenario would rapidly show how unfounded the hopes of reform had been. The previous opposition to Perestroika took on the aspect of open hatred and dissent against the Soviet reformers. In a way, conservative communists could claim to have been right by predicting that reforms would lead to nothing good, from their point of view. The Italian communists alone maintained their commitment to the "invented tradition" of reform communism, and followed a postcommunist path by deciding to establish a new democratic party of the Left soon after the fall of the Berlin Wall. The PCI's conversion implied going beyond the communist and social-democratic traditions. Gorbachev still thought of himself as a convinced advocate of socialism, despite the growing problems he had to face within the Soviet Union. But his idea of "humanistic socialism" now repudiated much of the Soviet experience. For a couple of years, Soviet reformers and Italian postcommunist leaders maintained their common ideas and links. Few other subjects would adopt similar perspectives. Most notably, this happened in South Africa, where in 1990 the communist party endorsed the ideas of "democratic socialism" in its relationship with the African National Congress. In Eastern Europe, the only communist party really inspired by reform ideas, the Hungarian party, suffered a heavy defeat in free elections, revealing its limited popular support. Those parties able to hang on to power undertook only cosmetic changes, as was the case of the Bulgarian Communist Party. Communists preferred to pursue nationalistic ideas, even reaching extreme conclusions as in Serbia, or go back to their sectarian origins as small trade unionist factions, especially in Western Europe and Latin America. For their part, the ruling communists in Asia had obviously chosen totally different paths even before 1989, by combining authoritarianism, nationalism, and the market economy.

Gorbachev's reforms were meant to bring about change in the communist world, above all in terms of political culture, in the expectation that new energies would be released to promote a renewal of socialism. Gorbachev took the legacy of reform communism to its extreme consequences by acknowledging the hopeless marginality of the international communist movement and the need to abandon the very notion of such a movement. This invited opposition and disappointment among the large majority of both ruling and non-ruling communist parties. Gorbachev came to imagine a "third way" between social democracy and the communist tradition, and he sought convergence with the European Left as the only realistic perspective. He maintained that this objective would have to be pursued alongside a gradual "reform-from-above" of the Soviet-type systems. However, 1989 in fact brought the trajectory of reform communism and "humanistic socialism" to an end. Gorbachev and his leading group represented the ultimate evolution of reform communism. They showed how the perspective of reform meant change not only for communist political ideas and institutions, but also for their identity as such. Their eventual historical role was to wipe away the main revolutionary tradition of the twentieth century.

Silvio Pons is professor of contemporary history at the Scuola Normale Superiore of Pisa. He is the president of the Gramsci Foundation in Rome. He has written extensively on the Cold War, the Soviet Union, European communism, and the global history of communism. His main publications include: *Stalin and the Inevitable War* (Frank Cass, 2002); *Reinterpreting the End of the Cold War* (Frank Cass, 2005); *A Dictionary of Twentieth-Century Communism* (Princeton University Press, 2010); *The Global Revolution: A History of International Communism* (Oxford University Press, 2014). He is the general editor of the *Cambridge History of Communism* (Cambridge University Press, 2017).

Notes

1. *V Politburo TsK KPSS*, 43.
2. Pons and Di Donato, "Reform Communism."
3. Pons, "Western Communists."
4. *V Politburo TsK KPSS*, 312.
5. A crucial source for understanding Gorbachev's evolving attitude toward the communist parties is Chernyaev's diary. See Chernyaev, *Sovmestnii iskhod*.
6. See the chapter in this volume by Peter Ruggenthaler.
7. See the chapters in this volume by Wanda Jarząbek and Támas Baranyi.
8. See the chapter in this volume by Stefan Berger and Norman LaPorte, as well as the one by Andreas Stergiou.
9. See the chapters in this volume by Aldo Agosti and Dominique Andolfatto.
10. See the chapter in this volume by Maximilian Graf.
11. Pons, *The Global Revolution*, 309–10.
12. Chernyaev, *Sovmestnyi iskhod*, 793.

Bibliography

Chernyaev, A. *Sovmestnii iskhod: dnevnik dvukh epokh 1972–1991*, Moscow, 2008.
Pons, Silvio. *The Global Revolution: A History of International Communism 1917–1991*, Oxford, 2014.
_____. "Western Communists, Mikhail Gorbachev and the 1989 Revolutions", *Contemporary European History*, Vol. 18, No. 3 (2009), 349–62.
Pons, Silvio, and Michele Di Donato. "Reform Communism," in *The Cambridge History of Communism: Vol. 3., Endgames? Late Communism in Global Perspective, 1968 to the Present*, ed. Juliane Fuerst, Silvio Pons and Mark Selden, Cambridge, 2017, 178–202.
V Politburo TsK KPSS: Po zapisami Anatoliya Chernyayeva, Vadima Medvedeva, Georgiya Shakhnazarova (1985–1991), Moscow, 2006.

Index

Abuladze, Tengis, 109, 110
Adamec, Ladislav, 37
afganos, 303, 305
Afghanistan, 43, 95, 189, 249–250, 261;
   and invasion, 180, 205, 219, 241–242,
   303, 316
"aktivs," 260
Algeria, 62
Alliance of the Left and Progress
   (Synaspismos tis Aristeras kai tis
   Proodou), 266
Andreeva, Nina, 189, 190
Andropov, Yuri, 93, 106–108, 184
Androulakis, Mimis, 266
Anguita, Julio, 308–315, 317
Anschluss, 288
anti-communism, 258
Armenia, 70–72, 192
Asemblea Federal (Federal Assembly),
   310
Athens, 259–260
coup, 57, 61, 74, 115, 161, 164; and
   Moscow, 59, 115; and August 1991,
   73, 113–115, 181, 271; and d'état, 203,
   210–211; and Poland, 241–242, 244,
   250
Austro-Communism, 279–280, 291
Autobiografía de Federico Sánchez, 302

Axen, Hermann, 225, 287
Azcárate, Manuel, 300
Azerbaijan, 70–72, 192

Bahro, Rudolf, 219
Baier, Walter, 289, 291
Baikal (Lake), 58
Bakker, Marcus, 242, 247
Baku, 70
Baltic republics, 56–57, 72–73, 192
Baudouin, Jean, 205
BCP (Bulgarian Communist Party), 37,
   39–40, 46, 328
Beckett, Francis, 216
Beijing, 95, 287, 327
Békés, Csaba, 89
Belavezha Accords, 115
Belorussia, 63, 192
Belovezhskaya Pushcha, 57, 62, 73
Benn, Tony, 226
Bennite Left, 224, 226
Berecz, János, 98
Berghianu, Maxim, 164
Beria, Lavrentiy Pavlovich, 92
Berlin Wall, 2, 5, 14, 16, 39, 43, 170, 194,
   207–209, 216, 218, 251, 268, 311, 317,
   326–327
Berlin, Jack, 216, 226–227

Berlinguer, Enrico, 8–9, 179–181, 185, 301
Bernstein, Eduard, 4
Berolina Travel, 227
Bertolissi, Sergio, 196
Bessarabia, 170
Bettanin, Fabio, 196
BGS (Britain-GDR Society), 217, 227–228
"Big Brother," 15
Bil'ak, Vasil, 34, 45
Bilal, Enki, 203
Bobu, Emil, 161
Boffa, Giuseppe, 183, 186–187, 196–197
Bogomolov, Oleg T., 35
Bolshevik, 62–64
Bonn, 93, 133–134, 144, 207, 217,
Brandt, Willy, 9
Brașov, 169
Bratislava, 65
Brezhnev, Leonid, 59; and leadership, 8
Brezhnev Doctrine, 1, 42, 126, 133, 326
Bristol University, 220
Brouwer, Ina, 249
Brucan, Silviu, 164
Bufalini, Paolo, 185
Buffet, Marie-George, 208
Bukovina, 170
Bulgaria, 37–40, 46, 108, 288
Burtica, Cornel, 164
Bush, George H. W., 44
Butorac, Franjo, 111

Cambio, 311
Cambodia, 95
Cambridge, 220
Campbell, Beatrix, 220
Caratan, Branko, 109
Carrero Blanco, Luis, 300
Carrillo, Santiago, 299–306, 311
Catholic Church, 120, 125, 168
Ceaușescu, Elena, 170
Ceaușescu, Nicolae, 14, 28, 33, 40–43, 45, 153–155, 157–170, 202
Central Committee, 28, 34, 72, 91, 95, 108, 110–111, 134, 137–138, 141, 143–145, 162, 166, 187, 191, 219, 225, 226, 260, 268–271, 285, 300–301, 303–304, 318
Central Europe, 291, 325, 327
CGT (*Confédération générale du travail*), 210
Charta 77, 186, 243, 244
"Charter of Paris for a New Europe," 11
Chater, Tony, 220, 224–226
Chebrikov, Viktor, 71
Chechnya, 68
Chernyaev/Chernayev, Anatoly, 162, 325, 327
Chernenko, Konstantin, 38, 64, 94, 106–107, 134, 164
Chernobyl, 185
Chervonohrad, 74
Chiaromonte, Gerardo, 187
Chiesa, Giulietto, 184, 187–188, 191, 192, 196
China, 39, 67, 90, 95–96, 165, 182, 194, 205, 217, 241, 250, 327
Chinese Communist Party, 205
"class struggle," 245, 285
Claudín, Fernando, 299
Cold War, 3–5, 10–11, 38, 99, 114, 218, 224, 237, 250, 267, 303, 307, 323; and Gorbachev, 89; and Second, 90; and Romania, 169; and "new," 181–182; and PCI, 183; and PCF, 207; and West European communist parties, 258; and KPÖ, 291
Comecon (Council for Mutual Economic Assistance), 13, 91, 93–95, 98–99, 137, 264
Comintern (Communist International), 27, 257
Comisiones Obreras, 303, 314
Comité Federal, 318
Commission on Security and Cooperation in Europe, 162
Common European Home/House, 42, 126, 190, 286
Commonwealth, and communist, 90; and of Indipendent States, 115; and socialist, 121

communism, 2–10, 12–16, 43, 90, 98, 115, 126, 137, 139, 181, 194–195, 205, 208–209, 212, 218–223, 228, 237, 240, 247–248, 250–251, 256, 258, 268, 278, 291, 299, 302, 303, 305–306, 311–315, 317, 318–319, 323–324, 326–328
Communist Party of Poland (KPP), 124
Complex Programme, 94
Conference on Security and Cooperation in Europe (CSCE), 124, 167; and Kremlin, 45
Congress of People's Deputies of the Soviet Union, 58, 110, 143
Consultative Economic Council of the Prime Minister (*Konsultacyjna Rada Gospodarcza przy Prezesie Rady Ministrów*), 120
Cook, Dave, 220
Cooper, Julian, 193
Cossutta, Armando, 185
Council of State (*Rada Państwa*), 120
counterrevolution, 4, 272, 281
coup d'état, 203; and August 1991, 3, 13, 59, 113, 317; and PCF, 210–211; and Poland, 242, 244
CCG, Communist Campaign Group, 224
CPB, Communist Party of Britain, 224, 226
CPGB (Communist Party of Great Britain), 4, 14, 216–221, 223–230, 326; and Eurocommunism, 218; and "Really Existing Socialim," 221–222
CPN (Communist Party of the Netherlands), 15, 236–251
CPSU (Communist Party of the Soviet Union), 1, 3–4, 6–7, 9–10, 15, 27, 30, 37, 43–46, 55, 59, 93, 108, 119, 121–123, 126, 135, 137–138, 140–144, 161–162, 179, 182–188, 190, 192, 194–196, 203–204, 222–223, 225, 236–237, 239–240, 242–243, 246–247, 250–251, 259, 262, 271, 280, 282–287, 290–291, 299–302, 305; and Gorbachev, 71, 106, 108, 110, 134; and Politburo, 71, 140; and SED, 133, 282; and Stasi, 136; and Central Committee, 144, 186, 301; and PCE, 317
Craxi, Bettino, 11
Crimea, 70
Crimean Tatars, 69–70
Croatia, 109, 112, 114
Cruise missiles, 133, 180, 242
CSCE (Commission on Security and Cooperation in Europe), 11, 45, 167; and follow-up conference, 11, 124
Cuba, 204
Cultural Forum, 162
Cunhal, Álvaro, 326
Cyprus, 4, 38
Czechoslovakia, 35–36, 45, 47, 64–65, 105, 136, 167, 186, 204, 219, 239, 243, 261, 281, 285, 288, 290; and invasion, 42–43, 45, 218, 220, 249–250, 299, 316

Damanaki, Maria, 270
Danish Socialist People's Party, 270
Dannenbaum, Anne H., 158
DC (Democrazia Cristiana), 179
de Boo, Jan, 247
De Gaulle, Charles, 211
de Groot, Paul, 237–238
Delors, Jacques, 94,
Demichev, Pyotr Nilovich, 107
"democratic alternative," 180
"democratic socialism," 197, 223, 228, 265, 300, 302, 327
Die Alternative, 219
Dienstbier, Jiří, 37
Dietz Verlag, 138
"Discussion Club for the Support of Glasnost and Perestroika," 39
Dizdarević, Raif, 106, 111
Djuranović, Veselin, 106
Dobrynin, Anatoly Fyodorovich, 108, 222
Dolgikh, Vladimir Ivanovich, 107
Donets'k, 74
Dragasakis, Giannis, 266
Dubček, Alexander, 44, 92
Dutch Communist Party, 237

East Berlin Conference of European Communist Parties, 240, 259
East Berlin, 43–44, 134, 139, 143–144, 216, 218, 221, 224–227, 239, 301; and "Austro-Communism," 279; and Gorbachev, 41, 144, 217; and CPGB, 218, 226; and Poland, 219
East German foreign intelligence (HVA), 155
Eastern Bloc, 4, 7–8, 27, 32, 37, 43, 45, 93–95, 99, 115, 126, 133, 202–203, 241, 259, 264–265, 278, 302, 313; and Bulgaria, 38; and Gorbachev, 92, 122; and KPÖ, 282; and Hungary, 30; and "New Thinking," 44; and PCF, 209; and Poland, 42
Eastern Europe, 2, 5, 8, 12–14, 259, 269–271, 287, 290, 308, 312–318, 40, 90, 95, 105, 111, 126, 158, 169, 182, 194, 208, 211–212, 223–224, 228, 240–241, 244–245, 249, 251, 324–328
Eastern Studio, 168
Eberlein, Walter, 283
Einheit von Wirtschafts- und Sozialpolitik, 136
Einhorn, Barbara, 227
Eliou, Elias, 259
"entangled" history, 12
"Esquerra Unida," 309
European Community (EC), 115, 261, 264–266, 269, 286–288
Eurocommunism, 8–9, 13, 100, 181, 205, 212, 218, 264, 279, 281, 291, 300–305, 311–312, 314–315, 323
Eurocommunismo y Estado, 301
European Commission's White Book, 265
European Council, 258
European integration, 93, 126, 264, 286
European Nuclear Disarmament, 227
European Parliament, 220, 270, 315
European United Left group, 270

Falin, Valentin, 286
Farakos, Grigoris, 257, 262–263
Fazekas, János, 164
Fedorov, Rafael P., 43

Felfe, Werner, 226
Ferghana Valley, 71
Ferretti, Maria, 196–197
FIAT, 180
Fifth Republic, 211
"Fifth Point," 64
Fischer, Ernst, 280–281
Fischer, Oskar, 33
Fiterman, Charles, 208, 211
Florakis, Charilaos, 257, 262
Foa, Renzo, 191
France, 64, 181, 203, 208, 211, 229, 303
Franco, Francisco, 157, 298–300, 304, 312
Franco, Nicolás, 299
Francoism, 300, 305
Frankfurter Allgemeine Zeitung, 97, 166
"Fraternal Parties," 27, 28, 34, 43, 46, 122, 279, 282–283, 288
"Fraternal States/Countries," 35, 42
FRG (Federal Republic of Germany), 33, 38, 45
Friedrich Ebert Foundation, 120
Funderburk, David, 158
Fürnberg, Friedl, 281

Gabanyi, Anneli Ute, 156
Gallego, Ignacio, 305–308, 313
Gandhi, Indira, 67
GDR (German Democratic Republic), 3, 7, 31–33, 40–41, 43, 94, 132–139, 141–146, 167, 202, 207–208, 216–220, 224–228, 283–284, 287–288, 326
Geimer, William M., 159
Geneva, 184
Geneva Refugee Convention, 33
Georgia, 57, 61, 72–73
Gere, Mihály/Mihai, 164
German Communist Party, 218
"German Reich," 288
German reunification, 47, 132, 136, 182–183, 287
"German trauma," 288
Germany, 32, 64, 112, 288; and East (East Germany), 202, 204, 207–208, 217–218, 224, 226–228, 283–285, 288; and GDR, 133, 136; and West (West

Germany), 133, 138, 144, 207, 219, 227
Gheorghiu-Dej, Gheorghe, 94
Giannaros, Grigoris, 266
Gill, Ken, 220
Glasnost, 1–2, 5, 14, 16, 28, 31, 39, 61, 72, 88, 96–98, 118, 121, 123, 128, 135–136, 141, 143–144, 170, 185, 191–192, 203–204, 217, 222, 229, 236, 246, 249, 256, 262, 266, 268, 271, 283, 290
Glemp, József, 125
Gollan, John, 219
Gorbachev, Mikhail, 1–2, 4–16, 27–33, 35, 37–38, 40–46, 55–62, 64, 67, 69–74, 88–91, 94–98, 106–115, 118–119, 121–127, 132–145, 153–154, 158–167, 169–170, 179, 181–197, 202–204, 206–210, 212, 216–218, 221–225, 227, 229, 236, 247–248, 256, 261–263, 271, 282, 286–288, 290–291, 306–307, 311, 313–314, 317, 323–328; and Ceaușescu, 160–162; and Honecker, 132, 135; and "New Thinking," 45, 90, 182; and Perestroika, 27–28, 41, 43, 45, 95, 113, 139, 142, 145, 169, 203, 212, 217, 229, 271, 287, 291, 307, 311, 313–314; and Reagan, 165, 184; and reforms, 5, 15, 38, 42, 45, 88–92, 96, 98–99, 105, 107, 110, 121, 141, 144, 202, 212, 217, 228, 230, 236, 246, 248, 251, 261, 268–270, 283–284, 286–288, 306, 323, 328
Goulag, 205
Govrin, Yosef, 162
Gramsci, Antonio, 181, 308
Gratchev, Andrei, 202
Great Britain, 64, 216
Greek Left, 256–257, 260–261, 263, 265–268
"Greek Left" (Elliniki Aristera, EAR), 263, 266
"Groen Links" (Green Left), 236–237, 240, 248–249, 251
Gromyko, Andrei, 106–107, 191
Grósz, Károly, 13, 32, 92, 97–98, 170
grósznoszty, 13, 97

Guerra, Adriano, 183–184, 189–190, 192, 196
"Guided Democracy," 67

Habsburg Empire, 63
Hager, Kurt, 138–139, 141
Havana, 141
Helsinki Final Act, 8, 11
Herbstritt, Georg, 161
Hermier, Guy, 211
Hicks, Mike, 224
historical actors, 5
"historic compromise," 179, 256
Hitler–Stalin Pact, 42, 123, 290
Hobsbawm, Eric, 229
Hoekstra, Henk, 246
Hoffmann, Hans-Joachim, 141
Honecker, Erich, 9, 28, 40–43, 45, 132–140, 142–146, 161, 202, 208–209, 217, 226, 284, 326
Horn, Gyula, 32–33, 92
House of Europe, 32
HSWP (Hungarian Socialist Workers' Party), 31, 44–45, 88, 90–92, 96–99
"humanistic socialism," 323, 325, 327–328
Humboldt University, 144, 216
Hungarian Human Rights Foundation (HHRF), 159
Hungarian Press of Transylvania (HPT), 163
Hunt, Judith, 220
Husák, Gustáv, 34–35

Ianaiev, Guennadi, 210–211
Ibárruri, Dolores, 303–304
Iceland, 326
Iglesias, Gerardo, 305–306, 311
Il Contemporaneo, 189
Il Messaggero, 9
Iliescu, Ion, 43, 160
"imperial overstretch," 133
imperialism, 91, 302; and Lenin, 264
India, 67–68
Indochina, 62
Indonesia, 67–68
Indonesian Communist Party, 238

"Iniciativa per Catalunya," 309
intelectual colectivo, 309
intelligenzija, 308
Internationalism, 193, 222, 286, 303; and "new socialist," 245; and proletarian, 217–218, 228–229, 257, 263, 271–272
"international Communism," 16
"international communist movement," 184–184, 190, 222, 236–239, 242, 246, 298–299, 314, 325
International Monetary Fund, 153, 155
Iotti, Nilde, 194
Iron Curtain, 1, 3, 7–8, 14, 31–33, 44–45, 205, 212, 218, 224, 236, 249–250
Izeboud, Elly, 243, 246
Izquierda Unida (IU), 15, 307–315, 317–318

Jackson–Vanik Amendment, 38
Jacques, Martin, 220, 224
Jakeš, Miloš, 34–36, 45
Jamestown Foundation, 159
Japan, 38, 64
Jaruzelski, Wojciech, 28–30, 44, 119–122, 126, 242, 244, 303; and "Plan," 124
Johnson, Monty, 220, 222–223
Jović, Borisav, 113–114
"July Concept," 38

Kádár, Janos, 13, 28, 90–92, 95–99, 166, 169
Kadijević, Veljko, 112–114
Kanapa, Jean, 4
Kapitonov, Ivan, 107
Kashmir, 67
Katyń massacre, 123
Kazakh Communist Party, 69
KGB, 6, 29, 34, 70
KKE (Greek Communist Party), 15, 256–266, 268, 270–272, 326
Kinnock, Neil, 219
Király, Károly, 163
KNE (Communist Youth of Greece), 267
Kohl, Helmut, 33, 134, 144, 182
Kolbin, Gennadii, 69
Komunist, 107, 110–111
König, Hartmut, 137
Köpeczi, Béla, 167
Koplenig, Johann, 280
Koslov, Alexey P., 223
Kosovo, 108
Kotz, John, 227
KPČ (Communist Party of Czechoslovakia), 35–37, 44–45
KPÖ (Austrian Communist Party), 4, 15, 278–291
Krapiec, Michał, 125
Krasucki, Henry, 210
Kreissekretäre (district secretaries), 138
Kremlin, 27–28, 31–32, 34, 38–39, 41, 43–45, 95, 122–123, 159–160, 162, 191, 208, 247, 264, 302
Krenz, Egon, 43, 132, 137, 139
Król, Marcin, 126
Khrushchev, Nikita, 3, 31, 60, 92, 185, 238, 299
Kryuchkov, Vladimir, 29
KSČ (Czechoslovak Communist Party), 34, 65
Kunaev, Dinmukhamed, 69
Kuznetskii Basin, 58
Kyrilenko, Andrei, 93

L'Humanité, 205, 207–211
L'Unità, 183–184, 187–189, 191, 194, 196
La Vie ouvrière, 210
Labour Party, 219–220– 222–224, 227
Lamond, James, 220, 227
Lane, Tony, 220
Latin America, 56, 157, 260
LCY (League of Communists of Yugoslavia), 13, 107
Le Peuple, 210
Le Pors, Anicet, 208
Lenin, Vladimir, 28, 62, 122, 124, 264, 306–307
Leningrad, 57, 140, 189, 194, 197
Leninism, 4, 8, 236, 240, 245, 248, 259, 301, 303, 313
Leroy, Roland, 203, 209
Liberman, Evsei, 96, 98–99

Liga für Völkerfreundschaft, 226
Ligachyov (Ligacëv), Yegor, 110, 189–191, 196
Lomas, Alf, 220
Lukanov, Andrei, 39

Macharski, Józef, 125
Manning, John, 226
Marchais, Georges, 202, 205–206, 208–209, 211, 316
Marcou, Lilly, 209
Marek, Franz, 280
Marković, Dušan, 115
martial law, 69, 118–120, 128, 180, 219, 261, 281
Marx, Karl, 41
Marxism Today, 219–221, 223, 227
Marxism, 181, 245, 303; and Soviet, 258
Marxism–Leninism, 4, 8, 11, 27, 128, 218, 220, 229, 257, 263–264, 307, 313
Matthews, George, 220
Mazowiecki, Tadeusz, 29, 44
McElvoy, Anne, 216
McGahey, Mick, 220
McLennan, Gordon, 216, 218, 220–221, 225–226
Meier, Viktor, 166
Mélenchon, Jean-Luc, 207
Mesić, Stipe, 114
Messner, Zbigniew, 123
MI5, 227
Middle East, 313
Milošević, Slobodan, 113
Mitdank, Joachim, 228
Mittag, Günter, 144
Mitterrand, François, 203, 208, 211
Mladenov, Petăr, 39
Mlynar, Ždenek, 186–188
Mock, Alois, 32–33
modernizers, 268, 270
Modrow, Hans, 139, 141
Moldova, 57, 61, 71–73, 161
Morning Star, 218–221, 224–226
Moro, Aldo, 303
Moscow University, 186
Moscow, 17, 28–46, 57–59, 70, 90, 93, 95, 98, 105–109, 111–112, 114–115, 122–124, 127–128, 133–138, 140, 142–144, 153, 157–158, 161–164, 166–167, 169–170, 181–186, 188–190, 192–194, 197, 202–203, 206, 208, 210, 217–18, 221–222, 224–225, 229, 237–248, 250, 257, 259–264, 278, 280, 282–283, 288, 299–302, 304–305, 307–308, 310, 317
Most Favored Nation (MFN), 154, 165, 168
Muhri, Franz, 280–281, 283–286, 288, 290
Mundo Obrero, 303
"mutual deterrence," 243
"mutual interdependence" (*vsaimosavisimost'*), 182
Myant, Chris, 220, 225

Nagorno Karabakh, 70–71, 189, 192
Nagorno-Karabakh Autonomous Oblast (NKAO), 70
Napolitano, Giorgio, 185, 189, 194
National Reconciliation, 299
National Security Agency (NSA), 160
National Unity Front, 120
NATO (Nord Atlantic Treaty Organization), 243, 246, 249, 261, 307, 316–318, 47, 105
Natta, Alessandro, 9, 181, 184, 325
N-Bomb, 242–243
Nelson, Daniel, 154
Németh, Miklós, 31–32
Neue Zeit, 142
Neues Deutschland, 138, 140, 142, 226
New Communist Party (NCP), 217
"new constructivist" approach, 7
New Democracy (Party), 267
New Economic Mechanism, 92
New Economic Policy (NEP), 124
New Left, 219–220, 308–309
"New Order," 67
"New Right," 261
"New Thinking," 8, 11, 27, 35, 43–44, 88–90, 92, 99, 125, 141–142, 182, 189, 323
Nicaragua, 313
Nicholson, Fergus, 220

Nicolescu, Paul, 164
NKAO (Nagorno-Karabakh Autonomous Oblast), 70–72
nomenklatura, 203
"Normalization," 34, 282
novoe myslenie ("New Thinking"), 182
Novoye Vremya (New Times), 302
Nowe Drogi (New Ways), 124
Nueva Izquierda, 309–310
Nyers, Rezső, 92–93, 97

Occhetto, Achille, 9, 187, 193–195, 197
October revolution, 133, 180, 188–189, 204, 229, 248–249, 257, 301–302
Olteanu, Constantin, 160
Orwell, George, 60
Ottoman empire, 63

Pacepa, Ion Mihai, 159
Pacifist Socialist Party (PSP), 236–237, 248
Palme, Olof, 9
Palmer, Mark, 88, 90
"Pan-European Picnic," 33
Papadimoulis, Dimitrios, 266
Papariga, Aleka, 269–270
Pasionaria, 304
PASOK (Panhellenic Socialist Movement), 256, 261, 263, 265–267
Patras, 260
Patriotic Movement of National Revival (*Patriotyczny Ruch Odrodzenia Narodowego*), 120
PCC (Political Consultative Committee), 42, 125
PCF (French Communist Party), 3–4, 7, 14, 181, 202–212, 324, 326
PCI (Italian Communist Party), 3–4, 8–9, 14, 16, 179–197, 238, 259, 315, 325–327
PCE, (Communist Party of Spain), 4, 15, 181, 298–319
PCPE (Partido Comunista de los Pueblos de España), 305
PCR/RCP (Romanian Communist Party), 14, 161, 166, 169, 202

PDS (Party of Democratic Socialism), 43
peace movements, 244, 281
People's Alliance (Iceland), 326
People's Republic of China, 90, 95
Perestroika, 1–16, 27–30, 34, 36, 38–41, 43, 45–46, 55, 58, 88–92, 94–99, 105, 107–115, 118, 121, 123–128, 132–135, 138–145, 153–154, 163–164, 169–170, 179, 181, 183, 186–190, 192–197, 203–204, 206, 208–212, 217, 229, 236, 246, 249, 251, 256, 262–263, 266, 268–272, 278–279, 282–284, 286–287, 289–291, 298, 307, 311–314, 318–319, 323–327; and anti-, 36, 190; and opponent/–s, 40–41, 45–46, 282; and reception/perception, 1, 12, 56, 62, 88, 112, 114, 118, 132–133, 143, 164, 169–170, 218, 222, 282–284, 287; and Soviet, 34, 107, 109–110, 114, 123, 154, 164, 206; and Soviet Union, 35, 138, 290, 307, 311
Pérez Royo, Fernando, 315–316
Pershing missiles, 133, 180, 242
Pertsov, Vladimir, 301
Peter the Great, 92
Pilon, Juliana, 168
Pinochet, Augusto, 157
Piraeus, 260
pluralism, 97, 125, 193, 195, 223, 246, 305
Pocock, Gerry, 218, 222–227
Politburo, 30, 35, 39, 70–72, 106–107, 118, 126, 128, 142, 188, 190, 206, 260, 268, 280–281; and CPSU, 71, 140; and Moscow, 41–42; and PCE, 302; and PCF, 205, 210; and SED, 132, 141, 223; and Soviet, 70, 121
Polityka, 125
Ponomiarow, Boris, 306
Pons, Silvio, 196
Popescu, Dimitru, 164
PPR (Dutch Radical Party), 236–237, 248
PPPS (People's Press Printing Society), 221
Poulantzas, Nikos, 260

Prague National Museum, 186
"Prague Spring," 34–35, 45, 65, 140, 186, 229, 281, 290, 302, 314, 324
Pravda, 140, 186
Prawo i Życie (Law and Life), 125
preustroistvo, 38, 46
Primate of Poland, 125
"Process of Rebirth," 38–39
przebudowa (reconstruction), 127
PSOE, Spanish Socialist Workers' Party, 314–315, 319
PSUC, Partit Socialista Unificat de Catalunya (Unified Socialist Party of Catalonia), 309
Punjab, 67
"purge," 34, 221, 303
PUWP/PZPR (Polish United Workers' Party), 13, 28–30, 44, 118–124, 127–128, 145

Queen Mary and Westfield College, 220

Rakowski, Mieczysław, 30, 127, 146
Reagan, Ronald, 5, 165, 182, 184, 247
Real socialism, 9, 141, 181–182, 302
"really existing socialism," 13–14, 216–219, 221, 223–225, 229, 236, 242, 245–246, 249–251, 285, 291, 316, 326
Realsozialismus, 133
"Red Book," 265
Red Square, 69–70, 248
Reed, John, 105
RFE (Radio Free Europe), 156, 161
reform communism, 6, 98, 218, 228, 230, 291, 324, 326–328
reformers, 65, 95, 97, 108, 165, 188–190, 221, 226, 270, 281–282
Reformsozialismus, 133
renovadores, 305, 308–310, 315, 318
Repentance, 109–110, 285
revolution/–s, 4, 13, 27, 59, 124–125, 169, 188, 190–192, 203–204, 209–211, 229, 249, 251, 258, 268, 271, 286–289, 291, 316, 325; and 1956, 97; and Chinese, 205; and communist, 211, 299; and "Copernican," 247; and peaceful, 132, 144–146; and Perestroika, 3; and Portuguese, 300; and Romanian, 162; and World, 323
Révolution, 210
Reykjavik, 182
Ribbentrop–Molotov Pact, 170
Rinascita, 183, 186, 189–190, 192–193, 195
Rizospastis, 262, 266, 268
Romania, 3, 31, 40–41, 43, 91, 94, 99, 153–170, 202, 204, 285, 289, 326
Romanian Defense Council, 42
Romanov empire, 63
Rosen, Moses, 168
Rosiewicz, Andrzej, 127
Rossiyskaya Gazeta, 88
RSFSR (Russian Soviet Federated Socialist Republic), 57–59
Rubbi, Antonio, 192
Rudé Pravo, 140
Rusakov, Konstantin, 93
Russia, 13, 54–59, 61–64, 66, 68, 73, 92, 111–112, 196, 203–204, 210–211, 217, 230, 300
Russian Federation, 68, 290–291

Sacharov, Andrei, 186
Salonika, 260
Sartorius, Nicolás, 315
SB-*Służba Bezpieczeństwa* (Security Service), 119
scala mobile, 180
Schaffer, Gordon, 227
Schöpflin, George, 168
Schreuders, Gijs, 244
Schultz, George, 159, 165–166
SDI (Strategic Defense Initiative), 182, 247
SED (Socialist Unity Party of Germany), 3–4, 7, 10, 14–15, 28, 33, 36, 40–43, 132–146, 216–220, 223–227, 229, 279–285, 287–288, 291
SEKE (Socialist Labor Party of Greece), 257
Semprún, Jorge, 299, 302
Serbia, 112–114

Seven Days, 225
Sharapov, Viktor, 39–40
Shatrov, Mikhail, 142
shestidesyatniki ("the '60s generation"), 324
Shevardnadze, Eduard A., 33, 37, 41, 113, 121, 123, 307
Siberia, 123
Sieber, Günter, 227
Silbermayr, Walter, 289
Slavic Union, 73
Slovenia, 112
Smithfield Market, 222
"snatch," 185
"social actor," 12
social democracy, 7, 99, 310, 316, 328; and European, 8–9, 180
Social Economic Council to Parliament (*Rada Społeczno Gospodarcza przy Sejmie*), 120
"Socialism with a human face," 229, 259, 281
Socijalizam, 108–109, 111
socjalistyczna odnowa ("socialist renewal"), 127
Sohn, Susanne, 289
Solidarność, 29, 44, 59, 119, 125–126, 128, 242, 281
Solomentsev, Mikhail Sergeyevich, 107
South Africa, 313
Soviet Bloc, 31, 90, 94–96, 105, 128, 155, 168, 258, 268, 284, 287, 311–312, 314–316, 318–319, 323
Soviet Empire, 2, 5, 43, 113
Soviet Union, 2, 5–8, 10–11, 13–15, 28, 30, 35–38, 41, 43–44, 46, 55–58, 60–69, 72–74, 128, 132–144, 154, 157–158, 161–164, 166–170, 180–182, 185, 187, 196, 203–204, 210, 217, 220–223, 228–229, 236–241, 243–251, 257–259, 261–262, 268, 270–271, 281–284, 286–288, 290–291, 298–302, 304–308, 310–315, 317, 319, 324–327
Sovietskaja Rossija, 140, 189
Spanish Civil War, 299, 303, 305, 309, 312

SPD (Social Democratic Party of Germany), 3, 9
Spira, Leopold, 286
Sputnik, 41, 142, 225
Stalin, Josif, 28, 41, 58–60, 63–64, 69, 105, 109–110, 142, 190, 221, 238, 261, 299, 307, 324
Stalinism, 4, 204, 271, 285, 290–291, 299, 311
START Agreement, 182
Stasi, 136–138, 140–142, 144, 219, 227, 285
Stern, 138
Stipsic, Karl, 168
Stošić, Branko, 111
"Straight Left," 220, 224
Strauß, Franz Josef, 134
Suharto, 67–68
Sukarno, 67
Sumgait, 70–71
Sung, Kim il, 162
Superpower/-s, 89, 95, 165, 241, 243, 246–247, 283–284
Supreme Soviet, 190–191, 197
Suslov, Mikhail, 93
Sychov, Vyacheslav, 94
Synaspismos, 266–267, 270–271
SYRIZA-party, 263

Tanjug, 111
Tarver, John, 226
TASS (Technical, Administrative and Supervisory Section), 220–221
Taylor, Graham, 218, 221, 226–228
Taylor, Sheila, 226–228
Teutschbein, Frank, 225
Thälmann, Ernst, 218
Thatcher, Margret, 9, 216, 219, 222
Thatcherism, 219, 223
The Hunting Party, 203
The Times, 222
Theater heute, 141
"theory of the two camps," 237, 241
"third way/-s," 4, 324, 328; and doctrine, 8
Third World, 307

Tiananmen Square, 194, 217, 223, 287, 327
Tito, Josip Broz, 65, 66, 112, 280
Togliatti, Palmiro, 194, 238, 280
Transición (Transition), 300
transnational activity, 5
transnational influences and entanglements, 8
Transnationalism, 5
Transylvania, 158, 163–166, 168
Treaty of Maastricht, 310
Tribunal of State, 120
Trybuna Ludu, 126
Tsar, 63, 92
TUC (Trades Union Congress), 221
Turin, 180

Ukraine, 13, 63, 72–74
United Kingdom Treasury, 155
United States, 62, 112, 154–155, 158–159, 164–165, 168, 182, 237, 241–243, 246–247, 301–302, 307
University of London, 220
US Congress, 159, 165, 167
uskorenye (acceleration), 134, 135
USSR, 1, 4–5, 10–11, 14, 28, 30, 33, 35–36, 43, 46, 55, 58, 61–64, 66, 73, 94–96, 106, 111, 115, 121, 126, 154, 158, 161, 163, 170, 180–186, 189, 191, 193–195, 197, 203–205, 208–211, 258, 262, 271–272, 283, 287, 290; and Cold War, 323; and collapse, 271; and market economy, 31; and modernization, 222; and social trends, 57

Vanovitch, Kathy, 227
VCN (League of Communists of the Netherlands), 245
"Velvet Revolution," 45, 59, 65, 194, 223, 290
Verdet, Ilie, 164
Vietnam, 62, 204, 241
Volksstimme, 279, 285, 287, 289
Volos, 260
Vranitzky, Franz, 288

Warsaw Pact, 29–30, 32–33, 37, 41–45, 47, 91, 121, 123, 125–126, 153, 161, 165, 182, 239, 242–243, 249, 281, 299
Washingtonian, 159
Weg und Ziel, 279, 282–283
Weimar Republic, 217
Western Europe, 2, 5, 8–10, 16, 95, 164–165, 217, 262, 300, 302, 304, 315, 327–328
West European Communist Parties, 3–4, 14, 258, 262, 278, 280–281, 288, 315
Wiener Tagebuch, 286
Willerding, Hans-Joachim, 137
Wilson, William, 220
Wimmer, Ernst, 282, 285
Wimmer, Philipp, 282
Wolff, Jaap, 242, 247
Woman's Advisory Committee, 220
Workers' Party of Ireland, 270
working class, 180–181, 241, 245, 259, 269
World Bank, 153–154
World War II, 3, 56, 60, 62–63, 65, 69, 123, 218, 237, 278–279, 291, 314

Xiaoping, Deng, 96

Yakovlev, Aleksandr N., 35, 41, 89–90, 113, 124, 190
Yazov, Dmitry Timofeyevich, 112–113
Yeltsin/Eltsin, Boris, 56–58, 68, 73, 110, 135, 188, 191, 196–197, 203–204, 290; and "affair," 204
Yevtushenko, Yevgeny, 136
Yugoslav Institute of International Politics and Economics, 107–108
Yugoslav People's Army, 112–113
Yugoslavia, 8, 40, 64–65, 105, 107–108, 110–115, 285, 304; and Socialist Federal Republic of, 115

Žarković, Vidoje, 111
Zedong, Mao, 238
Zero Solution, 182
Zhivkov, Todor, 37–40; and "Process of Rebirth," 38; and "perestroika light," 38

www.ingramcontent.com/pod-product-compliance
Lightning Source LLC
Chambersburg PA
CBHW071332080526
44587CB00017B/2809